DEATH ROW

1993

Published Annually

Publisher
Glenn Hare

Vice President
Gerald Mortimer

Editors
Dan Burger
Amy Little

Art
Margaret Anderson
Kristin Maxwell

Editorial Assistant
A. Gregory

Typesetting
June Roper

Contributors

Leslie Boellstorff, reporter for the *Omaha* (Neb.) *World-Herald*

William Brown, organizer of a pro-capital punishment group, Amicus U.S.A.

Renee Busby, reporter for *The Mobile* (Ala.) *Press Register*

Lawrence Buser, reporter for *The Commercial Appeal* in Memphis, Tenn.

Kathy Barrett Carter, reporter for *The Newark* (N.J.) *Star Ledger* and columnist for the *New Jersey Law Journal*

John D'Anna, editor for the *Tribune Newspapers* in Mesa, Ariz.

Kathy Fair, reporter for the *Houston Chronicle*

Enid Harlow, works with Amnesty International USA's program to abolish the death penalty

Erin Mathews, free-lance writer, former reporter for *The Salina* (Kan.) *Journal*

Dennis McDougal, free-lance writer, former *Los Angeles Times* reporter

Tom Miller, reporter with the *Kansas City* (Mo.) *Star*

Carol Rust, reporter for the *Houston Chronicle*

Bruce Westfall, reporter for *The Columbian* in Vancouver, Wash.

Sean Whaley, reporter for the *Las Vegas Review Journal* in Carson City, Nev.

Janet Zimmerman, reporter for the *San Bernardino* (Calif.) *Sun*

Copyright © 1992 Glenn Hare Publications

A Division of Dyna Corporation
6300 Yarrow Drive
Carlsbad, CA 92009

ISBN 0-9624857-2-1

WE NEED FURTHER DEATH ROW INFORMATION

We believe this publication to be the most complete single source of information regarding death row inmates available. It is a useful reference for many law enforcement agencies, legal professionals, and journalists.

It is our intent to continue to provide a compendium of this important information on a regular basis in the future. But we could use your help.

Any writing, photographs, or original drawings regarding death row inmates will help us in our effort to chronicle capital punishment. Please write, or call, to give us details on any materials you may have that would be meaningful in future Death Row publications. Contact: Death Row Editor, Hare Publications, 6300 Yarrow Drive, Carlsbad, CA 92009. Phone: (619) 438-2511.

ACKNOWLEDGEMENTS

Many organizations have contributed information that was instrumental in the production of the series of Death Row books. With their efforts we have been able to compile one of the most comprehensive source books pertaining to criminals convicted of capital offenses.

Behind the scenes at these various organizations are countless individuals who have assisted us in our endeavor. We would like to thank the following organizations and their courteous staffs:

State Departments of Corrections
Arizona Department of Corrections
State of Arizona Attorney General
Alabama Department of Corrections
Arkansas Department of Corrections
California Department of Corrections
Colorado Department of Corrections
Somers State Prison (Connecticut)
Delaware Department of Corrections
Florida Department of Corrections
Georgia Department of Corrections
Idaho Department of Corrections
Illinois Department of Corrections
Indiana State Prison
Kentucky Department of Corrections
Louisiana Department of Corrections
Mississippi Department of Corrections
Potosi Correctional Center (Missouri)
Montana Department of Corrections
Nebraska Department of Correctional
   Services

Nevada Department of Prisons
New Jersey Department of Corrections
New Mexico State Prison
North Carolina Department of Corrections
Southern Ohio Correctional Facility
Oklahoma State Penitentiary
Oregon State Penitentiary Salem
Pennsylvania Department of Corrections
South Carolina Department of Corrections
Tennessee Department of Corrections
Texas Department of Criminal Justice
Utah Department of Corrections
Mecklenburg Correctional Center (Virginia)
Washington State Penitentiary

Organizations
American Correctional Association
Luce Press Clippings, Inc.
NAACP Legal Defense and Education
   Fund, Inc.
U.S. Department of Justice

The responsibility for the presentation of material in this book, however, lies solely with Hare Publications.

DEATH ROW

Volume 3   1993

DEATH PENA

THE QUESTION

Rational people the world over agree that to deliberately take another person's life is an appalling act. When that act is committed with particular savagery or when multiple victims are involved or the victim is a child or a police officer, the crime seems to cry out for vengeance.

Certainly no one disputes the need for severe punishment. One can only stand in awe of the indescribable anguish suffered by the families and friends of those who have been murdered. And one can understand a mother, father, husband, wife or child of a murder victim calling out in his or her initial rage for the death of the murderer.

But when a society allows the desire for revenge to become premeditated violent homicide as an instrument of social policy, that society sinks to the level of its most detestable criminals. To give a government the power to kill its own citizens is to give it a totalitarian and impermissible power. The claim that the death penalty deters others from committing murder is frequently offered in a vain attempt to justify the use of this most extreme and barbaric punishment.

Studies proliferate on both sides of the deterrence question, yet Amnesty International finds no conclusive evidence that the death penalty deters violent crime more effectively than other harsh penalties already available. The more severe a sanction, the more substantiation of its deterrent value must be demanded before it can be selected for use

BY ENID HARLOW

LTY DEBATE

OF DETERRENCE

Capital punishment defines who we are as a people. It is a matter of life and death that not only determines sentencing policy but proclaims our ultimate values and professed morality. This issue reflects a deeper ideological premise: our commitment to human rights, to social decency, and to a fundamental social order. Our deepest beliefs ultimately decide this issue. Human rights begin when justice establishes an ultimate penalty for an ultimate crime.

Men tolerate government to ensure justice, to maintain fair and proportional sentencing structure, and to sustain an effective deterrent inhibiting criminal acts.

DEATH PENALTY

The Deterrent Argument

Webster's Unabridged Dictionary traces deterrence from the "Latin root *deterrere* meaning to frighten from: to discourage or keep from doing something through fear, anxiety, doubt." The threat of punishment restrains or prevents potential killings. Reasonable individuals are deterred through simple cost-benefit analysis.

The death sentence contains two distinct types of deterrent value: specific deterrence and general deterrence. Specific deterrence deters an individual from further criminal homicide. When Ted Bundy was executed, he was specifically deterred from ever killing again. Permanently! He received his just deserts. Executing the guilty insures that the

BY WILLIAM BEATY BROWN

over a less severe sanction. The burden of proof in this matter must rest with those who would authorize the use of capital punishment and that burden, in Amnesty International's view, has not been met.

The Studies

Deterrence studies run the gamut from Isaac Ehrlich's now largely discredited 1975 research suggesting each U.S. execution deters up to eight homicides[1] to William Bowers' study positing a "brutalizing effect" of capital punishment, based on his findings that two to three homicides occur after a month in which an execution has been carried out.[2]

When one looks at the incidence of violent crime in neighboring states such as Illinois and Michigan—the former with the death penalty, the latter without—one sees that the crime rates are so similar the availability of capital punishment simply cannot be a factor. It must also be understood that most murders are committed in a moment of panic or rage or when under the influence of drugs or alcohol, or out of some personal derangement. In none of these circumstances is a person likely to say to himself: "If the penalty is 25-years-to-life imprisonment, I'll do it; if the penalty is death, I won't." Those who commit murder for hire don't believe they'll ever be apprehended so the availability of a death sentence doesn't enter their thinking.

It is often argued that even if capital punishment provides no proven deterrent effect, execution of convicted murderers is necessary to protect society from the chance (no matter how remote) that they will one day be released from prison and murder again. However, the evidence shows that of all offenders released on parole, convicted murderers present one of the lowest risks of recidivism.

A recent study by James W. Marquart and Jonathan R. Sorensen tracked 558 convicted murderers in 30 U.S. states who were originally sentenced to death but whose sentences were commuted under *Furman v. Georgia* (the 1972 U.S. Supreme Court ruling that struck down capital sentencing statues in Georgia and Texas as being "cruel, unusual, arbitrary, wanton and freakishly imposed" and invalidated all similar statutes throughout the U.S.). The Marquart study followed

these 558 persons over a period of 15 years to see if they would kill again. Five hundred and fifty-one never did so. Tragically, seven did. Four killed other prisoners; two killed prison guards; and one killed his girlfriend and then himself after being released to society. Another four of the original number were shown to be innocent. So had we executed all of them, we would have killed 558 people to save seven and in the process would have taken four innocent lives.[3]

Available Sentences

While no definitive proof that the deterrent value of capital punishment exists, effective alternatives to the death penalty do. The general public, however, is on the whole seriously misinformed about the actual length of these alternative sentences.

A common misperception is that a person sentenced to life for murder serves an average of seven years before being released on parole. This is simply untrue. As explained in a study by Ronald Tabak and Mark Lane, if a person in New York, for instance, (most states now have penal laws similar to New York's) is convicted of the highest degree of homicide (second-degree, in New York) and sentenced to 25-years-to-life, he or she *must* serve 25 years before even becoming eligible for parole. Furthermore, if other crimes were committed in conjunction with the murder, minimum sentences for those crimes may be added onto the murder sentence, conceivably making the defendant ineligible for parole for most, if not all, of his or her natural life. Someone convicted in New York of second-degree murder who was also convicted of first-degree robbery might be sentenced to 25-years-to-life for the murder, plus 12.5 for robbery. Such a person would not even be eligible for consideration for parole until he or she had served 37.5 years behind bars.[4]

When, as regrettably happens upon occasion, a convicted murderer is released from prison after a short period of time and murders again, the claim is invariably raised: "If he'd received the death penalty in the first place, he couldn't have been paroled and done it again." This argument, too, is invalid for it asserts that a death penalty statute would prevent murders committed by people killer will never escape, be paroled, or kill again. Specific deterrence is both moral and 100 percent effective.

General deterrence opens a far different argument. The theory of general deterrence is that by punishing someone for a crime we deter another from committing that crime in the future. At best this is a theoretic and statistical guessing game. It is neither a certain nor moral basis for policy. Nor is it intended as a justification or goal of capital punishment. It may be a side benefit.

Common sense provides most of the logic we seek. Imagine a state where criminals are put to death for murders only if committed on Monday, Wednesday, or Friday. If general deterrence is not connected to punishment then killings should fall randomly on each day of the week. Would anyone be so foolish to test this idea? The point is simple. A cost-benefit analysis will have some impact on the decision to murder.

Execution to Murder Ratio

This cost-benefit analysis is apparent from the raw numbers of killings which took place from 1935 to 1965. Executions peaked in 1935 before steadily declining only to bottom out in the 1960s. In direct proportion to the decline of executions, the frequency of murder rose until reaching a 300 percent increase.

Records show a decreasing frequency of murders from 1930 through 1955. During that period, 3,617 executions were carried out (that's about 144 execution a year or approximately three per week) making a death penalty a real and frightful sentence. In 1935 the annual murder total was 10,587 compared to only 7,418 in 1955 (a 30 percent decrease over 20 years). The FBI saw reason to expect the trend to continue. Potential killers saw reason to expect the sentence to be carried out.

In the 1930s, 1,600 criminals were executed; 1,300 in the 1940s; 717 in the 1950s. By 1961 the number of executions dropped to only 51, then to zero in 1968. A moratorium on executions remained during the next 10 years.

Unfortunately, murderers did not slow down the frequency of killings. In 1968, 12,500 innocent victims fell; 18,520 in 1972. In 1975, the data listed 20,510 murders—

three times the frequency rate of the 1930s.

In addition to the dramatic 300 percent increase, there was a disturbing new factor. In 1966 the FBI reported a rapid increase in "stranger" murder, those committed by professional criminals while in the commission of some other crime; the rate jumped from 14.8 percent in 1966 to 22.2 percent by 1974. This is alarming because if any group is likely to understand the changes in prosecution and sentencing it is this class of criminal—deterrable killers.

The Implied Threat

Criminals understand that even if a longer jail sentence is incurred by killing, it is mitigated by "good time" or early release programs. In Nebraska, for example, in 1992 the state legislature doubled the automatic "good time" for all convicted felons from three months per year to six months per year. If sentenced to 20 years for murder, the convict receives six months "credit" for each of the 20 years. That is a total of 120 months (10 years) deducted immediately upon sentencing.

Today, first-degree killers are going to prison only to receive parole much sooner than either the public or the victim's family expected. The convicted could also be granted release because of legal "trial error" discovered by an appeal process. In fact, a life sentence in most states actually means about three to 20 years and then parole.

Not even a death sentence carries any immediate or real threat. Nationally, in 1982, a total of 70 death row inmates left death row: 34 had their sentences and convictions vacated; 20 had their sentences lifted, but convictions upheld; 10 had their sentences commuted; two died by suicide; two were killed by another inmate; two were executed.

Isaac Ehrlich, an econometrician from the University of Chicago, completed a deterrence study using a standard method from his field. The method is successfully used to gather economic factors and to accurately predict and avoid particular problems in the future. This method allows for the variables that factor into this equation (e.g., prosecution, conviction, and medical influence). Abandoning the usual methodology of comparing murder rate with legal status of the death penalty, Ehrlich built paroled within a few years of their convictions. Yet a person paroled after serving such a short time could not have been convicted of the highest degree of homicide (since he received less than the most severe sentence) and therefore could not initially have received the death penalty, which constitutionally cannot be imposed for violent crimes other than the most severe degree of homicide.[5]

Famous Cases

Two highly publicized cases illustrate the point. In 1984 Mauricio Silva was convicted in California for three murders, all committed within a week of his release from prison on parole. Silva's original conviction had been for manslaughter, not first-degree murders. Since the death penalty is unavailable for manslaughter, Silva could not have been executed for his first crime, preventing the subsequent ones.

Jimmy Lee Smith, of "Onion Field" fame, was convicted of murdering a Los Angeles policeman the same year he was paroled from prison. Many people said he should have received the death penalty the first time and the policeman would still be alive. But Smith was originally convicted on theft and drug charges, not murder charges, and

therefore could not legally have been executed for those crimes.[6]

FBI Statistics

Proponents of the death penalty, and especially politicians running for office, are fond of saying their endorsement of capital punishment proves they are "tough on crime." They insist this supposed toughness (which does nothing whatever to address the real causes of crime) will result in fewer murders in their community, particularly of police officers. FBI statistics prove just the opposite.

During 1976-1986, according to the FBI, the 12 states that actually carried out executions reported 340 law enforcement officers killed. This represents an officer-killed ratio of 4.9 per million population. During the same years, the 13 states without death penalty statutes reported 143 law enforcement officers killed, or an officer-killed ratio of 2.7 per million.[7]

Those Most Likely

Edmund (Pat) Brown, Governor of California from 1959 to 1967, offers two poignant examples of the lack of deterrent value of capital punishment even among those most closely connected to the process and therefore most likely to be deterred.

"Crime comes out of the conditions people are living in. Once we improve the reality of people's lives we could be tearing down jails, not building them."
—Ronald Hampton
National Black
Police Association

California's first gas chamber was built at San Quentin in 1937, using labor conscripted from the prison. One of the hardest and best workers was a journeyman plumber serving a term for robbery with violence. This man spent weeks installing the system of pipes and gauges which made the chamber work, and was even present at several successful tests as live pigs were quickly killed.

a multiple-regression analysis. His conclusion was "one cannot reject the hypothesis that punishment in general, and execution in particular, exert a unique deterrent effect on potential murders ... an additional execution per year over the period (1933 through 1967) in question may have resulted, on average, in 7 or 8 fewer murders."

This is supported by hard evidence provided by California State Supreme Court Justice Marshall McComb. His list of responses from criminals asked why they did not use a weapon, or failed to kill witnesses included: "I knew if I used a real gun and that if I shot someone in a robbery, I might get the chair." And, "I think I might have escaped at the market if I had shot one or more of them. I probably would have done it if it wasn't for the gas chamber."

Thomas Aquinas, from his 13th century monastic search for social order, *Summa Theologica*, wrote, "It is not always that one obeys the law, but sometimes it is through the fear of punishment." But today endless appeals have become a "ponderous impotence" in our judiciary. Fear is far from the mind of a criminal who understands the avenues of appeal litigation.

Deterrent to Reasonable Criminals

A 1971 report from the Los Angeles Police Department on 99 criminals apprehended while committing robbery, assault, and other crimes reveals this insight. Of those who carried no firearm, or at least had not used one, 50 respondents had deliberately chosen not to use them out of fear of execution, seven were unaffected by the death penalty because it was no longer enforced, 10 said they were undeterred by the death penalty and would kill whether it was enforced or not, and the remaining arrestees said they would not carry a weapon due to a fear of being injured or

injuring others. This supports the notion that capital punishment is effective in deterring reasonable people, even reasonable criminals.

For other specific examples, Frank Carrington's book *Neither Cruel Nor Unusual*, provides dozens of examples. For instance, Robert D. Thomas, alias Robert Hall, an ex-convict from Kentucky; Melvin Eugene Young, alias Gene Wilson, a petty criminal from Iowa and Illinois; and Shirley R. Coffee, alias Elizabeth Salquist, from California, were arrested April 25, 1961, for robbery. They had used toy pistols to force their victims into a back room where the victims were bound. When asked why they used toy guns, all agreed that real guns were too dangerous, and if someone were killed during a robbery they would all receive the death penalty. In 1961 the fear of execution was still a meaningful sentence.

The threat of severe punishment inhibits the impulse to kill, but no punishment will ever eliminate all crime. Problems of deterrent value lie in the criminal's belief of "getting away with it." Since the courts refuse to carry out an execution with any certainty, and never with swiftness, there exists only a vague probability of execution.

Hugo Adam Bedau, a leading opponent of capital punishment, has made an objective observation on deterrence studies. Because of the variables at play (e.g., whether or not an

"When people begin to believe that society is unwilling or unable to impose upon criminal offenders the punishment they 'deserve' then there are sown the seeds on anarchy."
—Potter Stewart
Supreme Court Justice

He was subsequently released on parole. Within a year, he shot to death three members of his family, was sentenced to death and wound up seated in the very device he had helped to build.

Brown's second story concerns a convicted robber and inventor assigned to maintenance duty in the room housing the electric chair in Ohio's state prison. Seeing a flaw in the design of the machine, this man invented a set of iron clamps that held the condemned person's legs more securely in place. Upon his release, he committed a murder, was sentenced to death and ultimately executed in Ohio's electric chair, his legs secured by clamps of his own invention. The former Governor remarks:

When you add to these the hundreds of equally true stories about policemen, prosecutors and prison guards—people whose working lives revolve around the death penalty—committing capital crimes and being executed for them, you begin to realize that whatever else it may be, the death penalty is no deterrent.8

Street Sense

Ronald Hampton, executive director of the National Black Police Association and law-enforcement officer for 20 years, said he's out there every day on the streets of D.C., "talking to all kinds of people, not all of them good, nor all with good intentions." He believes, "Crime is based on opportunity. Very few people actually plan to commit a crime." Today, longer jail sentences are imposed and capital punishment threatens to become an option in the District. "Even so," said Hampton, "no one is thinking about the penalty. People are thinking about getting away with it, surely not about the death penalty. To have the death penalty just to say we have it won't do any good.

"People in law enforcement," Hampton continued, "see the death penalty as another tool they can put in their belt to fight crime. When they really get personal about it, when a police officer is killed, that's when they say we need the death penalty. But the criminal justice system is designed to take all the personality out of it. There's no room for personal opinion there. Just do the job. The death penalty doesn't do that. It won't stop anything.

"If we look at the death penalty as a deterrent," Hampton pointed out, "people in law enforcement ought to be able to see the deterrent value in it. They can't see it as that. They put it to use as vengeance. They hold it over the head of someone who has already committed a crime. 'We're gonna kill you,' they say, 'because you killed a police officer.' They don't see it as a way to stop crime, or as any deterrence *before* the crime is committed."

Officer Hampton said experience tells him: "Crime comes out of the conditions people are living in. Once we improve the reality of people's lives we could be tearing down jails, not building them."

International Perspective

China: Amnesty International recorded 1,650 death sentences and 1,050 executions in China in 1991, illustrating the dramatic increase in the use of the death penalty that began in that country in 1990. Executions of drug dealers are being highlighted to frighten people into avoiding heroin. Even so, drug use is spreading rapidly in China and heroin is widely distributed.9

Uganda: In Uganda the death penalty is increasingly used as a measure to curb the rising numbers of rapes. Yet rather than showing any deterrent effect, the levels of rape continue to rise despite the lethal penalty.10

Malaysia: Since 1983 Malaysian roads are dotted with ominous billboards posted as warnings to local citizens and foreign travelers "Be Forewarned: Death for Drug Traffickers Under Malaysian Law." As of June 1990, 104 persons have been hanged and 200 sit on Malaysia's death row on drug charges. Yet Amnesty International finds: "Despite hundreds of executions, there is no clear evidence of a decline in drug trafficking which could be clearly attributed to the threat or use of the death penalty." Even Malaysia's own deputy minister of Home Affairs admits his country's mandatory death penalty for drug trafficking has failed to curb either drug trade or abuse.11

Iran: Another of the 23 countries that use

execution has taken place in the last 10 to 15 years is more important than the mere fact it is a legal option), "the deterrence factor can't be disproved nor confirmed by current standards." To compare the murder rates in a state without a death penalty to a state in which the penalty exists but has not been used for years is to compare a difference too subtle for mathematical calculations.

There is not likely to be a resolution of the general deterrence argument. It is too abstract for statistical formula. It is an argument attempting to prove the negative. You can not prove someone was deterred because there is no evidence when a murder is *not* committed.

The Moral Argument

Capital punishment is a first-principle moral issue and therefore immune to numbers, variables, and formulas. General deterrence, while a valuable side-benefit, is not sufficient to justify the states' right to execute a killer. If we based justification of the penalty on general deterrence, we run into an immediate problem: It is immoral. To punish a convicted killer with a death penalty in order to deter someone in the future is holding the present person accountable for a future crime committed by someone else. That is immoral. Moral punishment is based on individual culpability and accountability.

The only principle that leads to the justification of capital punishment is *punishment*. To pay back criminals, to get even, to hold them accountable for their evil acts—acts which violate the social agreement.

You will not find a notable western political philosopher who opposes the death penalty. Five hundred years before Christ, Socrates began a discussion on justice which continues today. Each successive normative political philosopher passes on a deepening agreement on the necessity of capital punishment in the administration of good government.

The purpose of creating government is self-preservation. To ensure our preservation, we initiated an agreement long ago and formed a sacred pact. A social contract, which provides the foundation of every other agreement formed. This contract provided a road away from a life that was "solitary, poor, nasty, brutish, and short." In brief, we have all

agreed to abide by the laws of the society and to be protected by society. Previously, we lived in a primitive setting where self-preservation was determined by survival of the fittest. But even the most fit were sometimes murdered by lesser inhabitants who were smart enough to attack while their victim slept. This was a world where "every man was at war with every man."

U.S. Supreme Court Justice Potter Stewart put it succinctly, "The instinct for retribution is part of the nature of man, and channeling that instinct in the administration of criminal justice serves an important purpose in promoting the stability of a society governed by law. When people begin to believe that organized society is unwilling or unable to impose upon criminal offenders the punishment they 'deserve,' then there are sown the seeds of anarchy — of self-help, vigilante justice, and lynch law.

"Punishment is the way in which society expresses its denunciation of wrong doing: and, in order to maintain respect for law, it is essential that the punishment inflicted for grave crimes should adequately reflect the revulsion felt by the great majority of citizens for them. It is a mistake to consider the objects of punishment as being deterrent or reformative or preventive and nothing else ... The truth is that some crimes are so outrageous that society insists on adequate punishment, because the wrong-doer deserves it, irrespective of whether it is a deterrent or not."

Justice, in other words, is fundamental to the stability of a moral community. Justice is an end in itself. There need be no further benefit other than the moral satisfaction harvested. Justice has no instrumental purpose. "And what about when a man believes he has been done an injustice? Doesn't his spirit in this case boil and become harsh and form an alliance for battle with what seems just; and, even if it suffers in hunger, cold and everything of the sort, doesn't it stand firm and conquer, and not cease from its noble efforts before it becomes gentle, having been called in by the speech within him...?" Socrates in this dialogue from *The Republic* was struggling to convey the same message as Justice Stewart.

We do justice when we punish offenders in

the death penalty for drug offenses is Iran. In 1974, the government of the Shah of Iran announced that during the past two-and-a-half years 239 drug smugglers and peddlers had been executed. Yet far from providing any deterrent effect, these mass executions were followed by an enormous increase in heroin abuse and trafficking, leading to an officially released figure of 3 million heroin addicts by mid-1980.[12] Iranian newspapers have reported a yearly average of 600 executions nationwide since 1988. And still the tide of illicit drug trafficking continues to rise. One daily paper reported in January 1989 that narcotics confiscations rose from 1,600 pounds in 1975 to 112,000 pounds in 1985.[13]

A Lottery Of Life

Approximately 20,000 persons commit capital murder in the United States annually. Of these, maybe 200 are sentenced to death. Are they the 200 most vicious, heinous criminals in the country? Hardly. They are people who, through a process no better than a lottery, drew a prosecutor who chose to seek death rather than life, a jury who voted to recommend it (or perhaps did not, but was overruled by a judge) and a judge who decided to impose it. Furthermore, they are overwhelmingly educationally and economically disadvantaged. (More than 90 percent of the people on death row cannot afford to hire an attorney.) They tend disproportionately to be people of color. (Although only 12 percent of the U.S. population is black, blacks constitute nearly 40 percent of the nation's death row population.) Their victims—even though blacks and whites fall victim to murder at the same rate—are almost always white. (Since 1944 the United States has executed only one white person for killing a black person, and he had previously been convicted of nine other murders, all of them of white). Those on our nation's death row are often mentally retarded or mentally ill. They have frequently suffered extreme abuse as children. They are sometimes children themselves. (The U.S. is one of only six countries in the world that, in clear violation of international human rights standards, executes people who were under the age of 18 at the time of the crime.[14]) They are occasionally innocent.

Add such variables as incompetent counsel, perjured testimony, prosecutorial misconduct, inadequate police investigation, availability of handguns, possibility for political gain, sensationalized media coverage, and a host of others that regularly play their part in the criminal justice system, and it becomes impossible to say that directing one man or woman to the death chamber and another for the same crime to a prison cell is the act of a rational and enlightened society.

Enid Harlow works with Amnesty International (AI) USA's program to abolish the death penalty. AIUSA is an impartial, worldwide human rights organization that is unconditionally opposed to the death penalty.

REFERENCES

[1] Isaac Ehrlich, "The Deterrent Effect of Capital Punishment: A question of Life and Death," *American Economic Review* 65, 1975. pp. 397-417.

[2] William J. Bowers with Glenn L. Pierce and John F. McDevitt, *Legal Homicide, Death as Punishment in America, 1864-1982*. Northeastern University Press, Boston, 1984. p. 298.

[3] James W. Marquart and Jonathan R. Sorensen, "A National Study of the Furman-Commuted Inmates: Assessing the Threat to Society From Capital Offenders," *Loyola of Los Angeles Law Review*, vol. 23, Nov. 1989, no. 1. pp. 5-28.

[4] Ronald J. Tabak and J. Mark Lane, "The Execution of Injustice: A Cost and Lack-Of-Benefit Analysis of the Death Penalty," *Loyola of Los Angeles Law Review*, vol. 23, Nov. 1989, no. 1. pp. 125-126.

[5] Ronald Tabak and Mark Lane, "The Execution of Injustice." pp. 119-120.

[6] Tabak and Lane, "The Execution of Injustice." pp. 120-121.

[7] *Law Enforcement Officers Killed and Assaulted, 1985*, FBI Uniform Crime Reports, Washington, D.C.: U.S. Department of Justice, 1986. p. 10.

[8] Edmund G. (Pat) Brown with Dick Adler, *Public Justice, Private Mercy, A Governor's Education On Death Row*, Weidenfeld & Nicolson, New York, 1989. pp. 156-157. (Used by permission of Grove Press, Inc.)

[9] AIUSA, China Report, 1992.

[10] Amnesty International News Release, "Uganda: Time For Action to Safeguard Human Rights," Sept. 9, 1992.

[11] "Opinion," *The Sacramento Bee*, Monday, Jan. 7, 1991. B13.

[12] Amnesty International, "The Death Penalty: No Solution to Illicit Drugs," Dec. 1986, p. 6, and *Appendix: A Survey of National Laws & Practices*, p. 12.

[13] *New York Times*, Dec. 4, 1991.

[14] The other five countries are: Iran, Iraq, Nigeria, Pakistan and Bangladesh. Amnesty International USA, "The Death Penalty and Juvenile Offenders," Oct. 1991, p. 79.

proportion to their culpability and to the gravity of their crimes. It is the community which establishes that gravity of the offense. The trial and a jury of peers decides culpability and blame worthiness of an offender. To abolish capital punishment would remove from the judge a punishment reserved for the most deserving butchers. The death penalty sets a standard. Once you give a prison sentence to a most vicious killer then an attorney for a less brutal killer will appeal for a lesser sentence on his clients behalf. Proportionality and fairness would argue powerfully in his regard.

Criminals as Victims

Today we are in the midst of an intellectual battle between long-held social beliefs of retribution and atonement and the vacant notion that criminals are the victims of a bad social environment and their rights are violated when punished for their acts. Abolitionists promote a theory that ultimately leads to a policy of not arresting killers and decriminalizing murder. If the threat of death is not a deterrent, then 25 years in prison is unlikely to deter. If deterrence is the only reason for punishment, and punishment does not deter, then why arrest killers?

Abandoning the concept of the ultimate punishment for the ultimate crime of murder begins an erosion of the order constructed by the social contract. We are now at the core of the engine driving the abolitionist movement. An agenda to devalue moral and legal history, replacing it with a preferred "humanistic" understanding. Ultimately they would abolish criminal law and replace it with an expanded version of civil law in which the state no longer has any direct interest in the action. Once the state is no longer the injured party, as it is in criminal law, then the only legal avenue of appeal for the victim is civil law, where suits can be filed against the killer much like an auto accident claim.

That would void the social contract, which provided a solution to the eternal war "of every man against every man." Given time, this would return society to the blood feuds, vigilante justice, and lynch laws Justice Stewart feared.

Abolitionists want us to feel guilty over our gut anger at the butchery of innocent vic-

tims. But in truth, the impulse to hurt a hurter is among the noblest qualities we have. Especially when we are not the victim but still insist that punishment is enforced on the victims behalf. It shows our deep caring for the suffering of others. It makes us angry, an anger which springs from moral indignation, a gut anger at the injustice to the victim. The community revulsion toward the murderer is inbred and axiomatic in a just society. Only where it is forced out of us would that nature change. And who would wish to live in a society where no one cares about his neighbor's pain!

The solid, unquestioned authority by which capital punishment is sustained is the moral argument. It begins very simply: *Life is sacred.* The innocent victims life not the killers.

The Social Contract

Punishment asserts that acts of butchery will not be tolerated. Not to deter some abstract crime in the future, but to seek retribution. It is meant to get even with a criminal for what he did to one of us: the law-abiding, innocent victim. To denounce butchery and thereby re-establish that we will not tolerate that behavior. By reaffirming societal values, we are brought back to the shared security of the social contract. The security of a just world. "In many ways," writes Leon Sheleff, "attitudes to capital punishment are a probing test of a person's deepest beliefs ... looming over the specific fate of a particular individual are larger issues such as the sanctity of life, the meaning of death, the purpose of sovereignty, the rights of the individual, the suffering of those victimized, and the basis of the social bond."

Capital punishment, with its impact on criminals and its clear symbolic message, defines how deeply our society values human life. To powerfully denounce the act of heinous murder with the grave imposition of execution carried out with the solemn judgment of the state, literally defines our most profound value: *The Sanctity of Life.*

William Beatty Brown is the Founder and Chairman of Amicus U.S.A., an organization that advocates the ethical use of capital punishment inclusive of full due process protection.

THE RISE AND FALL OF NEW JERSEY'S DEATH ROW

KATHY BARRETT CARTER

THE EXECUTION CHAMBER

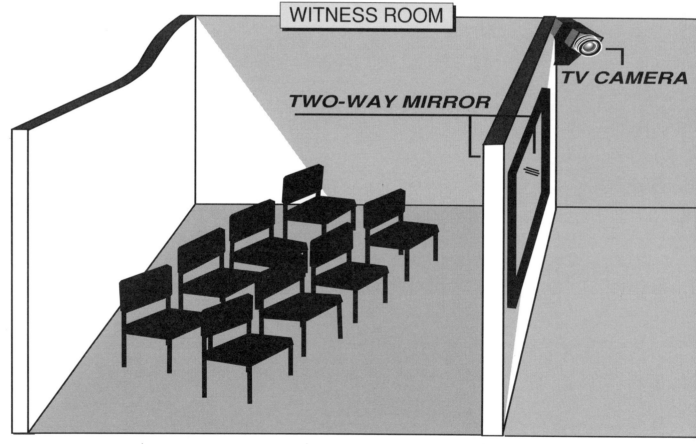

WITNESS ROOM

TWO-WAY MIRROR

TV CAMERA

1. Prior to execution, the condemned inmate receives a sedative designed to leave him calm, but conscious.

2. The sedated inmate is wheeled into the execution chamber on a gurney. An intravenous tube is connected to the inmate's body.

3. Two execution technicians—each paid $500—pour fluids into a machine that will send poisons through the IV tube into the condemned person's body. Neither executioner will know who administered the three deadly drugs—one to induce unconsciousness, one to stop breathing, and another to stop the heart.

Responding to smoldering public frustration with crime and a justice system that seemed to coddle criminals, the New Jersey Legislature voted to reinstate the death penalty in the summer of 1982.

The Garden State would become the 37th state to re-enact capital punishment after the landmark 1972 U.S. Supreme Court ruling in *Furman v. Georgia*, which led to the invalidation of death penalty laws throughout the nation.

Supporters of New Jersey's capital punishment law hailed its passage, saying it would at the very least prevent vile, heinous murderers from killing again. Opponents decried its re-enactment, saying it was a step backward for a civilized society and would do little to deter crime.

Armed with the new law, prosecutors swiftly began to apply it. Thomas Ramseur, an Irvington, N.J., man who stabbed his 54-year-old girlfriend to death in May 1983 as her two grandchildren watched, was the first to be sentenced to death.

Serial killer Richard Biegenwald, who lured young girls with offers of marijuana, would be next. He was sentenced to death for the December 1983 shooting death of Anna Olesiewicz of Camden, N.J. He was later convicted of three other murders.

New Jersey's death row population would swell to 29 within just a few years after the return of the death penalty, but just as rapidly, it would plummet.

Like dominoes dropping, the court would strike down 33 consecutive death sentences

Although the first execution under New Jersey's 1982 death penalty law is several years off, the Department of Corrections is ready. According to the law, executions will follow these explicit instructions:

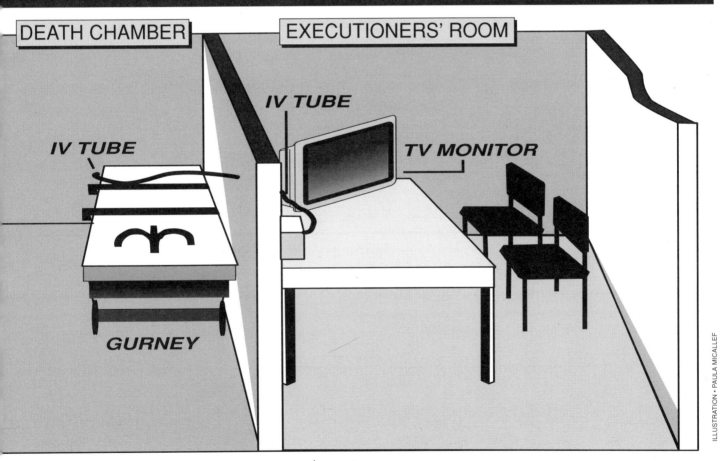

DEATH CHAMBER

EXECUTIONERS' ROOM

IV TUBE

IV TUBE

TV MONITOR

GURNEY

ILLUSTRATION • PAULA MICALLEF

4. The law says the witnesses should include the comissioner of corrections, two physicians, six adult witnesses, up to two clergy, and eight journalists.

5. The procedure is supposed to last four minutes after which time the physicians who witnessed the execution will examine the inmates' body and issue a certificate of death.

before it would uphold one in early 1991. To date, the justices have reversed the capital sentence of 35 convicted murderers. While a small number of those defendants still face new capital trials, most have escaped the death penalty. Either the court has held the inmate was ineligible for the death penalty, or frustrated prosecutors have accepted a plea bargain where the defendant gets 30 years or more without possibility of parole.

Millions of dollars later and more than a decade after the Legislature, opinion polls show 73 percent of New Jerseyans support the death penalty. But no one has been strapped to the gurney in the death chamber at New Jersey State Prison in Trenton; no one has been sedated and injected with a lethal dose of drugs.

Many of those who battled to get a death penalty statute on the books have discovered that the long, hot summer of legislative deal-making and debates was just the first of many hurdles to be jumped before the law would result in an actual execution.

Assistant Public Defender Dale E. Jones, who oversees death penalty appeals, said he does not expect anyone to be executed in New Jersey until well into the 21st century. Prosecutors hope it will come sooner but concede it is still many years away.

Who will be the first to face New Jersey's death chamber? Although three men are now death row inmates, only Robert Marshall and Marko Bey have had their death sentences affirmed by the state's top court. Either one is a likely candidate.

Marshall's case is perhaps the most sensational in the state. A successful insurance agent in the shore community of Toms River, N.J., Marshall paid a Louisiana hitman $65,000 to kill his wife, Marie, so he could collect $1.4 million in life insurance money and run away with his lover, the assistant principal at a local school. He arranged to have Marie, a 42-year-old housewife and mother of the couple's three teen-age boys, shot on the way home after they had gone out for dinner and gambling in Atlantic City.

Marshall originally told police his wife had been shot and he had been knocked unconscious by robbers after pulling off of the Garden State Parkway into an isolated pic-nic area to fix a flat tire. That story would quickly unravel, and police arrested Marshall and charged him with his wife's murder.

The crime rocked the state and became fodder for a best selling novel, *Blind Faith* written by Joe McGinnis, and a made-for-television movie.

The other capital murder sentence upheld by the court is the case of Marko Bey, from Asbury Park, N.J., who abducted, raped, beat and strangled to death Carol Peniston, a 46-year-old school board secretary and ex-wife of a local police officer. Bey attacked Peniston as she was leaving night school. It was his second murder.

He was spared the death penalty by the state's high court for his first murder because he was a juvenile at the time, and New Jersey's death penalty statute was amended to exclude anyone under 18. However, the Peniston murder occurred just weeks after Bey's 18th birthday, making him eligible for the death penalty.

● ● ● ● ● ● ●

Based on the experience of other states, people in New Jersey's criminal justice system said they anticipated that the road to an actual execution in New Jersey would be long and winding. Nationwide more than 2,600 people are on death row and only slightly more than 100 have been executed.

Couple the national trends with the New Jersey Supreme Court's long reputation for being exacting when it comes to protecting the rights of accused criminals, prosecutors knew getting the New Jersey high court to affirm a death sentence would be a Herculean task. But many say rulings of the state Supreme Court have turned that admittedly long road into a tortuous trail.

Prosecutors have accused the court of having an ulterior motive for not upholding the death penalty. At a point, New Jersey's Supreme Court was frequently compared with California's highest court under Rose Bird. She presided over a court that reversed 50 of the first 52 death sentences it reviewed until an angry populace waged a bitter battle to unseat her and other members of the court who had voted to overturn death sentences.

New Jersey critics say two court rulings are responsible for nearly emptying death row. The first came in 1988. Five years after prosecutors started using the death penalty to prosecute defendants, the state's highest court issued a ruling that led to the reversal of the sentences of 15 of the 29 people then sentenced to die. In that decision, the court said that the trial judge had failed to properly explain to the jurors how to weigh the aggravating and mitigating factors.

Under New Jersey's death penalty statute capital trials are divided into two parts. In the first phase the jury must determine guilt. If found guilty of capital murder, a second hearing is held. In that phase the jury weighs the *mitigating* factors—things which would lead the jury to have mercy on the defendant, such as youthfulness or a troubled family background—against the *aggravating* factors, those things that would cause the jury to determine he should receive death. The brutality of the crime is usually among the aggravating factors.

In the early days of the New Jersey death penalty statute it was unclear how these things should be weighed and whether the jury had to unanimously agree on both the aggravating and mitigating factors.

In 1988, the court would hold that the jury had to unanimously agree that the aggravating factors outweighed the mitigating. If one person disagreed, the convicted murderer would get 30 years without possibility of parole. The court also said jurors had to be told that if they could not agree the defendant would get a minimum of 30 years.

Because those instructions had not been given in many cases tried prior to 1988, the court would churn out a series of decisions that reversed the death sentence and required a new penalty phase trial.

Equally significant but more disturbing to prosecutors was the court's ruling in *State v. Walter Gerald*. In that case the court said the death penalty only applies to defendants who intended to kill their victims. Based on the justices reading of the statute's legislative history and relying on the New Jersey Constitution, the court said

it would be "cruel and unusual punishment" to execute someone who did not intend to kill his victim.

Rather than strike down the law as unconstitutional, the court said in every capital case the jury would have to determine whether the accused had committed "knowingly and purposeful murder"— what some states call first-degree or premeditated murder—or inflicted serious bodily injury that resulted in death, also known as second degree murder. The latter could result in a 30-year sentence but not execution, the court found.

The decision was contrary to the position held by the U.S. Supreme Court and meant that fewer people would be sentenced to death in New Jersey.

Neil Cooper, former chairman of the County Prosecutors Association's Capital Punishment Committee, said that decision "clearly emasculated the death penalty statute."

Walter Gerald was found guilty of beating to death a man in a suburban community outside of Atlantic City during a burglary in 1982. Gerald and two other men broke into the home of an

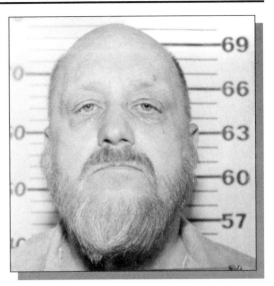
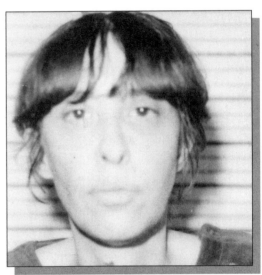

Among the killers on death row in New Jersey who have had their sentences reversed are Richard Biegenwald (top), Marie Moore (center) and Thomas Ramseur (bottom).

elderly man and attacked the man, his son, and a daughter who was there caring for the men. According to court testimony, Gerald hit the man in the head with a lamp, dropped a television set on his head, and stomped on his face with so much force that sneaker prints were visible at the time of autopsy.

Though rushed to the hospital, the son, who was 59, died that night from the beating. The older man, who never returned home from the hospital, died several months later.

The Gerald decision would result in the reversal of nine capital murder convictions. It was more devastating that the prior ruling on aggravating and mitigating factors, because murder convictions that were struck down based on what people now call "the Gerald factor" required a whole new trial, except in cases where the court otherwise commuted the sentence to 30 years.

In many cases prosecutors, dreading the prospect of another capital trial, simply accepted plea bargains, which in all cases meant the person would be in prison for the rest of his life.

Deputy Attorney General Boris Moczula, who supervises capital appellate cases, said retrying cases years after the crime occurred is risky because memories fade with time.

Among the more notorious cases reversed on Gerald grounds was that of Nathaniel Harvey. Authorities alleged that Harvey entered the unlocked patio door of a garden apartment in Plainsboro, N.J., and woke the tenant Irene Scnaps, a young widow. Scnaps punched Harvey in the nose. He would ultimately beat her to death with what the medical examiner called "a hammer like" object. Harvey is awaiting a new trial.

The so-called Gerald factor would apply in the case of Kevin Jackson who stabbed his victim 53 times, including 18 stab wounds to the genital area. Even though Jackson pleaded guilty, the court said the judge did not establish whether Jackson intended to kill his victim. Jackson was granted a new trial. In September, the jury spared his life and imposed a 30-year sentence without possibility of parole.

The court also found the Gerald factor

applied in the case of Bryan Coyle, who killed his paramour's husband, Seth Lemberg. Authorities said Lemberg came to Coyle's house demanding his wife return home. A scuffle erupted and spilled out into the street. Outside the house, Coyle shot Lemberg in the leg. As Lemberg attempted to crawl away, Coyle shot him in the back. The third and fatal shot, was at point-blank range to the back of Lemberg's head. At trial Coyle would argue he was only trying to keep Lemberg away from his wife. After his conviction was reversed by the court, a new jury sentenced Coyle to 30 years without possibility of parole.

Defense lawyers say the impact of the Gerald case has been overstated and misunderstood. Jones said the court is simply making a distinction between first-degree and second-degree murder. Under New Jersey's current crime code, the two are considered the same. In capital cases, however, Jones said it is appropriate to distinguish between the two.

Anger over the Gerald ruling galvanized legislative action and in 1992's November election, voters will have a chance to decide whether they agree with the New Jersey Supreme Court's view that executing killers who commit a second-degree murder is cruel and unusual punishment.

The public question, if approved at the ballot, would amend the state constitution to allow for the execution of people who inflict serious bodily injury that results in death.

Recent polls indicate that most of the state's residents favor exposing more killers to execution. A newspaper poll conducted in July 1992 showed 53 percent of voters want to expand the death penalty beyond cases involving premeditated murder.

The Coalition of Victim's Rights Organization, which has not publicly supported the death penalty, backs the constitutional amendment, according to James O'Brien, chairman of the group.

But former Sen. John Russo, the original sponsor of New Jersey's death penalty law whose father was killed in 1970 by an intruder, opposes the amendment. Neither he nor former Gov. Thomas Kean, who signed New Jersey's death penalty statute into law, intended for it to be broadly applied, Russo said.

"It was never our intention to apply the death [sentence] in cases where death was not intended," Russo said.

Russo said while the popular view may be to "hang the bastards," he thinks that is dangerous. When capital punishment is applied too often, Russo said, "it erodes public confidence and increases the danger of a mistake."

Tampering with the law at this juncture will do no good, said Russo.

But Moczula said the court ruling, aside from resulting in nine reversals, has given defense lawyers an opportunity to "exploit" the distinction between knowing and purposeful murder and serious bodily injury that results in death when, in fact, he said the difference is "razor thin."

"Juries are looking twice," Moczula said and deciding not to impose the death penalty based on this fine distinction.

Jones calls the issue "a tempest in the teapot." He said New Jersey juries have been reluctant to impose the death penalty even when the evidence established that a first-degree murder occurred. He said he believes jurors will be even more reluctant to do so in cases where the accused did not intend to kill the victim, particularly since they know the alternative is 30 years without possibility of parole.

For many jurors, knowing the defendant will not be paroled for 30 years is enough to convince them to spare a convicted murderer's life. Since jurors have been told that the alternative to death is 30 years, few death sentences have been returned in New Jersey. Moreover, it only takes one dissenter of the 12 jurors to result in a deadlock to make the judge impose the 30-year sentence. Leigh Dingerson of the National Coalition to Abolish the Death Penalty, a Washington-based organization, said, "Most states don't have a jury instruction on parole." She thinks that could be a big factor. Studies show juries do discuss parole and are concerned that if they don't impose death, the person will soon be returned to the community.

She said the New Jersey experience suggests that juries are less interested in executing people and more interested in making sure the public is safe.

Aside from the cases that were reversed based on the two primary factors, other reasons have led to reversals. For example, New Jersey's law requires the killer to have killed with his or her own hands. The only exception is people who hire a hitman.

That standard resulted in the commutation of the death sentence of Marie Moore, the only woman sentenced to die since New Jersey reinstated capital punishment. Moore, 42, of Paterson, N.J., was convicted of orchestrating a six-month reign of sexual abuse and torture that culminated in the slaying of her 13-year-old teen-age goddaughter, Theresa Feury.

Feury died from head injuries she suffered when she hit her head on the bathtub she was chained to every night. The girl's mummified body was found in an attic crawl space in Moore's house. Court records show the girl was killed by falling against the tub after being lifted by Ricky Flores, a 14-year-old who prosecutors said became Moore's enforcer and lover. He received two years at a juvenile facility for his role in the girl's murder. Moore was sentenced to 62 and one-half years without possibility of parole.

Moczula said many of the court decisions have been favorable to defendants.

The string of reversals, constant delays and other problems with the death penalty are not unique to New Jersey. Dingerson said of the 38 states and jurisdictions with the death penalty, "most haven't used it."

The death penalty, once considered a crucial weapon in the arsenal of every prosecuting attorney, has lost much of its sting in New Jersey as prosecutors come to the conclusion that it will be used sparingly.

Currently, there are only four death penalty trials underway in this state with 7.7 million people. The death row population has dwindled from a onetime high of more than 30, down to three men.

Kathy Barrett Carter has covered legal and legislative news for *The Newark* (N.J.) *Star* for over a decade. She is also a columnist for the *New Jersey Law Journal.*

> **Recent polls indicate that most of the state's residents favor exposing more killers to execution.**

U.S. METHODS OF EXECUTION

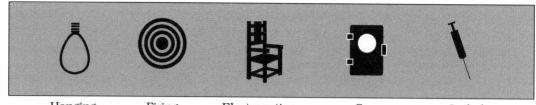

Hanging   Firing squad   Electrocution (introduced in 1890)   Gas chamber (introduced in 1924)   Lethal injection (introduced in 1977)

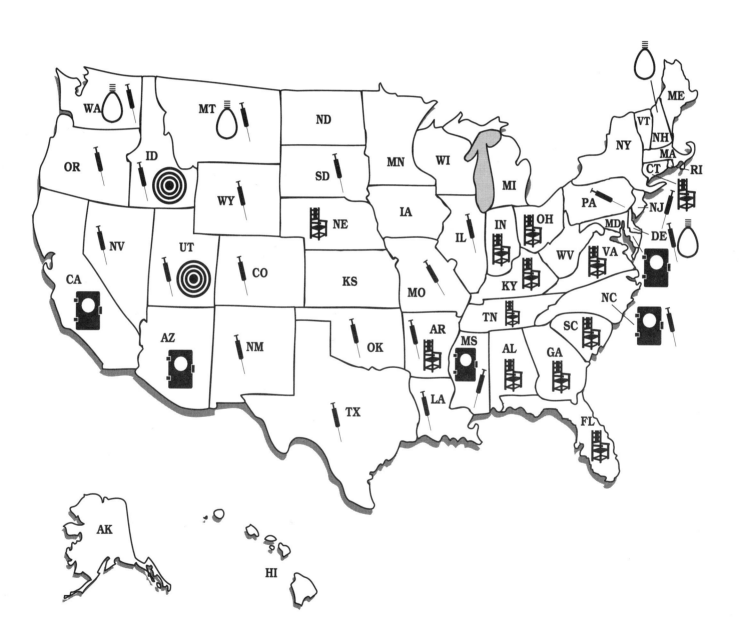

BUREAU OF JUSTICE STATISTICS 1991

CRIMINAL-HISTORY PROFILE OF PRISONERS UNDER SENTENCE OF DEATH

	NUMBER				PERCENT[a]			
	ALL RACES[b]	WHITE	BLACK	HISPANIC	ALL RACES[b]	WHITE	BLACK	HISPANIC
U.S. total	2,482	1,291	973	184	100%	100%	100%	100%
Prior felony convictions								
Yes	1,587	792	672	108	68.7%	65.7%	74.7%	62.4%
No	723	413	228	65	31.3	34.3	25.3	37.6
Not reported	172	86	73	11				
Prior homicide convictions								
Yes	181	82	81	15	8.3%	7.2%	9.5%	9.1%
No	1,998	1,053	769	149	91.7	92.8	90.5	90.9
Not reported	303	156	123	20				
Legal status at time of capital offense								
Charges pending	140	79	49	8	6.5%	7.0%	5.8%	5.1%
Probation	178	100	65	11	8.2	8.8	7.7	7.1
Parole	437	186	208	41	20.2	16.4	24.8	26.3
Prison escapes	41	25	13	2	1.9	2.2	1.5	1.3
Prison inmate	61	31	24	6	2.8	2.7	2.9	3.8
Other status[c]	29	16	11	1	1.3	1.4	1.3	.6
None	1,275	697	470	87	59.0	61.5	56.0	55.8
Not reported	321	157	133	28				

[a]Percentages are based on those offenders for whom data were reported.
[b]Includes whites, blacks, Hispanics, and persons of other races.
[c]Includes 12 persons on furlough or work release, 4 persons on mandatory conditional release, 4 persons out on bail, 2 persons residing in halfway houses, 2 persons residing in pre-release centers, 1 person confined in a local jail, 1 person under house arrest, 1 for whom charges were pending from the U.S. Army, 1 assigned to raod gang work, and 1 on an accellerated release program.

BUREAU OF JUSTICE STATISTICS 1991

TIME BETWEEN IMPOSITION OF DEATH SENTENCE AND EXECUTION, BY RACE, 1977-91

YEAR OF EXECUTION	NUMBER EXECUTED			AVERAGE ELAPSED TIME FROM SENTENCE TO EXECUTION FOR:		
	ALL RACES	WHITE	BLACK	ALL RACES	WHITE	BLACK
Total	157	94	63	85 mos	80 mos	93 mos
1977-83	11	9	2	51	49	58
1984	21	13	8	74	76	71
1985	18	11	7	71	65	80
1986	18	11	7	87	78	102
1987	25	13	12	86	78	96
1988	11	6	5	80	72	89
1989	16	8	8	95	78	112
1990	23	16	7	95	97	91
1991	14	7	7	116	124	107

Note: Average time was calculated from the most recent sentencing date. The range for elapsed time for the 143 executions was 3 months to 170 months. Some numbers have been revised from those previously reported. The average elapsed time for the 9 white Hispanics and 1 black Hispanic case was 84 months. They are included in the white and black categories in the table.

STATE EXECUTIONS IN 1991 AND STATUS OF DEATH PENALTY

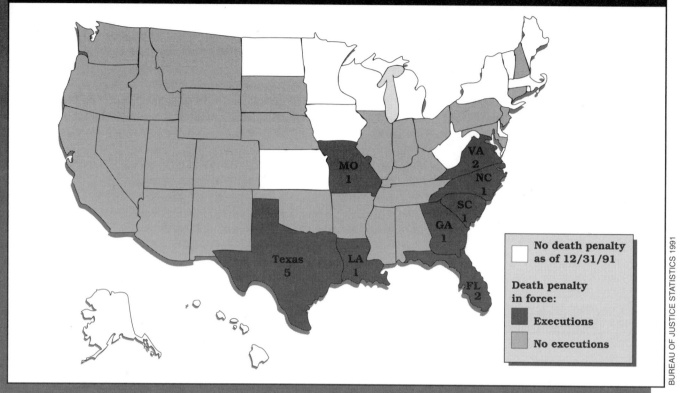

VA
2

NC
1

SC
1

GA
1

MO
1

Texas
5

LA
1

FL
2

No death penalty
as of 12/31/91

Death penalty
in force:

Executions

No executions

BUREAU OF JUSTICE STATISTICS 1991

NUMBER OF PERSONS EXECUTED, BY JURISDICTION IN RANK ORDER, 1930-91

STATE	NUMBER EXECUTED		STATE	NUMBER EXECUTED		STATE	NUMBER EXECUTED	
	SINCE 1930	SINCE 1977		SINCE 1930	SINCE 1977		SINCE 1930	SINCE 1977
U.S. TOTAL	4,016	157	New Jersey	74		Delaware	12	
Georgia	381	15	Maryland	68		New Mexico	8	
Texas	339	42	Missouri	68	6	Wyoming	7	
New York	329		Oklahoma	61	1	Montana	6	
California	292		Washington	47		Vermont	4	
North Carolina	267	4	Colorado	47		Nebraska	4	
Florida	197	27	Indiana	43	2	Idaho	3	
Ohio	172		West Virginia	40		South Dakota	1	
South Carolina	166	4	District of Columbia	40		New Hampshire	1	
Mississippi	158	4	Arizona	38		Wisconsin	0	
Louisiana	153	20	Nevada	34	5	Rhode Island	0	
Pennsylvania	152		Federal System	33		North Dakota	0	
Alabama	143	8	Massachusetts	27		Minnesota	0	
Arkansas	120	2	Connecticut	21		Michigan	0	
Virginia	105	13	Oregon	19		Maine	0	
Kentucky	103		Iowa	18		Hawaii	0	
Tennessee	93		Utah	16	3	Alaska	0	
Illinois	91	1	Kansas	15				

BUREAU OF JUSTICE STATISTICS

Capital Offenses, by State, 1991

ALABAMA Murder during kidnaping, robbery, rape, sodomy, burglary, sexual assault, or arson; murder of a peace officer, correctional officer, or public official; murder while under a life sentence; murder for pecuniary gain or contract; aircraft piracy; murder by a defendant with a previous murder conviction; murder of a witness to a crime.

ARIZONA First-degree murder.

ARKANSAS Capital murder as defined by Arkansas statute (5-10-101). Felony murder; arson causing death; intentional murder of a law enforcement officer; murder of prison, jail, court, or correctional personnel or of military personnel acting in line of duty; multiple murders; intentional murder of a public officeholder or candidate; intentional murder while under life sentence; contract murder.

CALIFORNIA Treason; homicide by a prisoner serving a life term; first-degree murder with special circumstances; train wrecking; perjury causing execution.

COLORADO First-degree murder; kidnaping with death of victim; felony murder.

CONNECTICUT Murder of a public safety or correctional officer; murder for pecuniary gain; murder in the course of a felony; murder by a defendant with a previous conviction for intention murder; murder while under a life sentence; murder during a kidnaping; illegal sale of cocaine, methodone, or heroin to a person who dies from using these drugs; murder during first-degree sexual assault; multiple murders.

DELAWARE First-degree murder with aggravating circumstances.

FLORIDA First-degree murder.

GEORGIA Murder; kidnaping with bodily injury when the victim dies; aircraft hijacking; treason; kidnaping for ransom when the victim dies.

IDAHO First-degree murder; aggravated kidnaping.

ILLINOIS Murder accompanied by at least 1 of 11 aggravating factors.

INDIANA Murder with 12 aggravating circumstances.

KENTUCKY Aggravated murder, kidnaping when victim is killed.

LOUISIANA First-degree murder; treason.

MARYLAND First-degree murder, either premeditated or during the commission of a felony.

MISSISSIPPI Capital murder includes murder of a peace officer or correctional officer, murder while under a life sentence, murder by bomb or explosive, contract murder, murder committed during specific felonies (rape, burglary, kidnaping, aircraft piracy, arson, robbery, sexual battery, unnatural intercourse with a child, nonconsensual unnatural intercourse), and murder of an elected official. Capital rape is the forcible rape of a child under 14 years old by a person 18 years or older.

MISSOURI First-degree murder.

MONTANA Deliberate homicide; aggravated kidnaping when victim or rescuer dies; attempted deliberate homicide, aggravated assault, or aggravated kidnaping by a state prison inmate who has a prior conviction for deliberate homicide or who has been previously declared a persistent felony offender.

NEBRASKA First-degree murder.

NEVADA First-degree murder.

NEW HAMPSHIRE Contract murder; murder of a law enforcement officer; murder of a kidnaping victim; killing another after being sentenced to life imprisonment without parole.

NEW JERSEY Purposeful or knowing murder; contract murder.

NEW MEXICO First-degree murder, felony murder with aggravating circumstances.

NORTH CAROLINA First-degree murder.

OHIO Assassination; contract murder; murder during escape; murder while in a correctional facility; murder after conviction for a prior purposeful killing or prior attempted murder; murder of a peace officer; murder arising from specified felonies (rape, kidnaping, arson, robbery, burglary); murder of a witness to prevent testimony in a criminal proceeding or in retaliation.

OKLAHOMA Murder with malice aforethought; murder arising from specified felonies (forcible rape, robbery with a dangerous weapon, kidnaping, escape from lawful custody, first-degree burglary, arson); murder when the victim is a child who has been injured, tortured, or maimed.

OREGON Aggravated murder.

PENNSYLVANIA First-degree murder.

SOUTH CAROLINA Murder with statutory aggravating circumstances.

SOUTH DAKOTA First-degree murder; kidnaping with gross permanent physical injury inflicted on the victim; felony murder.

TENNESSEE First-degree murder.

TEXAS Murder of a public safety officer, fireman, or correctional employee; murder during the commission of specified felonies (kidnaping, burglary, robbery, aggravated rape, arson); murder for remuneration; multiple murders; murder during prison escape; murder by a state prison inmate.

UTAH Aggravated murder.

VIRGINIA Murder during the commission or attempts to commit specified felonies (abduction, armed robbery, rape, sodomy); contract murder; murder by a prisoner while in custody; murder of a law enforcement officer; multiple murders; murder of a child under 12 years during abduction; murder arising from drug violations .

WASHINGTON Aggravated first-degree pre-meditated murder.

WYOMING First-degree murder including felony murder.

DEMOGRAPHIC PROFILE OF PRISONERS
UNDER SENTENCE OF DEATH

CHARACTERISTIC	YEAR-END	ADMISSIONS	REMOVALS
Total number under sentence of death	2,482	266	130
SEX			
Male	98.6%	98.5%	98.5%
Female	1.4	1.5	1.5
RACE			
White	59.0%	61.3%	51.5%
Black	39.6	38.0	45.4
Other*	1.4	.8	3.0
ETHNICITY			
Hispanic	8.0%	7.9%	5.8%
Non-Hispanic	92.0	92.1	94.2
EDUCATION			
7th grade or less	8.0%	6.5%	11.8%
8th	8.3	6.0	11.8
9th to 11th	37.3	36.9	37.0
12th	36.1	40.1	32.8
Any college	10.2	10.6	6.7
Median education	11th grade	12th grade	12th grade
MARITAL STATUS			
Married	28.8%	24.7%	25.6%
Divorced/separated	22.1	17.0	28.1
Widowed	2.5	3.6	2.5
Never Married	46.6	54.7	43.8

Note: Percentage and median calculations are based on those cases for which data were reported. Missing data by category were as follows:

	Yearend 1991	Admissions 1991	Removals 1991
Ethnicity	189	14	10
Education	313	49	11
Marital Status	183	19	9

*Consists of 23 American Indians and 13 Asians present at year-end 1991, 1 American Indian and 1 Asian admitted during 1991, and 2 American Indians and 2 Asians removed during 1991.

EXECUTION BY STATE AND METHOD, 1977-91

State	Number executed	Lethal injection	Electrocution	Lethal gas	Firing squad
Total	157	61	90	5	1
Texas	42	42			
Florida	27		27		
Louisiana	20		20		
Georgia	15		15		
Virginia	13		13		
Alabama	8		8		
Missouri	6	6			
Nevada	5	4		1	
Mississippi	4			4	
N. Carolina	4	4			
S. Carolina	4		4		
Utah	3	2			1
Arkansas	2	1	1		
Indiana	2		2		
Illinois	1	1			
Oklahoma	1	1			

Note: This table shows the distribution of execution methods used since 1977. As can be seen, the most frequently used method, electrocution, was used in 57% of the executions carried out. Lethal injection accounted for 39% of the executions. Three states, Arkansas, Nevada and Utah, have employed two methods.

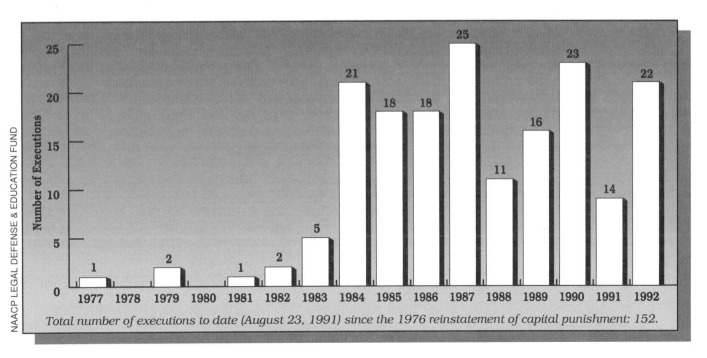

Total number of executions to date (August 23, 1991) since the 1976 reinstatement of capital punishment: 152.

OMAHA PD
NEBRASKA

HAROLD LAMONT OTEY

LESLIE BOELLSTORFF

On a balmy June Sunday in 1991, the family and friends of Harold Lamont Otey gathered at the Nebraska State Penitentiary to keep watch during the condemned man's last hours on earth.

As the clock ticked away in the prison's windowless lobby, the visitors took turns saying good-bye to Otey. It seemed ever more certain that Nebraska would carry out its first execution since 1959.

"I can't believe we're here to do this," lamented an ardent death penalty foe who befriended Otey through her volunteer work on death row.

Otey escaped death that night. The 8th U.S. Circuit Court of Appeals canceled his date with the electric chair with less than six hours to spare.

Even so, the episode made it clear that Nebraska's moral and legal struggle over the death penalty would be played out in the case of the man they call "Walkin' Willie."

• • • • • • •

The roots of Otey's nickname are tangled in the past. Expelled from high school after the 10th grade, kicked out of the Army, Otey went into itinerant work at horse tracks.

People said that was how he got his moniker—he was a horse walker.

Otey says he was actually a groom. He maintains that his nickname originated after he won a walking race in his home town of Long Branch, N.J.

Walkin' Willie now has spent 14 years on death row for the June 11, 1977, rape and murder of Jane McManus, an attractive 26-year-old photography student and part-time waitress who lived across the street from Omaha's Ak-Sar-Ben track.

He made the most of his borrowed time. He studied philosophy, politics and literature. He wrote three chapbooks of poetry. He befriended college professors and Nebraska's poet laureate, among others.

Even the nickname got polished up.

Walkin' Willie now signs his poetry "Wili."

In June 1991, his legal avenues exhausted, Otey and his supporters went to the Nebraska Board of Pardons to plead for his life. He had changed and grown, they said. He had become a better person than the man who murdered Jane McManus.

That kind of talk rankled McManus' survivors.

"I can't bring the friends Jane made in the past 14 years. Harold Otey took that away from her," sister Laura, now 39, told the board.

Her mother, Joan, now 66, told a newspaper reporter: "How can he even think he should be excused? He has to, every time he closes his eyes, remember what he did. He has got to vividly remember all that blood and the knife carving and the stabbing. And now he has the nerve to go before these three people and ask that his sentence be commuted. It just gags me."

The three-member pardons board, composed of the governor, secretary of state and attorney general, rejected Otey's clemency request in a 2-1 vote. Otey was scheduled for the electric chair in 30 hours time.

Lawyers scrambled to stop the execution. They hurriedly filed a federal court appeal raising the dregs of arguments already rejected by the courts. Even the lawyers admitted the 8th Circuit probably granted the stay of execution more because it was offended by the hasty execution date than the merits of the appeal.

The 8th Circuit eventually rejected the appeal. By that time, Otey's lawyers found a new argument. In a lawsuit not yet decided by Federal Judge Warren K. Urbom, they claim that Otey was not treated fairly by the Pardons Board.

●●●●●●●

Jane McManus gazes soberly out of a photograph, a self-portrait taken in the year before her death. Her solemn mouth and haunted eyes seem to carry a reproach from beyond the grave.

She had been asleep on the sofa that night, the night Harold Otey walked by the rental house she shared with her sister, Martha.

Walkin' Willie, then 25 years old, was heading back to his quarters at Ak-Sar-Ben. He'd been out partying and he was hungry. He was thinking about finding a place to eat.

He saw Jane McManus through the window and decided to let himself in.

"There was this chick asleep on the sofa," he told police in a tape-recorded confession.

Entering the house through an open door, he prowled around looking for something to steal. He found some marijuana joints and a stereo.

"She must have woken up and I surprised her," he said. "And I grabbed her by the throat. I had this fish knife. ... She asked what I was doing and I said I was going to rob her. Then I told her I was going to rape her. ... She started to fight me back."

Otey cut her on the top of the forehead to show her he wasn't kidding.

"Once I cut her, the rest was easy," he said.

After raping her on a downstairs couch, Otey ordered McManus to find some money. She left a bloody trail as she led him upstairs.

"I noticed she was bleeding pretty bad from the cut and I panicked," Otey said. "I started stabbing her. ... I hit her with a hammer and she started pleading with me to kill her. She said 'kill me, kill me.' OK, I figured. I went that far. Why not?"

Unsure whether McManus was dead, Otey strangled her with her belt. He hit her four or five times on the head with a hammer he

found on top of a dresser. Then he covered her face with a pillow, because he couldn't stand the sight.

He left the house with the stereo and with some amphetamines he said he found in a dresser. Otey estimated that he killed McManus at 3:30 a.m., after being in the house for about half an hour. He returned an hour and a half later to find his knife and destroy evidence.

Then he headed back to the track.

●●●●●●●

McManus' brother, John, found her body, nude and covered with blood, lying on her bedroom floor at about 9:45 a.m. The contents of her purse were scattered about her. The house had been ransacked.

Her autopsy showed she had been raped and sodomized. She had at least 15 major stab wounds, including two that penetrated 5 inches into her abdomen. She had suffered at least one blow to the head with a blunt instrument. Injuries to her larynx showed she had been strangled with her belt, found lying on her bed.

Police had few clues to the identity of McManus' attacker. They interviewed her former boyfriend, but let him go without charging him. They examined the knives in the house but found none that matched the murder weapon. They searched an acquaintance's home, but found nothing to connect that person with the slaying.

Then, in mid-July, Otey struck again.

A woman driving home to her apartment in a suburb southwest of Omaha noticed a white convertible following her as she pulled into her garage stall.

Moments later, as she pushed her key into the lock of her apartment door, a man grabbed her from behind. He cupped one hand over her mouth and put a long-bladed fish knife to her neck.

He dragged the woman back into the garage, but fled when she screamed.

Within a half hour of the attack, Douglas County Sheriff's deputies and suburban police officers spotted and chased a car matching the description of the convertible. They forced it to stop at a roadblock, but the driver escaped on foot.

On the front seat of the abandoned car was a long, sharp knife with a bone handle.

Then the pieces started to fall together. The race track worker who owned the car told police he lent it to Otey that morning. A man who'd put Otey up at his house said he'd seen Otey with a stereo resembling the one taken from the McManus house. Police found letters and other Otey writings that seemed to indicate he was the killer.

Police had enough to get an arrest warrant for murder.

But Otey was gone.

• • • • • • •

Acting on a hunch, homicide Sgt. Charlie Parker posted wanted posters at every race track in North America. A worker at a Chicago-area track told police he had purchased a stereo from Otey. It was the one stolen from the McManus house.

Authorities found the stereo speakers at a Detroit track.

They found Otey himself at the Florida Downs track near Tampa, Fla. Otey wasn't working there—he'd come in to place a bet. A worker recognized him and alerted an off-duty sheriff's deputy working as a security guard. When Otey tried to flee, the deputy commandeered a taxi cab to chase him down.

During the next two days, Otey talked with police for more than eight hours. He gave a detailed account of the McManus murder and told the police he committed at least 10 rapes in six years.

"I got off on seeing the fear in her eyes," he said of his first rape. "I think it was knowing I was man enough to force somebody into doing something that they didn't want to..."

• • • • • • •

Harold Lamont Otey was born Aug. 1, 1951, the third of 13 children in a family that lived in a public housing project in Long Branch, N.J. He and one of his brothers had the same father, but he didn't know the fathers of all his siblings.

By the time he was four, he moved in with an aunt and uncle in Bryn Mawr, Pa. The family was getting too big for his mother, Julia Wheeler, to handle. For a time, Otey was told his mother didn't want him, according to lawyer Vic Covalt. Otey ultimately took the last name of his uncle, Napoleon Otey.

In a videotape played at his Pardons Board hearing—he was not allowed to attend in person because of concerns about security—Otey described a cruel childhood in Bryn Mawr. His aunt and uncle whipped him with a razor strap and occasionally locked him alone and naked in the basement.

A neighbor, Juanita Ramsey, confirmed the whippings. She remembers Otey being afraid of water. When she talked with his uncle about it, he told her "I'm holding his head down under the water, trying to get rid of the fear."

Still, Otey had more advantages than many children of poverty, according to Assistant Attorney General J. Kirk Brown, who told the Pardons Board that Otey got a 10-speed bike and Lincoln logs for Christmas when he was a kid.

In the videotape, Otey said his aunt and uncle had "black bourgeois values."

"They were not wealthy, I mean they probably had only a couple thousand dollars in their savings account," he said. "They owned their own home, they owned their car, they had a back yard, they went to church every Sunday and all their furniture and stuff was paid for, and they lived that middle-class lifestyle, as if the world was entirely theirs.

And their values were ingrained in me through belts."

His aunt died when Otey was 14 and his uncle sent him back to his mother's house. He took to sleeping in the streets and working at race tracks because her house was too crowded with children.

He got kicked out of school in the 10th grade for violent behavior. He got his general equivalency diploma while in the Army, but washed out of military service after being prosecuted 17 times for rules violations.

"They give you these tests, similar to the Iowa test they give in school," he told police about his Army stint. "My scores were too high to be in infantry and not high enough to get—well, they were high enough to get into computer school, but computer school was four years and there was no way I was going to be in computer school."

He said he began raping women in about 1972. He told of three attempted rapes during the summer McManus was killed. Asked why he singled out one woman for a rape attempt, he said "because she was in a car by herself."

● ● ● ● ● ● ●

Walkin' Willie's case went to trial in April 1978, only 54 days after his arraignment in Douglas County District Court. His attorney, Assistant Public Defender Tom Riley, had been preoccupied with jury trials in other cases in the four weeks before Otey's trial date.

Fully expecting his request would be granted, Riley went to Judge John T. Grant the day before the trial was scheduled to begin and asked for more time to prepare.

Grant denied the request.

"I am not going to let you do that to me, Mr. Riley," the judge told him. "You have a bunch of lawyers over there and you are one of them ... but I am not going to let the fact that Mr. (Tom) Kenney (head of the public defender's office) won't hire another investigator stop us from doing what we have got to do. Everybody has got to do their thing."

Riley had done little or no legal research on the case before he was thrust into the courtroom to defend Otey. He had interviewed only five of 45 witnesses endorsed by the state. The ex-boyfriend of McManus—who supposedly had confessed to her murder—was not questioned by Riley until almost immediately before prosecutors called the man to the witness stand.

Riley had planned to contact other witnesses when they returned with "the horses" to the city on May 3, 1978.

It was all over by then.

●●●●●●●

On April 13, 1978, the jury found Otey guilty of first-degree murder in the commission of a sexual assault. The most damning piece of evidence against him was that detailed, explicit confession in which he described McManus' death and bragged of his "life of rape."

On June 20, 1978, a three-judge sentencing panel sentenced Otey to death by electrocution.

Citing his confession as well as robbery and burglary charges that were pending against him in New Jersey, the panel concluded that Otey had a significant history of prior criminal acts, one element to be considered in the sentencing decision.

Since then, Otey's lawyers have argued that neither the confession nor the New Jersey charges should have been used against him. No convictions ever resulted from the New Jersey charges, which were dismissed in 1989.

The lawyers also maintain that police failed to properly advise Otey of his rights before questioning him and continued to question him even after he asked for a lawyer.

Parker, now deputy chief of the Omaha Police Department, said police officers "couldn't stop Otey from talking" upon his arrest in Florida.

"I have listened to many confessions," Parker said. "From what he told us ... I am convinced that nobody else in the world was in that house. Nobody else in the world killed Jane McManus. There is just no doubt."

The Nebraska Supreme Court affirmed Otey's sentence in 1979 and affirmed it twice again in 1982 and 1991. The conviction and death sentence also survived one federal court challenge.

His case now is viewed as a test of Nebraska's will to carry out the death penalty.

"I hear laughter across the State of Nebraska. It is the laughter of murderers who know they are safe. It's the laughter of gang members and drug dealers who know they are safe because they can see there is always some technicality, some loophole that will keep them safe," Attorney General Don Stenberg said when a state court judge first ruled in Otey's favor on the Pardons Board argument.

Among other things, Otey's lawyers argued that Stenberg acted as both prosecutor and judge when he allowed his staff to present evidence against Otey during the hearing. Stenberg argues that such rules do not apply to the Pardons Board because a pardon is an executive "act of grace" that can be granted or denied for any reason or no reason at all.

In an editorial, the *Omaha World-Herald* called the delay a "de facto" repeal of the death penalty.

"Lawyers litigate and judges judge, but Nebraska's death penalty remains a fiction," the editorial said. "Old age may be a bigger threat. In effect, the criminal justice system has repealed the very capital punishment law it was pretending to uphold."

Death penalty opponents, however, complain that the state is unseemingly eager to carry out Otey's death sentence.

Angry about the Attorney General's aggressive pursuit of Otey's execution, State Sen. Ernie Chambers of Omaha told news reporters a female assistant attorney general seemed to be deriving too much satisfaction from her work.

Noting that the late Supreme Court Justice William O. Douglas described capital punishment as an orgasm for the public, Chambers suggested that Assistant Attorney General Sharon Lindgren "will have to achieve that elsewhere. Maybe with a vibrator. I doubt she can get a man."

Chambers, the Nebraska Legislature's only black member, is a longtime foe of capital punishment. He has attempted to repeal capital punishment every year since it was put back on the books in 1973, the year after the U.S. Supreme Court declared all then-existing death penalty laws unconstitutional.

Chambers nearly succeeded in 1991, when his repeal proposal netted 25 cosponsors—enough votes for passage. But the Otey case galvanized death penalty proponents and support for repeal fell away.

The senator nevertheless promises to continue his efforts to abolish the death penalty.

Otey's former lawyer, Gerald Soucie, now of West Chester, Pa., said death penalty politics have prevented serious examination of legitimate legal questions about Otey's case.

"Wili's turned into a political football for the death penalty, instead of looking at his case on the merits and that's just a crying shame," said Soucie, who spent nearly 10 years on Otey's case before moving out of state in 1991.

"As I see it, it goes all the way back to 1978."

• • • • • • •

At times, Otey has implied he is innocent of Miss McManus' murder, possibly because of the legal questions about the validity of his confession.

In a 1991 interview with "The Drummer," an alternative newspaper in Ames, Iowa, Otey portrayed himself as something of a political prisoner.

"I get angry, but I don't sit in my cell and dwell on it," he said. "I don't hate the judge, I don't hate the witnesses, I don't hate the jury, I hate the system. This can happen to anybody; it's happened many times before. You don't know how many innocent people have been lynched or who are spending their whole lives in the penitentiary."

Yet during the two-day hearing before the Pardons Board, lawyer Covalt made no attempt to dispute Otey's guilt.

Otey does not talk about the slaying, Covalt said, because he cannot admit to himself he was capable of the crime.

"He has made a very sincere effort to kill that moment in him," the lawyer said. "He hates that in himself more than you do. This is his day of judgment."

Nearly two months later, Otey wrote to Mrs. McManus and her family. That letter said:

Dear Mrs. McManus:

I do not know where one begins to say they are truly sorry for the grief, despair, turmoil and continuous pain caused by an inane and senseless notion. I know that whatever I shall say will neither bring your daughter, friend, part of your soul back, nor will it convince you of the nightmarish shell of an existence I have lived these many years on death row. It has taken me this long to realize I had to apologize to you, to let you know that I am aware the scar shall never completely heal, but at least, the endeavor to reconcile the bitterness must come from me.

Contrary to much belief, I am human, I still feel and though I cannot say that any member of my immediate family was taken prematurely from this life by murder, I have tried very hard to live your hurt, share your listlessness, accept this emptiness I envision are whenever memories of Jane McManus long to stay with you. I know how long the nights must be, the difficulty still to adjust to this loss and any explanation thereof. I wish that I could give you the words with which to understand this. I cannot. I do not know them. Though back then I recall that I did not operate with a heart, a mind, maturing and facing the meaning of life I have come to learn what beauty, truth, living is and I want all of you to know that I am sorry that Jane McManus did not have this same opportunity to find herself, grow into the adulthood she was born to enjoy.

Truthfully,

Harold Lamont Otey

P.S.—If you care to believe that I am doing this to save my butt, scratch that. I can never be whole again, can never be alive again. I just want the hating to stop. No one grows, no one heals when that is happening. This country is bent on destroying, it needs to be focussed on values, not anger.

The McManus family did not accept Otey's apology.

Leslie Boellstorff is a reporter for the *Omaha* (Neb.) *World Herald*. She specializes in the legal system and the prison system. She has covered Nebraska's death row since 1986.

> **The Otey case galvanized death penalty proponents and support for repeal fell away.**

MISSOURI

MISSOURI

RAY AND FAYE COPELAND

TOM MILLER

COPELAND

The little farm house, potted plants hanging out over the small porch, looked no different than hundreds of others scattered across rural northern Missouri. There was a barn, a couple of sheds, small holding pens and the usual assortment of barnyard sights: an old tractor, a flat trailer, an aging pickup truck.

But the yellow frame farm home of the elderly Ray and Faye Copeland was certainly no ordinary farm, and the Copelands were far from the ordinary farm couple.

The farm was the headquarters for a brutally efficient killing operation that spanned at least three years, time during which Ray, 75, and Fay, 69, would recruit transients, winos and drifters from far-away homeless shelters with the promise of a job, and then rope them into a bad-check scheme to buy cattle. After acquiring the livestock, Ray Copeland would put a .22 caliber slug through their heads.

The dead men—their hopes for a fresh start in life tragically snuffed out—would then be stripped of any identification and trucked to an isolated barn or old water well for burial. The brutal cycle would be repeated. Sometimes it began the next day after one murder had taken place.

The bodies of five victims were eventually found, but most officers on the case feel certain there were more victims, yet the bodies simply have never been located.

The aging Copeland couple—they marked their 50th wedding anniversary in separate jail cells after the case broke— is now apart, in prisons 150 miles away from each other. If they live long enough, they will both be executed by lethal injection in the state's death chamber at the prison in Potosi, Mo.

They are the oldest couple ever sentenced to death in America.

● ● ● ● ● ●

Ray and Faye Copeland lived in self-imposed isolation on their small farm near the tiny Missouri farming town of Mooresville and the county seat community of Chillicothe. They seemingly scratched out a modest living on the 40 acres of hard soil, worked hard, traveled around the state to cattle sales, and Ray worked odd jobs. They were left alone. No questions asked, no problems, no prying.

Ray and Faye were products of the Depression-era Arkansas Ozarks. She was raised in a dirt-floor house by strict, religious parents; he was a son of a sharecropper, and started stealing—even from his own family—while in his teens. She'd known little but hard work all her life; he'd seemingly been in constant search of the angle that would cut him a few illegal dollars.

Most of the rural Midwest had suffered through severe hard times through the early 1980s, with farm after farm abandoned to bankers or richer neighbors. Ray himself had gotten into a financial bind, nearly losing his farm once when a batch of small operating loans came due. His farm was then signed over to a son, and the financial crisis passed. The couple never lived a fancy life, having few possessions, never traveling or eating out. Faye worked cleaning motel rooms in a $20-a-night motel in Chillicothe after years of hard work on an assembly line in a factory that made work gloves. Any money Ray made was apparently turned over into more cattle purchases.

Like much of the rural Midwest, where

the solitary life is wanted by many, the Copelands pretty well wanted to be let alone, and that was how they hoped things would stay.

But a lifetime of questions—hard, brutal, painful questions—opened in the fall of 1989, when nagging doubts from a persistent deputy coupled with a bizarre telephone call to a crime-stoppers hot line combined to blow the case open.

Livingston County Deputy Gary Calvert had been nosing around the activities of Ray Copeland for several months, but despite strong instincts that told him something was wrong, he had not been able to put anything together against the crusty old farmer.

The soft-spoken Calvert, as the chief deputy for long-time Sheriff Leland O'Dell, had been getting sizeable bad checks from cattle sales barns—checks for as much as $7,000—written by folks nobody in this county of 15,000 ever heard of. The checks, which bounced from a number of small banks in the area, couldn't be cleared up, Calvert discovered, because the check-writers had seemingly vanished.

But, in Calvert's many trips around the county, and as he talked to the sales operators and others around the area, he found the check-writers were linked back to Ray Copeland.

"They'd say, 'Old Ray hires these guys, brings 'em in here for work,' and 'I've seen 'em at the sales' and that kept me wondering what was really going on," Calvert says.

He even talked to Ray Copeland a couple of times, but the farmer—always dressed in his blue bib overalls—claimed no knowledge of the men. "He'd tell me he didn't know a thing about any men or bad checks," Calvert says. Ray stands about six feet four inches, though he's stooped in his later years, and he appears to be partially deaf, often cupping his massive hand around his ear during conversation. But he'd stare Calvert in the eyes and quickly and bluntly deny any knowledge of the drifters.

Deputy Calvert still couldn't quite figure out what was happening, and usually dismissed the notion that Ray Copeland might have killed the drifters. The assumption

was, early on, that if Ray was involved in helping the men write the checks, he'd probably given them a hundred bucks and simply sent them on their way.

That all changed in late September when frightened former Copeland employee Jack McCormick, on a drunken drive West from Missouri, stopped and called a Nebraska Crimestoppers hotline.

The 56-year-old McCormick, stretching the facts with the aid of vast amounts of cheap liquor, said he'd seen a human skull and other bones on the Copeland farm, and that Ray Copeland had been killing people he'd hired to work for him.

McCormick, who at times resembles an aging leprechaun, continued on his round-about trip West after the phone call. It was several days before Jack McCormick was finally arrested in Washington. He was charged with vagrancy and was issued a Missouri warrant for writing bad checks. He repeated his Copeland story to anyone who'd listen. Meanwhile, the information from the phone call convinced Calvert and others that they needed to quickly search the Copeland farm.

When McCormick was arrested and safely returned to Missouri, he repeated his story and a massive search was planned for the Copeland farm.

Warrants were sought charging the Copelands with conspiracy to aid McCormick in writing the bad checks. The couple was arrested and then a small army of officers swarmed onto the Copeland farm.

Searchers used shovels and backhoes, tracking dogs from a Kansas prison and found animal remains and lots of trash.

But they found no skulls and no human bones.

The increasing frustration was eased, however, by other things they did find: a closet jammed with an odd assortment of men's clothing and a crudely lettered list of names, some which matched those on the bad checks. Some of those names, ominously, had an X after them. The list was in Faye Copeland's handwriting, keeping with her role as the family secretary because Ray Copeland couldn't read or write.

And the headline-making news of the

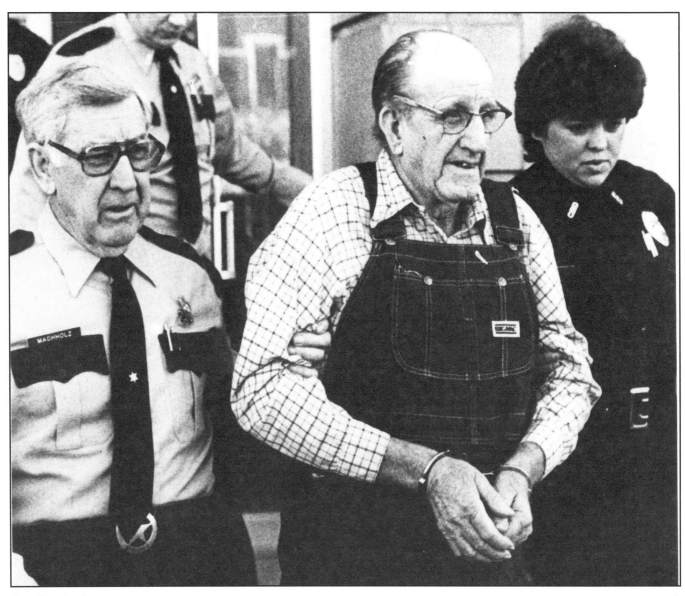

massive search on the Copeland farm
sparked hundreds of phone calls to the
sheriff's office. Other farmers said they'd
hired Ray Copeland over the years for odd
jobs painting barns, clearing brush, filling
abandoned water wells in backroad pas-
tures.

A nosy neighbor even called and said
she'd spied on the Copelands, seeing a variety of "bums" around the place over the
years.

The search widened, and finally after
days of futile searching, two bodies were
found buried in shallow graves, head to
foot, in the dirt floor of an isolated barn a

few miles from the Copeland farm.

Then two more bodies were found in another barn, and finally, the fifth body was
found at the bottom of an abandoned water
well, weighted down with a log chain and
concrete block.

The community was stunned by the de-
velopments. Not that anyone ever thought
Ray or Faye were saints, but no one suspected they could be this cold and calculat-
ing.

As the investigation continued and murder charges were filed, officers re-created
the scheme as worked by the Copelands.

Ray, sometimes alone, sometimes with

**Ray Copeland
used drifters in
his cattle buying
scam because
after he killed
them he knew
they wouldn't
be missed.**

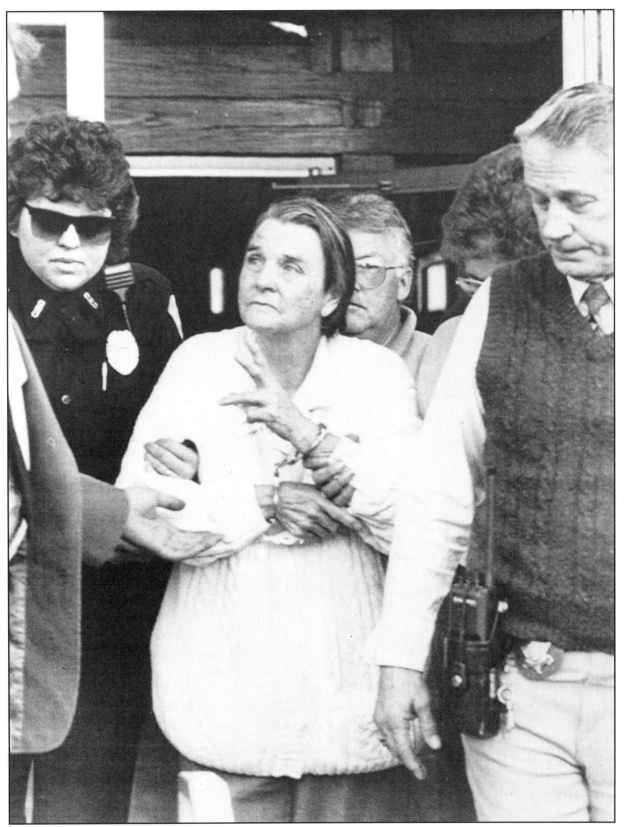

After Faye Copeland was sentenced to death, her husband
commented, "Well, those things happen to some."

Before the bad checks could surface, Ray took his 1957-vintage Marlin .22 rifle, and shot the drifters and buried them.

Faye, would travel to Springfield or Joplin, Mo., or perhaps to Bloomington, Ill., and visit homeless missions in the run down parts of town.

He'd say he was a big-time Missouri cattle buyer, but because he was getting old and hard of hearing, he needed someone to help him on his farm and in his cattle buying operations.

He'd promise the men $50 a day and room and board, and pepper the prospects with questions—Do you have relatives? Are you married? Do you have a car? If the men would answer "no" he'd drive his point home: If you come to work for me, you must not be in contact with your family, you must not tell others where you are, and you won't need a car. He would even grill them once in a while to see if they knew anything about farming and cattle, and even bought one worker a pair of overalls so he'd "look farm."

Once those tests were passed, he'd take them back to Missouri to the farm, setting them up in the second bedroom of the small house.

Sometime after they'd arrive, the pair would travel to a small nearby town, and Ray Copeland would have the man open a post office box, to establish an address. Then he'd give the drifter a few hundred dollars to open a checking account in the drifter's own name.

The two would then "practice" cattle buying at sales barns scattered across the region, waiting for the personalized printed checks to come from the bank.

Once the checks arrived, usually in about a week, the operation would begin in earnest. Ray had specific instructions for the drifters: He would let them out a few hundred yards from the sale barn so they wouldn't be seen together. They'd sit apart at the sale, and Ray would tip his cap to signal when a bid should be made. The drifter would then buy the cattle with his own check, taking advantage of the often lax security and check verification procedures at the sales barns.

Ray would then load up the cattle—usually small lots of fewer than a dozen—and either re-sell them on the spot or hold them a few days at his farm and then re-sell them.

Ray Copeland got the "good" money, the sale barn would soon be getting a bad check returned.

But, before the bad checks could surface, Ray took his 1957-vintage Marlin .22 rifle, and shot the drifters and buried them.

In some cases, the bodies were wrapped in black plastic before burial.

It was cold, efficient, and it was working. Nobody was tracing the bad checks back to Ray or Faye Copeland.

And it was the best plan old Ray had ever developed. For years, since he was a teenager, Ray had been stealing cattle or writing bad checks or forging checks. He'd served at least three separate jail and prison terms either in his native Arkansas or in Illinois, where he lived before moving to Missouri.

In searching his past, it's as if he kept trying to perfect the final plan.

At one point, years earlier, he would hire drifters and then have them write "Ray Copeland" on the checks, and then claim it wasn't his signature. Not very slick, admittedly, and it landed him in jail.

One of Ray's sons has a chilling recollection of a trip to an Illinois town with his father decades earlier. They passed a young hitchhiker, and Ray launched into a tirade: "Welfare bums! Living off everybody else... somebody ought to take them out and shoot 'em!" Al Copeland still shudders at that memory of his father.

● ● ● ● ● ●

The "secrets" of Ray Copeland's "success" for so many months were many.

First, and perhaps tragically, his victims weren't missed. They were men who'd often been out of contact with their families for years, and they had perfected the art of staying undiscovered.

Secondly, Ray's hands were not on the bad checks. He didn't write them, there was nothing to trace him to the bad paper.

And, thirdly, he buried the bodies in areas so isolated that they likely would not have been found. As it was it took dozens of officers searching and re-searching to find the five bodies. Others probably went undiscovered.

And, some officers will admit, if Ray Copeland had not violated his own tests and hired the colorful Jack McCormick, the whole plot may have never opened up.

Jack McCormick, 56, was once fired from a funeral home job because he took a loaded coffin to the wrong burying yard. He was a conman in his own right, and quickly figured out the Ray Copeland scam.

He just as quickly became wary about his own safety, and managed to get away from Ray. He said later that Ray had asked him to find a 'coon' in a barn, and as Jack McCormick poked around with a stick, he looked up and saw Ray Copeland taking aim at him with that old rifle.

Jack McCormick knew enough to get out of there, and kept up his spiel until Ray Copeland took him to town and Jack could make his break. He "test drove" a car from a used car lot, keeping it for several days as he made his escape.

McCormick's alertness and his flight—he kept the check book and dropped bad paper clear to the West Coast—led to Copeland's downfall.

The victims, all dead from neat .22 shots to their heads, were:

Paul Cowart, 21, Dardanelle, Ark., shot and killed on May 1, 1989. A high school dropout, Cowart had roamed since his late teens. He'd stopped at a homeless mission in southern Missouri when hired by Ray Copeland;

John William Freeman, 27, Tulsa, Okla., killed Dec. 8, 1988. Freeman's father died in Vietnam, and he had drifted much of his life since leaving high school. Recurring bouts with alcohol made him a target for Ray Copeland;

Jimmy Dale Harvey, 27, Springfield, Mo., killed Oct. 29, 1988. Years of problems, in-

The Copelands never lived a fancy life. They had few possessions and never traveled or ate in restaurants. They marked their 50th wedding anniversary in separate jail cells.

It was cold, efficient, and it was working. Nobody was tracing the bad checks back to Ray or Faye Copeland.

cluding a brief jail term for burglary, had Harvey in a homeless mission when Ray Copeland hired him. His family said he suffered from epilepsy and had trouble holding a job;

Wayne Robert Warner, 40, Bloomington, Ill., killed Nov. 19, 1986. He was about to marry a woman he'd met at an AA meeting, but took the Copeland job offer to set himself up with paying work. He battled alcohol problems from an early age;

Dennis K. Murphy, 27, Normal, Ill., killed Oct. 17, 1986. Murphy had graduated high school and even attended college, but started roaming in his early 20s and was in an Illinois homeless mission when hired for the Missouri farm job.

• • • • • •

For Livingston County prosecuting attorney Doug Roberts—who'd never handled a capital murder case in his three terms in office—the Copeland case proved to be a massive undertaking. He requested and got help from the state's attorney general's office, and prosecutor Kenny Hulshof joined in the effort.

The Major Case Squad, a combined force of state, county and city law enforcement officers, spent days and weeks gathering stacks of evidence in the odd case. There would be no witnesses to the shootings, but they had a ballistics match from the Copeland gun and slugs found in three of the victims, and they would match the checks to the dead check writers. And, they had the clothing—some of it marked with the initials of the victims—and the chilling list of names found in Faye Copeland's kitchen.

It looked like a solid case, and there was considerable public pressure to prosecute them to the fullest extent of the law.

But Roberts soon discovered that the high-profile Copeland case was going to be a political one, too, with Attorney General Bill Webster (a candidate for governor) taking the unusual step of flying to Chillicothe to announce the state was seeking the death penalty.

There were some nagging doubts about the depth of Faye Copeland's involvement in

the scheme, but first degree murder charges were filed against her, too.

Two of the five Copeland children lived in Chillicothe. They had little trouble believing their father could be involved in something like this, but refuse to this day to believe their mother was involved. They repeated stories of him beating them when they were youngsters, and believed Faye would have no say in anything her husband did or wanted to do. Defense attorneys sought and received a separate trial, and Roberts offered Faye a greatly reduced sentence if she would tell them all she knew and provide information about the location of more bodies. Her public defender, David Miller, urged her to consider the offer.

She refused, saying she had no information and telling lawyers, "I ain't done nothing."

Her trial was scheduled first, as her husband continued to be evaluated by psychiatrists. The handsome third floor courtroom in the Livingston County courthouse was the scene of the trial.

Faye wept virtually non-stop through her trial, heard in Chillicothe by a jury brought in from another county, and Roberts summed up his prosecution:

Her lawyer tried to convince jurors that Faye was the meek wife, never prying into her husband's business, a product of a "traditional marriage." He argued that Faye had no knowledge of Ray's business dealings.

But Roberts hammered away at the list of names and the preparations Faye would make for the new workers. "She's guilty," he told jurors, "clear up to the top of her old grey head."

The jury quickly agreed and set death as the punishment.

Faye Copeland never took the stand in her own defense. After her conviction, she wailed "I never done nothing!"

The next day, Sheriff O'Dell took Ray Copeland to a state hospital for another examination. As they drove along, the sheriff asked Ray if he'd heard what the jury did to his wife of 50 years. He said he hadn't heard, and the sheriff said, "They gave her death."

Ray calmly told the sheriff: "Well, those

Neither Ray
nor Faye
Copeland
testified in
their own
defense. Each
received the
death penalty,
but appeals
have yet to
be heard.

things happen to some."

Ray's trial was to follow, and Roberts finally agreed that the expensive trials had ripped the county apart enough, and that in all likelihood, the couple would die of natural causes before they could be executed.

Roberts engineered a plea agreement of life in prison without parole for both Copelands, only to have the state's attorney general and the trial judge strongly object.

Roberts' efforts at a plea led to his removal from the case—an extremely rare development in Missouri courts—and Hulshof took the case against Ray Copeland.

Aggressive public defenders argued that Ray was senile, suffering from a variety of health problems. "His brain is shriveling as we sit here," one lawyer said.

Hulshof didn't give Ray much slack, however. He hammered home the brutality of the crimes, telling jurors his victims were simply

men trying to get their lives together, only to be cheated by Ray Copeland.

"Ray must pay," Hulshof told jurors.

Again, an out-of-town jury quickly agreed, and fixed punishment as death by lethal injection.

Ray Copeland, like his wife, never took the witness stand. He told lawyers after his conviction: "I'll be alright."

Since Missouri resumed executions in 1989, the average time between conviction and execution has been nearly 10 years.

The Copelands, however, seem to have thrived in prison, getting proper medical care, a first for him, and finding activities to fill their days.

Appeals are yet to be heard in both Ray and Faye's cases.

Tom Miller is a reporter for the *Kansas City* (Mo.)
Star. He wrote a book, "The Copeland Killings,"
detailing the tragic saga.

RANDY STEVEN KRAFT

DENNIS McDOUGAL

Shortly after 1 a.m. on Saturday, May 14, 1983, two California Highway Patrolmen pulled over a 1979 Toyota Celica along a remote stretch of the San Diego Freeway in Orange County, about 60 miles south of Los Angeles. The driver, Randy Kraft, was a respected 38-year-old computer analyst from nearby Long Beach. He had been weaving a bit and, when he made an illegal lane change, Officers Howard and Sterling switched on their red lights.

But they wrote no traffic citations that night.

Terry Lee Gambrel, a 25-year-old U.S. Marine stationed at nearby El Toro Marine Air Station, was drugged and dying in the passenger seat next to Kraft. His pants were down to his knees and his hands were bound with the laces from his shoes. He had been garrotted with his own belt. Shortly after paramedics arrived, Gambrel was dead.

As Orange County Prosecutor Bryan Brown would tell a jury five years and four months later, the two CHP officers stumbled headlong into a 12-year nightmare of murder, mayhem and unprecedented depravity. They had unwittingly caught up with Randy Steven Kraft, a modern day Jack the Ripper with a seemingly limitless blood lust for young hitchhikers, especially U.S. Marines.

The investigation launched that night would reveal a string of sex-thrill killings dating back to 1971. Though prosecutors have only found enough evidence to positively link Kraft to a little over 40 murders, a so-called encoded "death list" in Kraft's own hand enumerates a total of 61—and possibly 67—victims in all.

Even now, almost a decade after his arrest, Kraft maintains his total innocence of all charges. He still has investigators puzzling over such notations on his list as "Navy White," "Angel" and "Marine Down." Ominous entries such as "Hawth Off Head" and "Marine Head BP" are all too clear, however, when linked with other evidence. They represent victims whose bodies have been bludgeoned, hacked, decapitated, dismembered and strewn from the freeways that crisscross Southern California since Kraft began his bloody rampage 22 years ago.

The list came to be known as Kraft's "score card." If the list is accurate—and homicide experts say there is little doubt that it is—Randy Kraft claims the dubious distinction of killing more human beings than anyone in modern U.S. history.

More than Charles Manson.

More than Ted Bundy.

More than John Wayne Gacy.

More, in fact, than all of them combined.

Randy Kraft, a wiry, sandy-haired gay who had led a quiet existence in a Long Beach suburb with a long-term live-in companion, is without a doubt, the nation's most prolific, most methodic and most heinous, serial killer.

How and why he led his double life and how he managed to elude police for 12 years is a riveting, if uncomfortable, story.

• • • • • • •

At one point, in 1975, he was actually hauled in for questioning in the disappearance of Keith Crotwell, a 19-year-old Long Beach youth. Crotwell's friends and family conducted a neighborhood search that pinpointed Kraft as the most likely suspect and led to his formal questioning at police headquarters in downtown Long Beach. But in a

PHOTO · LEO HETZEL

Homicide experts
believe Kraft's
"score card"
indicates he has
killed more human
beings than anyone
in modern history.

calm, innocent voice, Kraft convinced detectives that he had picked the teen-ager up and given him a ride to Orange County. He dropped him off unharmed and never saw Crotwell again, Kraft told police.

Neither did anyone else. Three months after Kraft's release, the young man's head was discovered floating near the jetty at Long Beach Marina. His torso and limbs were found later in the year in the Laguna Hills a hundred miles south of Long Beach. His hands have never been found.

If police had made the Crotwell-Kraft connection in 1975, they would have cut short

eight more years of terror in which an estimated 45 more victims were claimed.

But the horrifying nature of what law enforcement was up against had not yet hit home in Southern California. Police had a sense that they were dealing with some new and particularly vicious kind of evil, but they didn't know how evil. The concept of the serial killer who murders for recreation, for pleasure and for his own perverse game of cops-and-robbers was still too hard a concept for most in California jurisprudence to believe.

When hitchhikers began disappearing at an alarming rate along the web of freeways that link the Southern California Megalopolis, vague warnings began to go out to schools, colleges, military outlets. Don't hitchhike. Don't ride with strangers.

By the late 1970s, the universal paranoia that something profoundly wicked might be stalking the Southern California night was reality. In 1977, police in Riverside—some 100 miles from Kraft's home in Long Beach—arrested Patrick Wayne Kearney for murdering and dismembering the body of a drifter he picked up. Kearney came to be known as the "Trash Bag Killer" because of his method of dismembering victims, putting the parts in a large plastic trash bag and disposing of the bags in the California desert.

Police ultimately linked 21 murders to Kearney and believed they had checked the evil stalking the freeways.

But the mysterious disappearances, followed by the discovery of mutilated bodies, continued to haunt Southern California.

Shortly before Christmas, 1980, Los Angeles police followed a van to a parking lot in Hollywood and broke out their weapons when they heard screams coming from inside.

PHOTO • LEO HETZEL

When they opened the van doors, police caught William George Bonin in the act of sodomizing a young hitchhiker he had bound and gagged. The ensuing investigation re-

Donnie Crisel, a 20-year-old marine (above right) was found dead June 16, 1978. His body, like many of Kraft's victims, (one of which is shown here) was found near a Los Angeles freeway.

vealed that Bonin, an unemployed truck driver, had been using the van as a mobile rape and murder salon. He was not so tidy as Kearney, however, and simply tossed the lifeless bodies out onto freeway embankments.

A total of 20 killings were attributed to Bonin and his band of five teenage cohorts. Bonin came to be known in the headlines as "The Freeway Killer."

With Bonin and Kearney both behind bars, law enforcement breathed easier.

And, still, the freeway murders persisted.

There were inconsistencies between the bodies being found by the freeways and the kinds of killings linked directly to Kearney and Bonin. Kearney always used a .22 caliber derringer, placed to the left temple of a hitchhiker sitting in the passenger seat next to Kearney. He never drugged them before murdering them. Bonin beat his victims to death, but did not dismember them.

The bodies that were now showing up along the freeways with alarming frequency were almost always strangled. Sometimes they were mutilated. Sometimes they were not. All of them had traces of drugs and, usually, alcohol in their systems.

But the most striking differences between the fates of the hitchhikers who thumbed rides with Kearney or Bonin and those who rode with Randy Kraft are spelled out by the Trashbag Killer and the Freeway Killer themselves.

"I am not the wooden stake," Kearney protested during his confession.

"I don't cut the dicks off little boys," Bonin snarled indignantly to the jury during his 1982 trial.

As heinous as their crimes were, even Kearney and Bonin put some sort of inexplicable, self-imposed limits on their depravity. Kraft did not.

● ● ● ● ● ● ●

Following a five-hour labor, Opal Lee Kraft gave birth to her fourth and final child at 2:18 p.m. on March 19, 1945. A few days later, the *Long Beach Independent* reported that Mr. and Mrs. Harold H. Kraft of 4212 Gaviota St. had a boy. Mrs. Kraft had a normal pregnancy and delivery. Randy was as healthy as his three older sisters: Kay, Doris and Jeannette.

Harold and Opal Kraft moved to California three years earlier, in 1942. He became an assembly line worker at Douglas Aircraft. She was a housewife. He was 39 and she was 33 when Randy was born.

"They were a little bit on the strict side with middle western conservative attitudes," recalled Duane Eastburn, Kraft's former brother-in-law.

Others were more harsh in their assessment.

"His father was a very unpleasant man and I hear tell there's a good possibility that there was child abuse involved," said Ann Manley, one long-time acquaintance of the family. "At the same time, he (Randy) was overindulged. He was the youngest with three older sisters."

"I used to rock him in my arms and sing him to sleep as a baby," recalled his sister Doris, 12 years his senior. "He was a very calm baby."

When he was still an infant, he fell off the couch, breaking his collarbone, shortly after his first birthday. But a far worse occurrence—one that the family now believes may have had long-term devastating effects—took place a year later.

"Dad had taken us out to look at a house that he was thinking about buying on Beach Boulevard," Doris remembered. "And it had large concrete steps up to the porch. And Randy fell down and he hit his head and was unconscious and we had to take him to the medical clinic—the only one in the town."

He was unconscious when they arrived at the medical clinic. He came to, was treated and released, apparently with no further complications, according to his sisters. The clinic's records were destroyed in the early 1970s.

In 1948, when Randy was three, the family left the growing metropolis of Long Beach to live in the small town of Westminster about 15 miles away. The Kraft family became active members of the Westminster First Presbyterian Church. Doris sang in the choir. Mrs. Kraft chaired the Deacons committee. Randy spent Sundays in Bible study classes, usually taught by his oldest sister, Kay.

"I often wondered if there was the kind of father-son relationship that Randy wanted and didn't have," said Eva Boyd, wife of the church's pastor. "Harold Kraft was never around. I mean, a lot of the men didn't come to church, but they at least showed up for progressive dinners and the festivals. Whenever I saw Randy he was always with his sisters and his mom. Harold was always ... distanced."

In junior high, Randy was promoted to accelerated classes. Even then, the towheaded kid with the freckles and the flat-top butch haircut showed no propensity for violence.

"Everybody liked him," remembered classmate Jim Hulsey. "You wouldn't fight with Randy Kraft. He didn't fall into that category. There would be plenty of reasons to fight with other people but you wouldn't fight with Randy."

He wasn't totally cerebral. He began dabbling with the saxophone and learned to be a power hitter and runner on the softball diamond, but academics is where he shined. The only time he ever got animated was over politics.

"We were both someplace to the right of Attila the Hun," said Billy Manson, his best friend in high school. "Nixon was a liberal, Barry Goldwater was OK, but our real hero was William F. Buckley, Jr."

He was a model student. Most of his teachers gave Kraft good grades. He graduated near the top of his class, winning a scholarship to the prestigious all male Claremont College.

"First of all, in the '60s homosexuality was not accepted," said Randy's college classmate Russell Chung. "Everyone was still in the closet. In the '60s you had an image of a homosexual as someone who was effeminant and had strange mannerisms. And you didn't suspect someone who appeared to be straight and had a hidden, secret life. That was completely something that you wouldn't imagine at that time."

And especially not at a place like Claremont.

But there were other changes in the air. At the beginning of his college career, drugs, civil rights and homosexuality were terms as foreign to Randy and the other students as Cambodia, Laos or Vietnam. But all of that started to change during Randy's four years at the school.

"By the time we'd hit college, I think he'd be-

come agnostic or atheist, I'm not sure which," said his old friend Bill Manson. "He was a rationalist in one sense or another anyway."

Randy took on a part-time job tending bar at The Mug, a Garden Grove cocktail lounge with a gay clientele. While he was tentatively emerging from the closet, bringing male friends home to meet his parents, he continued to live his double life at Claremont.

By the time he was a junior, Randy had traded his Mercury in for a classic white Jaguar XK convertible and sported longer hair, a mustache and, briefly, a beard. Occasionally, some heard rumors that Kraft and at least one other student might be involved in sadomasochistic "bondage and discipline" parties off-campus.

"The most bizarre thing about Randy as a person was that he would disappear with regularity," said his roommate that year. "Maybe two, three times a week. At odd hours of the night. Like you'd be going to bed and he'd be going out. He'd been up all day. And then he'd go out and about and whatever."

He also began to suffer from migraine headaches and chronic stomach trouble. His friends diagnosed it as stress brought on by the usual pressure of midterms and finals along with the threat of the draft looming after his student deferment lapsed at graduation. He began taking Valium to calm himself down.

Bill Manson got married that summer to a girl he'd met at college in Illinois. Randy hitchhiked back to the wedding in upstate New York. They had both changed, but Manson didn't know how much. Randy was four-fifths out of the closet by then. He lived near the beach and cruised the growing gay bar scene in the burgeoning homosexual community of Long Beach. He appeared to have come to grips with the worst of his misgivings about his politics, his sexuality and his future. Most of the time, he seemed well-adjusted and at peace with himself.

But there were moments when all did not seem so well and intimate friends glimpsed a facet of Randy Steven Kraft they did not want to see.

"We used to have these big soul search things," said his Claremont roommate. "There was a time when I was a senior and he was a junior and he looked at me one night. ... We were out somewhere and he said, 'You know, there's a part of me that you will never know.'"

Twenty-five years later, the roommate still shudders as he recites Randy's words, a chill attached to each syllable. He shakes his head in a futile effort to shake away the memory.

"And he was right: there was a part of him that I never knew."

• • • • • • •

In June of 1968, Randy joined the Air Force. Records show he scored in the mid-90s in just about every category of the recruiting aptitude tests, but despite his college degree, he entered as an enlisted man. He also was granted a "secret" security clearance.

Kraft was stationed at Edwards Air Force Base in Southern California. He posed for his boot camp graduation photo wearing a scarf, leather flight jacket and airman's patent leather visor hat, looking as dashing as a still from a Spencer Tracy movie. The reality was not nearly so romantic. For the next year, he painted test planes.

He used to write his former college roommate. One letter in particular was disturbing.

"At the top, like a letterhead, he had drawn a boat with 'S.S. Kraft' written on the bow and the boat was sinking," the roommate remembered. "Then he wrote this letter mainly about the fact that he was going to have to get out of the service because he couldn't stand the pressure of worrying about being discovered about his lifestyle."

The following year, Randy was discharged for his homosexuality. He began an odyssey of odd jobs and college computer classes during the next few years, living in beach area apartments while he struggled with his identity. By 1970, his day-and-night lifestyle was firm: by day, hard-working upwardly-mobile young member of the growing Long Beach gay community and, by night, drug-dabbling cruiser and "chicken hawk."

In March of 1970, Randy picked up a truant 13-year-old junior high student at the beach and took him home. After drugging the boy with beer and drugs, he sodomized and forced him to orally copulate him. Then he left for work. Nearly 20 years would pass be-

PHOTO • LEO HETZEL

fore the boy told his story on the witness stand. At the time, he was so hurt, confused and embarrassed that he only told his parents and police about the drinking. A police report was filed, but Kraft was never even questioned about it.

One and a half years later, on Oct. 5, 1971, Wayne Joseph Dukette, 30, was found at the bottom of a ravine off Ortega Highway. The corpse was bloated and rank, but deputies could tell even from several yards up the hillside that it was naked.

The coroner said the man had been dead two weeks. The sun and wind and morning dew had erased any marks on the body or other telltale signs of foul play. His blood alcohol level at the time he died was .36. The medical examiner settled on acute alcohol poisoning as a cause of death.

Police discovered his car still parked next door to a beach area bar where he worked nights. He was the bartender at the Stables, located next door to Broom Hilda's and just down Pacific Coast Highway from the Buoys Shed in Sunset Beach. All three were gay hangouts. It was apparent after detectives asked just a few questions that Dukette had been gay.

His car may have been on the blink the

night he disappeared or he may just have gotten so resoundingly drunk that he needed a ride home. But the trail was two weeks cold before his body was even discovered, so the odds of discovering the good samaritan who helped him get naked and dumped him off the Ortega Highway were slim or none. On Oct. 8, Wayne Dukette was buried without ceremony in Pacific View Memorial Park in Newport Beach.

The entry "Stables" which appears near the top of the list found in the trunk of Kraft's car 12 years later is generally accepted by law enforcement as representing the first—or nearly the first—of Kraft's victims. Though Kraft was never charged, that first victim is believed to have been Wayne Dukette.

Edward Moore was the earliest of the 16 murders with which Kraft was eventually formally charged. On Dec. 26, 1972, the crumpled body of the 20-year-old U.S. Marine was spotted by a passing motorist at approximately 1:45 a.m. on the westbound offramp of the 405 and 605 freeways in Seal Beach. He wore only one sock. The other sock was jammed into his rectum. He wore a jacket with a USMC patch and a Confederate flag sewn on it. "Ed Moore" was stenciled on the waistband of his jockey shorts. There was a rabbit's foot tied to one of the belt loops of his trousers.

He was dumped from a car. It probably slowed down, but it didn't stop. The last time anyone remembered seeing him alive was in the barracks at Camp Pendleton about 6 p.m. on Christmas Eve.

His face had been beaten with a blunt instrument, possibly a pipe. The autopsy showed that the face injuries had occurred minutes before death. What killed him, though, was the garrotting. Red ligature marks ringed his neck. Faint red rings encircled his wrists and ankles too, leading investigators to conclude that he had been tied up during his ritual killing. There were also fingernail scratches and a bite mark on his genitals.

• • • • • • •

Moore was the first of several Marines or other service men who disappeared from Pendleton, El Toro and other military bases during the next decade. Those that were found had usually been drugged and sexually mutilated.

Marines were not the only victims of this freeway phantom though. Young hitchhikers were also favorite prey. Few of these young men were gay, though some of the victims who were eventually attributed to Randy Kraft, had been picked up in gay bars.

One veteran lawman who recognized what kind of a monster he was facing years before he was able to catch up with Kraft was Orange County (Calif.) Sheriff Det. Jim Sidebotham. A tall, laconic homicide investigator with more than 20 years on the force, Sidebotham puzzled daily for years over the sick and dangerous foe he faced. When Patrick Kearney was arrested, he cheered along with hundreds of other law enforcement officials. His cheering died when he learned that Kearney did not choke his victims.

Cheers went up again with Bonin's arrest but, again, the cheering stopped when it became apparent that the Freeway Killer could not have committed the homicides Sidebotham had come to know all too well. Kraft apparently learned through trial and error what dosages of beer and drugs to give to a prospective victim before raping and carving them up alive. He had the process down to a science by the time Sidebotham joined the growing number of detectives who were stalking this killer.

Hours after Kraft's arrest in 1983, while investigators were still combing Kraft's Toyota for evidence, Sidebotham tried questioning him. Kraft maintained his innocence, wanted to see a lawyer and lapsed into silence on key questions surrounding the evidence pulled from his car and home—a silence that he has sustained for almost a full decade.

Besides empty pill bottles and a cooler in the back seat of the Toyota full of ice and Moosehead lager, police discovered several dozen Polaroid pictures of various unidentified young men in different stages of undress. Several of the young men appeared to be lifeless.

Sidebotham joined the search. The investigators carefully gathered fibers and hairs, labeling them for future reference. They conducted chemical tests, searching for traces of blood, bits of cloth. They dusted for fingerprints.

Then, in a notebook in the trunk of the car, one of the detectives made a chilling discovery. There, in neat, block print, was a list of odd, seemingly unrelated names or phrases. Cryptic phrases, such as "2 in 1 Hitch" and "2 in 1 Beach." Only months of research and correlating spelled out the meaning of those phrases: that Randy had apparently bagged two victims on those occasions instead of his usual one.

The list bore 61 entries. For Sidebotham, it added up to one simple, if deeply disturbing, fact: Randy Kraft was the one he had been looking for.

A search of Kraft's home turned up even more evidence. Victims' clothing, shoes, ID cards and more Polaroid pictures. Sidebotham had to requisition a computer system to keep track of it all.

Kraft began preparing his defense. He had simply picked up a groggy Marine hitchhiking back to his base. He realized something was wrong with Gambrel and was racing to the nearest hospital when the Highway Patrol pulled him over.

He went through a series of attorneys, finally settling on a team of three former public defenders. Throughout the many court delays, Kraft lived in solitary in the Orange County Jail where he was protected from the other prisoners. He read extensively and became a jailhouse lawyer. Along with his defense team, he was allowed by Judge Donald McCartin to cross-examine witnesses and aid in his own defense.

The trial of Randy Kraft began in the Santa Ana Courthouse in September of 1988 where he was formally charged with 16 murders committed over 11 years. The trial lasted nearly a year and cost more than $10 million.

According to testimony, Kraft usually selected white male hitchhikers as his victims, many of whom were drugged, sexually mutilated and strangled.

As a computer troubleshooting specialist for defense contractor Lear Siegler, Kraft also traveled throughout the nation in the early '80s. In addition to exporting his computer expertise, he also exported murder. During the penalty phase of his trial, prosecutors

linked Kraft to eight other slayings. At least six killings in northern Oregon have been attributed to him. Another two victims were garrotted and sodomized in Grand Rapids, Michigan.

He was also implicated in another 29 deaths in California, Michigan, and Oregon, but those cases never got an airing in court at all. Prosecutors from Michigan and Oregon were eager to have their turn at Kraft, but it appears as though California will be the state that sends him to the gas chamber.

Orange County Superior Court Judge Donald McCartin upheld the recommendation of a 10-woman, two-man jury to send Kraft to the gas chamber for killing 16 young men over a 12-year period in Southern California. After the sentence was read, Kraft, speaking publicly one of the few times in his 13-month trial, denied committing any of the murders for which he was convicted the previous May.

"Burn in hell!" shouted Darwin Hall, the father of one of Kraft's victims, as Kraft disappeared into a courtroom holding tank following his sentencing. Kraft never looked back.

On Nov. 30, 1989, one day after being sentenced to die in the gas chamber, Kraft accompanied Orange County sheriff's deputies on an hour-long flight to San Quentin's death row.

Only one other defendant in California history had been convicted of more serial killings. A jury found Juan Corona guilty of murdering 25 migrant farm workers after their bodies were unearthed in fruit orchards near Yuba City in 1971.

As in all capital cases, Kraft has been granted automatic appeal. He has acquired a computer while on Death Row and filed several pro per habeas corpus writs with the California Supreme Court, maintaining his innocence. In his briefs, Kraft simply ignores the obvious questions about photos, drugs, blood, victim souvenirs and the body of Terry Gambrel in the front seat of his car. Instead, the briefs dwell on his contention that the prosecution failed to present sufficient evidence to convict him.

No formal appeal has yet been pursued on his behalf.

Dennis McDougal is a former *Los Angeles Times* staff writer and author of "Angel of Darkness," a book detailing the Randy Kraft case.

Prosecutors linked Kraft to eight other slayings. He was also implicated in another 29 deaths.

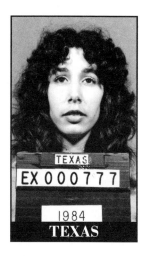

EX 000777
TEXAS
1984
TEXAS

KARLA FAYE TUCKER

CAROL RUST

TUCKER

Karla Faye Tucker always looks forward to visits.

Wearing a solid white, prison issue uniform, a white scarf keeping her dark, rambunctious curls from her fresh-scrubbed face, she chirps answers to friends' questions, frequently punctuating them with references to Jesus.

Her eyes are bright. She softly teases, jokes and chatters, the smile rarely leaving the lips she's daubed lightly with coral-colored lipstick to make her look nice for her "guests." But the 32-year-old Texas Department of Corrections inmate is careful not to let her conversation wander too far into the future or the past.

As one of four women on Texas' death row, and the one likely to die the soonest, her future is uncertain.

She's had one execution date struck down by a state appeals court, but she could receive another any day.

And it was her past—one that resembles a rough Harley ride down a treacherous highway while high on drugs—that put her here: a tiny concrete building enclosed by concertina wire in the Gatesville's Mountain View Unit, which houses women whose crimes are so ghastly and heartless that the perpetrators were sentenced to die.

●●●●●●●

As a wiry tomboy growing up in the Houston area, Tucker dreamed of fame as the first woman quarterback for the NFL. She scorned anything sissy, and thumbed her nose at anything that remotely resembled authority.

She could fistfight any man and have a decent chance of winning. She could outdrink anybody, outsmoke anybody and still be shooting up bathtub-manufactured speed after the last person had refused any more. She once dislocated her shoulder during an 82-foot dive, but she didn't regret it. She'd lived up to her reputation of never turning down a dare.

Few people crossed Karla Faye Tucker, and the ones who did paid dearly.

Like Jerry Lyn Dean. He'd made her angry more than once. First, she came home from a stint as a call girl in a cheap hotel in a West Texas oil town, and there he was asleep in her bed with her roommate. Worse, his Harley Davidson was parked in the middle of her living room floor, leaking oil onto the carpet.

Her roommate later told Karla that Dean had beaten her up. Karla punched his nose and broke his glasses, requiring a trip to a hospital emergency room to get the glass out of his eye. She got word from friends in the biker-doper crowd she and Dean hung around with that Dean had threatened to burn her with a blow torch—not to kill her, but to mess up her face.

"I'd like to see him try," was her response.

In retrospect, sitting in her tiny cell on death row, she realizes the whole scene was just a lot of tough talk, a contest of who could sound like the "badder bad ass."

But back then—after 72 hours of shooting Dilaudid, heroin, Methadone and speed, interlaced with the handfuls of tranquilizers she and her two buddies took like so many M&Ms—Karla started taking the talk seriously.

And when one of her friends, after another round of tequila, said, "If I don't do something, I'm going to climb the walls," the three formed a plan as they sat around the kitchen table.

Didn't they all hate Jerry Lyn Dean? Wouldn't this be a great opportunity for a reconnaisance mission, the ones like her live-in lover, Danny Garrett, told her of during his time in a special forces unit in Vietnam? They'd go to Dean's house and case the place, so they could return and steal the motorcycle parts with which he was building a bike.

Everybody knew the best way to get to a biker was to steal his wheels.

A week before, Karla had found a set of keys to Dean's apartment in her washing machine, where her former roommate—now Dean's estranged wife—had done her laundry. The three set out, agreeing that Karla and Danny would go inside the apartment while their friend, Jimmy Leibrant, kept watch outside.

They would later say they hadn't counted on Dean being home, asleep with a woman he'd met that afternoon at a pool party. They would later say they hadn't counted on the tools of Dean's trade—mattocks and picks for laying cable—scattered about the house.

PHOTO · HOUSTON CHRONICLE

Karla Faye Tucker found her fame not with a passing arm, but with a pickax—the one she left buried in the chest of a woman on June 13, 1983, minutes after she used it to kill Dean.

A jury found her guilty the year following Dean's murder, after days of grisly testimony by Leibrant and police investigators.

She rarely has the nightmare anymore: the one that haunted her sleep, with blood spattering anew on the walls of an apartment bedroom each time she brings the pickax down and hears the thud of flesh against bone. It is a nightmare in which one of the victims begs her to go ahead and kill her because the pain is too great. It's the same one in which she grins maniacally at Leibrant as she wiggles the tool to get it out of her victim's shoulder

so she can plunge it in again.

When Karla dreams now, she has a baby, one she is raising, she says, "the way I know the Lord would want me to." Sometimes she dreams she is walking free and going from one prison to another to minister to the women there, "so they can know Jesus, too."

But when she awakens, she remembers her hysterectomy at age 15 that precludes her ever having children. She remembers the death sentence that precludes her ever walking free.

But Karla Faye Tucker believes in miracles—her dramatically changed life is one in itself, she says.

And her supporters do, too. They aren't just members of the prison ministry group who have befriended her, the ones Karla cred-

Karla Faye Tucker used a pickax in the grisley slayings of two people. Some believe that she is a female Charlie Manson, a cold-blooded killer trying to save herself by claiming to be a born-again Christian.

its for "leading me to the Lord." They include former prosecutors, police officers and a former U.S. judge who is an outspoken advocate of the death penalty. They include two members of the victims' families who are convinced Karla has genuinely changed.

Her supporters are conducting a letter-writing campaign to convince the Texas Board of Pardons and Paroles to commute her sentence to life. Ronald Carlson, the slain woman's younger brother, says Karla can do more good alive than dead.

But there are others who remain certain that Karla is a female Charlie Manson, a cold-blooded killer who is trying to save herself by claiming to be a born-again Christian. Dean's mother still celebrates the birthday of her youngest child, the one whose murder at age 26 occupied newspaper headlines for weeks.

Longtime friend Dale Boudreaux of Houston remembers Dean as "the kind of guy who would give you the shirt off his back." He believes Karla should pay for his friend's life with her own.

Karla knows either side could win. But for now, all she can do is wait, knitting furiously to finish Christmas presents before the holiday—or her execution date—arrives.

● ● ● ● ● ● ●

"Everybody thinks you have to have a horrible childhood to end up on death row," she says, "but I didn't. I had a wonderful childhood; I just made a lot of bad choices."

Those choices included smoking marijuana at 8 and shooting heroin at 10. They included skipping so much school she failed the seventh grade three years in a row, at which time she dropped out completely. They included prostitution, starting with showing her breasts to a man who picked her up hitchhiking in exchange for money, and evolving into a career of flying around the country as a call girl, and transporting drugs for her older circle of friends on the side.

Her mother was more of a friend to Karla and her two older sisters than a parent. "We shared drugs like lipstick," she told Los Angeles-based author Beverly Lawry, who chronicled Karla's life in her book, *Crossed Over*. Her mother's friends taught her how to perform oral sex on men, Lowry wrote.

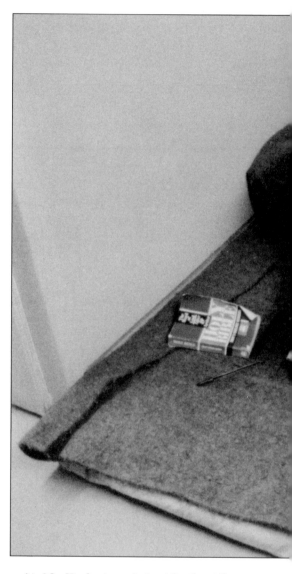

At 13, Karla traveled with the Allmann Brothers as a groupie. As she got older, she got wilder. Her marriage at 18 fell apart when her mother died and she ceased to care about anything anymore.

She had barely gotten her maiden name back when she met Danny Garrett, 14 years older than her, with tales of adventure that made her want to be like him. So much so that when he suggested the reconnaisance mission, she couldn't have said no if she wanted to.

When the police arrived at the north Houston apartment, the radio was playing. An overhead light turned on in a bedroom was the only other sign of life.

Police found Dean's naked body, half on

PHOTO · HOUSTON CHRONICLE

and half off a mattress on the floor. A woman in a T-shirt lay in the corner, a pickax sticking out of her chest.

Across town, Karla and Danny didn't try to hide their crime: They bragged about the murders, intently watching news reports about them on television. Karla even claimed she had an orgasm each time she'd plunged the axe into her victims.

Then their boasts turned to threats they'd "off" anybody who squealed about the deaths, they said. Family and friends who knew about murders began to fear that Karla and Danny might imagine them as traitors as they continued to shoot more speed and downers. Doug Garrett, Danny's brother, and Kari Tucker, Karla's sister, were so afraid that they

moved out of the apartment they shared and stayed with Danny's ex-wife. They took turns sleeping while guarding each other with a shotgun.

Houston Police Sgt. J.C. Mosier had gone to high school with Danny, and couldn't have been more surprised when he heard two investigators mention Danny in connection with the murders.

"Danny didn't have anything to do with them, did he?"

"Maybe not, but he knows some of the people involved," they replied.

Mosier knew that didn't sound right, so he called Danny's ex-wife to see what was going on with his high school acquaintance. She told him about the dopers he'd been hanging

TEXAS PENAL CODE

The punishment for murder with malice aforethought shall be death or imprisonment for life if:

(1) the person murdered a peace officer or fireman who was acting in the lawful discharge of an official duty and who the defendant knew as a police officer or fireman;

(2) the person intentionally committed the murder in the course of committing or attempting to commit kidnapping, burglary, robbery, forcible rape, or arson;

(3) the person committed the murder for remuneration or the promise of remuneration or employed another to commit the murder for remuneration or promise of remuneration;

(4) the person committed the murder while escaping or attempting to escape from a penal institution;

(5) the person, while incarcerated in a penal institution, murdered another who was employed in the operation of the penal institution.

Under the present law, a person convicted of capital murder may be sentenced to one of two sentences—death or life imprisonment.

If the jury answers three questions with yes the sentence is death. The questions are:

(1) Did the defendant act intentionally and should he have known someone might be killed?

(2) Is there a probability that the defendant would in the future commit criminal acts of violence that would constitute a menace to society.

(3) Was the conduct of the defendant in killing the deceased unreasonable in response to the provocation, if any, of the deceased?

TEXAS DEPARTMENT OF CRIMINAL JUSTICE

with. Mosier gave her a phone number and asked her to get Doug to call him.

He got a call back almost immediately and arranged to meet with Doug.

"Doug broke down crying when he saw me, he'd been so scared," Mosier recalls. When Doug told him what had happened, Mosier persuaded him to wear a wire and get confessions from Karla and Danny on tape.

Brother and sister turned brother and sister in.

• • • • • • •

Attorney Henry Onckene had seen a lot of things in his career, but the day the court appointed him to defend Karla Faye Tucker, he went home and told his wife he wasn't sure if he could do it.

It wasn't just the crime, which was horrid enough, Karla didn't seem to realize, or care, what she'd done. Her speech was slurred from drugs, her hair and clothes unkempt. She looked at him as if looking through a fog.

As the drugs left Karla's body, her eyes brightened and her speech became clear. "Because of the drugs, she'd never had an opportunity to be anything else," Oncken says. "She was completely different from the person I'd first met."

After she was given the death penalty, she became the key witness against Danny Garrett. She made no deals for a reduced sentence, prosecutors insist. Karla Faye was

WOMEN ON DEATH ROW, 1992

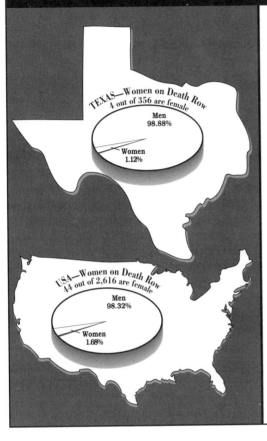

TEXAS—Women on Death Row
4 out of 356 are female
Men 98.88%
Women 1.12%

USA—Women on Death Row
44 out of 2,616 are female
Men 98.32%
Women 1.68%

Women under sentence of death

State	Total	White	Black	Hispanic
Total	45	28	17	2
North Carolina	6	5	1	0
Alabama	5	4	2	0
Oklahoma	4	3	1	0
Ohio	3	0	3	0
Texas	4	3	1	0
Florida	5	3	1	1
Illinois	2	0	2	0
Indiana	2	1	1	0
Mississippi	1	0	2	0
Missouri	4	3	0	1
Arizona	1	1	0	0
California	2	2	0	0
Kentucky	1	1	0	0
Nevada	1	0	1	0
Pennsylvania	2	0	2	0
South Carolina	1	1	0	0
Tennessee	1	1	0	0

Since 1977, one woman, Velma Barfield, has been executed. She was put to death in North Carolina's gas chamber Nov. 2, 1984, for killing a man.

NAACP LEGAL DEFENSE AND EDUCATION FUND

the first person they'd known of to testify against someone after receiving the death penalty.

The man who she testified she still loved received the death penalty, too. Like Karla, he has appealed his case.

Today, Oncken and his wife Jackie visit Karla in prison. The former U.S. judge and his wife say they sometimes feel like parents to the convicted murderer.

Karla's attorney, George Secrest, orders books for his client, who has received her high school diploma and 30 hours of college credit since she has been on death row.

Detractors say it's normal for inmates to exhibit a change, especially those given the death sentence. And even if she has changed, argues Joe Magliole with the U.S. Attorney's office in Houston, does that diminish her crime? "Are we going to go over the heads of a duly appointed jury every time someone changes?"

The Rev. Gary Breed of the Family Life Training Center in Hungerford, which sends a ministry group regularly to prisons to help people like Karla, says he hopes the letter-writing campaign to have Karla's sentence commuted will show state officials, "They're either going to have to start executing them more quickly or accept the fact that people can change."

At the very least, Oncken hopes they'll accept his belief that Karla has changed. "I'm not saying we should let everyone off of death row, and I'm not saying that other people on death row haven't changed," he said. "I just haven't gotten to know everyone on death row like I have Karla.

Carol Rust has been a feature writer at the *Houston Chronicle* for 2 1/2 years. Previously, she worked as a feature writer and columnist for the *Beaumont* (Texas) *Enterprise*. During her tenure there, she also worked as assistant city editor and copy editor, and was a stringer for the *New York Times* and the *Dallas Morning News*.

ARIZONA

ROBERT HENRY MOORMANN

JOHN C. D'ANNA

MOORMANN

Just an hour drive southeast of the sprawling metropolis of Phoenix, the sleepy town of Florence lies like a jewel amid the lush cotton farms that line the banks of the Gila River Valley in defiance of the sere, bleak desert of Central Arizona.

Named after the daughter of a former governor, the town has a wide, old-fashioned main street, friendly folks, and a picture-postcard courthouse that harkens back to territorial days.

But just across the highway, a cigarette toss from the Blue Mist Motel, an ominous eight-foot chain-link fence wears a crown of barbed wire and marks the outer perimeter of the Arizona State Prison.

Deep inside the massive complex of stone and steel, lies the state's gas chamber, that put Donald E. Harding to death on April 6, 1992 for killing two men. It was the state's first evecution since 1963, paving the way for Moormen.

On July 11, 1991, with a fresh seal of approval from the state environmental officials who had worried that lethal cyanide gas could leak into the atmosphere, the chamber stood ready to receive Robert Henry Moormann.

The day before, the paunchy 43-year-old was handcuffed and shackled and then escorted to the Death House, where he spent the night just 15 feet from his destiny. Then, on the day that was to be his last, he scrawled in his crude, almost juvenile handwriting his last request: "two hamburgers with everything, lots of french fries, three Cokes—cold—and three large pieces of cake."

He never got to eat it.

Moormann was spared by the stroke of a judge's pen just hours before he was to pay the ultimate price for smothering his elderly, adoptive mother and cutting her body into two dozen pieces in the shower of Room 22 at the Blue Mist Motel while on a 72-hour compassionate leave from prison.

The stay of execution was an act of mercy unlike any Moormann had ever shown in his three decades as a kidnapper, child molester and ultimately, murderer.

• • • • • • •

Robert Henry Moormann was born an unwanted child in a cruel world. The year was 1948. His mother drowned shortly after he was born in Tucson, Ariz. His father, a military man, gave the boy to his grandparents to raise after receiving orders for a transfer.

But Moormann's grandfather was an alcoholic who abused him, and the boy was quickly handed over to a Catholic social services adoption agency. He was shuffled from one foster home to the next, seven in all, before Henry and Maude Moormann, a desperate, childless couple in their late 30s were told there was a 2-year-old boy available.

The agency let the couple take the child overnight, but Henry Moormann, a strapping, sandy-haired Navy veteran with a Jesuit college education, had an uneasy feeling and suggested to his wife that they try for another child. Fearing that the chances of adoption would decrease if they passed this opportunity, Maude tearfully demanded that they keep the boy.

Henry gave in, and they took young Robert home to their modest Elm Street bungalow in Flagstaff. They had no way of knowing he would bring them so much pain.

Nestled among the stately Ponderosa

DEATH ROW III

pines 7,000 feet above sea level, the Flagstaff of the early 1950s was where big timber, the mighty Santa Fe railroad, and the charming neon-lit motor courts of Route 66 came together to make an idyllic alpine town. It was the perfect place to raise a family.

The Moormanns, who had suffered a miscarriage earlier in their marriage, did their best to be loving, devoted parents and worked hard to raise their son with wholesome, middle-class values.

Henry Moormann ran the town's taxi company, which he started after the war, and it provided a respectable income that allowed his family to live in comfort.

An avid outdoorsman, Henry taught Robert to hike, hunt and fish in the shadow of the majestic San Francisco Peaks just outside of town, while Maude, a ravin-haired Oklahoma gal with Cherokee blood, gave up her job teaching at a nearby Indian school to devote herself to the full-time job of mothering her new son.

Indeed, doting on the child became her obsession. Young Robert was never allowed to stray far from her watchful eye, and she jumped to protect him from even the most minor childhood mishaps. The boy could do no wrong in her eyes. If he broke something, had a tantrum or spoke out of turn, she jumped to his defense, saying he was a good boy and didn't mean to do it.

As an overprotected, only child, Robert was painfully unprepared for the cruelty he would face at the hands of other children when he went off to school. Pudgy, flat-footed and uncoordinated, he wore thick glasses to compensate for his bad eyes. His trouble assimilating was reflected in his grades; he was labeled a "poor achiever" with "low intelligence," and he constantly lagged behind kids his own age.

He was shuffled from public schools to Catholic schools to special schools in California and New Mexico, but he always flunked out or ran away. He wound up back in Flagstaff at College Elementary, a school near Northern Arizona University where student teachers learned to work with difficult children.

In between being shuffled from school to school, he was shuffled from doctor to doctor; they all knew something was different about the boy, but none could say for sure what the problem was. One diagnosed him with mild cerebral palsy. Another offered a similar theory of slight retardation. And yet another traced the boy's troubles to a pair of auto accidents when he was a baby and suggested he suffered a brain-stem injury after being thrown through the windshield in one of them.

The constant shuffling of schools and doctors took its toll on the boy, and he became more and more withdrawn. As he grew more distant, his mother grew more strident in her attempts to protect him, almost smothering him in a misguided attempt to

> He was shuffled from doctor to doctor; they all knew something was different about the boy, but none could say for sure what the problem was.

DEATH ROW ARIZONA

Method:	Gas Chamber			
Last Execution:	April 6, 1992			
	Donald E. Harding			
Total Inmates:	102			
Race:	White	Black	Hispanic	Native American	Unknown
Male:	66	12	19	3	1
Female:	1				

At 13, Moormann was accused of molesting a little girl and sent to a boarding school for troubled boys. While he was home for Christmas, he shot his adoptive mother in the stomach with a .22-caliber relvolver.

shelter him from all that was unkind. Her mothering almost cost him his eyesight in the fourth grade, when an eye doctor prescribed a patch over his weak left eye in order to strengthen his weaker right eye. Robert refused to wear it because of the way his classmates teased him, so his mother put a thick coat of transparent fingernail polish over the left lens of his glasses, thinking it would work as well as the patch. It almost blinded him, and perhaps was a factor in his continuing failure as a student.

While Robert had trouble in school, he had an easier time learning to take advantage of his mother. He became an accomplished liar and a constant runaway. Regardless of how outlandish his tales, his mother always believed him. She dismissed his running away as a phase he was going through. And even through there were whispers that he had strange notions toward young girls, particularly after he was caught tying up a neighbor child at the age of 11, he always found a place in his mother's forgiving arms.

At 13, Robert was accused of molesting a little girl and was sent to Valley of the Sun School in Phoenix, a boarding school for troubled boys. His parents still had no idea of how troubled he had become. While home for the

Christmas holidays, he took to his bed sick. When Maude Moormann sat down at his bedside to read to him from the *Arizona Sun*, Flagstaff's newspaper, he slipped a .22-caliber revolver from beneath the sheets, pulled the trigger and shot her in the stomach. Even though friends and family members felt otherwise, Maude Moormann insisted the shooting was an accident. She spent weeks in the hospital. Because of the way the bullet was lodged in her liver, her doctors opted not to remove it. She supposedly carried it there until the day she died, but in one of several macabre twists to the tale of her murder 22 years later, the slug could not be found when the coroner reassembled what was left of her body for autopsy.

After the shooting, Moormann was returned to Valley of the Sun School. Soon he was arrested for being a runaway in possession of a deadly weapon and sent to the Fort Grant juvenile correctional facility in southwestern Arizona. It was the first of two stays there. The second time was at age 17 for molesting yet another little girl. He was released at 18 and began taking the drug Mellaril to control his sexual urges.

He returned to Flagstaff, where he received a General Equivalency Diploma in 1967, the same year his father died. The cause of death officially was listed as a massive coronary, but others said his 57-year-old heart had been broken by the boy he never wanted.

Robert, who had grown to a hefty five-foot 10 and still wore his thick glasses, was left alone with his mother. She continued to hover over him and provide a home with the generous estate her husband left.

Not fit for the draft because of his flat feet, poor vision and slow reading and learning ability, Robert held a series of odd jobs for the next two years. He was employed as everything from a busboy for the Flagstaff Holiday Inn to a recreation aid for the U.S. Forest Service before he enrolled at Plaza Mall Barber College. Although he successfully completed the course, he never used his barber's license, and went back to work as a busboy for the Franciscan Cafe. He held this job until Jan. 25, 1972, the day he officially entered the criminal world as an adult.

By his own account, the crime that first sent him to prison was premeditated, but it didn't happen the way he planned. Moormann, who had stopped taking his Mellaril weeks earlier, borrowed a .22-caliber Colt pistol from a friend. All his life, he said, he had been made to feel stupid and inferior by women, and the gun made him feel strong. He was going to use it to kidnap a friend of his mother's and make her do everything he wanted. But when he went over to her house that Tuesday morning and talked to her, he lost his nerve and couldn't bring himself to pull the gun.

He left in his mother's 1969 Chevy Malibu and began driving aimlessly around the slush-covered streets of Flagstaff with feelings of rage, failure and humiliation simmering in his soul. As he drove past an elementary school, he spied the woman's 8-year-old daughter, a bright-eyed, tow-headed child who was on her way home for lunch. She knew Moormann and though nothing of getting in the car with him, especially after he told her that her parents had said it was OK for her to have lunch with him.

Moormann drove her to the Flamingo Motel, where he had earlier rented Room 49. It was the room in which he had planned to humiliate the girl's mother. Once inside, he showed the trembling child the gun and told her not to scream. Promising he would not hurt her, he took off the sobbing child's clothes and then his. He handcuffed her,

and then he lay down on the bed with her. He made her touch him and then forced her to put her mouth on him. He then tried to have sex with her, but was unsuccessful.

Several hours passed, and as the child's parents were beginning to worry about why she had not returned from school. He dressed her against the winter chill and told her he was going to take her to Las Vegas to marry him. If her parents wanted her back, they would have to pay him $500. He put her in his mother's car, and the two of them headed west through the snow-covered pines along Route 66.

When they reached the jumble of motels, bars and truck stops known as Ash Fork, he rented a room and continued the violations that began in the Flamingo Motel. Back in the car, they turned north onto the back roads that led them through the snow-covered rock, sage brush and scrub oak to the far northwest corner of the state.

After driving most of the day, they checked into a motel in Meadview, a small town on the Arizona side of Lake Mead. He forced himself on the girl a third time, and then later that night, they continued on toward Las Vegas. Less than an hour later, the car became mired in the mud near Temple Bar, Arizona, 10 miles from the nearest paved road. They spent the rest of the night shivering in the car, while Robert Moormann began to contemplate what he had done.

While stunned police and family members mounted an intense manhunt for Moormann and the girl in Flagstaff, he had the car's AM radio tuned to an Oklahoma station and never knew the furor the child's disappearance was causing. But he did know he was in more trouble than he had ever been in, and he began to consider his options.

The thought of suicide came to mind. He could simply put the gun to his head and pull the trigger and it would all be over. Then he looked at his sleeping victim's innocent face and realized she could not fend for herself in a cold, desolate wasteland like the Arizona Strip.

At daybreak, he put the gun in the waistband of his pants and set out on foot, carrying the girl most of the way until they reached State Route 93, just east of Hoover

By his own account, the crime that first sent him to prison was premeditated.

Dam and the Nevada state line.

Along the way she asked him if she would have to do anything nasty again. He promised her she wouldn't.

Once they reached the roadway, nearly 48 hours after the odyssey began, Moormann and the girl were picked up hitchhiking along the highway by a family in a motorhome. The woman gave the frightened and exhausted little girl cookies and milk and put her to bed, while Moormann explained that he was taking her to see her uncle in Las Vegas.

When pressed for details, he changed his story, and the couple grew suspicious. Feeling their distrust, he pulled out the gun, emptied out the bullets and gave them to the couple. Then he told them to take him to the Las Vegas police station.

The girl was tearfully reunited with her parents, and Moormann waived extradition and was sent back to Flagstaff. He was sent to the state mental hospital in Phoenix for evaluation, and after being found competent to stand trial, he was taken back to Flagstaff, where he pleaded guilty to kidnapping and was given an open-ended sentence of nine years to life in the Arizona State Prison in Florence.

• • • • • • •

Moormann's prison career was unremarkable. He showed "good institutional adjustment," took classes, received weekly sex offender counseling and worked at the usual menial prison jobs. He tried to develop hobbies—horticulture, stamp collecting—and with his mother's financial backing, he tried to start a mail order laminating business, which went nowhere.

After six years of repeated requests for parole, he was finally released to a halfway house in Phoenix in January of 1979.

Moormann again sought his mother's financial help in the hopes of starting another business, a driving school, even though parole officer Jess Medrano had forbidden him from buying a car. He continued with the counseling he had started in prison and seemed to be adjusting to life on the outside.

Moormann still continued to express "wild sex fantasies," but his counselors didn't be-

lieve he was a threat. He began visiting prostitutes but had trouble performing. During one visit, he was rolled for $200, and to add insult to injury, he contracted syphilis. He later said that he became impotent with women because of the incident, but that he had "always had a problem with young children."

The stress of Moormann's relatively unstructured life on the outside grew greater and greater, and he began to have trouble living with the terms of his probation.

Only nine months after his release his parole was revoked, and he was sent back to Florence. This time, Moormann appeared devoted to bettering himself. He took a business management course, continued sex-offender counseling and completed an assertiveness training course. He also joined the Jaycees and became a member of the Church of Jesus Christ of Latter-day Saints.

His good behavior earned him the right to a furlough to visit with his mother. No one paid attention to the one-sentence notation in his prison file that said he should be kept away from her. That oversight later cost the state $100,000 in a wrongful death settlement with Maude Moormann's siblings.

On Thursday, Jan. 12, 1984, 74-year-old Maude Moormann boarded a Greyhound bus to Mesa, a Phoenix suburb just 50 miles from Florence. A friend met her at the station and drove her to the state prison to pick up her son. He had been given three days to spend with his mother in Florence.

With her son at her side, Maude stepped into the bright sunshine of a mild Arizona winter and breathed the crisp morning air. But her heart was heavy. She had already told Robert that she would be moving back to Oklahoma in April to live out her last years in peace. This would be her last visit.

They were driven a short mile to the Blue Mist Motel, a non-descript one-story block building. Maude had stayed there before when she came to visit her son. This time, she checked into Room 22, almost in view of the prison guard towers across the highway.

She never checked out.

That night in the room, Robert Moormann sat on one of the twin beds and showed his mother a codicil to her will, a document he drafted in prison that would have left her entire $300,000 estate to him.

She refused to sign it, telling him that it would be a mistake to leave him with that much money, that people would take advantage of him like they always had. She told him he would be better off if the money were held in trust for him like she planned, and that he would be able to live comfortably off the interest from her estate.

Robert would not be denied. Using strips torn from towels and bedsheets, he tied his aging mother to the bed and gagged her. Then he placed a pillow over her face and held it there.

As the last stars of the cold Arizona night faded from the sky, Robert left the motel room and walked three blocks west to a Circle K convenience market. He bought a

At the Blue Mist Motel, in Florence, Ariz., Moormann tied his mother to a bed and gagged her. Then he placed a pillow over her head and held it there until she stopped breathing. He then methodically cut her body apart limb by limb and disposed of the parts throughout the city.

box of white plastic garbage bags, a bottle of Pepto Bismol, a can of Lysol disinfectant spray, and a bottle of 409 cleaner. He also bought an Ecko serrated steak knife and a $23.95 folding Buck knife with a leather sheath. As he handed over $32 and waited for his change, he told the clerk that his mother had told him to buy the Buck knife as a present for a friend.

Robert walked back to the motel and told the manager his mother wasn't feeling well. He then asked for a supply of linen and towels, saying that he would make up the room himself so the maid wouldn't have to disturb her.

He locked himself in the room and stripped off his boots, jeans and blue prison work shirt. He then pulled off his mother's floral-print flannel nightgown, carried her lifeless body into the bathroom and put her in the tub.

What happened next shocked the tiny town and was described by Pinal County prosecutor Al Stooks as the grisliest crime he's ever seen.

Using the razor-sharp Buck knife to cut through the flesh and the steak knife to cut through gristle, Robert Moormann methodically cut his mother apart limb from limb.

He flushed nine of her fingers down the toilet—he lost one—so she couldn't be identified by her fingerprints.

He stuffed the rest of her in the garbage bags, cleaned the blood from the brown-tiled floor with the cleanser he had bought and then waited for nightfall.

On Friday night, George Johnson, who owns a pizza restaurant not far from the Blue Mist, flagged down police officers Don Thuesen and Keith Hyland and told them something strange was going on. He explained that Moormann had approached him with a suspicious request to put some "cow guts" and "spoiled meat" in his dumpster. Johnson, a prison employee who knew Moormann, also said that Moormann had mentioned that he was on furlough and that his mother was ill.

About 11 p.m., Thuesen and Hyland went to the Blue Mist to look in on Moormann and his mother. he told them that his mother was feeling better and had left with a friend earlier in the evening. he invited the officers into the room. Nothing seemed amiss, Maude Moormann's terry-cloth slippers were next to the bed, and her beige leather purse was on the nightstand. The officers did, however, notice the room was extremely cold with the air conditioner running, and they detected a "medicinal smell" coming from the bathroom.

They reported the incident to their supervisor, then left to continue their rounds. Two hours later, they returned to the motel and parked. Moormann stepped out into the chill of the clear January night and told them he was getting worried about his mother because she had not returned and had been without her blood pressure medication for nearly eight hours. The officers radioed in a missing persons report. When Florence Police Capt. T.J. Horrall drove to the motel, Moormann brought him and Thuesen and Hyland into his room again. This time, the officers noticed small, brownish red spots on the floor and wall, and the floor appeared wet. Then, Moormann began to tell Horrall a different story about his mother's disappear-

TRIAL COURT PROCEEDINGS

Presiding Judge: Richard N. Roylston

Prosecutor: W. Allen Stooks

Start of Trial: March 26, 1985

Verdict: April 4, 1985

Sentencing: May 7, 1985

Aggravating Circumstances

Prior conviction punishable by
    life imprisionment

Pecuniary gain

Especially heinous/cruel/depraved

Mitigating Circumstances

None sufficient to call for leniency

ance. This time, he said he had gone to purchase a knife as a gift for someone, and when he came back she was gone.

Horrall asked Moormann about the "cow guts", and he replied that a cousin had given him 25 pounds of hamburger that spoiled and that he flushed it down the toilet. At 1:20 a.m., the officers left, but Horrall told Thuesen and Hyland to keep an eye on Moormann. Fifteen minutes later, Moormann left his room to use a pay phone. The officers radioed for instructions, and Horrall ordered them not to let Moormann back into the room. He had just learned that an hour and a half earlier Moormann had given a box of raw bones to Corrections Lt. Luther Damman as a gift for the prison dogs.

Thuesen and Hyland told Moormann he could wait in their squad car until his mother returned. At 2:30 a.m., two prison officials arrived, and out of Moormann's earshot, told Thuesen and Hyland that the box of bones Moormann had given Damman contained human body parts.

Thuesen then placed Moormann under arrest for suspicion of first degree murder:

"I wonder if I need an attorney," Moormann told them. "I will leave it up to you guys if I need an attorney." As they drove to the station Moormann offered to make a full confession. Speaking into a tape recorder, he told Thuesen and Horrall, "Well, my mom and I had a—we had an argument, and during it I hit her a few times and then it got worse and I lost my cool and I tied her up—and she kept on me, talking things about my real family, and I don't remember the exact time and I suffocated her. Then I panicked and I dissected her."

Police began searching trash bins in town and found the grisly evidence of his crime. Maude Moormann's head was found in a dumpster behind the motel, and in another macabre twist in the investigation, her feet were found in a bin behind Foot's Drive-in. Whether it was a coincidence or a sick attempt at humor was never established.

The next day, a search of Moormann's prison cell turned up a draft of the forged will dated Jan. 13, 1984, the day Maude Moormann was murdered. The document provided to be the evidence prosecutor

Stooks needed to prove to the jury that the crime was premeditated, an allegation Moormann labeled "B.S."

Moormann claimed that he had been having sex with his mother and had put the pillow over her mouth to keep her quiet.

"Mom and I had been having an affair for years," he said. "That night I accidentally hurt her. I just put the pillow over her head to knock her out, not to kill her." He said he had seen his father use a pillow the same way to calm his mother down without hurting her, but the autopsy did not find evidence that Maude Moormann had been sexually violated.

During his nine-day trial, which began March 26, 1985, defense attorney Tom Kelly argued that Moormann was criminally insane and delusional, referring to a wife he never had and insisting his father was still alive. Stooks countered that the dissection was too meticulous to have been done during a lapse of sanity, pointing to the fact that the flesh had been so expertly removed from the bones he had given to the prison lieutenant that it took a prison doctor to tell they were human.

Stooks introduced a photograph of Maude Moormann's severed head into evidence after the defense refused to stipulate to the identity of the victim. Robert Moormann was unmoved when he was shown the photo, and sat emotionless during the proceedings, fidgeting occasionally with his thick, black-rimmed glasses.

The burly defendant never took the stand to testify in his own defense.

It took a jury only two hours to convict him of first degree-murder. On April 30, 1985, Judge Robert O. Roylston sentenced him to die.

Moormann still has about two years' worth of federal appeals. He hopes he never gets as close to the gas chamber as he did the first time, but if he does, he says he will put more thought into his last request.

"Next time I have to go through it, I'm going to order something special," he says. "Maybe something like steak with all the trimmings, or shrimp."

John C. D'Anna is the metro editor of *Tribune Newspapers* in Mesa, Ariz.

Defense attorney Tom Kelly argued that Moormann was criminally insane and delusional.

VERNON MADISON

RENEE BUSBY

On April 18, 1985, around 5:30 p.m., Mobile Police Corporal Julius Schulte was dispatched on a missing child report to a residence at 1058 Etta Avenue on the north side of Mobile, Ala. A mother had reported her daughter missing after she failed to come home from school.

For Schulte, it was a routine call. A 20-year veteran of the Mobile Police Department, he had spent 12 years in the Juvenile Division. He had been on hundreds of similar calls.

But this call was different. It would be his last. As he sat in his unmarked police cruiser in front of the house where the child lived, he was shot twice in the back of the head.

Schulte, referred to as "Mr. Friendly" and "The Peacemaker" by his fellow police officers, remained on life support machines at the University of South Alabama Medical Center until April 24, 1985, when the machines were shut off. His 20-year career came to an end as he was pronounced dead at the age of 53.

• • • • • • •

The assailant was Vernon Madison, 42, a Mississippi parolee who had been in a failed common-law marriage with Cheryl Greene, the woman who made the missing child report to police. Angry that Greene called the police, Madison thought she had accused him of kidnapping her child. Greene was also shot by Madison that night. She remained hospitalized for several days after being shot in the back, and then was released from a Mobile hospital.

The turmoil and domestic squabbling that converged on the house that night resulted in Schulte's death. Madison had moved out of the house and ended the relationship with Greene two weeks prior to the shooting. One week later, Madison threatened her.

When Greene arrived home from work on April 18, she became concerned because her 10-year-old daughter, Kimberly Hughes, who normally went to a neighbor's house after school, wasn't there. Her fear turned to panic when she read a note on the kitchen table that read: "You call the shots, I'll play the game, bitch. Call your cop friends." Greene's daughter still was not home at 5:30 p.m.

Greene didn't have a telephone so she went to a neighbor's, a minister, and called Madison's relatives. When Madison's mother said she hadn't seen Kimberly, Greene called 911 and reported her daughter missing. As she walked back to her house, she found Madison standing in the yard, angry because he thought Greene had accused him of kidnapping Kimberly. But Madison left the house, saying he was going to look for Kimberly. Greene then went back to the minister's house, hoping someone would call with information.

Around 6:15 p.m., Kimberly called and said she had been with Greene's friend, Lillian Buff Trapp. Greene and Trapp met while Trapp was an inmate in the city jail. Greene was employed by the county as a paralegal in the jail.

When Kimberly safely arrived home, Greene called 911 and told them the missing child report was simply a matter of miscommunication. Schulte, however, was already on his way to the house. Greene, afraid to stay at the house because of Madison's threats, was packing her clothes to leave and stay with Trapp.

Madison, meanwhile, had gone to Mary

PHOTOS • *THE MOBILE (ALA.) PRESS REGISTER*

Prior to the fatal stabbing of Julius Shulte in 1985, Madison was sentenced to 35 years in prison after being convicted of robbing and shooting a man in 1970. While he was in a Mississippi prison for this crime, he was convicted of two more violent crimes. In 1973, he assaulted and attempted to kill another inmate and in 1977, he assaulted a prison corrections officer.

McCord's home in Prichard, a suburb just north of Greene's house, and persuaded her to drive him to Greene's to get the remainder of his belongings from her house. McCord had befriended Madison before when the two were living together in the late 1970s, before Madison was sentenced to prison in Mississippi for armed robbery.

McCord agreed to drive him to the house. Before they got to the street where Greene lived, Madison instructed the woman to park around the corner and remain in the car until he came back.

Once at the house, Madison again argued with his former wife, and questioned why she accused him of kidnapping her daughter. Schulte had already pulled up in front of the house, while Madison was inside arguing with Greene. The police officer never got out of his squad car.

Realizing he may be faced with a possible domestic situation that could lead to trouble, Schulte called for backup around 7:27 p.m., but it was too late.

Trapp walked outside and told Schulte there had been a misunderstanding about Kimberly missing, and that she had picked her up from school. She said there was trouble and arguing going on and she asked Schulte to stay until Madison left and they were all safe.

Trapp went back inside the house where Madison and Greene were arguing. "He was arguing because he thought she called the cops on him and she told him she didn't call the cops on him, that she called the juvenile authorities because she thought Kimberly was missing and she didn't know what had happened," recalled Trapp.

Madison, Greene, Kimberly and Trapp walked out of the house, then Greene and Madison walked up to Schulte's car. Greene told the officer that Kimberly's disappearance was a misunderstanding, and that she had to leave her own house because she was being threatened by Madison. Still upset that he had been accused of taking Kimberly, Madison told Schulte he didn't like being blamed for something he didn't do.

Schulte assured Madison that he was not there to arrest anyone, but his sole concern was the safety of the child. The police officer

then informed Greene that a marked police unit would be sent back with her when she returned to the house to get the remainder of her possessions. At that point, Madison made the statement, "Oh yeah, wait a minute," and walked away.

He walked to McCord's car parked a block away, retrieved a .32 caliber pistol he had left in her purse earlier that night, and told her to forget about him. Madison walked back to Etta Avenue, and strode up to Schulte's car. He fired two shots in the back of Schulte's head, turned and fired another shot at Greene and her daughter. Greene fell to the ground after being hit in the back.

Trapp remembers it like this: "The next time I saw Vernon he was standing parallel or almost parallel to me and I saw a gun. I saw him aim a gun at Ofc. Schulte and I saw two flashes and then I saw the blood drip down Schulte's face," recalled Trapp. Kimberly said Madison then turned the gun toward her mother and made the statement, "Here, bitch, if you want to play this game, I can play it too," then shot Greene. By this time, Ofc. John Joseph Wynne had arrived as backup. As he stepped out of his car with his shotgun, he heard the shots, and then saw three women—Trapp and Kimberly dragging Greene.

Greene said she never saw who shot her. She said she heard two "pops," and fell to the ground.

"As I approached Ofc. Schulte, he was sitting up in the car swaying backward and forward. I could see blood coming from his left temple. He was mumbling, but I could not understand what he said," Wynne recalled.

Dr. Robert Mudd later testified at the trial that Schulte's gunshot wounds to the head were similar to the types of wounds suffered by Robert Kennedy when he was assassinated.

After the shooting, Madison went to the Roger Williams Housing Project on the north side of Mobile, where his mother lived, and told his brother, Michael McMillan, he was in trouble and he needed help.

McMillan stated to Mobile police after the shooting that he saw a gun protruding from Madison's pants, but at trial he recanted the story, and said he saw something bulging from the pants, but didn't know what the object was. He said he never saw Madison with a gun.

Michael and another brother, Nathaniel, drove Madison to a house off Broad Street on the south side of Mobile, and from there they went to another house about two miles away.

During both stops, Madison's brothers waited in the car while he went inside. When they left the second house, they drove across town to Radney Funeral Home, where Madison asked his friend, Ollie Lee Doss, to drive him to Bay Minette, Ala., a small city on the opposite side of Mobile Bay. He told Doss he had just shot a police officer. Doss refused, and when Madison left, employees at the funeral home called the police and gave them a description of the maroon Chevrolet Monte Carlo.

Two minutes after midnight, Ofc. Ronnie Burch spotted the car fitting the description in downtown Mobile. He pulled the car over, patted the three men down, and searched the car. Madison was in the back of the car when stopped.

Burch found a .32 caliber pistol in the back of the car under the right passenger's seat—later determined to be the gun that was used to kill Schulte.

Madison was arrested without resistance, and taken to the Mobile City Jail, where he was booked on an attempted murder charge. The charge was enhanced to capital murder after Schulte died. Murdering a law enforcement officer in the state of Alabama is a capital offense, punishable by death in the electric chair, or life in prison without the possibility of parole.

• • • • • • •

At his trial in September 1985, Madison pleaded innocent by reason of a mental disease or defect, and attempted to prove he suffered from a mental disease that prevented him from understanding right from wrong the night he shot Schulte. The defense's case focused on testimony from a psychologist and psychiatrist, who both testified Madison suffered from paranoia and an anti-social personality disorder that prevented him from realizing the criminal nature of his conduct.

One of the defense's psychiatrists testified that during stressful situations, Madison sees himself as a "combat soldier and anyone in front of him is the enemy," and the enemy has to be eliminated.

Defense witness Dr. John Renick, a Mobile psychiatrist, testified Madison told him that at the time of the shooting, he was under a lot of stress because his sister had been murdered one month before during a shooting at a Mobile nightclub. Renick said a person under stress with the type of mixed personality/paranoia disorder does "not have much capacity to discern what's right and what's wrong."

But a rebuttal witness for the state testified that during a battery of psychological exams, Madison "faked being bad." Psychologist Dr. C. Van Rosen testified that after examining Madison, he determined Madison knew right from wrong the night of the shooting, and was able to conform his conduct according to the law.

Rosen said although Madison had a personality disorder, that did not mean Madison was "crazy."

Witnesses testified Madison often said he wanted to kill a police officer.

After a week-long trial before Mobile County Circuit Judge Ferrill D. McRae, the jury entered the courtroom with its verdict, after deliberating 44 minutes. The courtroom was a sea of blue as Mobile police officers filled the benches. Defense attorney Arthur Madden protested the police presence, saying it prejudiced his client. "The court is full of police officers for the sole purpose of influencing that jury to return a verdict of a capital offense," Madden told the judge, arguing that the courtroom be cleared. But McRae said under the Constitution of the United States, trials are open to the public, and he refused to make the officers leave.

The all-white jury convicted Madison, who is black, of capital murder. Schulte was white.

Before attorneys made their arguments in the trial's sentencing phase, Aldonia McMillan, Madison's mother, begged for mercy for her firstborn son, who was one of nine children. "I come asking you to have

At his second trial in September 1990, a jury of six blacks and six whites again convicted Madison of capital murder, and recommended he be sentenced to die in the electric chair.

mercy on my child. I don't condone killing. My child is sick. Give him another chance. I tried to be a mother," she said, weeping. As he had throughout the trial, Madison showed no emotion as his mother pleaded with the jury to spare her son's life.

Mobile County District Attorney Chris Galanos told the jury it was not allowed by law to hear any evidence of Madison's prior criminal history. In the sentencing phase, however, the state could introduce any prior convictions.

He told the jurors this was not the first incident of violence demonstrated by Madison. Galanos said Madison, in 1970, was sentenced to 35 years in prison after being convicted of robbing and shooting a man. The district attorney pointed to two more convictions of violent crimes committed by Madison while he was in prison in Mississippi. One conviction was assault and battery with intent to kill another inmate in 1973. The other was an assault on a prison corrections officer in 1977.

"Life without parole in this case, I would respectfully submit, would be fraud. It would mock the dead—Julius, in this case—and would jeopardize presently living human beings. There is a time to keep silent and there is a time to speak, and if anyone is to tell him enough is enough, it's going to be you," Galanos told the jury.

Madison's court-appointed attorney, Arthur Madden, argued for the other possible sentence—life without parole. "My client is going to spend the rest of his life in the penitentiary. He will die there, and the only question is whether he will die by the hand of God or by the hand of many, by your decision."

It took the jurors 45 minutes to decide Madison should die in the electric chair. Eleven of the jurors voted for the death sentence, while the other juror voted to recommend life in prison without the possibility of parole.

The district attorney said after the trial there was clear and convincing evidence that Madison was not insane. "He was just mean," added Galanos.

Schulte's widow, Betty Jean Schulte, a Catholic Social Services worker in Mobile, remained silent throughout the trial, and later declined to talk to reporters.

Madison, who did not testify during his trial, issued a hand-written statement to the media after his trial. Madison signed the statement using his African name, Ajeka Kenyatta. "I wasn't deluded by the outcome of this case, for it is typical of the oppressor. Every black man, woman and child in this country is under a death sentence. We have no sovereign right. Justice is the oppressor, not the black man."

After the jury's verdict, a police dispatch went out over the police radio that Vernon Madison had been convicted of killing the veteran officer of 20 years, and the jury had recommended death.

On Nov. 12, 1985, Judge McRae followed the jury's recommendation and imposed the death sentence, saying the murder of Julius Schulte was a "pitiless and totally amoral act committed by a man whose life history is but one sequel after another of violent, assaultive acts against other human beings and total disregard for our law." Madison walked out of the courtroom vowing to be back. And he was.

A capital murder conviction in Alabama is automatically appealed to the Alabama Court of Criminal Appeals, and eventually to the Alabama Supreme Court. In 1989, the Alabama Supreme Court reversed Madison's death sentence and capital murder conviction, ruling the state had failed to give race-neutral reasons for excluding blacks from the all-white jury that convicted Madison. A new trial was ordered.

At his second trial in September 1990, a jury of six blacks and six whites again convicted Madison of capital murder, and by a 10-2 vote, recommended he be sentenced to die in the electric chair. Again, Madison asserted the insanity defense. Madison, as in the first trial, did not testify.

For Schulte's family, it was a painful reminder of the events that had occurred five years before. Mrs. Schulte continued to remain silent, but her son, Michael Schulte, made a brief statement to the media after the second trial. "I don't think there was any dispute that he did it. I believe in the death penalty. I think it would have been a detri-

ment to the community to allow him to stay in prison for life," Shulte said. Unlike the first trial, this trial was void of police presence. Only a few police officers attended.

Before McRae imposed sentencing on Nov. 14, 1990, a three-page, hand-written statement from Madison to the judge was read in court. Madison said the testimony against him was all lies. "I am by no earthly means evil or an abusive person, but I will defend myself, my loved ones and my life and property and if I am to die for doing those things, then don't anticipate on me giving up my life without defending it by any

Schulte was referred to as "Mr. Friendly" and "The Peacemaker" by his fellow police officers at the Mobile (Ala.) Police Department. His 20-year career came to an end when Vernon Madison shot and killed him.

means necessary in court and above all with the mighty sword of my God to aid me for I am not a murderer nor a hateful or vindictive soul, even when I should hate, I don't and I pride myself on being above the ignorance of men with natures for truly my God does not dwell in such a being. I am not some wild beast nor am I insane."

After the statement was read, McRae again followed the jury's recommendation and sentenced Madison to death—a sentence which was automatically appealed.

Madison never told his story in court, but in an interview with a probation officer who was preparing Madison's pre-sentence report for the judge, Madison recounted the events of that night as he remembered them.

Madison claimed when he heard Kimberly was missing, he went to Etta Avenue.

He said he became upset when he learned Greene had called the police, but he denied he became angry. Instead, he said he went to look for Kimberly. When he returned to Etta Avenue, he met his mother, who said Kimberly was home safe.

According to Madison, Greene knew all along that her daughter was with Trapp, and that she fabricated her daughter's disappearance to make it appear he was causing trouble. He denied he was at the house causing trouble. He said he went back to Greene's house to get the rest of his personal belongings.

He said when Ofc. Schulte arrived, Greene talked to him in hushed tones, which Madison claimed attempted to make him look bad. Madison said he felt Schulte failed to show him respect. He also claimed to not remember the shooting or any details of the night of the shooting. "I just snapped," he told police in a statement.

Schulte, according to Madison, never identified himself as a police officer. Madison said he wanted to simply protect himself, get his property and leave. Witnesses who testified at trial that he wanted to kill a police officer were lying, Madison said.

● ● ● ● ● ● ●

Madison was born in Mobile, Ala. His parents, Willie Seals and Aldonia Madison, never married and when Vernon Madison

was two, his mother married Nathaniel McMillan. Vernon was the oldest of nine children.

Madison was abused as a child by his stepfather. Once when he was 11, McMillan tried to smother him with a pillow. At age 9, he was struck in the face by his stepfather, and had several teeth knocked out. When he was 12, his stepfather deserted the family and, as the oldest, Madison had to manage the household and children while his mother worked. Madison lived with his mother until he was incarcerated in the Alabama Industrial School.

His criminal life began March 3, 1965, when he was a 15-year-old student at Blount High School. He was arrested for assault after he became belligerent with the school librarian. The librarian, Ethel Porter, threw a ruler at Madison, who then threw a knife at Porter, striking her in the neck causing a superficial wound. Madison was expelled from the Mobile County Public School System.

Five months later, Madison was charged with disorderly conduct after he threatened a man with a knife during an argument over who should get a grass cutting job in the Toulminville area of Mobile.

In November 1965, Madison was charged with assault with intent to murder after he stabbed another juvenile, William Ryne, in the heart with a 6-inch butcher knife.

His adult criminal record began in January 1968 when he was charged with assault with a gun, and sentenced to 60 days in jail. On November 20, 1970, Madison and three other men robbed the McGee Street Grocery in Prichard, Ala. Madison entered the store with a handgun and ordered all of the employees to get on the floor. Madison pistol-whipped the manager in the face and shot one round in the floor upon leaving. Later, Madison and another man robbed the Jet Package Store in Meridian, Miss., at gunpoint. One of the customers was shot during the robbery. Madison was sentenced to 35 years in prison for armed robbery, and while in prison was twice convicted of assault.

In 1973, Madison received a 10-year sentence, which was to run consecutively with his 35-year sentence, when he was convicted of assault and battery with intent to kill for stabbing another inmate in the Mississippi State Prison in Parchman, Miss.

Following another prison incident in March 1977, Madison pleaded guilty for the aggravated assault of a prison guard and was given 20 years. Five years of the sentence was suspended, and the remaining 15 years was to run concurrently with his other sentences. Madison was incarcerated in the Mississippi State Penitentiary from May 28, 1971, until his parole on May 31, 1983.

A corrections officer described Madison as "one of the most dangerous inmates ever at this institution."

In 1970, he began living in a common law relationship with Mary Elizabeth McCord. They had one child. Madison, released from prison in 1983, was unable to continue his relationship with Mary McCord. In July 1983 he married Ronetta Dixon. They separated in July 1984.

He met Greene in September 1984, and they began living together with Greene's daughter.

His last employment was a three-month stint in 1984 as a grounds keeper for the University of South Alabama. He was laid off due to a shortage of work.

● ● ● ● ● ● ●

In 1992, the Alabama Court of Criminal Appeals reversed and remanded Madison's case. His third trial was scheduled for late 1992. This appeals court ruled that a psychologist's testimony in the 1990 trial about Madison's mental state was inadmissible because he testified about facts that were not in evidence at trial.

Meanwhile, prosecutors have criticized appeals court rulings that have reversed several capital murder convictions in Mobile cases—including Madison's case. "I think our appellate courts now hold us to the unrealistic standard of giving a capital defendant a perfect, as opposed to a fair, trial. You can put any case under a microscope for years and probably find something wrong. Somewhere along the line, the question of guilt or innocence has been obfuscated by these hypertechnical legal arguments," commented District Attorney Galanos, who has

prosecuted Madison both times.

The actual costs of appeals in capital cases is not known. Assistant Attorney General Ken Nunnelley, with the Attorney General's Capital Litigation Division in Montgomery, Ala., said there's no way to gauge the amount spent on the time-consuming appeals for death row inmates. "It would be virtually impossible to figure it out. It's hard for us to tell how much time we spend on a given case. Unlike law firms, we don't keep up with the amount of time spent on each case," stated Nunnelley, who is one of two attorneys that handles death row appeals for the state of Alabama. Madison's last trial in 1990 cost the state of Alabama around $25,000.

Debbie Herbert with the Alabama Department of Corrections estimates it costs between $16,000 to $18,000 annually to clothe, house and feed death row inmates in Alabama.

Some medical experts who testified in Madison's 1990 trial were paid more than Madison's court-appointed attorney. According to records in the Alabama comptroller's office, Paul Brown, Madison's court-appointed attorney, was paid $2,620 for his in-court appearance, which totaled 65.5 hours, and $1,000 for his out-of-court preparation, which totaled 196 hours.

Brown had submitted a bill for $3,290 for his out of court preparation, but the maximum amount of court-appointed attorney can be paid in Alabama for out-of-court time spent preparing the case is $1,000.

While Brown feels the amount of money the state pays to represent indigent capital defendants is low, he said he is committed to helping indigent defendants in death penalty cases. "When you believe in what you're doing, that the death penalty is wrong, then it is somewhat of a labor of love," stated Brown.

Madison now sits in the Mobile County Metro Jail, awaiting his third trial.

The Schulte family sits and waits also—for the end to a seven-year ordeal.

"Somewhere along the line, the question of guilt or innocence has been obfuscated by hypertechnical legal arguments."
—Chirs Galanos
Mobile County, Ala.,
District Attorney

Renee Busby is a reporter for *The Mobile* (Ala.) *Press Register* and has covered state courts for the past six years. She has covered both of Madison's trials.

ALABAMA

GERALD ARMOND GALLEGO

SEAN WHALEY

Gerald Armond Gallego never met his father, but he is following in his old man's footsteps just the same. Like his father, Gallego waits for death in a small prison cell, sentenced to die for murder.

And barring any court victories, he will be executed for his crimes just like his father was 38 years ago.

Unlike his father, however, Gallego earned notoriety for his crimes. Convicted of the heinous murders of three young women and one man in Nevada and California, Gallego is best known by the infamous moniker, "sex slave killer."

Gallego was born in Sacramento, Calif., on July 17, 1946, while his father was serving a stint in San Quentin.

Nine years later, on March 5, 1955, Gerald Albert Gallego became the first man to die in the Mississippi gas chamber. Gallego's father was sentenced to die for the murder of a Gulfport, Miss., policeman, and for the killing of a jailer in an escape. He was recaptured a few days later.

The younger Gallego began his criminal activities as a teen-ager, logging numerous arrests for theft and burglary. He served a prison sentence for robbing a motel. His crimes were serious, but never deadly.

He married five times, sometimes failing to get a divorce from his previous spouse, resulting in bigamous unions.

It wasn't until age 32, in the late summer of 1978, that the 5-foot-7-inch Gallego began his life as a serial killer. When he was captured two years later, his fifth wife would attribute 10 murders to his name.

He became known as the "sex slave" killer for his fantasy of wanting to lock up young girls and make them available at his beck and call for sex.

As a result of testimony from Charlene Gallego, now Charlene Williams, an accomplice in all 10 murders, Gallego was sentenced to death for four of the crimes. He was never tried for the six other killings Williams alleged he committed in statements to police.

Gallego only admitted to one killing, the shooting of Craig Miller in November 1980, and that was committed while under the influence of drugs and alcohol he said at his California trial.

He further denied having any "sex slave" fantasy.

In a letter to a newspaper reporter, Gallego wrote, "So far, the press has made me out to be a mass murderer, a killer of young girls, and that's not the truth. Maybe someday I will ask you to sit down with me and listen to my side of the facts."

Gallego never granted that interview.

Charlene Williams, the only daughter of a middle class Sacramento couple, was introduced to Gallego by friends in the fall of 1977. At age 20, she already had two failed marriages.

Her first, in 1975 to a military man, ended six months later in an annulment. Her second, in 1976, ended in divorce after only a few months.

Williams, a major witness in the Nevada murder trial, recalled how impressed she was with Gallego, describing him as "a nice, clean cut, good looking type of fellow." The day after they met, he sent her a dozen roses with a card that read: "To a sweet girl, Gerry." Two weeks later, they were living together. Eventually, they married in Reno in 1978.

At first, the relationship went well. Williams called Gallego considerate.

Barring any court victories, Gallego will be executed for his crimes just like his father was 38 years ago.

But before long, Gallego dominated Williams, telling her how to fix her hair and what clothes to wear. He took her paycheck from a meat wrapping plant and controlled how her money was spent.

Their relationship suffered sexually, with Gallego occasionally impotent. It was always her fault, according to Williams.

One day Gallego confessed his secret fantasy to Williams, "fantasies of having women —girls—and keeping them in this cave-like thing, and they would be there whenever he wanted them," she said.

Gallego's fantasy became reality one September morning in 1978. "When we got up one morning, Gerry said, 'Come on, you're going to kidnap me a girl.'" Thus began what Williams later described as the two-year murder spree of Gerald Gallego.

According to law enforcement officials, Gallego did not act out his fantasy until September 11, 1978, when he kidnapped and killed Kippi Vaught, 16, and Rhonda Scheffler, 17.

Vaught and Scheffler were shopping at the Country Club Plaza shopping mall in Sacramento that day.

Williams didn't remember exactly how she lured two girls to the couple's customized van. But after they entered the vehicle,

PHOTO - AP WIDE WORLD

Gallego came in with a handgun, and the two teen-agers had only a few hours to live.

Gallego drove the girls into the Sierra Nevada, east of Sacramento, on Interstate 80. He sent Williams home to get their Oldsmobile, and ordered her to return at midnight.

Only Gallego knows what happened during the hours he was alone with Vaught and Scheffler. When Williams returned with the car, Gallego drove everyone to a desolate area near Sloughhouse, a small town southeast of Sacramento. He took the girls, one at a time, behind the car.

"I heard what I thought were pops." Williams said. "Then Gerry came back and told me to move over and he got into the driver's side. He sat there only a moment.

"Gerry said, 'One of the girls is still wiggling.' He got back out. He shot them again."

The girls were found two days later. Vaught had been shot twice in the head, and Scheffler had been shot three times.

Gallego told Williams that he had raped Scheffler, but the girls were too old for his desires.

Eight months later they moved to Reno,

and again Gallego tried to act out his fantasy.

Brenda Judd, 14, and Sandra Colley, 13, went to the Washoe County Fair in Reno on June 24, 1979. The Sparks teenagers were to meet up with other family members later in the day.

They met Gerald Gallego instead.

Williams tried to lure these girls into the van with a job offer, but the girls said first they needed to check with their parents. Gallego and Williams drove around Reno looking for other potential victims.

Later they returned to the fair. They found Judd and Colley, who now decided to accept Williams job offer. Once in the van, however, Gallego again entered with a pistol.

The girls, imprisoned in the back of the van, were driven to Lovelock, a small town about 100 miles east of Reno on Interstate 80. Gallego stopped the van at a picnic area off the highway. Williams recalled how the girls pleaded with her to let them go. "One of the girls asked, 'Why us,'" Williams said. "I just told her to do what he said. I might have been able to (help them) but I did not."

Gallego raped both girls, then killed them and buried them in the desert. Their bodies have never been found.

Gallego struck again 10 months later. Karen Chapman Twiggs and Stacey Redican, both 17, were dropped off at Sunrise Mall in Sacramento by Twiggs' mother, Mary Ann, on April 24, 1980. She would pick up the girls later in the day.

Both girls grew up in Reno. After the Twiggs family moved to Sacramento in 1979, Redican, described by her mother as "rebellious" was allowed to move there and live with Karen and her family.

On April 23, 1980, Gallego came home from his bar tending job at the Bob-Les Club in north Sacramento, and said he "wanted a girl." According to Williams, Gallego went on the prowl the next day. Again, Williams lured the two girls into the van. Gallego entered the van with a handgun and bound the girls' hands and feet. He asked the girls if they were "worth anything," and Redican said she had a relative in Reno who might give him money.

Gallego drove to Reno and made Williams take the wheel at Verdi, Nev. Gallego raped the teen-agers while she drove.

Williams then stopped at a supermarket in Reno, where Gallego bought a hammer. Gallego continued the drive from Reno to Lovelock. He turned on a dirt road, and they arrived at the remote Limerick Canyon well after dark. He gook Redican out of the van, then returned for Twiggs. Later, he showed Williams the two shallow graves where the girls were buried.

Hunters found their bodies July 27, 1980. Both girls' hands were trussed in an uncommon type of macrame rope. The rope would eventually provide a valuable clue for prosecutors to link Gallego to the slayings. An autopsy showed both girls were bludgeoned to death with a blunt, hammer-like instrument.

Gallego struck again on June 8, 1980, picking up pregnant, 21-year-old Linda Aguilar while she was hitchhiking along the coast of Oregon. Her body was found buried in the sand at Gold Beach, Ore.

The next month, Virginia Mochel, 34, was kidnapped as she left her job in a Sacramento tavern on July 17. A mother of two, her body was found in Yolo County just west of Sacramento.

Gallego's final two murders proved to be his undoing. Craig Miller, 22, and Mary Elizabeth Sowers, 21, were students at California State University, Sacramento. The couple, engaged to be married, was at the Arden Fair Mall in Sacramento in the early morning of Nov. 2, 1980, when they were kidnapped by Gallego at gunpoint.

Miller's body was found at Bass Lake in Eldorado County east of Sacramento the day of the kidnapping. Sower's body was found three weeks later in a ditch east of Sacramento in Placer County.

But a witness noted the license plate of the car that drove the couple away. The car was traced to Williams, who was identified by witnesses as one of the kidnappers.

Williams, brought in for questioning, denied any knowledge of the crime. She said her name was Mrs. Stephen Feil, a false identification Gallego devised.

The couple fled Sacramento the same day, but the law was not far behind.

On Nov. 3, 1980, Gallego made Williams phone her parents to ask for money. But on Nov. 17, the couple was arrested by the FBI as they collected their money in Omaha, Neb.

Williams finally decided to talk to investigators, and in June, 1982, told police about the Miller-Sowers killing and of Gallego's eight other victims.

In exchange for testimony against Gallego in both Nevada and California courts, Williams pleaded guilty to two first-degree murder charges for the deaths of Miller and Sowers and received a sentence of 16 years, eight months in prison.

On February 25, 1983, Williams pleaded guilty in Nevada to two charges of second degree murder in the Redican-Twiggs slayings. Nevada officials agreed with the sentence imposed in California, which did not allow for any time off for good behavior. The sentence was to run from Nov. 17, 1980 and be carried out in Nevada.

Gallego's first trial was in California for the murders of Miller and Sowers. He acted as his own attorney at the November, 1983 trial held in Martinez, California.

Sacramento County Prosecutor James Morris rested his case after playing a tape that recorded a conversation between Gallego and his mother-in-law, Mercedes Williams, whom he called mom. The recording was made surreptitiously on Dec. 7, 1980, when she visited Gallego at the Sacramento County Jail.

On the tape, Gallego said, "I'm not sorry at all, Mom. And I'll tell you something else. I don't feel cheated because, I'll tell you, Charlene has been good to me the last three years, Mom.

"Hey, it's not the length of life, it's the quality."

Gallego told his mother-in-law that his defense in the Williams-Sowers killings would be diminished capacity because he was using the hallucinogenic drug LSD at the time of the crimes.

In presenting his defense, Gallego said he went to the Arden Fair Mall with the intent to rob someone, not to find a victim to kidnap and rape. The robbery turned into a kidnapping, however, and Gallego said he planned to drop the couple off out of town somewhere.

Both girls' hands were trussed in an uncommon type of macrame rope. The rope would eventually provide a valuable clue for prosecutors that linked Gallego to the slayings.

But Gallego said Miller attacked him, and in fighting him off, he shot him. Gallego said he killed Miller while under the influence of drugs and alcohol, and that his wife killed Sowers to cover up his crime.

Gallego also denied telling Williams about a sex slave fantasy.

The jury did not believe him. On April 11, 1983, Gallego was found guilty of two counts of first degree murder and two counts of kidnapping. The jury of seven women and five men deliberated for 14 hours.

In June, the same jury returned a sentence of death on Gallego for his crimes.

As the California trial concluded, Richard Wagner, the prosecutor in Lovelock, Nev., charged Gallego in Pershing County for the deaths of Brenda Judd and Sandra Colley, and for the killings of Karen Chapman Twiggs and Stacey Redican.

Wagner said he wanted Gallego tried in Nevada because this state would be more likely to execute him for his crimes, even though the cost of the trial would be a hardship on the thinly populated Pershing County.

The Gallego case took an unusual turn in Nevada before it even began.

In January 1984, *Sacramento Bee* newspaper columnist Stan Gilliam wrote a column urging Californians to send a $1 to help cover the cost of the Nevada trial. Donations poured in. One donor wrote in an accompanying letter, "We are counting on the people of Nevada to see that justice is done. In other words, hang the so-and-so."

Many donors perceived that California would never execute Gallego, but Nevada "would do it right."

Eventually 1,785 people contributed more than $26,000 to the cost of the trial, which came in at $72,000. One $2 donation came from New Guinea.

Williams again testified in the February preliminary hearing in Lovelock about both sets of murders. When shown the pictures of Twiggs and Redican, she said, "Those are the girls I led out to the van from Sunrise Mall." Later, when asked about inconsistencies in her descriptions of the crimes, she said, "I know it sounds sick, but they all looked the same."

Gallego held over for trial on the Twiggs-

Redican case, but the court ruled there was no evidence, other than Williams' testimony, linking the Judd-Colley killings to Pershing County. Independent corroboration of Williams' testimony was required.

State Public Defender Tom Perkins tried to get the trial moved out of Pershing County. He commissioned a poll that showed 97 percent of the population knew about the case, and 87 percent thought Gallego was guilty. A change of venue was not granted, however.

Gallego did not allow his attorney to make an insanity plea on his behalf. Instead, Gallego maintained he was innocent of the crimes.

Gallego's trial began May 23 and lasted less than two weeks. The trial drew international attention from the media.

In addition to Williams' testimony, Wagner presented a picture as evidence showing Gallego camping in Limerick Canyon with friends a few months before the killings. They were camped in the exact spot of the graves of Twiggs and Redican.

Also linking Gallego to the crimes was the unusual macrame rope used to bind the hands of the girls. Identical rope was found in the trunk of a sportscar that belonged to Gallego.

Unlike the California case, Gallego was silent throughout the Nevada trial. He did not take the stand and made no comments in the courtroom.

Williams, who stands under 5 feet, explained on the stand how she became involved in the crimes with Gallego and did nothing to stop her husband. Williams said he dominated her so completely, that she felt she had to help him fulfill his fantasy of kidnapping young girls to rape and murder.

"It wasn't love, it was needing someone," she said. "He ... he was my security."

Williams also said she was afraid of Gallego. "I was afraid he'd kill me if I ever made him mad enough," she said. "I knew the only way he'd end our relationship was to kill me because I knew too much."

Wagner introduced the Vaught and Scheffler murders to show "a common plan or scheme," in Gallego's killing of Twiggs and Redican.

Perkins attempted to discredit Williams' testimony, and in his closing argument said that if her story sounded too horrible to be true, then maybe it was false.

But Wagner said, "This statement, 'Charlene's story is too horrible to be true,' you want horror? That's horror, and it's true. If it were not, I would walk out of this courtroom right now, but think of the horror in this case and what she testified, too."

A jury of six men and six women took less than four hours to convict Gallego of the two murders. The same jury sentenced him to death for the crimes, despite testimony from clinical psychiatrist Joan Cartwright that Gallego had the mental age of five or six. Cartwright admitted, however, that Gallego registered an IQ of 94 in an intelligence test, making him of average intelligence.

After the jury voted for death, Wagner said he would follow the appeal through the courts and see the sentence carried out. He vowed to be present when it was. He also said that Gallego's father was more of a man than Gallego because his father admitted what he had done.

Gallego continues to maintain his innocence of all crimes except the Miller killing. Yet his conviction and death sentence was upheld by the Nevada Supreme Court on December 20, 1985.

In an appeal for postconviction relief, Gallego's attorney, Richard Cornell, told the court there was a "possibility" that Williams, not Gallego, killed the women out of a "violent homosexual nature." But the court rejected the second appeal in September 1989.

Justice John Mowbray expressed irritation with the case's ongoing appeals. "The American people are fed up," he said. "The law is completely ineffective. This man should have been taken out, executed promptly and forgotten."

Mowbray is not the only one upset at the court delays in Gallego's and other death penalty cases. Donald Redican, the father of Gallego victim Stacey Redican, is also frustrated. He testified before the Nevada Legislature in support of legislation to speed up the appeals process in death penalty cases. "The federal court system absolutely stinks," he said. "We have federal judges sitting on these cases. The cases are complex and a great responsi-

bility, but if they can't resolve the issues in four years, they should resign.

"The appeals process should take no longer than five years," Redican said. "Anyone who does this kind of crime has no concern for society. But the federal system won't respond." The death penalty is absolutely necessary in cases like Gallego's, he said. "It would at least be a deterrent in his case," Redican said. "If he was released tomorrow he would start killing again."

In 1990, Gallego filed another petition citing 19 grounds for the overturn of his Nevada conviction and sentence. Cornell also brought up numerous inconsistencies in Williams' statements about the killings. A state district court rejected the petition.

Gallego appealed the denial to the Supreme Court, which rejected his claims in August, 1992. His attorney requested a rehearing. Even if the claims are rejected by the state, Gallego can still pursue an appeal in the federal courts.

Williams is serving out her 16-year, eight-month sentence at the Nevada Women's Prison in Carson City. She is scheduled to be released from prison on July 17, 1997.

Last year the Nevada Department of Prisons planned to release her from prison for completing her sentence. Her release was based on good behavior, and prison officials were not allowed to keep her behind bars solely because of the agreement made with Nevada and California officials.

California then refiled murder charges against Williams for the Miller and Sowers killings, saying Williams' failure to serve the full term would make her prior agreement void. She stayed in Nevada's prison, however.

Gallego is housed at the Ely State Prison, located near the Utah border. He spends his time on death row with 59 other men and one woman.

If and when the state obtains the authority to execute Gallego, it will be done by lethal injection at the Nevada State Prison in Carson City.

Gallego will then be able to join his father.

Sean Whaley has been a reporter in California and Nevada for the past 12 years. He has spent the past three years as a capital bureau reporter in Carson City, Nev., for the *Las Vegas Review Journal.*

> "The law is completely ineffective. This man should have been taken out, executed promptly and forgotten.
> —Justice John Mowbray

WESTLEY ALLAN DODD

BRUCE WESTFALL

It was Aug. 20, 1989, and Westley Allan Dodd awoke startled and scared out of a vivid dream.

He was on a beach. He watched as small plants and animals around him were mysteriously jerked down out of sight. Suddenly, an oval of sand sunk away as if through an hourglass. Standing there was the devil.

Dodd woke with a start. The devil really exists, he thought. Would he make a deal?

First, last and always William and Cole Neer were brothers. They played together, fought with each other and when they were threatened, they knew how to fight—or run—together.

Though they played with other kids in the Vancouver, Wash., housing project where they lived, the neighbors took note that William, 10, and Cole, 11, were inseparable.

Perhaps the bond had something to do with their difficult past and present. Their father, Clair, was an unemployed auto glass installer who had come west from North Dakota looking for work. Clair's marriage to the boys' mother, Arlene, a full-blooded Sioux Indian, had failed. The Pacific Northwest was a green land, verdant and tree-filled— the perfect place for a fresh start.

Clair had three sons: William, Cole and Robert. At 5, Robert was too young to tag along with his older brothers when they pedaled their bicycles out of Skyline Crest, a drab, congested cluster of low-income duplexes in Vancouver's McLoughlin Heights.

Vancouver, a city of 40,000, lies next to the broad Columbia River. It was here that the Hudson's Bay Company established a fort in the early 1800s. It was for a time a stronghold of fur trading and commerce, a foothold for settlement of the pioneer West.

As time passed, however, Vancouver's twin settlement, Portland, Ore., just across the river, outgrew its companion city to become the dominant metropolis of the region.

Though Vancouver existed in Portland's shadow, most people didn't mind.

After all, Vancouver had kept a certain pleasant parochialism, a sense of small-town identity that Portland, with its urban hills, had long ago lost.

People knew their neighbors and their neighborhoods and more than anything, people in Vancouver could feel safe.

Not that Clark County didn't have its share of troubles. Occasionally there were murders. There was, for example, the case of a man bludgeoned to death with a ballpeen hammer and left to rot in a sleeping bag on a remote country road. But residents could take comfort in that fact that he was not a local, but a victim of a Portland drug deal gone bad.

Occasionally men murdered wives or girlfriends. But those were simple domestic disputes taken to extremes. The urban nightmare of stranger-to-stranger violence was almost unknown. So it was, then, that Vancouver considered itself immune from the violence of the big city.

As Labor Day, 1989 approached, Vancouver was basking in a soft, warm, Northwest summer coming to a close. By early September, the bright sun of mid summer had started to slide south giving off an oblique light that was a prelude to fall.

Soon, the city's presumed innocence would come to an end, as well.

Among the 200,000 souls in and around Vancouver was a man who had become a hunter, a stalker of children. A man driven by fantasies of sex, torture and death.

Westley Allan Dodd was unremarkable in appearance. Thin and wiry with a wisp of a mustache and goatee, Dodd, 28, was a quiet, reliable shipping clerk at a Vancouver paper plant.

His supervisors saw potential in the man who followed orders, showed up on time and demonstrated a little initiative. A promotion was in his future, they believed.

Dodd lived in a Vancouver studio apartment that was really the converted back end of a home owned by white-haired Vivian Shay, a strict Jehovah's Witness who regarded Dodd as a model tenant.

Yet this man, who appeared to be just an ordinary boy next door, was extraordinarily disturbed.

He had come to Vancouver on the heels of a failure: jilted by his girlfriend, a woman who claimed that Dodd fathered her child. Yet she deserted the Navy veteran and left him in a Yakima, Wash., motel room in July of '89. It was another in a string of adult relationships that soured. Psychiatrists would say that's why he turned to children.

Broke and alone, he sold some of his meager possessions for gas money to drive to Vancouver where his father, Jim, lived. It was July, and Dodd—like Clair Neer a year or two before—believed Vancouver would offer a place for a fresh start.

Vancouver would make a fine hunting ground, he wrote in his diary. It was a chilling sign that behind Wes Dodd's dark, expressionless eyes, a monster lurked.

David Douglas Park is a spacious, 68-acre table top of land that drops away on three sides toward the flat, prosperous retail center of Vancouver.

The broad, grassy park is a magnet for picnickers, and its six baseball diamonds are nearly always busy.

On the south edge, the park falls away into a thickly wooded canyon isolated by Douglas fir trees and spindly vine maples.

The broad trail at the bottom, with its natural colonnade of pillar-like firs, was an isolated and fascinating place for youngsters where they could ride bikes and play. Up in the park, or on the bustling four-lane road just a few yards away, nobody would know anyone was on the trail.

William, known as Billy, was a sly and outgoing 10 years old. He was a natural athlete who liked to play jokes. His brother, Cole, was a year older and more serious. Cole loved to draw. His father regarded him as something of an artist. Together, they mowed the lawn and watched out for their brother, Robert, an epileptic.

The boys also shared a passion for baseball. Between them, their father estimated they had 7,000 baseball cards. To earn money to expand their collection, they would bicycle to the nearby Vanco Driving Range to collect golf balls that had sailed over the fence. The owner would buy them back for a few cents apiece.

That's where they told their father they were going that carefree Labor Day afternoon, the last time Clair would see them alive.

The night before, Westley Dodd hardly slept.

He spent four hours in David Douglas Park Sept. 3, according to his diary. While he saw a handful of children he believed he could kill, the circumstances weren't right; too many kids together or a father following too close behind.

Despite the frustrations of the day before, he awoke the next day refreshed and optimistic. "Now ready for my second day of the hunt," he wrote in his diary. "Will start at about 10 a.m. and take a lunch so I don't have to return home." There was one worry. If he had to kill a youngster in the park, "I'd lose my hunting ground for up to two to three months," he wrote.

Nobody could say just where or how Wes Dodd came by his sadistic pedophilia, sexual gratification in molesting and harming youngsters. But his evolution began at 13 or 14. That was when he first exposed himself to neighborhood kids from an upstairs window of his Richland, Wash., home.

Dodd himself didn't understand it, he would say later. He remembered that he was never good enough for his father. He said he was slapped around a few times. But he wasn't sexually abused as a child. His parents divorced when he was 15, the climax of years of fighting, he said. But that wasn't really a reason for what he did.

It was a thrill, and maybe that's all there

Among the 200,000 souls in and around Vancouver was a man who had become a hunter, a stalker of children.

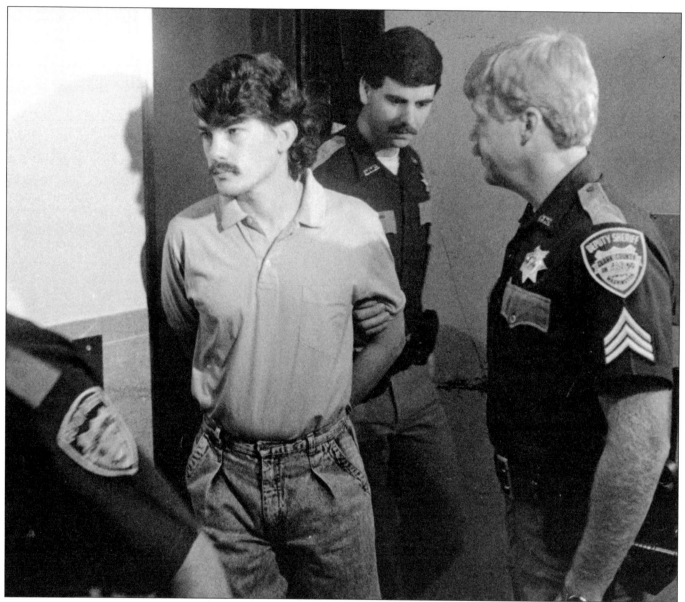

A mere two days after the murders of the Neer brothers, Dodd wrote in his diary, "I must go find another child. I think I get more of a high out of killing than molesting." Less than two months later, Dodd kidnapped, molested and hanged a four-year-old boy.

was to it. There was a certain satisfaction, and by the time Dodd reached his middle teen-age years, he had grown bolder at seeking it out.

He approached young boys in isolated settings—a park, perhaps—and questioned them. "What would you do if I told you to take your pants down?" he would ask. Sometimes they did. Sometimes they didn't. But the behavior, driven by forces unknown, drew the attention of police. He was caught

molesting children four times between the ages of 15 and 27. In none of those incidents did he serve much jail time, however. And in each case he walked away from counseling.

In his other life, the one outsiders knew, Dodd was a musician, an average clarinet player and a model student who earned the right to be a summer counselor at a Seattle-area music camp.

At Richland's Columia High School, Dodd was known as a quiet loner who didn't date and didn't socialize. He took a girl out once, but he later described the experience as "long and boring."

He graduated with a 3.0 GPA, worked in a grocery store for a year and then followed his brother into the U.S. Navy.

By his account, Dodd's Navy recruiter was stunned at his high IQ and begged him to volunteer for submarine duty.

While he trained in the prestigious branch of the Navy, Dodd became only a submarine shopkeeper. Within two years, he was drummed out of the Navy with a general discharge. There were allegations that he frequented video game parlors, attempting to solicit sex from young boys.

After the Navy, he fell into a patchwork of jobs over the next few years. He drove a truck, worked at a gas station and by 1987 had become a Seattle-area security guard.

By his own count, Dodd had sexual contact with youngsters as many as 80 times as he bounced from one Northwest community to another.

His most serious brush with the law came in July of 1987. Dodd tried to lure a 9-year-old boy into an empty building while he was serving as a security guard at a construction site in Seattle.

The youngster escaped and called police. Originally, Dodd was charged with kidnapping. But he finally pleaded guilty to a reduced charge of attempted unlawful imprisonment, a misdemeanor. He was sentenced to a year in sexual therapy. That's how he ended up on the doorstep of Seattle psychiatrist Dr. Kenneth Von Cleave.

Dr. Von Cleave was shocked by what he heard. In a long interview, Dodd spun what Von Cleave called the "most extensive sexual history I have ever seen in someone that age. If you have a dictionary definition of a pedophile, Wes Dodd's picture should be next to it," he would say later.

Dodd visited the psychiatrist regularly for about a year. But when his court-ordered probation was up, he walked away.

He went to work in a Seattle-area convenience store. "Everybody liked him. We trusted him completely," the owner said.

By the time he came to this relatively peaceful river town, he carried with him increasingly vivid fantasies of molesting and killing children. But he had to have a plan. And in the scrupulously neat handwriting of his diary, it began to unfold some two weeks before Labor Day, 1989.

"As a result of my dream ... I believe in Satan and am prepared to enter a contract with him," Dodd wrote after his dream of the devil on the beach. "I will trade my soul and my services before and after death in exchange for the conditions on the following page.

"I will exchange my soul for a long happy life as a pedophile."

Dodd listed 10 conditions of his bargain with the devil. The first and most important: "I must never be reported to or caught by authorities."

Though Billy and Cole told their dad they were going to pick up golf balls Sept. 4, they had strayed over to David Douglas Park and the steep inviting canyon on the park's south edge.

At 6:20 p.m., Dodd approached the boys as they explored the canyon. He told them to come with him. They followed the dark-haired man.

The hunt was over.

"I found two boys down near the center section of trails. They had their bikes," he told police later. "I walked up to 'em and said, I want you two to come with me. You can bring your bikes with you if you want."

Dodd and the two boys walked west on the secluded trail downhill toward Andresen Road, a busy, four-lane street near the edge of the park. They could hear traffic rush by, but the summer foliage concealed them from view. They walked up a slope off the worn path to the base of a large tree.

"Told 'em I wanted one of 'em to pull their pants down. I wouldn't let 'em go 'til one of 'em did," Dodd said. "Billy said, 'Him.' Cole asked, 'Why?' and I said 'Because I told you to.' So he did."

Cole, the quiet one, did as he was told. Dodd performed oral sex on the youngster.

"I kept tellin' 'em everything's gonna be okay, I wasn't gonna hurt 'em." They told Dodd that they had to go because they were hungry and their dad would be mad. "I said to tell him they got lost." Billy started to whimper. Dodd told the youngsters, "OK, there's just one more thing." In a single smooth motion, Dodd pulled a 6-inch fillet

In a single smooth motion, Dodd pulled a 6-inch fillet knife from under his pant leg and stabbed Billy in the stomach. Then he turned to Cole and stabbed the older brother in the chest again and again.

By his own count, Dodd had sexual contact with youngsters as many as 80 times as he bounced from one Northwest community to another.

knife from under his pant leg and stabbed Billy in the stomach. Then he turned to Cole and stabbed the older brother in the chest again and again.

Billy, wounded but not dead, sprang to his feet and clutching his stomach, he ran toward the busy roadway perhaps 50 to 60 feet away. Dodd bolted after him. Just a few feet short of the road Dodd caught Billy, and spun him around by the arm. For an instant, their eyes met.

"I'm sorry, I'm sorry," was all Billy could say.

Dodd plunged the knife into the boy two or three more times. Billy dropped to the ground, just short of safety.

Dodd half-walked and half ran up to the spot where Cole had fallen. He was on his back, head turned to one side. His eyes were open and vacant. He was clearly dead.

Dodd walked back toward his car, an ancient, ill-running Ford Pinto station wagon. He passed a number of people. His left hand had some of the boys' blood on it. He concealed it inside his pants pocket. Later, nobody would have a clear memory of a stranger in the park that day. After all, what had just happened down the trail on the last day of summer was inconceivable.

Dodd checked his watch, the entire episode took less than 20 minutes.

He drove home and showered. He felt the blood pounding in his head. He was scared, but there was another emotion: a powerful rush of excitement.

Perhaps five minutes after the murders, a McDonald's hamburger cook named Chris Bridge dropped down off Andresen onto the wooded path. He stumbled across Billy, all bloody and pale. The teen-ager thought at first the boy had been struck by a car. He ran to a nearby convenience store and called 911.

By the time Vancouver police detectives Darryl Odegaard and Jeff Sundby arrived at the park, confusion reigned. One boy was dead, and it wasn't any car accident. But officers had found two bikes. Was it possible there were two murders?

Clair got worried when the boys didn't come home for supper. He spent a couple of hours searching the neighborhood in his car.

About 10 p.m. he called 911 dispatchers to report his two boys missing. Within minutes Patrol commander Bob Kanekoa, a stocky, soft-spoken Hawaiian, was on Clair's doorstep.

Kanekoa had carefully sorted through Polaroid photos of the dead boy, looking for a picture that would not convey the violence by which Billy died.

But as he entered Clair Neer's home, he saw a large picture of Billy and his brothers. The Polaroids would not be needed. He asked Clair to sit down.

"I'm afraid I have some very unfortunate news," Kanekoa said. Then he watched the life drain out of the father's face.

About 2 a.m., a searcher discovered Cole's body. It was a blow to everyone. "It's the middle of the night in a forest. The innocence of a child. It's something you're never able to explain," recalled Odegaard, a beefy, tough-minded cop who hated loose ends. But he was now caught up in a case with enough loose ends for a lifetime.

A manhunt was on. The murders were fresh and police knew the first few hours were crucial. Day and night police scoured the forest in search of clues. They filled 15 grocery sacks with debris from the crime scene.

What they missed, amateur searchers found. One man brought in a rusty scythe to the police department, convinced it was the murder weapon.

Detectives waded through dozens—hundreds—of phone calls. But there was precious little to go on.

That night Dodd went to bed and got a couple of hours sleep before reporting to work as a shipping clerk at a local paper plant. Word of the murders had spread.

Dodd's appetite for news was insatiable. He watched television and clipped articles from the local newspapers. Two days after the murders he wrapped the knife in newspaper and threw it in a dumpster at work. It was never found.

His co-workers talked about the killings, but Dodd kept his mouth shut. Police released a composite drawing that Dodd believed looked dangerously like him. "I was afraid to go to work after that came out," he told detectives later. "I was afraid somebody would notice it and make a phone call."

But his perversions were stronger than fear. A mere two days after the murders Dodd wrote in his diary, "I must go find another child. I think I get more of a high out of killing than molesting."

Police were lost, and as the days wore on, Dodd realized the murder investigation was going nowhere. His obsession with boys only grew. "I didn't want to do it in a place like that again. I wanted to have more time, so I decided kidnapping a boy would be good thing to do," he told detectives.

He prayed to Satan for help in finding another victim.

September grew into October. The nights became cooler and the Northwest foliage began to blush brilliant fall colors. By then, Dodd's mania had again reached a full boil.

He began to plan the abduction of another young victim. If anything, he was becoming more fixated. The planning excited him nearly as much as the sex itself.

He drew a rough plan of a torture rack. He purchased X-acto® knives and tweezers. He wrote that he needed the tools to perform "exploratory surgery and use what I learn later to operate on live boys."

He imagined surgically exploring a youngster's genitalia. He couldn't stop thinking about mutilation. He imagined playing games with victims in which they would roll dice or pull lots from a hat to choose how they would die.

This time, he would lure a victim to his home where he could abuse and kill a boy at his leisure.

Lee Joseph Iseli was a blond, winsome 4-year-old playing with his brother Sunday, Oct. 29, 1989, at Richmond School in his southeast Portland neighborhood.

Lee was watching some other boys play football when a dark-haired man came up from behind. He was wearing a hat that said, "Don't worry, be happy."

"I asked Lee if he wanted to make some money," Dodd said. " I asked him if he wanted to have some fun and play some games. And he was a little hesitant. I reached my hand out. He took it and walked off with me."

Lee's 9-year-old brother Justin told police that one minute Lee was playing nearby on

WASH STATE PEN
933606
DODD   W   7 90

WASH STATE PEN
933606
DODD   W   7 90

PHOTO • DAVID TINNEY/THE COLUMBIAN

In his early teens, Dodd began to show signs of pedophilia. At 13 or 14, he first exposed himself to neighborhood kids from an upstairs window of his Richland, Wash., home.

the playground when Justin looked again, he was gone.

On the way to Dodd's Vancouver apartment, Lee Iseli began to cry, but Dodd reassured the youngster, saying, "We're going to have some fun." When the two arrived, Dodd told the boy he had to be quiet because "a neighbor lady didn't like kids."

Dodd molested the boy before dinner then took Lee to a nearby McDonald's for a hamburger, then to K-Mart where he bought the youngster a "He-Man" action figure.

"There was one time when he said, 'Can I go home?'

And I said 'Aren't you having fun? I thought you were going to spend the night with me.' And he said, 'Oh, yeah.' And he forgot about wanting to go home." Dodd said.

The man molested the boy throughout the night, even telling him once, "I'm gonna kill you in the morning." Lee Iseli didn't believe it. But about 5:30 a.m., about the time Dodd had to get up for work, he arose, put his hands around the neck of the 4-year-old and tried to choke the life out of him.

"I thought he was dead, but he wasn't," Dodd said. "He'd lay on the bed and start breathing again." So Dodd tied a rope around the youngster's neck and hung him in the closet. When he went to work, he placed the body of Lee Iseli on his closet shelf. "He was a bright kid. He could identify me," Dodd explained.

After work, Dodd took the boy's corpse out of the closet, sodomized it, then loaded it in a couple of garbage sacks, drove to a nearby lake and dumped the naked body on the ground.

He burned the rope and most of Lee's clothes. But he kept the boy's underwear and continued to collect newspaper stories in a briefcase under his bed.

A 67-year-old pheasant hunter found Lee Iseli's body the next morning, two months after the murders in David Douglas Park.

Police conducted a painstaking grid search of the area on hands and knees, but they found absolutely no clue to the killer's identity.

Although the Neer brothers and Lee Iseli were children and all three had been murdered, police believed the similarities stopped

there. The Neers were stabbed, the Iseli boy strangled. The Neer brothers showed no evidence of being sexually molested. Lee Iseli had been.

Police believed the crimes to be the work of two different killers.

Police agencies went their separate ways. As the Iseli investigation accelerated, led by Portland police and the Clark County Sheriff's Office, Vancouver police detectives Odegaard and Sundby were growing increasingly lonely and frustrated. Their case idled along in neutral, going nowhere. They had a gut feeling the person would kill again. Fact is, he already had.

For Westley Dodd, the pace quickened after Lee Iseli's murder. His search for victims now centered on Clark county movie theaters. The night of Nov. 13, two weeks after Lee Iseli was murdered, Dodd went to the New Liberty Theater in nearby Camas. Playing was a movie called, "Honey, I shrunk the kids."

As Dodd settled into a back seat in the theater, 6-year-old James Kirk, bright-eyed with a floppy brown head of hair, walked by on the way to the restroom.

Dodd quietly followed him in. "You're going to come with me. I won't hurt you," he told the boy. Dodd picked up the youngster and started to exit the theater.

But James Kirk would have none of it. He screamed and cried as Dodd walked onto Third Street toward the corner where he parked his car. The moviehouse owners, alarmed by the boy's tantrum, followed the pair out the door.

At the corner Dodd had to make a decision. He realized he couldn't carry a kicking, screaming boy to his car. He set James down, quickly walked to the Pinto and drove off.

It would take a soft-spoken construction worker to accomplish what up to now, dozens of cops could not.

William Graves, a concrete foreman and boyfriend to James Kirk's mother, found out what had happened. Graves, thin and wiry but ready for trouble, hustled onto the street. A passerby pointed the direction in which Dodd drove off.

Graves hopped into his own car, drove a

few blocks and found a stalled car with a skinny dark-haired guy bent over the engine near the town paper mill.

Sure he was the one, Graves coolly approached the man and asked if he could help. As Westley Dodd bent over the engine again, Graves cranked Dodd's arm into a hammerlock and the two marched back to the theater.

The nights in Camas are usually quiet, so the attempted kidnapping at the town's only theater drew plenty of police attention. It didn't take Camas Police Sergeant Don Chaney long to put two and two together. He learned that Dodd lived less than a mile from David Douglas Park. He learned that Dodd worked at a paper plant near Vancouver Lake.

He picked up the phone.

Within the hour, three homicide detectives huddled with Dodd in the Camas Police Chief's office. After about 45 minutes of questioning, Portland Detective C.W. Jensen suggested that Dodd might want to get something off his chest.

The killer bowed his head. Tears started to well up in his eyes. He asked for a glass of water. Then Dodd calmly confessed to all three killings. He told police he would have killed James Kirk, too, if he had just gotten him into the car.

Starting almost with the moment of his arrest, Dodd began a work of self-redemption.

Against the advice of attorneys he continued to talk to the cops. He was helpful to a fault. He refused to mount a defense on three aggravated murder charges. He shuffled in and out of court quietly, head down.

He pleaded guilty on July 11, 1990, a day that quite by coincidence would have been Cole Neer's 12th birthday. "Good for the son-of-a-bitch," snarled Cole's father.

He even refused to defend himself against Washington's death penalty. After some 20 hours of deliberations, a jury agreed that Dodd should die.

In the state of Washington, death row inmates can choose between lethal injection and hanging. Dodd told a television news reporter he wanted to hang, "mainly because that's how Lee Iseli died."

He wrote a primer for children, entitled "When You Meet A Stranger," telling them what to do should someone try to grab them. He based the publication on little James Kirk's escape from the Camas theater. "My name is Wes," he wrote. "I am the stranger you should stay away from."

Dodd became ever more determined to live right—and die— right.

He wrote to the parents of sex offenders, warning them that they should seek treatment for their children lest they turn out like him.

Dodd even offered to be an organ donor following his execution. He claimed also to have become a Christian, and asked that the Vancouver man who led him to Jesus to accompany him on that lonely walk to the gallows.

How soon that may be remains open to question. Dodd has steadfastly waived any rights to appeal his sentence. Growing impatient with the courts Dodd even threatened to take his own life by attacking a prison guard at the state penitentiary in Walla Walla. The guards would have to shoot him, he reasoned.

The image of the slightly built Dodd attempting to attack a grown prison guard seemed unlikely at best.

But his intent was clear. He ached to die at the hands of a hangman.

Deprived of victims by his capture, Dodd sits on Washington's death row, becoming more and more withdrawn. For 23 hours a day he remains in a 5-foot-by-12-foot cell. For one hour a day, he is allowed in a courtyard where there is a telephone and chin-up bar. He told a psychiatrist last June that he has no one to call and no desire to exercise.

He asked that his television set be removed. "I guess you would say I sit for the most part and stare," Dodd told the psychiatrist.

He is left with the memories of his crimes. The only way to halt them is to die, he believes. Dodd's death at the end of a rope, then, will not only be an act of atonement, but a final, violent cleansing of the soul. Perhaps a fitting end for a man whose failed relationships included a bargain that even the devil couldn't keep.

Bruce Westfall is a reporter for *The Columbian* in Vancouver, Wash.

> "I will exchange my soul for a long happy life as a pedophile."
> —Dodd

TENNESSEE

PERVIS TYRONE PAYNE

LAWRENCE W. BUSER

PAYNE

Millington, Tenn., 10 miles up the road from Memphis, is just about as American as it gets.

Most of its 18,000 people are linked in some way to the U.S. Naval Air Station's site of technical training.

And just off U.S. Highway 51 is a neatly manicured stadium that is home to USA Baseball, the training site of America's amateur teams that compete in the Olympics, the Pan Am games and the Goodwill Games.

Despite the trappings of All-American integrity, police here are accustomed to dealing with the rougher elements, rough unsavory characters and occasional murders. But etched in their memories forever will be the bloody afternoon of June 27 four years ago.

"It was the worst crime scene I had ever been on and I'd been on quite a few," recalls Asst. Chief Jere Orman, a 25-year veteran of the Millington Police Department.

Pervis Tyrone Payne was neat and muscular, 5 feet 7 inches and 176 pounds. He sometimes drank Geritol because he believed it would keep him strong and his energy level high. At Munford High School, Payne was a drummer in the band. As his lawyer would say later, Pervis Payne lived an exemplary life for 20 years.

If so, that all changed on a hot, sunny day in June, 1987.

The day began with Payne and a friend cruising around Millington, drinking beer and Geritol and admiring the glamorous, naked women in a Playboy magazine.

Payne's girlfriend, Bobbie Thomas, was visiting her mother in Arkansas. He expected her to return to her residence in the Hiwassee Apartments and planned to spend the weekend with her.

He stopped by her apartment several times before 3 p.m. but found no one home. During one visit, he left a gym bag with a change of clothes and three cans of Colt 45 Liquor on the doorstep.

Charisse Ann Christopher was a newly divorced mother of two young children—Nicholas Alan, 3, and Lacie Jo, 2. She was a petite brunette with soft brown eyes and a gentle, engaging smile.

She was working as a secretary at an oil company and lived across the narrow hallway from Payne's girlfriend in the four-unit, two-story apartment building.

Charisse, the only girl in a family of four, had visited her mother earlier in the day.

Neighbors say the commotion began around 3:10 p.m.

Nancy Wilson was relaxing in her first-floor apartment when she heard the screams, shouts and fast-moving footsteps. She heard the Christopher's door banging open and shut and then heart Charisse scream, "Get out, get out." Wilson would later surmise that Christopher was yelling not at an intruder but at her children in a desperate attempt to save their lives. The noise stopped for a moment but then became "terribly loud, horribly loud," she said. She considered going upstairs to investigate but quickly decided it was a matter for police.

At the same time, Laura Picard was sunbathing in the backyard when she heard what sounded like moaning coming from the Christopher apartment. She saw the back door slamming three or four times, but it would not shut. "And this hand, a dark-colored hand with a gold watch, kept trying to shut that back door," Picard would say later.

The Millington Police dispatcher received

the call from Wilson at 3:23 p.m. and immediately sent a squad car to the apartments.

Wilson went to her bathroom after calling police and noticed that the screams from upstairs had ceased. Then she heard footsteps, which she surmised to be in the upstairs bathroom. She heard the faucet being turned on and the sound of someone cleaning up. The footsteps then quickly moved across the floor again, out of the Christopher apartment, and the door was slammed shut.

Wilson then heard someone gallop down the stairs. She waited anxiously for police.

Patrolman C.E. Owen was alone in a squad car when he heard the broadcast for the Hiwassee Apartments just two minutes away.

When he arrived, he saw a black man in a white shirt and dark pants on the second-floor landing of the stairwell. The man picked something up and then bounded down the stairs where he was confronted by Owen.

The officer thought there may have been a domestic disturbance that had escalated to violence.

"He had blood all over him," Owen would later recall. "It looked like he was sweating blood." When Owen asked the man who he was, the man quickly responded, "I'm the complainant."

The officer grew suspicious and when he asked politely "What's going on up there?" The man struck Owen with the overnight bag, dropped the tennis shoes he was holding, and ran off, disappearing into another apartment complex.

Owen radioed for help when he could not keep up with the swift suspect.

Wilson, who had a master apartment key, with Owen and another officer opened the door to the Christophers' apartment. They each took a deep breath and entered what had become a chamber of horrors.

Blood covered the walls and the floor. A kitchen drawer was partially opened and a 13-inch butcher knife lay on the kitchen floor near three mutilated bodies.

Charisse Christopher and her daughter Lacie Jo were dead. Their eyes were still open in what soldiers call "the thousand-yard stare."

Charisse had been stabbed 84 times, including one wound that went through her left

side and out the back. Many of her wounds were to her arms and hands, defensive wounds that represented silent testimony to investigators.

"That woman put up one hell of a fight," Capt. Sam Wilson of the Millington Police said. "She tried to save her kids. When she was hollering 'Get out, get out' she wasn't talking to Payne. She was talking to her kids."

Tiny Lacie Jo was stabbed nine times in the chest, stomach, back and head. Three-year-old Nicholas, however, was alive, awake and able to respond to the officers. He too had multiple stab wounds, several of which went through him, slashing his liver, spleen and vena cava. His intestines spilled from his abdomen. Nicholas underwent seven hours of emergency surgery at Le Bonheur Children's Medical Center in Memphis. During surgery, he was given 1700 cc's of new blood as doc-

Pervis Payne entered the apartment of Charisse Ann Christopher, and stabbed her and her 2-year-old daughter, Lacie Jo, to death. Nicholas Alan, who also suffered multiple stab wounds, somehow survived.

tors tried desperately to maintain his normal volume of 1200 to 1300 cc's. Nicholas lived in intensive care for weeks and had to undergo two more operations but somehow survived his nightmare.

Police found three cans of Colt 45 Malt Liquor with Payne's fingerprints on them inside the apartment. Payne's fingerprints also were on the telephone and kitchen counter. His baseball cap was also found there. The adjustable strap was looped over Lacie Jo's arm.

Jere Orman was a police captain in 1987. He was spending his off-day mowing the lawn a block from the Hiwassee Apartments.

When screeching squad cars and officers running with shotguns caught his attention, Orman grabbed his service revolver and radio and headed to the scene. When Orman joined up with his partners, they said several residents lounging by the pool had seen the suspect run by. One of them had chased Payne a short distance. He led police to the apartment Payne had ducked into.

Orman advised the two women who lived in the apartment—acquaintances of Payne's—to step outside. Then he and two other officers carefully went inside where Payne was hiding in the attic. "Payne eased himself down from the attic and I drew down on him," Orman recalled. Payne was covered with blood and sweating profusely. Orman heard him breath heavily before he shouted to the officer. "Man, I ain't killed no woman."

Orman had not asked a question.

In Payne's pockets officers found a small packet of cocaine, a syringe wrapper and an orange cap from a hypodermic syringe. His gold watch had blood on it and there were scratches on his chest.

It was not until Orman went to the murder scene and saw the bodies of Lacie Jo and Charisse that he realized the horror of the crime.

"Had I been to the scene first I don't know what my reaction would have been," Orman says four years later. "Nobody had to face the test of what would you do (with a suspect) after seeing a child like that."

When Pervis Payne went to trial seven months later, he told a state Criminal Court jury in Memphis that a black man who

raced by him down the stairs that day had done the killings.

Payne said he heard a baby crying and went into the Christopher apartment where he found the victims bleeding and dying.

"I was about ready to get sick, about ready to vomit," Payne testified.

"I said don't worry, I'm going to help you. Don't worry. Don't worry." Payne said he panicked and ran from the officer because with the victims' blood on him—he said it was from kneeling and helping the Christophers—he feared he would be a suspect.

But on cross examination Payne's story began to unravel.

Prosecutor Thomas Henderson asked Payne how he got bloodstains on his left leg.

Payne explained that it must have happened when Mrs. Christopher "hit the wall. When she reached up and grabbed me."

It was the opening the veteran prosecutor was looking for.

"When she hit the wall?" Henderson bellowed, reciting each word slowly for emphasis.

A chilling silence overpowered the courtroom as jurors watched and awaited Payne's reply.

"When she—when she hit—when she hit, when I got ready to run up—when I got ready to vomit," Payne stammered.

It was a turning point in the trial and Henderson would not let Payne escape.

"Is that what you said, sir, that she got blood on you when she hit the wall?" the prosecutor barked again.

In frustration, Payne finally snapped. "That ain't, that's not what I said."

Evidence suggested that Payne sexually assaulted Christopher and that she resisted his advances. However, the medical examiner said the test results were not conclusive.

There was no evidence that anything was missing from the apartment.

The jury took six hours to return two verdicts of first-degree murder and another of assault to commit first-degree murder.

During the sentencing trial that immediately followed, prosecutors put on just two witnesses—Charisse's mother, Mary Zvolanek, and Millington Det. Sam Wilson.

Mrs. Zvolanek's brief testimony involved this exchange with the prosecutor: "Mrs.

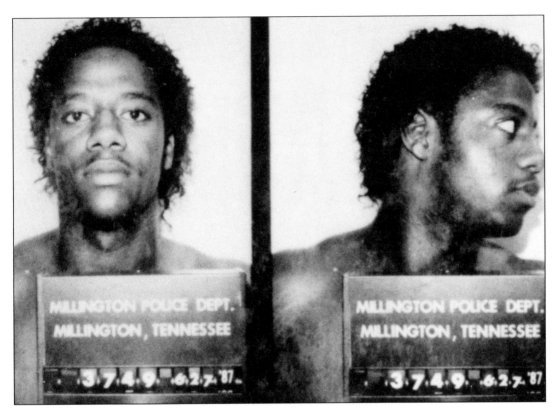

Police found three cans of Colt 45 Malt Liquor with Payne's fingerprints on them inside the apartment. Payne's fingerprints also were on the telephone and kitchen counter. His baseball cap was also found there. The adjustable strap was looped over Lacie Jo's arm.

Zvolanek, how has the murder of Nicholas' mother and his sister affected him?"

"He cries for his mom. He doesn't seem to understand why she doesn't come home. And he cries for his sister Lacie. He comes to me many times during the week and asks me, Grandma, do you miss my Lacie? And I tell him yes. He says, I'm worried about my Lacie."

Later prosecutor Henderson, in arguing for the death penalty, told the jury that young Nicholas would one day want to know "what type of justice" was issued on behalf of his dead mother and sister.

"With your verdict you will provide the answer," Henderson told them.

Prosecutors also described in heartbreaking detail the future for Nicholas, now a motherless child.

"His mother will never kiss him good night, or pat him as he goes off to bed, or hold him and sing him a lullaby," Prosecutor Phyllis Gardner said.

These are things, Henderson said, that illustrate why this crime was especially cruel, heinous and atrocious, and worthy of the death penalty.

Defense lawyers argued that such "victim impact evidence" unfairly prejudiced the jury, but the trial judge—and eventually the U.S. Supreme Court—ruled otherwise.

Still, the most memorable evidence for jurors in the trial was the color videotape made at the crime scene before the dead victims were removed.

Judge Bernie Weinman decided two minutes of the 10-minute tape was all the jury needed to see. There is no narrative.

"I couldn't talk," said then-detective Sam Wilson who made the tape while trying to cope with the macabre scene. "I just literally could not talk."

Wilson went back to the apartment a week later—on the Fourth of July—to clean up the blood.

"I couldn't let the family members go back in there and see it," Wilson says, "and I couldn't ask anybody else to do it."

Payne's defense lawyers put on four witnesses during the sentencing trial, including his parents, his girlfriend and a psychologist.

Bernice and Carl Payne, his mother and father, said Pervis was a good son who caused them no trouble and who worked hard with his father as a painter and carpenter. Carl

VICTIMS' RIGHTS

Four years to the day after Charisse Ann Christopher and her baby daughter were slashed to death in their small-town Tennessee apartment, their case became a landmark U.S. Supreme Court decision for victim's rights.

On June 27, 1991 the high court upheld the death-penalty conviction of their killer, Pervis Tyrone Payne, and gave prosecutors greater latitude in presenting so-called "victim impact" evidence in seeking the death penalty.

By a 6-3 vote, the newly structured Supreme Court overturned two previous rulings and said the Eighth Amendment does not bar a jury from considering evidence relating to the victim's survivors.

The ruling was hailed by victim's rights groups, many prosecutors and by the Bush Administration. Then-U.S. Attorney Richard Thornburgh made a rare appearance before the Supreme Court to argue for the decision.

"We've got to get away from considering only the character of the defendant," Thornburgh said. "Murder victims are not just faceless statistics."

The decision endorsed the opinion of the Tennessee Supreme Court that said in part:

"It is an affront to the civilized members of the human race to say that at sentencing in a capital case, a parade of witnesses may praise the background, character and good deeds of the defendant (as was done in this case) without limitation as to relevancy, but nothing may be said that bears upon the character of, or the harm imposed, upon the victims."

The U.S. Supreme Court's ruling overturned the 1987 and 1989 decision—Booth v. Maryland and South Carolina v. Gathers—in which victim impact evidence was condemned as inflammatory.

But the court has become more conservative with Bush-appointee Justice David Souter replacing Justice William Brennan and upheld the Payne case in light of the "evolving standards of decency."

"For the victim's survivors, it's an extremely important decision because it gives them an opportunity to participate in the case," says David Beatty, an attorney and spokesman for the National Victim Center in Fort Worth, Texas. "It has a cathartic effect and it helps them regain control of their lives."

Payne, then 20, was convicted and sentenced to death for the 1987 murders of Mrs. Christopher, 28, and her 2-year-old daughter, Lacie Jo. He was sentenced to 30 years for assault to murder her 3-year-old son, Nicholas, who survived his critical wounds.

In the sentencing trial, prosecutors emphasized the suffering of survivors and Nicholas' anticipated desire for Payne's execution.

They also noted the exemplary lives of the victims after several defense witnesses praised Payne as a hardworking, church-going young man.

At least some victim-impact information always trickles into trials as proof of the crime itself is presented.

But prosecutors say the ruling now gives them court-approved options to counter the character witnesses presented on behalf of the defendant.

"Now you can balance out some of that what-a-good-guy-the-defendant-is testimony from the defense," says Thomas Henderson, the lead prosecutor in the Payne case. "The decision will have an important impact but it's limited. It won't affect the actual verdict in many cases."

Defense lawyers such as James Garts, who represented Payne, say victim-impact information can have a powerful or subtle impact on a jury, depending on how prosecutors choose to use it.

He worries that juries will be inclined to issue death sentences based on emotions or "psychological intimidation" rather than on facts and reason.

But Henderson argues that what some lawyers call "psychological intimidation," others call "persuasive argument."

"It just depends on what side of the courtroom you're on," Henderson says. "I've always heard that love is a stronger emotion than hate. You can't just get up and ask them to execute the defendant out of hate. You've got to love the victim, too."

In the Payne trial, prosecutors told jurors of the suffering of survivors, most notably by the brief, heart-wrenching testimony of Mary Zvolanek, the children's grandmother.

"The whole tenor was emotional and it was a cumulative thing," recalls Garts, who suffered the wrath of the victim's friends and relatives during breaks in the trial. "It got so bad that they were cornering me and calling me dirt. Jurors were crying during closing arguments."

Memphis Attorney J. Brooke Lathram, who handled the appeal, argued that the death penalty should be decided only on what the defendant did, why he did it, the manner in which he did it and the kind of person he is.

The court's ruling, however, shifts the focus to the victim's character and worth in deciding whether the death penalty is warranted, he says. The question then becomes whether one victim's life was more important than another.

"A murder is no less heinous and the offender no less

deserving of punishment simply because the victim happens to be a derelict or a hermit who dies without survivors rather than, say, a beloved parent," Lathram argued in his Supreme Court brief.

Garts and Lathram warn of a scenario in which the prosecution hails the victim as a revered priest and the defense attorney counters that the priest once molested altar boys.

In providing their client a vigorous defense, lawyers will be put in the risky position of compounding the grief of survivors and possibly offending jurors, they say.

"I'm not sure how people are going to handle this," says Garts.

Prosecutor Henderson appreciates the apparent trick-bag in which his foes might be placed. "It puts them in the position of taking a cheap shot at the deceased ... which they've never passed up before."

Proponents of victim-impact evidence say lawyers must constantly make calculated decisions on how to try a case, including whether they should speak ill of the dead.

Also, they say, judges can rule during the trial how far lawyers can go in praising or damning a victim.

In many cases, prosecutors may choose not to highlight the character of the victim as in shootings over drugs.

"A lot of times you can debate all day, who was worse, the defendant or the victim," says Prosecutor Paul Goodman of Memphis. "The question is what the defendant did, not the character of the victim."

But Tennessee Attorney General Charles Burson says a jury still needs to be reminded that the victim was a unique individual and whose death is a loss to society.

"Otherwise you have a generic victim," Burson says. "To look at the full extent of the crime the jury has to look at the full extent of the harm."

Prosecutors say the court rules now are clear where they once were difficult to read.

"A lot of times you use up your evidence in the guilt phase but now we've got something left for sentencing," says Henderson, who handles many of the capital-murder cases in Memphis. "Now we've got somebody here with us. We can tell the jury about the victim.   —Lawrence W. Buser

was the pastor at the Millington church of God in Christ.

His girlfriend, Bobbie Thomas, testified that she had joined Payne's father's church and that Payne befriended her at a time when she had been through a troubled marriage. She described Payne as a very caring person who was devoted to her children.

Finally, a psychologist, Dr. John Hutson, told jurors Payne was borderline mentally handicapped based on tests he administered.

He also described Payne as "somewhat naive" and as one of the most polite persons he had ever seen in the jail.

The emotionally charged trial concluded with co-prosecutor Phyllis Gardner grabbing the murder weapon and stabbing a hole through a large diagram of young Nicholas.

"This is what he did to them," Gardner said as she stabbed exhibit 24 with exhibit 25. "Did they deserve it? Are you going to let it go unpunished?"

As in the first phase, the jury took six hours to return its verdict: Payne shall receive the death penalty for the murders.

He now sits on death row with some 95 other inmates at Riverbend Maximum Security Institution on the west side of Nashville.

The last execution carried out in Tennessee was in 1960.

Capt. Sam Wilson sits in his cramped office in Millington, staring once more at the bloodiest crime he has ever seen.

He says he would be happy to help Payne's execution along.

"I think I could pull the switch myself and have no qualms about it," says Wilson, who, barring that, "would buy a ticket to it."

But Wilson knows that will not snuff out the terrible memories that will torment him forever.

"I carry it with me," Wilson says, drawing slowly on a cigarette. "I remember the scene and each bit of evidence. I could probably recite my court testimony verbatim. It was the worst because of the kids. It was so senseless.

"I just wish somewhere along the way I could go back to him and just say why?"

Lawrence W. Buser covers the Criminal Courts for *The Commercial Appeal* in Memphis, Tenn.

DANIEL EUGENE REMETA

ERIN K. MATHEWS

Somewhere along the road, James C. Hunter Jr. noticed that his thumb had lost its touch. None of the drivers who saw him standing with thumb outstretched near the entrance to the Kansas Turnpike in Wichita would pull over and pick him up.

The tall, bearded, Amoret, Mo., man had hitchhiked to his brother's house in Austin, Texas, in a little over a day one month earlier. Getting back to his parents' Overland Park, Kan., home was turning out to be more of a chore. He had been traveling now for nearly three days, and he still had about 200 miles to go.

As he had done periodically on this long trip, 33-year-old Hunter found a convenience store with a pay phone and updated his father on his lack of progress. The senior James Hunter offered to pick up his stranded son himself, but "Charlie," as his family called him, turned down the ride.

"That's too far a drive for you," he said. "I'll get a ride and get home as soon as I can."

As midnight approached, Hunter returned to the store to warm up and drink some coffee. He had spent the better part of an hour looking out the front window when a woman approached him offering a free Bible. He gratefully accepted the gift and the motel room she offered to put him up in for the night.

It was past midnight when Hunter picked up his cowboy hat and two duffel bags and followed her to her car. During the 10-minute drive to a motel, their conversation turned toward the new day—Feb. 13, 1985.

"It's my unlucky day," Hunter said.

"Why would you say that? You shouldn't be so pessimistic," she chided.

"Just tell me something good about the 13th," he said.

After a shower and a good night's sleep, Hunter was able to flag down a car relatively easily. A 1971 Oldsmobile with Michigan plates pulled to the side of the road, and 27-year-old Daniel Eugene Remeta opened the passenger door.

Hunter's luck had just run out.

Remeta told Hunter that he and his two 18-year-old companions—Lisa Dunn of Traverse City, Mich., and Mark Walter of nearby Suttons Bay, Mich.,—were traveling around the country and were currently bound for Colorado to visit his relatives. Remeta offered Hunter an Old Milwaukee beer.

"As a matter of fact, I thought they were pretty polite," Hunter would later testify at his murder trial in northwest Kansas. "They seemed like a bunch of teen-agers having a good time."

As the hitchhiker settled into the cluttered back seat of the blue, two-door car spotted with red primer, he didn't recognize the seriousness of his situation.

This chance encounter with Remeta was the beginning of the end of Hunter's life. He would spend the next three years in prison after being convicted of multiple counts of felony murder, aggravated kidnapping, aggravated robbery and aggravated battery on a citizen and a law enforcement officer. Then, four days after a retrial jury acquitted him of all charges, a heart attack took his life.

Some residents of northwest Kansas still believe his sudden death was "God's justice."

Remeta, too, was on the last leg of his long and murderous journey when he ordered Walter to stop and pick up Hunter. The two guns in the car had already been used to kill two people and critically injure a third.

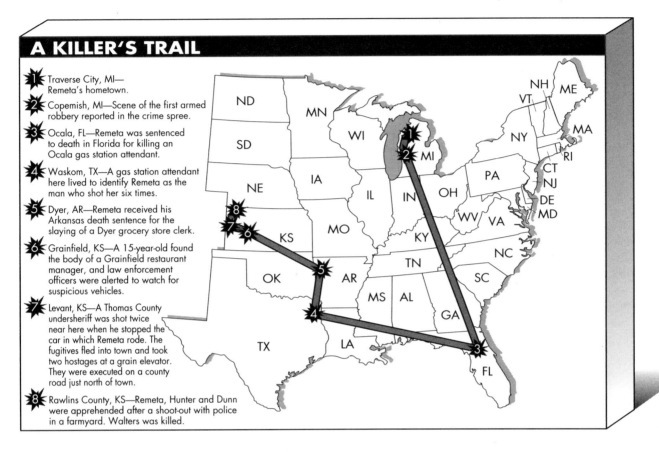

A KILLER'S TRAIL

1 Traverse City, MI—Remeta's hometown.

2 Copemish, MI—Scene of the first armed robbery reported in the crime spree.

3 Ocala, FL—Remeta was sentenced to death in Florida for killing an Ocala gas station attendant.

4 Waskom, TX—A gas station attendant here lived to identify Remeta as the man who shot her six times.

5 Dyer, AR—Remeta received his Arkansas death sentence for the slaying of a Dyer grocery store clerk.

6 Grainfield, KS—A 15-year-old found the body of a Grainfield restaurant manager, and law enforcement officers were alerted to watch for suspicious vehicles.

7 Levant, KS—A Thomas County undersheriff was shot twice near here when he stopped the car in which Remeta rode. The fugitives fled into town and took two hostages at a grain elevator. They were executed on a county road just north of town.

8 Rawlins County, KS—Remeta, Hunter and Dunn were apprehended after a shoot-out with police in a farmyard. Walters was killed.

Remeta would later be sentenced to death row in two southern states for those murders.

Before the day was over, Walter and three more people would be dead and several more would be injured. Remeta, Dunn and Hunter would be captured after a shoot-out with police.

In the next morning's *Colby* (Kan.) *Free Press*, the traditional Valentine's Day feature was at the bottom of page one. The banner headline across the top of the page was "Four dead, four injured in shooting spree." The paper also carried the news that the Kansas House was expected to pass a bill instituting the death penalty that day, but it would probably not survive a governor's veto.

Traverse City area law enforcement officers say Remeta was building up to his bloody crime spree long before he and Dunn actually got in Walter's car in late January 1985 and started toward Florida.

Community Police Officer Geoffrey Bobier vividly recalls his first encounter with Remeta, who was then 11 years old.

"He had assaulted a paper boy and was trying to rob him," Bobier said. "I grabbed him and had him down at the station. ... I was taking the information from him in regards to his home life, and I was struck by the fact of how hard this kid was.

"At one time I made the statement, 'You know you can't go on like this. When you get older they're going to wind up putting you in prison. What do you want to be when you grow up?' He looked me right in the eye and never cracked a smile or anything. He just said, 'I want to be a cop killer.' ... I knew he was lost at 11 years old."

Remeta was one of five children who grew up in the family home in a poor but well kept section of Traverse City, a community of about 17,000 people located in a scenic area at the southern tip of Grand Traverse Bay, an inlet on the northern end of Lake Michigan.

Traverse City, nestled among rolling hills, is known locally as "God's Area." The city offers both summer and winter sports opportunities to the hundreds of thousands of tourists who flock there each year. The National Cherry Festival held in July is the city's major annual attraction, celebrating the tart and sweet cherries that are an economic mainstay of the area.

Danny Remeta would begin his criminal career in Traverse City. He would end it on the flat plains of northwest Kansas, where wheat is king and the tallest structures in the small farm communities dotting the landscape are water towers and grain elevators.

"That's the first time I ever seen a grain elevator," Remeta later testified. "I didn't know what it was."

Remeta dropped out of school in the ninth grade and was enrolled in a Michigan reform school. Stuart Soule, Grand Traverse County magistrate, said a 14-year-old Danny Remeta told the officer transporting him to Maxey Boys Training School that he did not intend to stay.

"He actually escaped and came back to Traverse City before the officer got back," he said.

It was around that time when Soule, who was then a deputy sheriff, talked to Remeta and found out his goals in life were getting more grandiose.

"His goal was to kill a cop someday and go out west and join the Mafia and be a hitman," Soule said. "By that time, I'd taken Danny as a serious individual. He didn't have a sense of humor. He was very straightforward—somebody who said it like it is."

Although several of the Remeta children had had run-ins with police, middle-son Danny Remeta's criminal activity was "head and shoulders" above the rest. Bobier said. He was in and out of juvenile court until he was old enough to be sentenced as an adult for crimes such as assault, burglary, auto theft and criminal damage to property.

"His rap sheets gets progressively worse," Bobier said. "He went from little petty stuff to high court misdemeanors and felonies."

About the only time Remeta wasn't being arrested for something was when he was already behind bars, said Russ Casselman, Grand Traverse County detective.

Remeta had spent most of the 10 years between his 17th and 27th birthdays in prisons in Michigan and California. Prison records show that while incarcerated, Remeta continued to commit crimes including sodomy, in-

citing to riot and attacking a guard with a knife. He spent most of his prison time in solitary confinement.

Whenever he was released from prison, police were alerted that he was back in the area. If a call came in involving Remeta, three or four officers would respond.

"We never knew if he'd be armed or whether or not he'd try to take on a bunch of policemen," Bobier said.

Magistrate Soule described Remeta as "a strong-willed individual. You do it his way. He was a leader."

At a party in late December 1984, Remeta found someone willing to follow him. He had recently been paroled after serving three and a half years for larceny when he met Lisa Dunn. The paroled felon and the community college student who worked part-time busing tables at a local restaurant were partners in a card game that night and soon became romantically involved.

Remeta, who attracted Dunn with his boyish good looks, dark hair and dark eyes, made sure she got home on time and impressed her parents with his politeness on the phone, Dunn would later say. But one night after she stayed out too late, Dunn argued with her parents and moved out of the house and into a motel room with her new boyfriend. Remeta told his mother he and Dunn planned to marry.

Dunn, a gifted student who had never been in trouble with police, had earned a trip to Washington, D.C., to accept a 4-H award three years earlier. About three weeks after she moved in with Remeta, she would set out with him and Mark Walter, a former Catholic altar boy and the son of cherry farmers, on a completely different trip.

Dunn and Remeta had been talking about escaping the snow and bitter cold of Michigan for the sunshine of Florida when Remeta was arrested again—this time for smashing the windows of another man's car following an argument. Remeta's mother and Walter came up with $200 in bail money, and Remeta was released.

"That may have been the precursor to having him leave town and take off," Ofc. Bobier said. "He got his little band together, left and started pulling holdups. Of course, the next thing we knew it was on the national news: Hometown boy makes good."

Determined not to go back to prison, Remeta skipped his Jan. 28 arraignment and convinced Dunn and Walter it was time to go to Florida.

In preparation for the trip, Dunn stole her father's .357-caliber Magnum handgun from a bedside table. She testified that she believed she needed the gun for self-protection because she had been attacked and raped by two men when she went to Florida the previous year.

Remeta first put the gun to use on the night of Jan. 27, 1985, at the Gastown Party Mart convenience store in Copemish, Mich., about 25 miles southwest of Traverse City. After robbing 26-year-old store clerk Kathy Dinger of $275, he left her on the floor praying for her life. Remeta and his companions then headed south.

After they crossed the Florida line, Dunn became bothered by Remeta's attachment to the gun, which he nicknamed "Susie" and carried inside his coat. Remeta played Russian Roulette with "Susie" and even slept with the gun, Dunn testified.

Remeta became increasingly possessive of Dunn. He referred to her as his wife, Lisa Remeta, and told her what clothes she would wear. He said he wanted her to get pregnant.

During a trip to Disney World, Dunn testified that Remeta threatened to kill any innocent bystanders if she tried to escape. He also threatened her life and the lives of her family members.

"I just told him exactly what he wanted to hear," she said. "I knew that's the way to keep him happy is keep on telling him what he wants to hear."

Before the trio left Florida, the handgun would claim its first life. Sixty-year-old Mehrle "Shet" Reeder, a Tenneco gas station attendant in Ocala, Fla., would be shot four times just after midnight Feb. 8 during a robbery that netted Remeta and his companions about $50.

Instead of fleeing back toward Michigan, Remeta told Walter to head the car west. They raced along major highways through several southern states. Remeta was leaving behind the murder and the law enforcement officers who knew him, making his escape along a route as random and senseless as his crimes. His flight was fueled as much by beer as gasoline, and the car's back seat became cluttered with empty cans.

They followed Interstate 20 through Louisiana and had just crossed the border into Texas on Feb. 10 when Remeta saw the opportunity for another stickup at Le Fleur's Mobile Station in the tiny town of Waskom.

Camilla Carroll, 18, would not die after six bullets were pumped into her stomach and legs in that robbery. She would recover and identify Remeta as the man who took about $400 from the station and forced her into the Oldsmobile at gunpoint. Not far away, Remeta ordered her to get out and walk toward a stand of trees, she later testified. As she neared the trees, he fired.

The car sped back into Louisiana, where some of the money stolen in Texas paid for the purchase of a .22-caliber pistol at a flea market, according to Frank Garrett, an investigator for the Harrison County Sheriff's Department in northwest Arkansas.

They headed north the next day toward the small community of Dyer, Ark., a few miles east of Fort Smith along Interstate 40. It was there that the pistol was used to commit the next murder. On Feb. 11, Linda Marvin, 42, who had been working at Jim's Grocery to pay her college tuition, was robbed of more than $500 and shot six times.

After another day of driving, Remeta, Dunn and Walter got a motel room in Wichita, Kan. The group got a late start the next morning, and it was close to 11 a.m. when they saw Hunter trying to thumb a ride. Hunter told them he wanted a ride to Salina, about 90 miles to the north, where he intended to catch another ride from someone headed east on Interstate 70.

Hunter would later say the conversation was friendly at first. The former Marine was not alarmed when Remeta asked him if he could put a .22 back together and handed him a gun that would not fire. After Hunter reassembled the gun, Remeta loaded it and fired several shots out the window, Hunter testified.

At Salina, the car pulled through a McDonald's drive-through and the group stopped to buy a fresh 12-pack of beer. As the car approached the junction with I-70, Hunter became concerned when Remeta told Walter not to stop to let him out. But Remeta reassured him, saying he would get picked up by police if he hitchhiked at the intersection of two interstates and he would be better off to get out when they stopped for gas. The car turned west onto I-70.

Hunter had drunk three more beers by the time the Oldsmobile pulled into a gas station about 20 minutes later. He began preparing to get out, but Remeta would not let him leave the car's back seat. This time, Hunter became alarmed.

Remeta pulled from his coat several pairs of sunglasses and packs of cigarettes that he had stolen from the gas station. Hunter asked again to be let out as the car began rolling west down I-70.

"Then Danny Remeta said, 'I should have killed that one hitchhiker,'" Hunter would later testify. Remeta told Hunter they had picked up another hitchhiker earlier in the trip. That hitchhiker had refused Remeta's offer to steal a car for him, and now Remeta wished he had killed him.

Remeta, who had been drinking steadily during the trip, began to brag about his years in prison and the murders he claimed to have committed, Hunter said. Twice he ordered Hunter out of the car along the highway to join him as he urinated. One time he took a shot in Hunter's direction.

"Considering he wouldn't let me out I thought I was in a lot of trouble," Hunter said. "I didn't know if he was baiting me to run or what."

Remeta told Hunter he could get out at the Colorado border, but Hunter feared Remeta intended to kill him there.

It was after 3 p.m., when the Olds rolled up to a Stuckey's restaurant near Grainfield, a small northwest Kansas community. Minutes later, a 15-year-old boy entering the restaurant after school found the lifeless body of Stuckey's manager Larry McFarland crumpled on the floor.

Remeta would later say he shot 27-year-old McFarland twice because he "did not back away (from the cash register) fast enough."

Word of the shooting spread over police scanners throughout the region, and an eastbound highway patrol trooper reported seeing a suspicious-looking car headed west.

Thomas County Undersheriff Ben Albright spotted the car near the exit to Levant, an unincorporated community with fewer than 100 residents about 50 miles west of Grainfield. He activated the lights on his police cruiser, and Walter pulled the car off onto the exit ramp.

Hunter would testify that he was relieved to see Albright's car pull up. Remeta would say he was "more or less mad because I had to shoot him. When you shoot a cop, it's pretty hard to get away because they have the radio in the car."

Remeta confessed that he stepped out of the car and shot at Albright four times, striking him twice in the chest and arm before the .357 Magnum ran out of bullets. But in his testimony, Undersheriff Albright identified Hunter as his assailant.

Remeta left Albright for dead and got back in the Oldsmobile, but he looked back and saw the officer pick up his radio microphone. It was 4:07 p.m., and Albright's wife, Pat, who had come to the sheriff's office to visit her husband, listened stunned to his voice over the police scanner calling for an ambulance because he'd been shot.

During the shooting, Hunter had reached over the seat and picked up the pistol. He later said he planned to "shoot that rascal (Remeta)," but his finger slipped on the trigger and he accidentally shot Dunn. Remeta grabbed the gun, and the car flew down the exit ramp.

Remeta was looking for a fresh vehicle and hostages when he spotted the towering, white Bartlett and Co. grain elevator on the east edge of Levant. He told Walter to pull into the wide gravel parking lot. It was 4:15 p.m.

Fifty-five-year-old Glenn Moore and John R. "Rick" Schroeder, 28, had just stepped out of Moore's green Ford pickup in front of the elevator office when the Olds pulled up. A fellow employee said Schroeder, who had just begun work at the elevator three weeks before, greeted the newcomers with a smile—until he saw their guns.

Moore ran an elevator repair business and had been trying for several days to fix a broken auger in the grain dryer. Now, he and Schroeder watched in shock as Remeta broke out an office window and shot elevator manager Maurice Christie as he attempted to call authorities. Christie, 61, would survive, but the bullet that lodged near his heart would force him into early retirement.

Remeta then forced Moore and Schroeder into the bed of Moore's pickup, and he and Hunter hopped in back with them. Walter climbed behind the wheel, and Dunn—complaining about the pain of her bullet wound—slid into the jump seat.

The truck sped away from the elevator, turning north onto a dirt road that cut through the flat, snow-covered fields. About a mile down the road, Remeta beat on the window and told Walter to pull over.

Screaming obscenities, Remeta ordered Hunter, Schroeder and Moore out of the truck. The three stood side-by-side on the

road. Hunter told the jury he thought he was dead when he heard Remeta's next words: "I don't need no hostages, and I don't need no witnesses."

But Remeta ordered Hunter to step away from the hostages and get back in the truck. Hunter was checking on Dunn's wound when he heard the gunfire. Remeta said he had just fired a few warning shots when he climbed back into the truck.

Pursuing police, arriving at the scene minutes later, would discover the bodies of Schroeder and Moore, who had been shot in the head execution-style, lying face down in the road.

Walter revved the truck to 95 mph as the fugitives tried to escape north toward the Nebraska border. Still about 25 miles from the state line, they spotted a road block. Remeta ordered Walter to turn the truck around and pull into a farmyard.

Daniel Eugene Remeta and his girlfriend, Lisa Dunn, are escorted by authorities to trial.

PHOTO • SCOTT WILLIAMS/*THE SALINA (KAN.) JOURNAL*

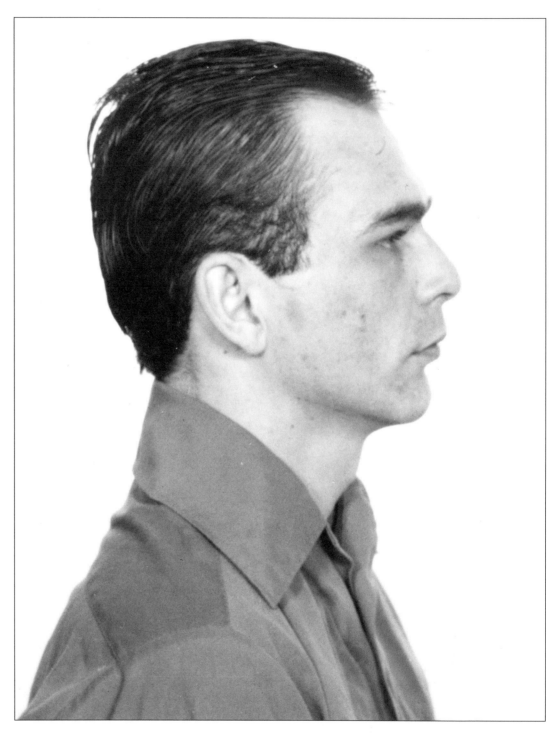

Remeta received five consecutive life sentences in Kansas before being extradicted to Florida. In Florida, as well as Arkansas, Remeta was given a death sentence. He currently awaits execution in Florida, as appeals proceed on his behalf.

No one was home at the L.A. "Bud" Roesch farm when the pickup pulled in near a shed. Hunter grabbed the pistol and ran to hide behind the metal building. Remeta said he told Walter to take Dunn into the house, but law enforcement officers were already on the scene when they stepped out of the truck.

Bullets began flying through the yard.

Officers on the scene said Walter was shooting at them. But Remeta, who was shot in the buttocks, later said it was he who returned fire with the .357. Walter, standing near the truck, was killed almost instantly. Dunn, trying desperately to crawl beneath the truck, was wounded. Hunter stayed out of the line of fire and was unhurt when he surrendered. None of the officers were injured.

The three surviving suspects were apprehended by 5 p.m. After their wounds were treated at a local hospital, Remeta, Dunn and Hunter were incarcerated in the Thomas County Jail and bond was set at $5 million cash for each. Rumors that lynch mobs were forming soon prompted Sheriff Tom Jones to move them to other undisclosed locations.

Initially, Remeta and Dunn told authorities that Hunter and Walter were the killers, but before their trial commenced in Colby, Kan., Remeta had confessed in media interviews to all of the Kansas shootings. Remeta, who has a tattoo of a dragon and sword on his left forearm, said the fantasy board game "Dungeons and Dragons" helped inspire the killing spree.

"Just because a few people got killed doesn't mean that I'm a psychopath, sick in the head, or just like doing it," Remeta told a Wichita television reporter in a jail cell interview.

In open court during the pretrial hearing May 13, 1985, he pleaded guilty to all charges.

Dunn and Hunter were tried together in June 1985 in Thomas County District Court. Remeta was called as a defense witness during the two-week trial, which was the first in Kansas history to be televised. Area residents who didn't crowd into the tightly secured courtroom watched with fascination as the proceedings were aired gavel to gavel on two local channels.

Attorneys representing both defendants argued that responsibility for the savage killings belonged to Remeta alone.

"I subjected you people to something no one should be subjected to," said Jake Brooks, Dunn's court-appointed attorney. "I subjected you to Daniel Remeta—a man who needs to control people. He's the kind of man who sees weaknesses in people quickly, and he uses those weaknesses to control them."

But after 12 hours of deliberation, the jury found both Dunn and Hunter guilty of all charges. They both received four life sentences to be served consecutively.

Dunn was granted a retrial by a federal judge. After her attorneys presented new evidence that she was a victim of "battered woman syndrome," she was found innocent by a jury in Shawnee County District Court on Sept. 2, 1992. Hunter was also granted a retrial and aquitted of all charges.

A pre-sentencing report about Remeta prepared by the Kansas Reception and Diagnostic Center described him as "contentious, provocative, rebellious, angry, hostile and dangerous."

"He's a predator who will physically hurt others," the report said.

Remeta received five consecutive life sentences in Kansas before being extradicted to Florida. He initially confessed to the murder of Florida gas station attendant Reeder, then recanted and blamed Walter for the slaying. Nevertheless, a Florida jury convicted him of the crime and recommended the death sentence.

An Arkansas jury was also convinced of Remeta's guilt in store clerk Marvin's murder, and he received a death sentence in that state as well.

Remeta currently awaits execution on death row in Florida, as appeals proceed on his behalf. Because he is not in custody in Arkansas, his appeals in that state are on hold.

Police, attorneys and the families of Remeta's victims are not the only ones wondering what could cause such a violent rampage.

Remeta's mother, Betty, said her family never had guns in the home and didn't even own a car.

"I'm a mother; I know how you feel. My thoughts and prayers have been with you each and every day," Betty Remeta wrote in a letter of apology to the victims of her son's crimes that was published in the Wichita (Kan.) Eagle-Beacon.

The letter said she never knew her son to be violent and could not understand what happened.

"He was no animal or monster turned loose on the streets," she wrote. "The rest of my life I'll ask myself why."

Erin K. Mathews is a free-lance writer and a former reporter for The Salina (Kan.) Journal.

"Just because a few people got killed doesn't mean that I'm a psychopath, sick in the head, or just like doing it."
—Daniel Remeta

RODNEY ALCALA

JANET ZIMMERMAN

Waves smashed furiously against the cliffs at Huntington Beach that June afternoon in 1979. The serious surfers whose wet-suited profiles usually dot the shoreline here in the early morning had long disappeared as the sun broke through the summer haze.

A scattering of tourists was beginning to emerge, stopping their cars along the dirt overhang to peer into the endless blue of the Pacific Ocean. On a good day, they might even catch a glimpse of Catalina Island, 26 miles offshore. When they'd gotten their fill of salt water and palm trees, they'd venture on to the seedy downtown of Huntington Beach, filled with head shops and outdoor hamburger stands where the locals hang out.

Teen-agers fresh out of school would catch the bus or hitch a ride with friends as they began work on their tans. They'd spread their towels on the hot white sand or perch on the cement retaining wall, listening to rock 'n roll music and maybe waiting for a friend who could score them some pot.

It appeared that this 20th day of June was like any other on this coastal city 50 miles south of Los Angeles—the beginning of a typical Southern California summer.

And it was, for almost everyone except 12-year-old Robin Christine Samsoe. It was here at 14th Street and Pacific Coast Highway that this blue-eyed 7th grader would peer directly into the face of death.

Death on that day took the form of a 35-year-old man named Rodney James Alcala. He was a lanky, soft-spoken ex-con with an insatiable appetite for young girls and violent sex.

Alcala wore a blue Hawaiian shirt. His hair was a thick, wavy black that hung below his shoulders and almost made him look like a woman. His weapon of choice was a 35 mm camera, which he used to befriend young girls who would pose for his promises of fame and fortune.

Robin and her best friend, 13-year-old Brigett Wilvert, were reclining on the cliffs at 14th Street when Alcala approached. Like dozens of girls before them, he asked to take their picture for a photography contest.

They agreed, flattered by the attention of an older man. It was a decision that would soon mean a slow and agonizing death for Robin Samsoe.

As Alcala focused his camera on the girls, he was interrupted by a woman who knew Brigett. When she asked what was going on, Alcala quickly walked away. But it wasn't the last they'd see of him.

Not long after, Robin and her friend headed toward Brigett's home. Robin was afraid she'd be late for her hour-long ballet class, so she hopped on Brigett's yellow 10-speed Schwinn and headed toward her home in an affluent area about a mile away.

At home Robin grabbed her blue dance bag and biked off to class at the Seacliffe Center dance studio, where the aspiring ballerina answered phones part-time so she could afford the lessons. She never arrived.

Police combed the city, but turned up no leads. Bulletins to other police departments went unanswered. Questioning of child-crime suspects proved fruitless.

Two weeks later, her nude, skeletal remains were found along a road near the Chantry Flats campground in the San Gabriel Mountains above Pasadena.

Aside from her long, honey-blonde hair, Robin was unrecognizable. Animals had

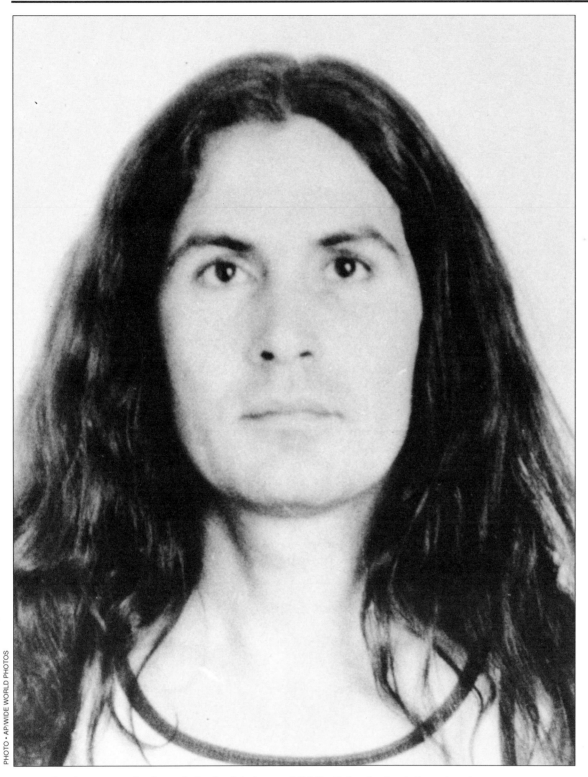

Prosecutors and police estimate that Alcala's IQ is as high as 160. The long-haired, UCLA film graduate used photography to befriend young girls who would pose for his promises of fame and fortune.

gnawed at her young body and she had to be identified through dental and X-ray records.

It was unclear whether she had been sexually abused. Authorities determined she'd probably been killed with the blood-stained butcher knife that was found in the nearby brush.

She was laid to rest in a small pink and white casket. Her classmates at Dwyer Middle School planted a pine tree on campus in her memory.

While her family and friends grieved, the widespread search for her killer began.

• • • • • • •

A police artist put together a sketch made from Brigett Wilvert's description of the beach photographer. Over the next month, investigators got dozens of calls from people who saw the composite drawing on the television news and recognized the subject as Rodney Alcala.

Finally, Alcala's parole officer called police and confirmed the reports. It was him.

Alcala was arrested July 24, 1979, in connection with Robin's slaying. He was living at his parent's Monterey Park home in Los Angeles County.

The evidence pointed strongly in Alcala's direction, police said. It opened a chapter on one of Orange County's most shocking and notorious murder cases.

After several delays, the trial opened in 1980. Prosecutor Richard Farnell argued that Alcala had sexually attacked Robin, then killed her to keep from being identified.

Farnell introduced three other cases for which Alcala was convicted in attacks on young girls. A Superior Court judge ruled the crimes showed a similarity to Robin's and allowed their introduction.

A jury took 11 days to convict Alcala of first degree murder and kidnapping. Jurors later recommended that Alcala should die in California's gas chamber for his crime and the judge agreed.

Alcala spent four years on death row.

Then the California Supreme Court, under the direction of Chief Justice Rose Bird, overturned his conviction. Justice Joseph Grodin, in a majority opinion for the high court, said the three prior crimes were not similar. Their introduction may have prejudiced jurors in the Samsoe case against Alcala, the court wrote.

So amid the outcries of prosecutors, police and the victim's family, Alcala was returned to Orange County for a second round. He came back into the ring smiling, but it wasn't for long.

Deputy District Attorney Tom Goethals took over the case in 1986. A fiery, well-established prosecutor, Goethals matched wits with the cunning Alcala.

They waged a long-standing personal battle. They exchanged words on several occasions, when Alcala poured over physical evidence on breaks and Goethals was assigned to watch over him. Alcala accused the prosecutor of being overzealous and politically motivated, while Goethals charged that Alcala was smug and dangerously smart.

"He always thought he could kick my butt because he thought he was smarter than I was," Goethals said. "Well, maybe he is, but like I told him, 'I'll be going home tonight, Rodney.'"

The tanned, bespectacled Goethals took a personal dislike for Alcala, more than he had for any other defendant. His crimes turned the stomach of this devout Catholic prosecutor and he wanted Alcala to pay.

"I think I could be the person who could go up there and execute Rodney Alcala," Goethals later said. "I'm sure that's the penalty he deserves."

Alcala is a "sexual carnivore ... and the prey is our children, the most innocent members of our society," Goethals said.

The stage was set for a stunning standoff.

But Goethals was dealt a blow early in the trial when the prosecution's key witness from the first trial no longer could remember events from the day Robin disappeared.

Forest ranger Dana Crappa testified in 1980 that she had seen a man who looked like Alcala dragging a blonde girl into the brush along Santa Anita Canyon, near where the corpse was found. That was the day Robin disappeared.

Crappa returned to the area five days later and found Robin's body. But she was so emotionally overwrought she did not report the siting for seven months, after the body had been discovered by another forestry worker.

The defense had a field day trying to discredit Crappa's testimony. Alcala's attorneys accused Crappa of concocting the story and later said authorities had brain-washed her with low-level hypnosis before she testified.

The defense won a small victory in the second trial, when the ranger-turned-nurse said on the stand that she had amnesia. Crappa believed she subconsciously blocked out all memory of the event because it was too painful. The slight, short-haired woman partially blamed herself for Robin's death because she didn't stop and question the man. She'd been wracked with nightmares over the incident.

Crappa's announcement shocked the

courtroom, especially the prosecutor. Goethals' case then hinged on the remaining evidence.

A pair of gold earrings had been found in a Seattle storage locker rented by Alcala shortly before his capture. Robin's mother, Marianne Frazier, identified the earrings as some her daughter was fond of wearing.

Alcala and his attorneys told jurors that he had owned those earrings for more than a year before Robin disappeared. Alcala claimed he was wearing one of the earrings on the Dating Game show in 1978, a tape of which was shown to the unconvinced jury.

Also found in the Seattle storage locker and at his parent's home were nearly 1,000 pictures of boys, girls and women, some of them nude. Dozens of the photos were of a long-haired Alcala, his back to the camera, wearing what appeared to be women's underwear.

One of the pictures was of a Sunset Beach girl who testified the photo was snapped the same day Robin disappeared.

Prosecutors claimed the material showed Alcala's abnormal interest in sex, especially with girls. So did another item found in the search—a 10-year-old videotape showing Alcala engaged in sex acts with three young women, they said.

The case seemed nearly sewn up.

But the prosecution was dealt another blow. Two snitches from the Orange County Jail recanted their testimony that Alcala had admitted to abducting Robin and slapping her until she passed out.

They said they'd concocted the story to gain concessions in their own legal cases. One of the men said he was motivated to testify because of a jailhouse code of ethics against child molesters.

Despite this, there was still some incriminating evidence remaining.

Robin's yellow bicycle was eventually traced to a thrift store 5 miles from Alcala's home, and 50 miles from the coastal neighborhood where the girl was abducted. The bike had been sold before investigators caught up to it.

And several girls, including Brigett Wilvert, identified Alcala as the man they had seen on the beach the day Robin disap-

peared. They said he was snapping pictures of girls and asked one to get "loaded" with him.

It was enough to convince jurors, who took three hours to return the same guilty verdict. One of the panelists characterized Alcala a dangerously intelligent man, devious and depraved.

Superior Court Judge Donald McCartin then upheld the jury's recommendation for the death penalty. Alcala had been dealt his second date with death.

"Mr. Alcala is as guilty as any man who has ever come through this court," the judge said. "For 20 years this man has been a vicious, malevolent individual who has preyed on the youngest members of society, and nothing has made any impression on Mr. Alcala.

"Death is the only proper penalty in a case such as this."

And so Alcala was returned to his old home—death row.

It's impossible, however, to discuss with Alcala the presumed terror of his young victim. He still denies any part in Robin's abduction or slaying.

Now 47, he spends hours in his solitary 5-foot by 11-foot cell in Northern California's San Quentin Prison concentrating on complicated legal issues. His thin wrists may be bound by metal shackles, but he's still as cocky as ever.

Alcala authored his own appeal to the seven-member Supreme Court, which was heard on October 8, 1992 in Los Angeles. A ruling was not yet issued at press time.

He still distrusts lawyers—he went through more than four during his trials. He says they make mistakes and overlook obvious facts.

In 1990, he granted a rare interview, but only on the condition that the reporter read his 400-page petition for a new trial. He then administered a 15-minute quiz to ensure its most minute details had been properly digested.

His chances of a new trial seem remote after two convictions and as many death sentences. He's grown older in prison, his curly black hair now streaked with the silver of age and dipping below the collar of

Alcala is a "sexual carnivore ... and the prey is our children, the most innocent members of our society."
—Tom Goethals

PHOTO • KATHI KENT RILEY

his prison-issue denims.

• • • • • • •

Little is known about Alcala's past. He couldn't control his urges, but somehow managed to keep his childhood a secret.

Prosecutors and police agree, however, that he is highly intelligent. There were estimates his IQ is as high as 160. But he's handicapped by an enormous ego and his manipulative personality, they say.

"It always seemed to me that 75 percent of the time Rodney was OK—ambitious, a contributing member of society," prosecutor Goethals said. "But occasionally Rodney's wires crossed. I don't know if it was environmental or hereditary, but if you were an attractive young woman, you didn't want to be around him at that time."

Alcala grew up without a strong father figure. His mother, Anna Maria German, remarried early in his life, but Alcala did not have a strong relationship with the man.

His mother testified at the penalty phase of Alcala's trial that he was "a good boy." He is one of four children and his brother is a retired Army general. Alcala performed well in Catholic schools and joined the Army after his high school graduation in 1961.

After his discharge in 1964, he earned a bachelor's degree in film at UCLA. "He was always on the honor roll," German told the court.

But Goethals painted a different picture of Alcala, whom he characterized as a vile man with no social conscience.

In 1963, Alcala had gone absent without leave from the Army. He turned up at his mother's home, where he exposed himself to his youngest sister, who became hysterical. Alcala told the court he wasn't sure whether he wanted to have sex with his sister at the time.

There apparently was no single, pivotal moment or incident that drove Alcala to a life of crime. That issue was never brought up at the trials.

At the second penalty phase of trial, Alcala's character witnesses included guards from San Quentin, who said he gave them no trouble.

Alcala also did graduate work in photography at New York University, but didn't finish before another murder turned up and he was named a suspect.

• • • • • • •

It wasn't the first time Alcala had been in trouble with the law, and it wouldn't be the last. One of his earliest encounters with authorities was one of the most telling about his perverted urges, prosecutors said.

In 1968, Tali Shapiro was walking to school along Sunset Boulevard in Hollywood when Alcala pulled up. He lured her into his car by claiming to be a friend of Tali's parents.

She ended up at a Hollywood home and was looking at a poster he wanted her to see when everything went black.

A suspicious bystander had seen Alcala pick the girl up on the street and followed them to the house before calling police. When officers arrived, Alcala, who was nude, parted a curtain and peered out. Instead of opening the door, he backed away and disappeared.

Police kicked in the front door. Tali was on the kitchen floor, lying in a pool of blood. The girl had a round, metal bar across her neck that Alcala apparently had used to restrain her. She eventually recovered, but Alcala had disappeared.

He was arrested three years later after a Concord, N.H., postal employee recognized his picture on an FBI wanted poster.

Alcala pleaded guilty to the attack in 1972 and was given an indeterminate sentence. He was paroled two years later.

But he didn't stay out of trouble for long.

Two months after his release, Alcala found 13-year-old Julie Johnson waiting to catch a school bus near Warner Avenue and Beach Boulevard in Huntington Beach. Alcala sat on the curb with her and talked awhile before offering to drive her to school.

She declined at first, then accepted his offer.

But Alcala didn't stop at her school. Instead, he told her he wanted to check out an apartment nearby. When she told him she wanted out of the car, he told her to be quiet.

Alcala drove to the cliffs area off Pacific Coast Highway in Huntington Beach, near the area where Robin Samsoe would meet up with him five years later. There he forced Julie to smoke marijuana with him, she testified.

When she tried to leave, he grabbed her by the leg. Alcala put his arm around her and kissed her forcefully.

Park rangers discovered the pair then and arrested them for smoking pot. The arrest sent Alcala back to prison for a three-year stint for violating parole. It was a familiar pattern for him.

A month after his June 1977 release, Alcala was questioned by New York police in the disappearance of a 24-year-old woman. Her body was found nearly a year later in a grave near the Rockefeller estate in Tarrytown, N.Y.

The woman's friends told police she was seeing a photographer named John Burger, a name Alcala allegedly gave authorities when he was arrested in 1971 in connection with the Hollywood attack. The case was dropped for lack of evidence.

Alcala also was questioned in connection with the June 14, 1979, slaying of a 21-year-old Burbank woman who was strangled in her apartment. Authorities said Alcala met the woman at a bar and danced with her, but she rejected his advances.

Blood stains at the scene matched Alcala's to a degree that would eliminate 90 percent of all other humans.

That case also was dropped because of the unreliability of the prosecution's key witness, a jailhouse informant.

Then Robin Samsoe disappeared and the cycle began again for Alcala. Only this time it was for good.

There was little sympathy for this articulate, audacious killer. Not from the judge, who called his claims of innocence "hogwash," and not from Robin's mother, who called him ruthless.

"When he dies, justice will be done," Marianne Frazier sobbed after the hollow victory of his second conviction. "He begged for his life, but I'm sure my daughter did too. He didn't spare her. There's no good reason to spare him.

"It's time to die."

Janet Zimmerman is currently a reporter with the San Bernardino (Calif.) Sun. In 1990, Alcala granted her an interview at San Quentin Prison, when she was a reporter with the Orange Coast Daily Pilot in Costa Mesa, Calif.

Blood stains at the scene matched Alcala's to a degree that would eliminate 90 percent of all other humans.

TEXAS

LEONEL TORRES HERRERA

KATHY FAIR

For three generations, the Herrera men stalked the small towns that dot the Rio Grande Valley in Texas, forging careers as drug smugglers and reputations as cold, cunning men who let nothing or no one step in their way.

They were chameleons: handsome, charming rogues who drank and played hard, who could turn into ruthless adversaries in the blink of an eye.

The most notorious of the clan is Leonel Torres Herrera, a high school dropout with a propensity for violence. In 1981, he murdered two cops in the span of just 10 minutes.

Herrera is under a death sentence for gunning down Enrique "Rick" Carrisalez, a 22-year-old rookie patrolman with the Los Fresnos (Texas) Police Department, who had stopped him for speeding. Herrera pleaded guilty to murdering Texas Department of Public Safety Trooper David Rucker and is serving a life sentence in that case. His execution was nearly carried out in March 1992, but a frantic, all-night legal battle waged by his lawyers spared his life and propelled Herrera's case back before the U.S. Supreme Court, cloaked in a mantle of innocence.

Defense lawyers laid the groundwork in 1990 for Herrera's claims that he did not commit the murders—despite his confession to one—when they began securing affidavits that swore Herrera had been the patsy and that the real killer was his brother Raul. The affidavits also claimed that Rucker ran protection for drug smugglers working in concert with a sheriff in a neighboring county. They even had an affidavit from an alleged eyewitness.

Prosecutors and law enforcement officers scoffed at the affidavits. All the witnesses who might have been able to verify the claims that Raul Herrera was the killer were conveniently dead. Another statement was tinged with revenge. It was given by Herrera's nephew, who may have been trying to even the score with his father when he blamed the murders on him.

Nonetheless, when the Supreme Court began its fall term in October 1992, Herrera's case was one of the first up, and its outcome has national importance. The court was asked whether the Constitution gives federal courts—which traditionally rule only on procedural matters in a trial—jurisdiction to hear a state prisoner's claim that he is not guilty, even if those claims arise a decade later.

It seems a rather innocuous legal argument, except that Herrera's lawyers couched the question in terms calculated to draw nationwide media attention: Is is unconstitutional to execute an innocent person?

"We don't have an innocent person here," Justice Sandra Day O'Connor told Talbot D'Alemberte, a prominent Florida trial lawyer and former president of the American Bar Association, who argued Herrera's case. "We have a person who has been convicted of the murder, and we have allegations that someone else may have committed the crime."

Prosecutors contend the case represents precisely the problem they face in carrying out capital punishment: endless 11th-hour delays often based on frivolous, and sometime fictitious, claims.

If the court allows Herrera to reopen his case, O'Connor acknowledged from the bench, "The burden this will put on the system of justice could be enormous."

● ● ● ● ● ● ●

Texas Highway 100 stretches for 26 lonely

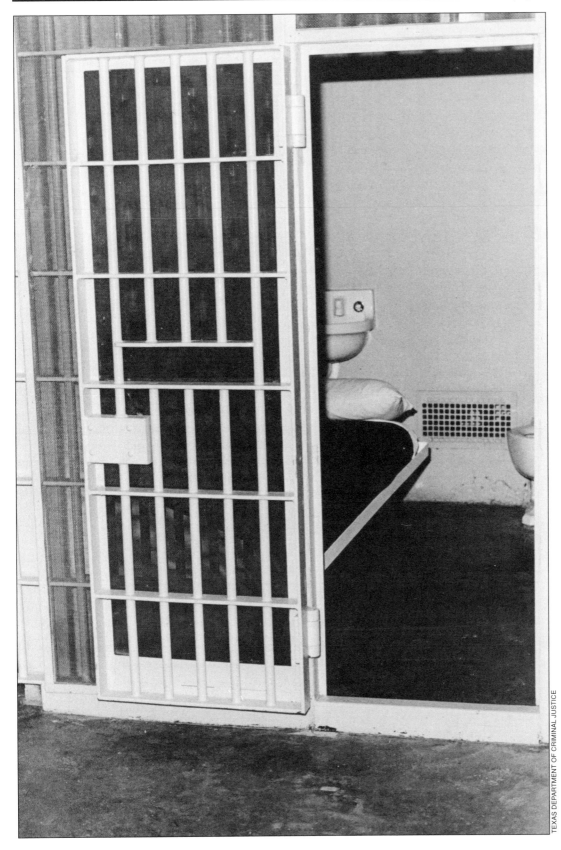

Herrera was provided a cell on death row after being convicted of murdering a 22-year-old policeman.

miles from Port Isabel, at the confluence of the Intracoastal Waterway and the Gulf of Mexico, to Los Fresnos, a one-stoplight town of 30,000 residents in the Rio Grande Valley.

Heavily traveled during the day by commuters and vacationers who use it as the main access to South Padre Island, the road becomes a dark, desolate route at night.

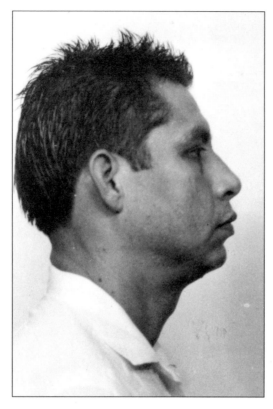

Such was the scene on the night of Sept. 21, 1981, when Rucker and Carrisalez, unbeknownst to each other, set up speed traps less than 10 miles apart on the highway.

About 9:30 that evening, Carrisalez stopped by the police station where his childhood chum, Enrique Hernandez, was waiting to accompany him on patrol. Hernandez, who operated a gas station in town with his father, hoped some day to become a cop himself and frequently accompanied Carrisalez.

Traffic was light, but as fate would have it, Herrera was barreling west on Highway 100, apparently heading home to the nearby town of Edinburg after picking up a load of dope on South Padre Island. He hit Rucker's speed trap first, at about 10:40 p.m.

By 10:50, both officers lay in the road. Rucker was dead from a gunshot wound to the back of his head so forceful it blew his left eye out. Carrisalez, mortally wounded in the chest, died eight days later in a hospital, but not before identifying Herrera as the man who gunned him down.

"Ironically, our whole conversation (that night) was dealing with things we had done together," Hernandez, now a narcotics officer with the Arlington (Texas) Police Department, would recall more than a decade later. "It was like something was telling me I'd never see Rick again."

Within minutes of the shootings, Herrera was the suspect. For one, authorities found his blood-splattered social security card on the road near Rucker's body. Second, Carrisalez had radioed the license tag of the 1978 gray Couger he was pulling over. Police quickly traced the plate to Herrera's common-law wife, Oralia Morales, at an address in Edinburg. And third, Hernandez had witnessed the shooting and gave police a description of Herrera and the car. Hernandez also later identified Herrera from photo and police lineups.

Within two hours of the shootings, police had recovered Herrera's car at Morales' house. Blood found on the fenders and interior eventually were determined to be the same type as Rucker's. Police also found traces of marijuana in the car, an imprint of a handgun that had been hidden in the carpet padding, and a sawed-off shotgun in the trunk.

Herrera was captured four days later, on Oct. 4, when police surrounded a house in a sparsely populated area a mile northeast of Edinburg. Herrera bolted out the back door and across an open field as two police officers pulled into the driveway. A state trooper hiding in the brush that ringed the open field fired one shot, and Herrera dropped to the ground, unscathed.

Inside the house, police found Herrera's blood-splattered jeans with the keys to the 1978 Cougar in a pocket. On Herrera, officers found one of the most damaging pieces of evidence used at trial: a letter he scrawled on the backs of five envelopes. The rambling letter read, in part:

"To whom it may concern: I am terribly sorry for those I have brought grief to their lives. Who knows why? We cannot change the future's problems with problems from the past. What I did was for a cause and purpose. One law runs others, and in the world we live in, that's the way it is. ...

"What happened to Rucker was for a certain reason. I knew him as Mike Tatum. He was in my business, and he violated some of its laws and suffered the penalty, like the

one you have for me when the time comes.

"*My personal life, which has been a conspiracy since my high school days, has nothing to do with what has happened. The other officers than (sic) became part of our lives, me and Ricker's (Tatum), that night had not to do in this. He was out to do what he had to do, protect, but that's life. There's a lot of us that wear different faces in lives every day, and that is what causes problems for all.*"

At the punishment phase of the trial, prosecutor Rey Cantu introduced testimony from witnesses at Edinburg General Hospital who had heard Herrera threaten to kill the six officers who were guarding him there.

He had been taken to the hospital after blacking out in his cell following a scuffle in a police interview room the evening he was arrested. During the interview, Herrera slugged a prosecutor from Hidalgo County in the face, knocking him unconscious. When officers rushed the room to subdue the suspect, Herrera and another officer were knocked to the floor. Herrera's lawyer, Jim Bates, contended the police had beaten his client with slapsticks, but authorities denied it.

Cantu also tried to show jurors a videotape of Herrera assaulting a TV cameraman in a courthouse hallway, but the judge ruled it inadmissible. The videotape had been made the day Herrera showed up for a hearing on an attempted capital murder charge for which he was later acquitted.

Nonetheless, the jury unanimously agreed that Herrera had deliberately killed Carrisalez and that Herrera was likely to commit acts of violence again. They sentenced him to die for his crimes.

Defense lawyers later argued that the jury was tainted because four members were either local police officers, related to police officers or knew the victims.

••••••

Leonel Herrera was born Sept. 17, 1947, the eldest son and one of five children born to a migrant farm worker and his wife. For years, his family made their way from South Texas to California picking olives or peaches. Family life, at least as described in affidavits for Herrera's appeal and in police records,

Herrera's defense lawyers claimed that his brother, Raul Herrera Sr. (left), was the real killer. All the witnesses who might have been able to verify that Raul was the killer were conveniently dead.

was not pleasant.

The family patriarch was José Maximillia Herrera, who once murdered a man he caught messing with one of his concubines. He regularly stomped and punched his wife and terrorized their children during binges induced by alcohol, marijuana and cocaine. He gave up migrant farming the year Leonel was born and turned to smuggling. He passed his legacy of booze, beatings and drugs on to two of his three sons and a grandson before dying in 1981 of a heart attack the day Leonel was sentenced to die.

Raul Torres Herrera Sr. was José's second son. A meat-cutter by trade, authorities long suspected—but could never prove—that he littered the rural roadsides with the dismembered body parts of victims of soured drug deals. A jealous, quick-tempered man with a lengthy criminal history, he once sent his wife to the store for shotgun shells, then casually loaded them and told her to run for her life. As she did, he shot her in the back of the knees while his young son, Raul Jr., watched. Raul Sr. was murdered in 1984, shot in the back of the head after threatening to kill a long-time associate.

Raul Herrera Jr. is a slim, baby-faced 21-year-old who apprenticed in the drug business at his father's knee. He's doing 20 years

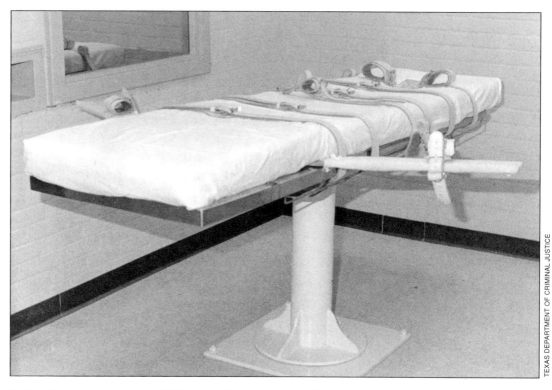

If executed, Herrera will be strapped to this gurney and given a lethal injection of drugs.

TEXAS DEPARTMENT OF CRIMINAL JUSTICE

in the Texas Department of Criminal Justice for aggravated assault. He was only 16 when he worked another man over with a baseball bat in a soured drug deal and was certified to stand trial as an adult.

Leonel Herrera had been an avid high school athlete until he dropped out of Edinburg High School during his sophomore year. He joined the Navy in 1967 and it was aboard a cruiser in international waters off Vietnam that his first violent response to authority figures is recorded. He was discharged two years later after being court-martialed for the brutal beating of a fellow sailor. Years later, his former commanding officer, Kenneth C. Wallace, now a retired rear admiral, recalled Herrera as "the most violent service-man on the ship (who) suffered no qualms or remorse about striking another shipmate." Herrera returned home, managed a convenience store with his mother and brother Raul, ran drugs with his dad, and fathered two daughters by his common-law wife. Along the way, he chalked up a lengthy record of pummeling friends, acquaintances, prosecutors and jailers, and shooting cops.

Authorities insist that Rucker and Carrisalez are not the first cops that Herrera shot. He was acquitted of the attempted capital murder of an Edinburg policeman in 1980. His lawyer in that case said the evidence against him was insufficient; prosecutors say he was acquitted because the Herrera family threatened to harm the family of a key state's witness.

"The Herrera men were involved with crime as a way of life for many years," notes Hector Villarreal, a former state district judge and now a defense attorney and liquor-store owner in Edinburg. He went to school with Raul Sr. and Leonel and has represented all of the Herrera men at one time or another.

"We're not talking about instances (of crime) when we talk about Leonel and Raul," he adds. "We're talking about careers. And I think it will continue with Raul Jr. He's a sociological nightmare. They are not the kinds of individuals who turned to crime because they had nothing else to do. I think they became criminals because they wanted to be."

It's against this background that prosecutors try to measure the credibility of the claims raised in the affidavits alleging Herrera's innocence.

Why, they ask, did Villarreal wait nearly 10 years before filing his affidavit claiming that Raul Sr. told him he had killed Rucker and Carrisalez?

Villarreal, who was representing Raul Sr. when Raul allegedly confessed, claims he told Leonel Herrera's trial attorney, Jim Bates, about the statement in 1984—after Raul Sr. was killed. By the time the affidavit was filed, though, Bates, too, was dead, killed by the jealous spouse of one of his divorce clients.

Then there's the matter of Raul Jr., who claims in his affidavit that he was in the back seat of the car when his father shot the officers and that another man, José Isabel "Chavello" Lopez, was riding in the front seat.

Prosecutors contend that Raul Jr. is simply trying to even the score with his father and Lopez: In 1983, Raul Jr. watched his father try to kill his mother. Then, in 1984, he was walking with his father when Lopez killed the father. Lopez ended up with a 10-year probated sentence for involuntary manslaughter.

• • • • • • •

More than a decade after the slayings, Herrera's case still strikes a raw nerve in a lot of people.

The judge who presided over Herrera's trial in Carrisalez' death was not pleased with the district attorney's decision to plea bargain in Rucker's case. His words—entered as part of the court transaction—echo the sentiment that many officers still hold:

"I do not think that the charges in this case should have been reduced," Judge Darrell Hester said. "If I had any discretion to do so I would have refused to accept the plea of guilty...to the lesser offense. I tried the companion case, I'm familiar with the facts of this case, and I feel very strongly that the indictment should have been prosecuted to the fullest.

"However, in checking the law...I am required to accept the defendant's plea...but I do state for the record that I feel like we have, to some measure, reduced the protection these peace officers are entitled to and, in some measure, lessened the value of one officer."

Hernandez still struggles with the nightmares about the night he saw his best friend gunned down. They are not as frequent as they were initially, but his memory still haunts him.

"I go to bed with this guy (Herrera)," he said. "At first it was every night I went to bed with him in my dreams. Later, as I became a police officer, I'd see him shooting me instead."

Kathy Fair covers the criminal justice system in Texas for the *Houston Chronicle* and writes extensively about death penalty cases.

Data for this listing was obtained from the NAACP Legal Defense and Education Fund (August 31, 1992) and newspapers from across the nation.

INMATE	STATE	SEX	RACE	JUVENILE
ABU-JAMAL, MUMIA	PENNSYLVANIA	M	B	

ADAMS, LARRY   **NEVADA**   **M**   **W**

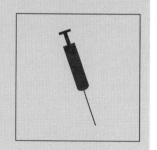

Larry Adams was convicted and sentenced to death for the August 1984 shooting murder of his wife and his daughter. During a violent fight, Adams shot his wife twice with one pistol and five times with another. Lora, the couple's 3-year-old daughter, was shot in the forehead while she was laying on the couch in the living room. The coroner's report revealed powder residue in Lora's left eye, indicating her eyes were open when her father shot her.

ABRAM, DONALD	MISSISSIPPI	M	B	
ADAMS, SYLVESTER L.	SOUTH CAROLINA	M	B	
ADAMS, THOMAS	NORTH CAROLINA	M	W	*
ADANANDUS, DWIGHT	TEXAS	M	B	
ADCOX, KEITH	CALIFORNIA	M	W	
ADKINS, CARL W.	TENNESSEE	M	W	
ADKINS, RICKY	ALABAMA	M	W	
AGAN, JAMES	FLORIDA	M	W	
AINSWORTH, STEVEN	CALIFORNIA	M	W	
ALBA, JOHN	TEXAS	M	H	

ALBANESE, CHARLES   **ILLINOIS**   **M**   **W**

Charles Albanese was convicted and sentenced to death for the 1980 and 1981 murders of his mother-in-law, grandmother and father. Albanese poisoned them with arsenic in an attempt to inherit the family business.

ALBRECHT, ALFRED	PENNSYLVANIA	M	W	

B Black; W white, H hispanic, A asian, N native american, U race unknown at press time.

ALCALA, RODNEY CALIFORNIA M H

In June 1979, 12-year-old Robin Samsoe of Huntington Beach, Calif., was abducted while riding a friend's bicycle to ballet class. About 10 days later, her skeletal remains were found, with her hands and feet missing, in the foothills more than 50 miles from her home. Investigators could not determine if she had been sexually assaulted or how many times she'd been stabbed because her flesh had been gnawed away by small animals.

Rodney Alcala, a UCLA graduate and one-time freelance photographer, was convicted in the killing. Prosecutors allege that Alcala had lured the seventh-grader to his car by promising to take her picture for a magazine layout.

This was not the first time Alcala was convicted in an assault charge. In 1968, Alcala kidnapped an 8-year-old girl from Hollywood, beating her and leaving her for dead. Police discovered her bleeding and unconscious with a steel bar across her neck. Alcala served two years for the crime.

Shortly after his release, Alcala abducted a 13-year-old girl. He was returned to prison for three years for the parole violation. In 1977, he was once again cited for violating parole—police found photographs of nude children and video tapes of Alcala engaging in sexual acts with young women. In 1978, he beat and raped a 15-year-old girl he picked up hitchhiking. While free on $10,000 bail in that case, he killed Robin Samsoe. Alcala was finally sent to death row in 1980, and is currently in the appeals process.

INMATE	STATE	SEX	RACE	JUVENILE
ALDERMAN, JACK	GEORGIA	M	W	
ALDRIDGE, RULFORD	TEXAS	M	B	
ALEXANDER, CARUTHERS	TEXAS	M	B	
ALEXANDER, GUY	TEXAS	M	W	
ALLEN, CLARENCE R.	CALIFORNIA	M	N	
ALLEN, DAVID	OHIO	M	W	
ALLEN, GARRY	OKLAHOMA	M	B	
ALLEN, HOWARD	INDIANA	M	B	
ALLEN, JEROME	FLORIDA	M	B	*
ALLEN, JOHN C.	OKLAHOMA	M	W	
ALLEN, KENNETH	ILLINOIS	M	B	
ALLEN, STANLEY	GEORGIA	M	B	
ALLEN, TIMOTHY	NORTH CAROLINA	M	B	
ALLEN, WANDA JEAN	OKLAHOMA	F	B	
ALLISON, WATSON	CALIFORNIA	M	B	
ALVAREZ, MANUEL M.	CALIFORNIA	M	H	
ALVORD, GARY	FLORIDA	M	W	

ALLEY, SEDLEY TENNESSEE M B

Alley was found guilty of the 1985 kidnapping, rape and murder of 19-year-old Suzanne Marie Collins, who at the time of her death was jogging in a Memphis area park. Collin's badly beaten body was discovered in the park the morning of the day she was to have graduated from avionics training at the Memphis Naval Air Station. Alley, 33, was sentenced to death on the murder conviction and to consecutive 40-year terms on each of the other two convictions.

INMATE	STATE	SEX	RACE	JUVENILE
ALLRIDGE, JAMES V.	TEXAS	M	B	
ALLRIDGE, RONALD K.	TEXAS	M	B	
ALSTYNE, GREGORY	TEXAS	M	B	

AMAYA-RUIZ, JOSE ARIZONA M H

Mark and Kimberly Lopez hired Jose Amaya-Ruiz, to take care of the stables at their ranch near Tucson. Mark and Kimberly had been married for a week and Kimberly was four months pregnant. On March 28, 1985, as Kimberly was talking to her sister on the phone, Amaya-Ruiz entered the house. He stabbed Kimberly 26 times with a kitchen knife while chasing her throughout the home. Finally, Amaya-Ruiz used Kimberly's handgun to shoot her in the ear. He fled in the Lopez' truck.

AMOS, BERNARD	TEXAS	M	B	

AMOS, VERNON FLORIDA M B

Vernon Amos and Leonard Spencer were first sentenced to death on Christmas Eve 1986. Together, Amos and Spencer killed Allen McAninch and Robert Bragman during a convenience store robbery and car heist in June 1986. Amos, borrowing law books from his friend and death row neighbor Ted Bundy, has represented himself in many appeals.

AMRINE, JOSEPH	MISSOURI	M	B	
ANDERSON, C. MICHAEL	NEBRASKA	M	W	
ANDERSON, JAMES	CALIFORNIA	M	B	
ANDERSON, LARRY NORMAN	TEXAS	M	W	
ANDERSON, RICHARD	FLORIDA	M	W	

ANDERSON, STEPHEN CALIFORNIA M W

During a May 26, 1980, robbery, Elizabeth Lyman was shot to death in her sleep. Stephen Wayne Anderson was convicted of breaking into the elderly woman's home and murdering her during a robbery that netted $112. His death sentence has been upheld by the California Supreme Court.

ANDREWS, JESSE J.	CALIFORNIA	M	B	
ANDREWS, MAURICE	TEXAS	M	B	
ANDREWS, WILLIAM	UTAH	M	B	
ANTHONY, FRANCIS	NORTH CAROLINA	M	B	
ANTWINE, CALVERT	MISSOURI	M	B	

INMATE	STATE	SEX	RACE	JUVENILE
APANOVITCH, ANTHONY	OHIO	M	W	
APELT, MICHAEL	ARIZONA	M	W	
APELT, RUDY A.	ARIZONA	M	W	

APPEL, MARTIN   **PENNSYLVANIA**   **M**   **W**

On June 6, 1986, Martin Appel and fellow Allentown, Pa., cab driver Stanley Hertzog killed three women during a bank robbery at an East Allen Township bank. In August 1986, Appel was sentenced to death. Appel, now 33, sits on Pennsylvania's Death Row.

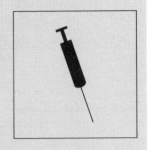

ARANDA, ARTURO D.	TEXAS	M	H	
ARBELAEZ, GUILLERMO	FLORIDA	M	H	
ARCHER, ROBIN	FLORIDA	M	W	
ARCHILETTA, MICHAEL	UTAH	M	H	
ARIAS, PEDRO	CALIFORNIA	M	N	
ARMSTRONG, LANCELOT	FLORIDA	M	B	

ARNETT, JAMES   **ARIZONA**   **M**   **W**

James Arnett stole a car in California, abandoned it in Arizona, and walked to a construction site outside of Lake Havasu City in Mohave County. On the night of February 9, 1976, Elmer James Clary arrived at the construction site in his truck. The next morning, Arnett asked Clary for food, but Clary refused him. Clary also declined to drive Arnett into the nearest town. Arnett then offered to sell Clary some jewelry. The two men walked to a shack to see the jewelry. Arnett entered the shack, got his rifle out of a pack, and shot Clary five times, killing him. Arnett then drove Clary's pickup into California, where he was arrested.

ARNOLD, JERMARR	TEXAS	M	B	
ARNOLD, JOHN D.	SOUTH CAROLINA	M	W	
ARTHUR, THOMAS	ALABAMA	M	W	
ARTIS, ROSCOE	NORTH CAROLINA	M	B	
ASAY, MARC	FLORIDA	M	W	
ASHFORD, JAMES	ILLINOIS	M	B	
ASHMUS, TROY	CALIFORNIA	M	W	
ATKINS, JOSEPH	SOUTH CAROLINA	M	W	
ATKINS, PHILLIP	FLORIDA	M	W	
ATWATER, JEFFREY	FLORIDA	M	W	

INMATE	STATE	SEX	RACE	JUVENILE

ATWOOD, FRANK ARIZONA M W

Frank Atwood had been convicted of lewd and lascivious acts and kidnapping an 8-year-old boy in California. In May of 1984, he was paroled from the kidnapping sentence. Atwood came to Tucson in September of 1984 in violation of his California parole. On September 17, 8-year-old Vicky Lynn Hoskinson was riding her bicycle home from mailing a letter. Atwood kidnapped the girl, molested her, and killed her. He left her body in the desert and fled to Texas, where he was apprehended. Vicky's body was not found until April of 1985.

AUSTIN, RICHARD	TENNESSEE	M	W	
AVENA, CARLOS	CALIFORNIA	M	H	

AVERHART, RUFUS INDIANA M B

Rufus Averhart was convicted and sentenced to death for the 1982 murder of an Indiana police officer during a bank robbery.

AYALA, HECTOR	CALIFORNIA	M	H	
AYALA, RONALDO M.	CALIFORNIA	M	H	
BABBITT, MANUEL	CALIFORNIA	M	B	
BACIGALUPO, MIGUEL	CALIFORNIA	M	H	
BACON, ROBERT	NORTH CAROLINA	M	W	

BAILEY, BILLY DELAWARE M W

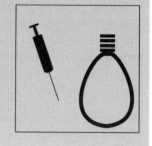

On March 28, 1980, 32-year-old Billy Bailey walked away from a Delaware work-release program and robbed a liquor store. Using a shotgun, he killed an elderly couple, Gilbert and Clara Lamberston. Baily was sentenced to hang, but a 1986 law has allowed condemned men facing the gallows to opt for lethal injection. His latest appeal is being reviewed by the Delaware Supreme Court.

BAILEY, JERRY	CALIFORNIA	M	W	
BAIRD, ARTHUR	INDIANA	M	W	
BAKER, LEE	PENNSYLVANIA	M	B	
BAKER, RONNIE	NORTH CAROLINA	M	W	
BALDREE, EARNEST O.	TEXAS	M	W	

INMATE	STATE	SEX	RACE	JUVENILE

BALDWIN, BRIAN — **ALABAMA** — **M** — **B**

Bryan Baldwin and Edward Horsley escaped from Hudson Prison in 1977. Hours later, they kidnapped North Carolina teenager Naomi Rolon. After raping and assaulting her, Baldwin and Horsley tried to kill her by running over Rolon with her own car, then stuffing her body into the trunk. Baldwin and Horsley abandoned the car off a rural Alabama road; they later returned to find Rolon was still alive. After more brutalities, Baldwin and Horsley killed Rolon with a hatchet then hid her body in a pile of brush. After their capture, Alabama authorities learned Baldwin and Horsley were escapees. They also learned Naomi Rolon was reported as missing. Baldwin and Horsley cracked under interrogation — both were convicted of murder and both were sentenced to death.

INMATE	STATE	SEX	RACE	JUVENILE
BANDA, ESEQUEL	TEXAS	M	H	
BANE, JOHN M.	TENNESSEE	M	W	
BANKHEAD, GRADY	ALABAMA	M	W	
BANKS, ANTHONY	OKLAHOMA	M	B	
BANKS, DELMA	TEXAS	M	B	
BANKS, GEORGE	PENNSYLVANIA	M	B	
BANKS, RANDY	ILLINOIS	M	B	
BANNISTER, ALAN	MISSOURI	M	W	
BARBER, DANNY LEE	TEXAS	M	W	
BARBER, TERRY	TENNESSEE	M	W	
BAREFIELD, JOHN KENNEDY	TEXAS	M	B	
BARNARD, HAROLD A.	TEXAS	M	W	
BARNES, ELWELL	NORTH CAROLINA	M	N	
BARNES, HERMAN	VIRGINIA	M	B	
BARNES, ODELL	TEXAS	M	B	
BARNES, WILLIS J.	TEXAS	M	B	
BARNETT, LARRY	OKLAHOMA	M	W	
BARNETT, LEE MAX	CALIFORNIA	M	W	
BARRAZA, MAURO	TEXAS	M	H	*
BARRETT, JOHN	FLORIDA	M	W	
BARRIENTES, ANTONIO	TEXAS	M	H	

BARROW, RONALD — **ILLINOIS** — **M** — **W**

Ronald Barrow was convicted and sentenced to death for the 1984 murder of 86-year-old Joseph O'Berto. Barrow was looking for rumored "barrels" of coins and $175,000 in hidden cash at O'Berto's home. Finding nothing, Barrow beat and shot O'Berto. He then stole $500 from his wallet.

INMATE	STATE	SEX	RACE	JUVENILE
BARTON, HERBERT	NORTH CAROLINA	M	U	

INMATE	STATE	SEX	RACE	JUVENILE

BARWICK, DARRYL   **FLORIDA**   **M**   **W**

Darryl Barwick was convicted and sentenced to death Aug. 21, 1992, for the May 1986 murder of Rebecca Ray Wendt. Barwick, who did not know Wendt, saw her sunbathing at her apartment complex, then attacked and stabbed her to death. In one appeal, he argued that racial bias may have tainted jury selection in his first trial. Barwick is white, the victim was white, and the jury was white. Barwick argued that the jury did not represent a fair cross-section of the community. The Flordia Supreme Court ordered a new trial for Barwick.

INMATE	STATE	SEX	RACE
BASEMORE, WILLIAM	PENNSYLVANIA	M	B
BATES, KAYLE	FLORIDA	M	B
BATES, WAYNE L.	TENNESSEE	M	W
BATTENFIELD, BILLY	OKLAHOMA	M	W
BATTLE, THOMAS	MISSOURI	M	B
BAXTER, NORMAN	GEORGIA	M	W
BEAM, ALBERT R.	IDAHO	M	W
BEAN, ANTHONY	CALIFORNIA	M	B
BEAN, HAROLD	ILLINOIS	M	W
BEARD, JAMES	ALABAMA	M	W
BEARDSLEE, DONALD	CALIFORNIA	M	W
BEASLEY, LESLIE	PENNSYLVANIA	M	B
BEATHARD, JAMES LEE	TEXAS	M	W

BEATY, DONALD   **ARIZONA**   **M**   **W**

On the evening of May 9, 1984, Christy Ann Fornoff, a 13-year-old news carrier, was collecting payment from her customers at the Rockpoint Apartments in Tempe, Ariz. Donald Beaty, the apartment custodian, abducted Christy then sexually assaulted and suffocated her in his apartment. Beaty kept the body in his apartment until the morning of May 11, 1984, when he placed it behind the apartment complex's trash dumpster.

INMATE	STATE	SEX	RACE
BEAVER, GREGORY	VIRGINIA	M	W
BEAVERS, RICHARD LEE	TEXAS	M	W
BEAVERS, THOMAS	VIRGINIA	M	W
BECK, ELI	GEORGIA	M	B
BEDFORD, DANIEL	OHIO	M	W
BEELER, RODNEY	CALIFORNIA	M	W

BEETS, BETTY LOU   TEXAS   F   W

Betty Lou Beets, 53, was sentenced to death in 1985 for killing her fifth husband, Dallas firefighter Jimmy Don Beets, for $100,000 in insurance benefits. She buried him in their yard. She was also charged but not tried in the murder of a previous husband, Doyle Wayne Barker, who was found buried behind a tool shed. Beets was spared temporarily when the Texas Court of Criminal Appeals ruled in 1984 that her crime technically did not fit the capital offense of murder for remuneration, since no third party was hired to perform the killing. The state Supreme Court reversed the decision.

BEETS, EDWARD   NEVADA   M   B

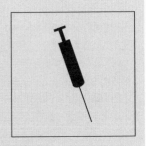

Edward Beets was convicted and sentenced to death for the March 1987 murder of a 71-year-old woman. Beets repeatedly hit her on the head with a hammer, then stabbed her in the neck and body with a knife when she tried to save her 28-year-old granddaughter from Beets' attack. The granddaughter tried to flee but was stabbed and then sexually assaulted with the hammer. Beets then went into the bedroom of a seven-year-old child, tied her up and sexually assaulted her.

BEHRINGER, EARL R.   TEXAS   M   W

BEJARANO, JOHN   NEVADA   M   H

In 1987, Bejarano shot a Reno, Nev., cabdriver to death with a sawed-off .22 caliber rifle. Bejarano, a 31-year-old Fresno, Calif., native, was convicted of killing Roland Wright, 62, during a robbery. He is appealing his case in federal court.

BELL, LARRY GENE   SOUTH CAROLINA   M   W

On May 31, 1985, Sharon Faye "Shari" Smith, 17, was abducted from the driveway of her Lexington County, S.C., home. About two weeks later, 9-year-old Debra May Helmick of Colombia, S.C., was also abducted. In 1986, Larry Gene Bell was convicted and sentenced to death for the kidnappings and murders of Smith and Helmick. Both convictions are being appealed.

While on death row, Bell was taken to a hospital where he received surgery to remove a tumor from his chest believed to be benign. The operation was performed under the watch of two armed guards.

INMATE	STATE	SEX	RACE	JUVENILE

BELL, RANDY ALABAMA M B

Turpin judicial experts say Randy Bell is the first person sentenced to die for killing someone whose body was never located. Bell maintains his innocence for the 1981 Christmas shooting of Charles Mims. According to the trial testimony of Michael Joe Hubbard, a key witness for the prosecution, Bell shot Mims in the back of the head and returned the next day to get rid of the body. In 1987, Bell offered to locate the body in exchange for life without possibility of parole. Mims' surviving relatives rejected his offer.

BELL, ROGER M.	TENNESSEE	M	B
BELL, RONNIE	CALIFORNIA	M	B
BELL, WALTER	TEXAS	M	B
BELL, WILLIAM H.	SOUTH CAROLINA	M	B
BELLMORE, LARRY	INDIANA	M	W
BELLO, CARLOS	FLORIDA	M	H
BELMONTES, FERNANDO	CALIFORNIA	M	H
BELTRAN, NOE	TEXAS	M	H
BELTRAN-LOPEZ, MAURICIO	FLORIDA	M	H
BELYEU, CLIFTON E.	TEXAS	M	W
BEMORE, TERRY D.	CALIFORNIA	M	B

BENEFIEL, WILLIAM INDIANA M W

On Nov. 3, 1988, Bill J. Benefiel was sentenced to die for the Feb. 7, 1987, murder of 18-year-old Delores Wells. On Sept. 18, 1991, the Indiana Supreme Court upheld the murder conviction and death penalty sentence. Numerous appeals are expected before an execution date may be set. Benefiel, now 35, has several appeal options open, including a direct appeal to the U.S. Supreme Court.

BENN, GARY WASHINGTON M W

Gary Benn was convicted and sentenced to death for the shooting deaths of his half-brother, Jack Dethlefsen, and friend Michael Nelson in February 1988.

BENNER, GLEN	OHIO	M	W

INMATE	STATE	SEX	RACE	JUVENILE

BENNETT, BABY RAY   **TEXAS**   **M**   **B**

At the age of 27, Ray Bennett was convicted of shooting Coyte L. Green, 70, during the 1985 burglary of Green's house. Bennett told police he first shot Green's dog, then shot Green when he tried to run. Bennett, according to a psychologist, laughed when describing to him how hard Green had been to kill. Green's body was stuffed in a car trunk and dumped under a Louisiana bridge.

BENNETT, EDWARD   **NEVADA**   **M**   **W**

In 1988, a Las Vegas, Nev., convenience store clerk, 21-year-old Michelle Moore, was shot to death. As she rang up a piece of candy, Edward Bennett, 19, pulled out a .45-caliber handgun and shot her in the face, killing her instantly. He then picked up Moore's head and marvelled in detached wonderment that he could see the floor through the bullet hole. Bennet's death sentence was upheld by the Nevada Supreme Court in Feb. 1990.

BENNETT, JACK	GEORGIA	M	W
BENNETT, RONALD	VIRGINIA	M	B
BENSON, RICHARD A.	CALIFORNIA	M	W
BERGET, ROGER	OKLAHOMA	M	W
BERNISCHKE, WILLIAM	INDIANA	M	W
BERRY, EARL	MISSISSIPPI	M	B
BERRY, WILFORD L.	OHIO	M	W
BERRYMAN, RODNEY	CALIFORNIA	M	B
BESARABA, JOSEPH	FLORIDA	M	W
BEUKE, MICHAEL	OHIO	M	W
BEY, MARKO	NEW JERSEY	M	B
BIBLE, RICHARD L.	ARIZONA	M	W
BIEGENWALD, RICHARD	NEW JERSEY	M	W
BIEGHLER, MARVIN	INDIANA	M	W
BIGBY, EUGENE	TEXAS	M	W
BIGSBY, ROOSEVELT	TENNESSEE	M	B
BILLIOT, JAMES	MISSISSIPPI	M	W
BIRDSONG, RALPH	PENNSYLVANIA	M	B
BIROS, KENNETH	OHIO	M	W
BIRT, BILLY SUNDAY	GEORGIA	M	W

BISHOP, RONALD P.　　　ARIZONA　　　M　　W

On January 18, 1976, Ronald Bishop, Fred Van Haelst, Catherine Leckliter, and her 2-year-old daughter met Norman Troxell at the Salvation Army Welfare Center in Phoenix, Ariz. The group left Phoenix in Troxell's car on January 20, and began traveling around the desert. On January 22, Bishop instructed Van Haelst to tell Ms. Leckliter and her daughter to take a walk far from the camp. When they had gone, Bishop asked Troxell to help him fix the car. As Troxell stood at the rear of the car, Bishop hit him several times on the back of the head with a claw hammer. After Troxell fell, Bishop removed Troxell's watch, wallet, and shoes, and tied his legs together. He and Van Haelst then dragged the still living victim to an abandoned mine shaft and threw him in. Bishop threw rocks on top of the victim before the group left the area in the victim's car.

BITTAKER, LAWRENCE　　　CALIFORNIA　　　M　　W

In 1979, Lawrence Bittaker and prison buddy Roy Norris set out on a mission to pick up young girls and brutally rape, torture and kill them. The pair would cruise down the coastal highways in Southern California, pick up the girls in a van nicknamed "Murder Mac" and then drive to the rugged San Dimas mountains. Bittaker earned the nickname "Pliers" for his use of pliers (as well as vice-clamps, an ice pick, a sledge hammer and coat hangers) during the torture of his victims. The Bittaker trial was one of the most brutal cases ever presented in California. A key element to the prosecution was a tape recording of one of Bittaker's victims crying and pleading for her life. Testimony indicated that he would play the tape in his van and that he thought it was "real funny." On February 1, 1981, after two days of deliberation, the jury convicted Bittaker of of kidnapping, torturing and killing five girls. In March 1981, he was sentenced to death. He remains on California's death row while his appeals process continues.

BIVINS, GERALD　　　INDIANA　　　M　　W

BLACK, BYRON　　　TENNESSEE　　　M　　B

In 1988, Byron Lewis Black, 35, of Nashville, Tenn., shot to death his girlfriend and her two young daughters. His death penalty sentence was upheld by the Tennessee Supreme Court Aug. 5, 1991.

BLACK, ROBERT　　　GEORGIA　　　M　　B
BLACKMON, RICKY D.　　　TEXAS　　　M　　W

INMATE	STATE	SEX	RACE	JUVENILE
BLACKWELL, MICHAEL	ILLINOIS	M	B	
BLAIR, JAMES N.	CALIFORNIA	M	B	
BLAIR, WALTER	MISSOURI	M	B	
BLANCO, OMAR	FLORIDA	M	H	
BLANKENSHIP, ROY	GEORGIA	M	W	
BLANKS, KENNITH	GEORGIA	M	B	
BLANTON, JAMES	TENNESSEE	M	W	

BLAZAK, MITCHELL	**ARIZONA**	**M**	**W**	

In the early morning hours of December 15, 1973, Mitchell Blazak and another man, armed with pistols, entered the Brown Fox Tavern in Tucson, Ariz. Blazak, who was wearing a ski mask, went to the bar and demanded money. When the bartender, Elden Baker, did not comply, Blazak shot him four times and then shot and killed John Grimm, who was sitting nearby. A second patron was wounded.

INMATE	STATE	SEX	RACE	JUVENILE
BLOOM, ROBERT S.	CALIFORNIA	M	W	
BLOUNT, JOHN	PENNSYLVANIA	M	B	*
BLUE, MICHAEL	TEXAS	M	B	
BLYSTONE, SCOTT	PENNSYLVANIA	M	W	
BOBO, TONY L.	TENNESSEE	M	B	
BOGGESS, CLIFFORD H.	TEXAS	M	W	
BOLDEN, CLIFFORD	CALIFORNIA	M	B	
BOLDER, MARTSAY	MISSOURI	M	B	
BOLENDER, BERNARD	FLORIDA	M	W	
BOLIEK, WILLIAM	MISSOURI	M	W	
BOLIN, OSCAR	FLORIDA	M	W	
BOLIN, PAUL	CALIFORNIA	M	W	
BOLTZ, JOHN	OKLAHOMA	M	W	
BONDURRANT, PAT	TENNESSEE	M	W	
BONHAM, ANTONIO N.	TEXAS	M	B	
BONIFAY, JAMES	FLORIDA	M	W	*

BONIN, WILLIAM	**CALIFORNIA**	**M**	**W**	

William Bonin was dubbed the Freeway Killer for his murder of 10 young men whose bodies were dumped alongside Southern California freeways. The victims, ranging in age from 12 to 19, were usually hitchhikers who were picked up by Bonin, sexually assaulted, tortured and strangled.

INMATE	STATE	SEX	RACE	JUVENILE
BONNELL, MELVIN	OHIO	M	W	
BONNEY, THOMAS	NORTH CAROLINA	M	W	
BOOKER, JOHN	MISSISSIPPI	M	B	

INMATE	STATE	SEX	RACE	JUVENILE
BOOKER, STEPHEN	FLORIDA	M	B	
BOOKER, WINFRED	OKLAHOMA	M	W	
BOOTH, JOHN	MARYLAND	M	B	
BOTTOSON, LINROY	FLORIDA	M	B	
BOUNDS, FRANK	ILLINOIS	M	B	
BOURQUE, SCOTT	LOUISIANA	M	W	
BOWDEN, ROOSEVELT	FLORIDA	M	B	
BOWER, LESTER L.	TEXAS	M	W	
BOWIE, BENITO	OKLAHOMA	M	B	
BOWLING, THOMAS C.	KENTUCKY	M	W	
BOX, CHRISTOPHER	CALIFORNIA	M	B	
BOYD, ARTHUR M.	NORTH CAROLINA	M	W	
BOYD, CHARLES A.	TEXAS	M	B	
BOYD, KENNETH	NORTH CAROLINA	M	W	
BOYD, MICHAEL	TENNESSEE	M	B	
BOYD, RONALD K.	OKLAHOMA	M	B	
BOYD, RUSSELL	INDIANA	M	W	
BOYD, WILLIAM	ALABAMA	M	W	

BOYDE, RICHARD   CALIFORNIA   M   B

Richard Boyde Jr. was sentenced to death for the 1981 kidnapping, robbery and murder of Dickie Lee Gibson, 31, a convenience store clerk and part-time football and wrestling coach. Boyde was aided by a nephew in forcing Gibson from the store after a $33 robbery. Boyde then shot Gibson three times in a nearby orange grove.

BOYLE, BENJAMIN H.	TEXAS	M	W	

BRACEY, WILLIAM   ARIZ/IL   M   B

Robert Cruz decided to have William Patrick Redmond murdered. Redmond owned a printing business in partnership with Ron Lukezic, and Cruz's ultimate goal was to take over the business. To carry out the murder, Cruz hired William Bracey and Murray Hooper from Chicago and Edward Lonzo McCall, a former Phoenix police officer.

On the evening of December 31, 1980, Bracey, Hooper, and McCall went to the Redmond home in Phoenix. Redmond, his wife Marilyn, and his mother-in-law Helen Phelps were home preparing for a New Year's Eve party. The men entered the house and forced the victims into the master bedroom. After taking jewelry and money, the killers bound and gagged the victims and made them lie face down on the bed. They then shot each victim in the head and also slashed Redmond's throat. Redmond and Phelps died from their wounds, but Redmond's wife survived.

Cruz and McCall were convicted of the murders following a joint trial. Cruz' conviction was reversed on appeal, but he was again convicted after two mistrials. Lukezic was convicted in a separate trial, but after obtaining a new trial, she was acquitted of all charges.

INMATE	STATE	SEX	RACE	JUVENILE
BRADFORD, BILL	CALIFORNIA	M	W	
BRADFORD, GAYLAND	TEXAS	M	B	
BRADFORD, MARK A.	CALIFORNIA	M	W	
BRADLEY, DANNY	ALABAMA	M	W	
BRADLEY, JERARD	PENNSYLVANIA	M	B	
BRADLEY, WILLIAM	OHIO	M	B	
BRANAN, DANNY	TENNESSEE	M	W	
BRANDON, TYRONE	ILLINOIS	M	W	
BRANTLEY, J. DAVID	GEORGIA	M	W	
BREAKIRON, MARK	PENNSYLVANIA	M	W	
BREAUX, DAVID	CALIFORNIA	M	W	
BRECHEEN, ROBERT	OKLAHOMA	M	W	
BREEDLOVE, MCARTHUR	FLORIDA	M	B	
BRENK, HERBERT	ARKANSAS	M	W	

BRETON, ROBERT   CONNECTICUT   M   W

When Joanne Breton, a 38-year-old divorcee, and her son went to bed the night of Dec. 12, 1987, all seemed in order in their Waterbury, Conn., apartment. The phones were left off their hooks, but that was becoming more the routine than the exception. Robert Breton, Sr. had been harassing the two for the past week. He knew and strongly disapproved of their plans for a trip to Florida, he did not want to be alone during the holidays. Decembers were always difficult for Breton, and this year no one had wished him a happy 41st birthday. At about 4 a.m., Breton broke into the home of his ex-wife and son. He crept into Joanne's bedroom and grabbed her. She started screaming for her son to call the police. After her son opened the door, Breton started chasing him into the hallway until he reached the stairwell. Breton fatally stabbed the boy, before returning to the bedroom to stab and kill a hysterical Joanne. Before leaving the scene, Breton paused at his son's body, and said "Thank you for the birthday card," and then plunged his knife into the boy's neck. On Oct. 3, 1989, Robert Breton was sentenced to death. He remains on Connecticut's death row on appeal.

BREWER, BENJAMIN	OKLAHOMA	M	W	
BREWER, BRETT	TEXAS	M	W	
BREWER, DAVID	OHIO	M	W	

BREWER, JOHN   ARIZONA   M   W

John Brewer and his girlfriend, Rita Brier, were having an arguement when Brier told Brewer that she was going to leave him. Brewer then locked the bedroom door and began to beat and strangle Brier. After a lengthy struggle during which Brewer bit Brier, tried to gouge her eyes out, and choked her with his hands, Brewer killed Brier by strangling her with a tie. Brier was 22 weeks pregnant at the time. After resting, Brewer took a shower. He then had sexual intercourse with Brier's corpse. Brewer walked to a nearby bowling alley, called the police, and turned himself in. Brewer pleaded guilty to first-degree murder.

INMATE	STATE	SEX	RACE	JUVENILE
BRIDDLE, JAMES M.	TEXAS	M	W	
BRIDGE, WARREN E.	TEXAS	M	W	
BRIDGES, EDWARD	CALIFORNIA	M	W	
BRIGHT, KENNETH	GEORGIA	M	W	
BRIMAGE, RICHARD	TEXAS	M	W	
BRIMMER, DAVID	TENNESSEE	M	W	
BRISBON, HENRY	ILLINOIS	M	B	
BRITZ, DEWAYNE	ILLINOIS	M	W	
BROGDEN, DONALD	NORTH CAROLINA	M	W	

BROOKS, GEORGE   **LOUISIANA**   **M**   **W**

George Brooks, 47, and his co-defendant and one-time roommate James Copeland, 29, were sentenced to die for the 1979 kidnapping, rape and murder of 11-year-old Joseph Cook Owen. Brooks and Copeland were accused of raping Owen at their home, then gagging him with a sheet and taking him to a site in Linvingston Parish, Louisiana, where they shot him in the back of the head as he knelt on the ground.

BROOKS, JOHN	LOUISIANA	M	B	
BROOKS, REGINALD	OHIO	M	B	
BROOM, ROMELL	OHIO	M	B	
BROWN, ALBERT	CALIFORNIA	M	B	
BROWN, ANDREW	CALIFORNIA	M	U	
BROWN, DAVID JUNIOR	NORTH CAROLINA	M	B	
BROWN, DAVID	OKLAHOMA	M	W	
BROWN, DEBRA	IN/OH	F	B	
BROWN, GARY	ALABAMA	M	W	
BROWN, GEORGE	FLORIDA	M	W	

BROWN, JAMES W.   **GEORGIA**   **M**   **W**

James Brown was convicted and sentenced to death for the 1975 murder of Brenda Sue Watson, a go-go dancer who suffocated after Brown raped her and stuffed her underwear down her throat.

BROWN, JOHN   **CALIFORNIA**   **M**   **W**

On June 11, 1990 John Brown shot his 77-year-old father, Wesley Brown, to death after an argument over the son's use of his father's car. The father angered his 45-year-old son by reporting the car stolen. Brown fired a .38-caliber pistol, putting three bullets into his father, before hearing him "grunt." Then, he panicked and left. After driving around the neighborhood for about 15 minutes, he said he went home to apologize.

INMATE	STATE	SEX	RACE	JUVENILE
BROWN, JOHN	LOUISIANA	M	W	
BROWN, JOHN W.	PENNSYLVANIA	M	B	
BROWN, LARRY	FLORIDA	M	B	
BROWN, PAUL A.	CALIFORNIA	M	B	
BROWN, PAUL A.	FLORIDA	M	W	

BROWN, RAYMOND **ALABAMA** **M** **W**

Raymond Eugene Brown first murdered in 1960. He was 14-years-old when he killed his aunt, his grandmother, and his great-grandmother in Ashland. By August 1987, a paroled Brown had made his way to Montgomery, where he murdered Linda LeMonte, 32, and her 9-year-old daughter Sheila.

BROWN, THOMAS JACK	NORTH CAROLINA	M	W	
BROWN, VERNON	MISSOURI	M	B	
BROWN, WILLIE	NORTH CAROLINA	M	B	

BROWNING, PAUL **NEVADA** **M** **B**

In 1985, Browning stabbed a Las Vegas jewelry store owner, 60-year-old Hugo Elsen. Browning, sentenced in 1987, is a Las Angeles native. He is appealing his case in district court.

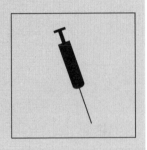

BROWNLEE, VIRGIL	ALABAMA	M	B	
BRUCE, KIRK	MARYLAND	M	B	
BRUCE, RENNETH	TEXAS	M	B	
BRUNO, MICHAEL	FLORIDA	M	W	

BRYAN, ANTHONY **FLORIDA** **M** **W**

On Aug. 12, 1983, 24-year-old Anthony B. Bryan kidnapped George Wilson. Wilson, a 43-year-old night watchman at a seafood wholesaler, had lent Bryan some tools to fix a luxury boat that Bryan had stolen. When the repairs failed, Bryan used his sawed-off shotgun to abduct Wilson from his home. He stole Wilson's car, tied him up, forced him into the back seat, drove him to an isolated area and killed him. Federal appeals court blocked Bryan's scheduled execution in 1990. An appeal is pending in the Florida Supreme Court.

INMATE	STATE	SEX	RACE	JUVENILE
BRYANT, JAMES	PENNSYLVANIA	M	B	
BRYANT, ROBERT	FLORIDA	M	B	
BRYANT, ROBERT PERNELL	PENNSYLVANIA	M	B	
BRYSON, WILLIAM C.	OKLAHOMA	M	B	
BUCHANAN, DOUGLAS	VIRGINIA	M	W	
BUCHANAN, LENWOOD E.	NORTH CAROLINA	M	B	
BUEHL, ROGER	PENNSYLVANIA	M	W	
BUELL, ROBERT	OHIO	M	W	

BUENOANO, JUDI	**FLORIDA**	**F**	**W**	

Buenoano's knack with poison earned her the nickname "The Black Widow." With insurance money as her reward, she poisoned a husband, son and boyfriend, and is suspected in the poisoning-murder of another boyfriend. Over the course of 1971 to 1983, these deeds would enable Judy to buy fancy cars and a diamond ring, have a face lift, put a down payment on a home, found a hair salon and nail business, and install a swimming pool at one of her homes. Buenoano was finally investigated after her boyfriend became suspicious after she took out a life insurance plan on him, then attempted to poison him and blew up his car. Her first husband's body was exhumed as a result and medical tests showed 10 to 95 times the lethal amount of arsenic in his system. Buenoano was convicted of first-degree murder and, on Nov. 26, 1985, sentenced to death in the electric chair for the murder of her first husband, James Goodyear. She currently sits on Florida's death row with four other women.

INMATE	STATE	SEX	RACE	JUVENILE
BUNCH, TIMOTHY	VIRGINIA	M	W	
BUNTION, CARL	TEXAS	M	W	
BUNYARD, JERRY	CALIFORNIA	M	W	
BURDEN, JIMMIE	GEORGIA	M	B	
BURDINE, CALVIN J.	TEXAS	M	W	
BURGENER, MICHAEL	CALIFORNIA	M	W	

BURGER, CHRISTOPHER	**GEORGIA**	**M**	**W**	

In 1977, Christopher Burger, a 17-year-old soldier at Fort Stewart, Ga., robbed, sodomized and murdered a soldier moonlighting as a cab driver. Burger barely escaped his fourth scheduled execution when a federal appeals court decided to make evidence about his childhood available.

INMATE	STATE	SEX	RACE	JUVENILE
BURGESS, RAYMOND	GEORGIA	M	B	
BURKE, MARK	OHIO	M	W	
BURKS, JOHN A.	TEXAS	M	B	
BURNAM, JEROME	PENNSYLVANIA	M	B	
BURNS, DANIEL	FLORIDA	M	B	
BURNS, WILLIAM	TEXAS	M	B	

INMATE	STATE	SEX	RACE	JUVENILE
BURRELL, ALBERT	LOUISIANA	M	W	

BURRIS, GARY INDIANA M B

In January 1980, Gary Burris shot to death an Indianapolis taxicab driver, 34-year-old Kenneth W. Chambers. Chambers' nude, bound and frozen body was found in an alley. He had been robbed of $30 and shot in the right temple. The Indiana Supreme Court ruling granted Burris a new trial on the grounds of ineffective assistance of counsel. Trial attorneys did not relate details of Burris' childhood.

BURROWS, JOSEPH	ILLINOIS	M	W	

BURTON, ANDRE CALIFORNIA M B

On Feb. 25, 1983, Andre Burton shot to death Gulshakar Khwaja in Long Beach, Calif. Khwaja is the mother of a man Burton robbed of $190 and shot in the eye. He was also found guilty of robbing two women at gunpoint earlier that day. Burton, now 28, is still in the appeals process.

BURTON, CHARLES	ALABAMA	M	B	
BUSH, JOHN EARL	FLORIDA	M	B	
BUSH, WILLIAM	ALABAMA	M	B	
BUSSELL, CHARLES	KENTUCKY	M	B	
BUTLER, JAMES	MISSOURI	M	W	
BUTLER, SABRINA	MISSISSIPPI	F	B	
BUTLER, STEVEN A.	TEXAS	M	B	
BYRD, JOHN W.	OHIO	M	W	
BYRD, MILFORD	FLORIDA	M	W	
BYRON, ROBERT	ILLINOIS	M	W	
CABALLERO, JUAN	ILLINOIS	M	H	
CADE, CLYDE	ALABAMA	M	B	
CAGE, TOMMY	LOUISIANA	M	B	
CAIN, JAMES R.	SOUTH CAROLINA	M	W	
CAIN, TRACY	CALIFORNIA	M	B	
CALDWELL, JEFFERY	TEXAS	M	B	
CALDWELL, RICHARD	TENNESSEE	M	W	
CALLAHAN, JAMES	ALABAMA	M	W	
CALLINS, BRUCE	TEXAS	M	B	
CAMACHO, FREDERICK	NORTH CAROLINA	M	A	
CAMACHO, GENARO	TEXAS	M	H	

INMATE	STATE	SEX	RACE	JUVENILE

CAMPBELL, CHARLES   **WASHINGTON**   **M**   **W**

Charles Campbell was convicted and sentenced to death for the 1982 murders of Renae Wicklund, her 8-year-old daughter Shannah Wicklund, and a neighbor friend Barbara Hendrickson.

CAMPBELL, JAMES BRYAN	NORTH CAROLINA	M	W	
CAMPBELL, JAMES	FLORIDA	M	B	
CAMPBELL, JEROME	OHIO	M	B	
CAMPBELL, KENNETH	TENNESSEE	M	W	
CAMPBELL, ROBERT	TEXAS	M	B	
CANAAN, KEITH	INDIANA	M	W	

CANAPE, RICHARD   **NEVADA**   **M**   **B**

In 1988, Canape, 36, killed 40-year-old Manuel Toledo, who ran out of gasoline near Apex, Nevada. Canape born in Honolulu, has a direct appeal to the Supreme Court pending.

CANNADAY, DOUGLAS	FLORIDA	M	W	
CANNON, JOSEPH	TEXAS	M	W	*
CANTU, ANDREW	TEXAS	M	H	
CANTU, DOMINGO	TEXAS	M	H	
CANTU, RUBEN	TEXAS	M	H	*
CAPEHART, GREGORY	FLORIDA	M	B	
CARD, DAVID L.	IDAHO	M	W	
CARD, JAMES	FLORIDA	M	W	
CARDENAS, FRANCISCO	TEXAS	M	H	
CARDONA, ANA	FLORIDA	F	H	
CARGILL, DAVID	GEORGIA	M	W	
CARLIS, LINDSEY	FLORIDA	M	B	

CARO, FERNANDO   **CALIFORNIA**   **M**   **N**

Eros Fernando Caro was sentenced to death for the 1980 killings of two 15-year-old cousins near Fresno, California.

CARPENTER, DAVID   CALIFORNIA   M   W

From mid-1979 to 1981, hikers in shore and mountain parks were found raped and brutally murdered off the scenic paths in Santa Cruz and Marin counties, in California. The man known as the "Trailside Killer," David Joseph Carpenter, was arrested in 1981. Carpenter, a printer, former salesman, ex-convict, child molester, arsonist, rapist and chronic stutterer, was convicted of seven brutal murders and an attempted eighth. Evidence also linked him to four additional trailside killings. Carpenter was given the death sentence and now sits on California's Death Row.

CARPENTER, JAMES	PENNSYLVANIA	M	B	
CARR, ANTHONY	MISSISSIPPI	M	B	

CARRERA, CONSTANTINO   CALIFORNIA   M   H

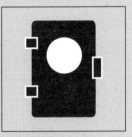

Constantino Carrera was convicted and sentenced to death for the 1982 robbery and double murder of Jack and Carol Hayes, managers of a Mojave motel. Carrera, then 20, and Ramiro Ruiz Gonzales (Ruiz), then 17, said they only planned to rob the motel. Yet when Carol Hayes reached for something, possibly a telephone to call for help, a killing spree ensued. Constantino slashed her arm, and with Ruiz repeatedly stabbed her 20 to 30 times. Jack Hayes, who had been sleeping, was visciously stabbed 14 or 15 times. One wound displayed the broken blade of a knife still embedded in Hayes' skull. Immunized witnesses testified that "they hit him with scissors in the head," and that when a knife used by Ruiz broke, "he went inside the kitchen and got a bigger knife." Witnesses also said they saw Carrera and Ruiz divide more than $100, and that they saw specks of blood on some of the money.

CARRIGER, PARIS   ARIZONA   M   W

On March 13, 1978, Paris Carriger entered a Phoenix jewelry store and forced the proprietor, Robert Gibson Shaw, into a back room. He tied Shaw's hands behind his back with adhesive tape. Carriger then killed Shaw by beating him over the head with a cast iron skillet and a ring sizer, then strangling him with his own necktie.

CARROLL, ELMER	FLORIDA	M	W	
CARROLL, ROBERT	ALABAMA	M	W	

INMATE	STATE	SEX	RACE	JUVENILE

CARTER, ANTONIO FLORIDA **M** **B**

Antonio Carter was sentenced to die for the 1986 slayings of Roy Patel, 34, and Fred Haberle, 53. Carter had been released from prison just four months earlier, where he served six years of a 15-year sentence for a 1979 robbery of a small grocery store. On April 15, 1986, Carter entered Patel's store, robbed him and shot him four times. Haberle, a wine salesman, was shot twice when he interrupted the robber-killer. Carter was arrested later in the day when a shopkeeper shot him in the leg during another robbery attempt.

INMATE	STATE	SEX	RACE	JUVENILE
CARTER, CLARENCE	OHIO	M	B	
CARTER, DARRYL	PENNSYLVANIA	M	W	
CARTER, DEAN	CALIFORNIA	M	N	
CARTER, DOUGLAS	UTAH	M	B	
CARTER, ERNEST	OKLAHOMA	M	B	
CARTER, JAMES D.	TENNESSEE	M	W	
CARTER, JOHNNY RAY	TEXAS	M	B	
CARTER, LOIS	NORTH CAROLINA	M	B	
CARTER, ROBERT ANTHONY	TEXAS	M	B	*
CARTER, TRACEY	CALIFORNIA	M	B	
CARUSO, MICHAEL	FLORIDA	M	W	
CARUTHERS, WALTER	TENNESSEE	M	B	
CASARES, JOSE	CALIFORNIA	M	H	
CASEY, GERALD	TEXAS	M	W	
CASTILLO, DAVID	TEXAS	M	N	

CASTOR, MARVIN INDIANA **M** **W**

In 1988, Marvin Castor was convicted of killing former Hancock County Sheriff Malcolm Grass during a shootout in the parking lot of a service station. Grass, then a sheriff's captain, was with FBI agents attempting to arrest Castor and his brother for an alleged extortion plot.

INMATE	STATE	SEX	RACE	JUVENILE
CASTRO, EDWARD	FLORIDA	M	H	
CASTRO, JOHN	OKLAHOMA	M	N	
CATLIN, STEVEN D.	CALIFORNIA	M	W	
CAUTHERN, RONNIE	TENNESSEE	M	W	

INMATE	STATE	SEX	RACE	JUVENILE

CAVANAUGH, PATRICK NEVADA **M** **B**

Patrick Cavanaugh killed Nathaniel "Buster" Wilson, 38, because he threatened to tell of a stolen check scheme. In 1980, he killed and mutilated of a member of the Coasters singing group in Las Vegas. Cavanaugh, a 47-year-old Camden, N.J., native, is pursuing his case in district court.

| CAVE, ALFONSO | FLORIDA | M | B |
| CAZES, VICTOR | TENNESSEE | M | W |

CEJA, JOSE ARIZONA **M** **H**

On Sunday, June 30, 1974, Jose Ceja went to the home of Randy and Linda Leon in Phoenix intending to steal a large shipment of marijuana. Upon entry, Ceja shot Linda (who apparently resisted him) twice in the chest, and then dragged her body from the living room to the bedroom where he shot her at least four more times in the head at close range. When Randy arrived home, Ceja shot him four times with Randy's gun, which Ceja had removed from a drawer in the house. Ceja loaded a suitcase he had brought with him with 12 kilos of marijuana. He removed the receiver from the phone and turned on the television to create an appearance that someone was home. He later attended the funeral of the victims, and offered to help police find the murderer.

CHABROL, ANDREW	VIRGINIA	M	W
CHAFFEE, JONATHAN	SOUTH CAROLINA	M	W
CHAMBERS, JAMES	MISSOURI	M	W
CHAMBERS, KARL	PENNSYLVANIA	M	W
CHAMBERS, RONALD	TEXAS	M	B
CHAMBERS, TONY	TEXAS	M	B
CHAMPION, STEVE	CALIFORNIA	M	B
CHANDLER, DAVID R.	FEDERAL	M	W

CHANDLER, JAMES FLORIDA **M** **W**

Jim Chandler was convicted and sentenced to death for the murder of an elderly couple in July 1980. He bludgeoned them to death, then stabbed them to make sure they were dead. Chandler was twice sentenced to death — first in 1981, then 1986 — for this double murder. His first sentence was overturned because of a legal technicality.

CHANEY, ANTHONY   ARIZONA   M   W

Anthony Chaney and Deanna Jo Saunders-Coleman were on the run from a string of burglaries in Texas and Colorado. They were driving a stolen pickup truck and were in possession of 11 stolen firearms. On September 6, 1982, Coconino County (Ariz.) Sheriff's Deputy Robert Cline, on routine patrol, checked the campsite where Chaney and Saunders-Coleman were staying outside of Flagstaff. After requesting a check on the stolen truck, Cline got out of his car and began talking to Chaney. Chaney pulled a gun on the deputy, had Deanna disarm him, and handcuffed him to a tree. Chaney and Deanna got into the truck and started to leave. As they did, John Jamison, a reserve deputy, arrived at the scene. Chaney jumped out of the truck and began firing at Jamison with a rifle. Using a hail of fire to pin Jamison down inside his car, Chaney advanced to point blank range and fired three fatal shots into Jamison. In addition to the fatal wounds, the deputy was struck by over 200 fragments of metal and glass from the shots fired into the vehicle.

Saunders-Coleman pled guilty to second-degree murder and received a 21-year prison sentence. She testified against Chaney.

CHAPPELL, WILLIAM	TEXAS	M	W
CHASE, RICKY	MISSISSIPPI	M	B
CHEATHAM, CHARLES L.	OKLAHOMA	M	B
CHENAULT, MARCUS	GEORGIA	M	B

CHERRY, ROGER L.   FLORIDA   M   B

Roger Cherry was convicted and sentenced to death for the 1986 June murders of an elderly couple. While burglarizing the Wayne's home, Cherry beat Mrs. Wayne, 77, to death. Mr. Wayne, 80, died of a heart attack during Cherry's unlawful entry into his home. Cherry then stole the couple's car. He received the death penalty for Mrs. Wayne's murder; life imprisonment with eligibility for parole in 25 years for Mr. Wayne's death; 17 years for burglary; and five years for a grand theft charge. The sentences were to run concurrently.

CHESTER, FRANK   PENNSYLVANIA   M   W

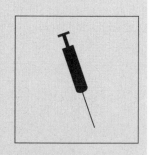

Frank Chester, 21, and Richard Laird, 25, were sentenced to die for the 1987 murder of Anthony Milano, who was tortured and whose throat was slashed. According to trial testimony, the two met Milano, 26, at a bar in December 1987. They insisted he take a ride with them, then attacked him because he was gay. Chester, who admitted pushing Milano to the ground, said it was Laird who repeatedly slit Milano's throat with a box-cutting knife.

INMATE	STATE	SEX	RACE	JUVENILE
CHILDRESS, JOHN	ILLINOIS	M	B	
CHILDS, JOHNNIE	GEORGIA	M	B	
CHINN, DAVEL V.	OHIO	M	B	
CHMIEL, DAVID	PENNSYLVANIA	M	W	

CHRISTENSON, SCOTT GEORGIA M W

Scott Christenson was convicted and sentenced to death March 1990 for the July 1989 murder and armed robbery of Albert L. "Bert" Oliver III. Christenson, 19, shot 31-year-old Oliver to death and stole his truck.

CHRISTMAS, MARC	FLORIDA	M	W	

CHRISTY, LAWRENCE PENNSYLVANIA M W

Larry Christy was convicted and sentenced to death for the 1980 killing of Thomas Volk, a security guard. Christy shot Volk three times in the head.

CLABOURNE, SCOTT ARIZONA M B

On the evening of September 18, 1980, Laura Webster, a University of Arizona student, was at the Green Dolphin Bar in Tucson, Ariz., with friends. She met Scott Clabourne and Larry Langston at the bar and agreed to leave with them. Clabourne and Langston then took Webster to the house of a friend of Langston.

Webster was repeatedly raped and sodomized, then strangled and stabbed in the heart three times. Her body was dumped in an arroyo, where it was found the next morning.

Langston pleaded guilty to murder and received a life sentence.

CLAIR, KENNETH	CALIFORNIA	M	B	
CLARK, ANTONIO	ARKANSAS	M	B	

CLARK, DAVID M. TEXAS M W

In February 1987, Beverly Benninghoff and Charles Gears were killed in a drug dispute. David Michael Clark and his fiancée, Mary Gober Copeland, thought Benninghoff and Gears had either stolen chemicals needed to manufacture methamphetamine or knew who had. Gears was stabbed 15 times, beaten and shot twice. Benninghoff was shot four times. Clark was sentenced to death Oct. 4, 1991.

CLARK, DOUGLAS	CALIFORNIA	M	W
CLARK, HERMAN ROBERT	TEXAS	M	B
CLARK, JACK	TEXAS	M	W

CLARK, JAMES DEAN ARIZONA M W

For most of 1977, James Dean Clark worked as a wrangler at a dude ranch in Elfrida, Ariz. In the early morning hours of December 4, 1977, Clark killed two other wranglers at the ranch: George Martin, Jr. and 17-year-old Gerald McFerron. Clark stabbed Martin numerous times in the chest and shot McFerron three times in the head. Both victims were asleep at the time of the attacks.

Clark then took a .357 Magnum and walked to the house of the owners, Charles and Mildred Thumm. After shooting Mr. Thumm twice, Clark shot Mrs. Thumm through the head as she slept. He took jewelry, credit cards and money from the Thumms, stole their car and, after slashing the tires of all the vehicles at the ranch, drove to El Paso. When Clark was arrested, the police found a souvenir he retained from the murders: the bullet that had passed through the head of one of the victims.

CLARK, JOSEPH	OHIO	M	B
CLARK, KENNETH	TEXAS	M	B
CLARK, LARRY	FLORIDA	M	B
CLARK, RICHARD	CALIFORNIA	M	W
CLARK, RONALD	FLORIDA	M	W

CLARK, TERRY NEW MEXICO M W

Terry Clark has the distinction of being the only person on New Mexico's death row. He was convicted and sentenced to death for the July 1986 murder, rape and kidnapping of 9-year-old Dena Lynn Gore. Her nude body was found in a shallow grave at a remote southeastern ranch. At the time, Clark was free on appeal of a conviction for another sexual assault against a 6-year-old girl.

CLARK, WILLIAM JOHN   **CALIFORNIA**   **M**   **W**

William Clark was convicted in 1984 of murder during the commission of arson. Clark set fire to his therapist's house because he wanted to make the woman suffer for cutting off his counseling. The therapist, Ava Gawronski, was seriously burned and her husband was killed. Clark later wrote to Gawronski threatening to harm other relatives. He received the death sentence in 1985.

INMATE	STATE	SEX	RACE
CLAYTON, JAMES	TEXAS	M	B
CLAYTON, ROBERT W.	OKLAHOMA	M	W
CLAYTON, WILLIE	PENNSYLVANIA	M	B
CLEMMONS, ERIC	MISSOURI	M	B
CLEMONS, CHANDLER	MISSISSIPPI	M	B
CLEVELAND, DELLANO	CALIFORNIA	M	B
CLINES, HOYT	ARKANSAS	M	W
CLISBY, WILLIE	ALABAMA	M	B
CLOUTIER, ROBERT	ILLINOIS	M	W
COBB, SEDRICK	CONNECTICUT	M	B
COBLE, BILLIE W.	TEXAS	M	W
COCHRAN, JAMES	ALABAMA	M	B
COCKRUM, JOHN	TEXAS	M	W
CODDINGTON, HERBERT	CALIFORNIA	M	W
CODE, NATHANIEL	LOUISIANA	M	B
COE, GLEN	TENNESSEE	M	W
COFFEY, FRED	NORTH CAROLINA	M	W
COFFMAN, CYNTHIA	CALIFORNIA	F	W
COHEN, MICHAEL	GEORGIA	M	B
COKER, ROCKY	TENNESSEE	M	W
COLE, TED CALVIN	TEXAS	M	W
COLE, WEST	MISSISSIPPI	M	B

COLEMAN, ALTON   **ILLINOIS/IND/OHIO M**   **B**

During the summer of 1984, Alton Coleman, along with his companion Debra Denise Brown, committed five murders and a variety of other criminal acts during a four-state crime spree. They were charged with crimes in Illinois, Indiana, Michigan and Ohio. One of the victims was 15-year-old Tonnie Storey, whose badly decomposed body was found in an abandoned building in Ohio. The cause of death was determined to be homicidal asphyxia.

INMATE	STATE	SEX	RACE	JUVENILE
COLEMAN, CALVIN	CALIFORNIA	M	B	
COLEMAN, CLYDELL	TEXAS	M	B	
COLEMAN, DEDRICK	ILLINOIS	M	B	
COLEMAN, MICHAEL A.	TENNESSEE	M	B	
COLEMAN, MICHAEL	FLORIDA	M	B	
COLEMAN, RUSSELL	CALIFORNIA	M	B	
COLINA, MANUEL	FLORIDA	M	H	
COLLIER, ROBERT	GEORGIA	M	B	
COLLINS, KENNETH	MARYLAND	M	B	
COLLINS, ROGER	GA/ILL	M	B	
COLVIN, EUGENE	MARYLAND	M	B	
COMBS, RONALD	OHIO	M	W	

COMER, ROBERT	**ARIZONA**	**M**	**W**	

On February 23, 1987, Robert Comer and his girlfriend, Juneva Willis, were at a campground near Apache Lake, Ariz. They invited Larry Pritchard, who was at the next campsite, to have dinner and drinks with them. Around 9 p.m., Comer shot Pritchard in the head, killing him. He and Willis then stole Pritchard's belongings. Around 11 p.m., Comer and Willis went to a campsite occupied by Richard Brough and Tracy Andrews. Comer stole their property, tied Brough to a car fender, and then raped Andrews in front of Brough. Comer and Willis then left the area, taking Andrews with them, but leaving Brough behind. Andrews escaped the next morning and ran for 23 hours before finding help.

Willis pleaded guilty to kidnapping and testified against Comer.

COMTOIS, ROLAND N.	CALIFORNIA	M	W	
CONE, GARY	TENNESSEE	M	W	
CONEY, JIMMY	FLORIDA	M	B	
CONFORTI, MICHAEL	PENNSYLVANIA	M	W	
CONKLIN, ROBERT	GEORGIA	M	W	
CONNER, KEVIN	INDIANA	M	W	
CONNER, RONNIE L.	MISSISSIPPI	M	B	
CONNOR, JERRY W.	NORTH CAROLINA	M	W	
CONNOR, JOHN WAYNE	GEORGIA	M	W	
COOEY, RICHARD	OHIO	M	W	
COOK, ANTHONY	TEXAS	M	W	

COOK, DANIEL WAYNE   ARIZONA   M   W

Daniel Cook, John Matzke, Kevin Swaney, and Carlos Froyan Cruz-Ramos worked at a restaurant in Lake Havasu City, Ariz., and shared an apartment. On July 19, 1987, Cook stole money from Cruz-Ramos. When Cruz-Ramos began searching the apartment for the money, Cook and Matzke tied Cruz-Ramos to a chair and began beating him with their fists and a metal pipe. Cook also cut Cruz-Ramos with a knife, sodomized him, and burned his genitals with cigarettes. After several hours of this torture, Matzke and Cook crushed Cruz-Ramos' throat with the pipe. When Swaney arrived at the apartment, Cook forced him upstairs and showed him Cruz-Ramos' body. Cook and Matzke then tied Swaney to a chair. Matzke went to sleep while Cook sodomized Swaney. When Cook was finished, he woke Matzke and the two men strangled Swaney with a bed sheet. Cook received the death penalty for both murders. Matzke pled guilty to second-degree murder and testified against Cook.

COOK, DAVID	FLORIDA	M	B
COOK, DERRICK L.	OHIO	M	B
COOK, JAMES	GEORGIA	M	B

COOK, KERRY M.   TEXAS   M   W

On June 9, 1977, 21-year-old Linda Jo Edwards' bloody body was found in the bedroom of a co-worker's apartment. She had been sexually mutilated and parts of her body that had been cut away with a knife and scissors were never found. Kerry Max Cook was sentenced to die for the slaying. He has since been granted a new trial.

COOK, ROBERT	PENNSYLVANIA	M	B
COOKS, CORNELL	OKLAHOMA	M	B
COOKS, VINCENT	TEXAS	M	B
COOPER, ANTHONY	SOUTH CAROLINA	M	W

COOPER, KEVIN   CALIFORNIA   M   B

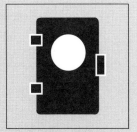

Kevin Cooper was convicted and sentenced to die in 1985 for four first-degree murders. In 1983, Cooper was an escaped prisoner who butchered F. Douglas Ryen and his wife, Peggy, both 41; their 10-year-old daughter, Jessica; and a visiting neighbor boy, Christopher Hughes, 11. Cooper was also convicted of attempting to murder Joshua Ryen, then 8, who survived a slashed throat. Investigators counted 140 wounds on the victims. At the time of his escape, Cooper was serving a term for burglary. He was mistakenly placed in a minimum-security section of the prison instead of a medium-security area.

INMATE	STATE	SEX	RACE	JUVENILE
COOPER, RICHARD	FLORIDA	M	W	
COOPER, VERNON F.	TENNESSEE	M	W	
COPELAND, FAYE	MISSOURI	F	W	
COPELAND, JAMES	LOUISIANA	M	W	
COPELAND, RAY	MISSOURI	M	W	
COPENHEFER, DAVID C.	PENNSYLVANIA	M	W	

CORAL, ROBERT	**ALABAMA**	**M**	**B**	

Robert Lance Coral shot 34-year-old Nancy Burt when she interrupted his robbery-in-progress at her apartment. While arguing for his life during closing remarks, Coral pointed to Burt's family and told jurors "nobody deserves to die." The prosecutors maintained Coral shot Burt to prevent her from identifying him.

INMATE	STATE	SEX	RACE	JUVENILE
CORBETT, RICKY	FLORIDA	M	B	
CORDOVA, JORGE	TEXAS	M	H	
CORLEY, EDWARD	TEXAS	M	W	
CORNELL, JOE	ARIZONA	M	W	

CORRELL, JERRY	**FLORIDA**	**M**	**W**	

Jerry Correll was convicted and sentenced to death for the 1985 quadruple murders of his 5-year-old daughter, his ex-wife, her sister and her mother.

CORRELL, MICHAEL	**ARIZONA**	**M**	**W**	

Michael Correll and John Nabors decided to rob Guy Snelling of money and drugs. On the night of April 11, 1984, Correll and Nabors went to Snelling's trailer and tied up Snelling and his girlfriend, Debra Rosen. When Robin Cady and Shawn D'Brito arrived at the trailer a short time later, they were also bound and gagged. Rosen was killed at the trailer by strangulation with a heavy shoelace knotted around her neck. Correll and Nabors took Snelling, Cady and D'Brito to a desert area north of Phoenix where all three were shot in the head. Snelling survived and lived to testify against Correll. Nabors committed suicide when police were about to arrest him.

INMATE	STATE	SEX	RACE	JUVENILE
CORRELL, WALTER	VIRGINIA	M	W	
CORWIN, DANIEL	TEXAS	M	W	
COULTER, DAVID	ALABAMA	M	W	
COULTER, ROGER	ARKANSAS	M	W	
COUNTY, CHARLES	TEXAS	M	B	
COX, JOHNIE M.	ARKANSAS	M	W	
COX, MICHAEL	CALIFORNIA	M	W	
COX, RUSSELL	PENNSYLVANIA	M	B	
COX, SUE	NORTH CAROLINA	F	W	
COX, TIEQUON A.	CALIFORNIA	M	B	
CRAIG, ANDREW	NORTH CAROLINA	M	B	
CRAIG, ROBERT	FLORIDA	M	W	
CRANE, ALVIN W.	TEXAS	M	W	
CRANK, DENTON ALAN	TEXAS	M	W	
CRAVATT, DARIAS	OKLAHOMA	M	N	
CRAWFORD, EDDIE	GEORGIA	M	W	
CRAWFORD, JOSEPH	OKLAHOMA	M	B	
CRAWLEY, DEWITT	PENNSYLVANIA	M	B	
CREECH, THOMAS	IDAHO	M	W	
CREWS, PAUL	PENNSYLVANIA	M	W	
CRISPELL, DANIEL	PENNSYLVANIA	M	W	
CRITTENDEN, STEVEN E.	CALIFORNIA	M	B	
CROSS, CHARLES	PENNSYLVANIA	M	W	
CROWE, SAMUEL	GEORGIA	M	W	
CRUMP, MICHAEL	FLORIDA	M	B	

CRUMP, THOMAS	**NEVADA**	**M**	**W**	

In 1980, Crump, 50, strangled a Las Vegas prostitute, 26-year-old Jodie Jameston. Crump, born in Muncie, Ind., is appealing his case in district court.

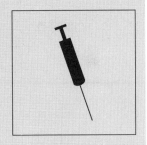

CRUSE, WILLIAM B.	**FLORIDA**	**M**	**W**	

William Cruse was convicted and sentenced to death for the 1987 murder of six people. Two of the six were police officers.

CRUZ, OLIVER D.	TEXAS	M	H	

INMATE	STATE	SEX	RACE	JUVENILE
CRUZ, ROBERT	ARIZONA	M	W	
CRUZ, ROLANDO	ILLINOIS	M	H	
CUDJO, ARMENIA	CALIFORNIA	M	B	
CUDJO, WILLIAM	OKLAHOMA	M	B	
CULBERSON, ALVIN	MISSISSIPPI	M	B	
CUMINGS, JERRY RAY	NORTH CAROLINA	M	N	
CUMMINGS, EDWARD LEE	NORTH CAROLINA	M	B	
CUMMINGS, RAYNARD	CALIFORNIA	M	B	
CUNNINGHAM, ALBERT	CALIFORNIA	M	B	
CUNNINGHAM, CALVIN C.	NORTH CAROLINA	M	B	
CURNUTT, MILLARD	TENNESSEE	M	W	
CURTIS, RONNIE ALLEN	FEDERAL	M	B	

D'AGOSTINO, FRANK	**NEVADA**	**M**	**W**	

Frank D'Agostino was convicted and sentenced to death for the April 1989 murder of a 27-year-old woman. D'Agostino stabbed her multiple times in the chest, neck and back. He then removed various personal items from her body, splashed it with rubbing alcohol and ignited it.

D'AMBROSIA, JOE	OHIO	M	W	
D'ANGELO, DOMINICK	FLORIDA	M	W	
DAILEY, JAMES	FLORIDA	M	W	
DAMATO, JOSEPH	PENNSYLVANIA	M	W	
DAMON, SHELLIE	SOUTH CAROLINA	M	B	
DANIELS, HENRY	PENNSYLVANIA	M	B	

DANIELS, JACKSON	**CALIFORNIA**	**M**	**B**	

On May 13, 1982, police officers Dennis C. Doty and Philip N. Trust went to the home of Jackson Daniels Jr. to take him to prison for a 1980 bank robbery conviction. Daniels, wounded in the robbery and paralyzed from the waist down, pulled a gun from between his legs and fatally shot both officers. Three days later, he was found hiding in a friend's closet.

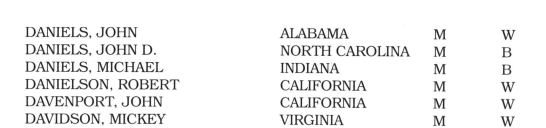

DANIELS, JOHN	ALABAMA	M	W	
DANIELS, JOHN D.	NORTH CAROLINA	M	B	
DANIELS, MICHAEL	INDIANA	M	B	
DANIELSON, ROBERT	CALIFORNIA	M	W	
DAVENPORT, JOHN	CALIFORNIA	M	W	
DAVIDSON, MICKEY	VIRGINIA	M	W	
DAVIE, RODERICK	OHIO	M	U	

INMATE	STATE	SEX	RACE	JUVENILE
DAVIS, ALLEN	FLORIDA	M	W	
DAVIS, CHARLES	OKLAHOMA	M	W	
DAVIS, CURFEW	GEORGIA	M	B	
DAVIS, DON	ARKANSAS	M	W	
DAVIS, EDWARD E.	NORTH CAROLINA	M	W	
DAVIS, FRANK	INDIANA	M	W	

DAVIS, GARY　　　　**COLORADO**　　**M**　　**W**

In 1987, Gary Lee Davis was convicted in the 1987 abduction, rape and torture-slaying of 33-year-old Virginia May. The Byers, Colo., farm wife was shot 14 times after Davis kidnapped her and forced her to have sex with him.

DAVIS, GEORGE	GEORGIA	M	B	
DAVIS, GIRVIES	ILLINOIS	M	B	
DAVIS, GREG	INDIANA	M	B	
DAVIS, GREGORY	MISSISSIPPI	M	B	
DAVIS, HENRY	FLORIDA	M	B	
DAVIS, JAMES	TEXAS	M	B	
DAVIS, JEFFREY	MISSISSIPPI	M	W	
DAVIS, JIMMY	ALABAMA	M	W	
DAVIS, JOHN MICHAEL	GEORGIA	M	W	
DAVIS, KENNETH	ALABAMA	M	B	
DAVIS, KENNETH	MISSISSIPPI	M	W	
DAVIS, LARRY	CALIFORNIA	M	B	
DAVIS, MARK	FLORIDA	M	W	

DAVIS, MICHAEL　　　　**ARIZONA**　　**M**　　**W**

On July 25, 1986, Michael Davis and Alfonso Salazar pulled the wrought iron bars from a window and entered the Tucson, Ariz., home of Sarah Kaplan. Kaplan was 83 years old, weighed less than 90 pounds, was 5 feet tall, and wore a patch on one eye. They beat her and strangled her with the telephone cord. Fingerprints belonging to both men were found at the scene. One of Salazar's prints was in blood. In a separate trial, Salazar was convicted and sentenced to death.

DAVIS, PERCY	LOUISIANA	M	B	

DAVIS, RALPH MISSOURI M B

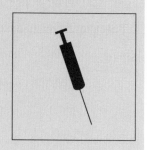

In 1986, Ralph Davis, a former insurance broker, murdered his wife, Susan Davis. Davis was convicted in March 1989. The trial was the first case in Missouri in which DNA "fingerprinting" was used as evidence.

DAVIS, RAYMOND	OHIO	M	W	
DAVIS, STANLEY	CALIFORNIA	M	B	
DAVIS, TIMOTHY	ALABAMA	M	W	*
DAVIS, TOMMY LEE	SOUTH CAROLINA	M	B	
DAVIS, TROY	GEORGIA	M	B	
DAVIS, VON CLARK	OHIO	M	B	
DAVIS, WILEY	OHIO	M	U	
DAVIS, WILLIAM PRINCE	TEXAS	M	B	

DAWSON, DAVID T. MONTANA M W

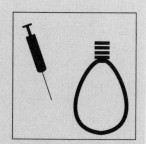

David Dawson was sentenced to die for the April 18, 1986, killing of three family members in a Billings, Mont., motel room he had rented. The victims, David and Monica Rodstein and their 11-year-old son, Andrew, were found in the room April 19 by Billings police detectives. They had been bound, gagged, injected with an unknown substance, then strangled with a telephone cord. Amy Rodstein, then 15, a daughter of the couple, survived.

DAWSON, HENRY NEVADA M B

Henry Dawson, 45, was sentenced to death for the March 1985 slaying of Leslie Gail Shepard, a convenience store clerk who resisted his sexual advances.

DAY, CHRISTOPHER	CALIFORNIA	M	B	
DE LA CRUZ, JOSE	TEXAS	M	H	
DEATON, JASON P.	FLORIDA	M	W	
DEBLANC, DAVID WAYNE	TEXAS	M	B	

INMATE	STATE	SEX	RACE	JUVENILE
DEBLER, SHELBY	MISSOURI	M	W	
DEBOUE, THOMAS	LOUISIANA	M	B	
DEEB, MUNEER M.	TEXAS	M	A	

DEERE, RONALD	**CALIFORNIA**	**M**	**N**	

On March 4, 1982, Donald Davis left work early to take his daughters, Melissa, 2, and Michelle, 7, fishing. He picked them up after school at their grandmother's home. The trio headed to their family's housetrailer for fishing gear. Davis went into a bedroom to get fishing poles. As he started out the door, 29-year-old Ronald Lee Deere, who had been hiding in an adjoining room, shot Davis between the eyes with a .22-caliber rifle. The frightened girls tried to escape out the front door. Michelle apparently was carrying her younger sister when Deere shot Melissa in the heart and Michelle in the stomach and in the head.

Testimony indicated that he may have killed the girls because they could have identified him. Apparently against Deere's will, appeals have been filed uncovering technical errors in the trial and delaying his death sentence.

INMATE	STATE	SEX	RACE	JUVENILE
DEGARMO, ROGER L.	TEXAS	M	W	
DEHART, ROBERT	PENNSYLVANIA	M	W	
DELAP, DAVID	FLORIDA	M	W	
DELK, MONTY ALLEN	TEXAS	M	W	
DELONG, WAYNE	VIRGINIA	M	W	
DELVECCHIO, GEORGE	ILLINOIS	M	W	
DEMOUCHETTE, JAMES	TEXAS	M	B	
DEMPS, BENNIE	FLORIDA	M	{B	
DENNIS, WILLIAM	CALIFORNIA	M	W	
DENT, OMAR	CALIFORNIA	M	B	

DEPASQUALE, VINCE	**NEVADA**	**M**	**W**	

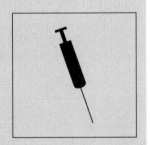

At Nevada State Prison in 1988, DePasquale, 32, killed his cellmate Ronald Cane, 46. DePasquale was sent to prison from Las Vegas where he was convicted of burglary, larceny and drug possession. A Las Vegas native, DePasquale's direct appeal to the Supreme Court has been denied.

INMATE	STATE	SEX	RACE	JUVENILE
DEPEW, RHETT	OHIO	M	W	
DEPUTY, ANDRE	DELAWARE	M	B	

INMATE	STATE	SEX	RACE	JUVENILE
DERRICK, SAMUEL	FLORIDA	M	W	
DESANTIS, STEPHEN	CALIFORNIA	M	W	
DESHIELDS, KENNETH	DELAWARE	M	B	
DESPAIN, LEROY	ARIZONA	M	W	
DETRICH, DAVID	ARIZONA	M	W	

DEUTSCHER, HENRY   **NEVADA**   **M**   **W**

A 51-year-old New Jersey native, Deutscher has been on death row since 1977, longer than anyone else in Nevada. He was convicted of killing Darlene Joyce Miller, 37, whom he met in a Las Vegas bar. The 9th U.S. Circuit Court of Appeals overturned his death sentence, but Nevada has appealed that decision to the U.S. Supreme Court.

DEVIER, DARRELL	GEORGIA	M	W	
DEXTER, CLARENCE	MISSOURI	M	W	

DIAZ, ANGEL   **FLORIDA**   **M**   **H**

Angel Diaz was convicted and sentenced to death for the 1979 murder of a Miami bar manager during a robbery. Diaz, a Puerto Rican who does not speak English, maintains his innocence.

DIAZ, ROBERT R.	CALIFORNIA	M	H	
DICKERSON, FREDERICK	OHIO	M	B	
DICKEY, COLIN	CALIFORNIA	M	W	
DICKS, JEFFREY	TENNESSEE	M	W	
DICKSON, MARTY W.	OKLAHOMA	M	W	
DIFRISCO, ANTHONY	NEW JERSEY	M	W	

DILL, JIMMY   **ALABAMA**   **M**   **W**

Jimmy Dill was sentenced to death for the February 8, 1988, robbery and killing of Leon Shaw, a known drug dealer. Dill, a reputed cocaine user, shot Shaw in the back of the head when he was refused cocaine on credit. Dill then stole $800 from Shaw. Although Shaw was alive when found, he eventually died in November 1988. After hearing his death sentence, Dill joked with his defense attorney, "I can't get probation?"

DILLBECK, DONALD	FLORIDA	M	W	
DINKINS, RICHARD	TEXAS	M	W	
DIVERS, JAMES	LOUISIANA	M	B	

INMATE	STATE	SEX	RACE	JUVENILE
DOBBS, WILEY	GEORGIA	M	B	

DODD, WESTLEY A.   **WASHINGTON**   **M**   **W**

Wesley Allan Dodd was convicted and sentenced to death for the sexual assault and murders of Cole Neer, 11; William Neer, 10; and Lee Iseli, 4. Dodd was also sentenced to 50 years in prison for the attempted murder of James Kirk, 6.

DOLEMAN, MARVIN   **NEVADA**   **M**   **B**

Doleman, 22, robbed and killed Las Vegas cabdriver Kenneth Marcum, 53, with accomplice Frederick Paine, 21, in 1990. Both men were sentenced to death in Nevada. Born in Grand Rapids, Mich., Doleman is appealing his case in district court. Paine, born in Florida, had his death sentence reversed by the Nevada Supreme Court and a new penalty hearing scheduled.

DOUGLAS, FRED BERRE   **CALIFORNIA**   **M**   **W**

Fred Douglas was sentenced to death for the 1982 strangulation deaths of Margaret Kreuger, 16, and Beth Jones, 19. An eyewitness of the murder testified Douglas promised to hire the young women as models. He took them into the California desert, where he sexually assaulted and killed them. Douglas then fled to Canada, and was later apprehended in Las Vegas. Court Judge Ronald E. Owen called Douglas a "sadistic and senseless killer" who took the young women's lives "to gratify some weird sexual fantasy." Douglas has called judges in U.S. courts "money-sucking, parasitical leeches that don't give a damn about a man's complete innocence."

DOWNS, ERNEST	FLORIDA	M	W	
DOYLE, DANNY	FLORIDA	M	W	
DRAIGHTON, ERICK	PENNSYLVANIA	M	B	
DRAUGHON, MARTIN A.	TEXAS	M	W	
DRAYTON, LEROY	SOUTH CAROLINA	M	B	
DREW, ROBERT N.	TEXAS	M	W	
DRINKARD, RICHARD G.	TEXAS	M	W	
DRINKWATER, RANDY	NEBRASKA	M	W	
DRISCOLL, ROBERT	MISSOURI	M	W	
DUBOSE, EDWARD	ALABAMA	M	B	
DUBRUCE, DERRICK	ALABAMA	M	B	
DUCKETT, JAMES	FLORIDA	M	W	
DUCKETT, ROBERT	OKLAHOMA	M	W	
DUEST, LLOYD	FLORIDA	M	W	
DUFF-SMITH, MARKHAM	TEXAS	M	W	

INMATE	STATE	SEX	RACE	JUVENILE
DUFFEY, STEVEN	PENNSYLVANIA	M	W	
DUFOUR, DONALD	FLA/MISS	M	W	
DUGAR, TROY	LOUISIANA	M	B	*
DUHAMEL, EMILE PIERRE	TEXAS	M	W	
DUNCAN, DAVID	TENNESSEE	M	B	
DUNCAN, DONN	FLORIDA	M	W	
DUNCAN, HENRY EARL	CALIFORNIA	M	B	
DUNCAN, JOE C.	ALABAMA	M	W	
DUNKLE, JON S.	CALIFORNIA	M	W	
DUNLAP, JOHN	IDAHO	M	U	
DUNN, KENNETH D.	TEXAS	M	B	
DUPLANTIS, DAVID	MISSISSIPPI	M	W	

DUREN, DAVID	ALABAMA	M	W

In October 1983, David Ray Duren and Richard David Kinder found a couple in a parked car and ordered them, at gunpoint, into the trunk. Duren and Kinder drove the car to Trussville, Ala., where they tied Charles Leonard and Kathleen Bedsole together and shot them both, after taking $40 from Bedsole's purse. Leonard survived and called the sheriff's deputies, who later arrested Duren and Kinder. Duren confessed to the murder on two separate occasions, and his only defense at trial was that he killed Bedsole by mistake while trying to kill Leonard.

DUROCHER, MICHAEL	FLORIDA	M	W

Michael Durocher was already a death row inmate when he was arrested for the murders of his 31-year-old girlfriend, Grace Reed; her 5-year-old daughter, Candice; and their 6-month-old son, Joshua. His first murder conviction was in 1989 for the 1988 murder of his roommate, Eddie Dwayne Childers. After smashing Childers' the head three times with a claw hammer, Durocher took Childer's body to a lake, poured two gallons of gasoline on the body and burned it. Durocher received a life sentence. He was convicted and sentenced to death in July 1989 for the January 1986 murder of Thomas J. Underwood III, who was murdered during an armed robbery. Durocher's second death sentence was handed down in March 1991.

DURR, DARRYL	OHIO	M	B
DUVALL, JOHN	OKLAHOMA	M	W
DYER, ALFRED	CALIFORNIA	M	B
EADDY, JIMMY	FLORIDA	M	W
EARHART, JAMES O.	TEXAS	M	W
EARP, RICKY	CALIFORNIA	M	W
EARVIN, HARVEY	TEXAS	M	B
EASLEY, ELBERT	CALIFORNIA	M	W

INMATE	STATE	SEX	RACE	JUVENILE

EASLEY, IKE　　　　　　ILLINOIS　　　M　　B

Ike Easley was sentenced and convicted to death for the 1987 stabbing death of Robert L. Taylor, 44, a prison superintendent. Easley, an inmate at Pontiac prison in Illinois, and fellow inmates Roosevelt Lucas, David Carter and Michael Johnson were part of a gang "hit" believed to be in retaliation for an earlier death of a fellow gang member.

EAST, WAYNE　　　　　　TEXAS　　　M　　B
EASTLACK, JOHN　　　　ARIZONA　　　M　　B

EATON, DENNIS W.　　　VIRGINIA　　　M　　W

On Feb. 20, 1989, Dennis Wayne Eaton, 32, decided to flee Shenandoah County, Va., to avoid a preliminary hearing on burglary charges. In a bizarre love triangle, Eaton was living with Walter Custer, Jr., and Ann McDonald, 24, who had a three-year-old son together. In order to eliminate Custer as a possible witness against him in the hearing, Eaton shot him twice in the face and once in the back using a .38-caliber pistol. He then walked next door to the home of Ripley Marston, shot him twice in the back of the head and took his wallet, the keys to his Ford Fairmont and some camping supplies. As Eaton and McDonald headed toward Texas, they stopped to pick up a six-pack of beer. At 11:30 p.m., Virginia State Trooper Jerry Hines unwittingly made a routine traffic stop. After retrieving a breathalyzer kit in his car and requesting for a "Signal 25" so other officers could hear his communications, he proceeded back to the car. Shortly after, the trooper was found dead face-down in a pool of blood. At 1:30 a.m., the Ford was observed in the drive-through lane at a fast food restaurant in Salem, Va. While officers surrounded the car, Eaton turned and fatally shot McDonald before turning the gun on himself. Eaton was the only shooting victim to survive. He was sentenced to death for Hines' murder and now sits on Virginia's Death Row.

EATON, WINTHROP　　　LOUISIANA　　　M　　B

ECHAVARRIA, JOSE　　　NEVADA　　　M　　H

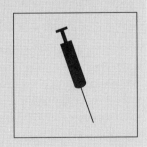

Jose Echavarria entered a Las Vegas bank in 1990 dressed as a woman when he displayed his hand-held revolver to a teller, the teller began to scream. An FBI agent, who happened to be in the bank, confronted Echavarria. The agent fired one shot and Echavarria dropped his revolver. He was placed in a chair, but jumped out of it and began struggling with the agent. The agent fell to the floor, Echavarria retrieved his weapon and fired three rounds into the agent. Echavarria fled to Mexico, where he was arrested. The agent died of his wounds. Echavarria was convicted and in May 1991 was sentenced to die.

INMATE	STATE	SEX	RACE	JUVENILE
EDDMONDS, DURLYN	ILLINOIS	M	B	
EDELBACHER, PETER	CALIFORNIA	M	W	
EDGERTON, ANDRE	ILLINOIS	M	B	
EDMISTON, STEPHEN	PENNSYLVANIA	M	W	

EDMONDS, DANA	**VIRGINIA**	**M**	**B**	

On July 22, 1983, John Elliot was killed during a robbery. Dana Ray Edmonds was convicted of hitting the 62-year-old grocer on the head with a brick and slashing his throat during the robbery. Edmonds, now 30, is still in the appeals process.

INMATE	STATE	SEX	RACE	JUVENILE
EDWARDS, DANIEL	ILLINOIS	M	W	
EDWARDS, GEORGE	PENNSYLVANIA	M	W	
EDWARDS, THOMAS F.	CALIFORNIA	M	W	
EL-MUMIT, ABDULLAH HAKIM	LOUISIANA	M	B	
ELEM, DAVID	FLORIDA	M	W	
ELEY, JOHN	OHIO	M	B	
ELKINS, MICHAEL	SOUTH CAROLINA	M	W	

ELLEDGE, WILLIAM	**FLORIDA**	**M**	**W**	

William Elledge was convicted and sentenced to death for the murder of Margaret Anne Strack in August 1974. He raped her, then strangled her. After the killing, Elledge dumped Strack's body in a church yard. He then broke into a convenience store, where he found Edward Gaffney, 47. Elledge shot him in the back and side. He then stole Gaffney's money and even took the money inside of a donation box. Elledge then traveled to Jacksonville, where he killed a beach motel owner. Although sentenced to death for the Strack murder, Elledge received life sentences for the Gaffney and motel owner murders. He has been on Florida's Death Row since April 1975.

INMATE	STATE	SEX	RACE	JUVENILE
ELLIOT, MARCHAND	ARIZONA	M	U	
ELLIOTT, JOHN W.	TEXAS	M	H	
ELLIS, CYRIL W.	OKLAHOMA	M	B	
ELLIS, RALPH	FLORIDA	M	W	*
ELMORE, EDWARD LEE	SOUTH CAROLINA	M	B	
EMERSON, DENNIS	ILLINOIS	M	B	
EMERY, JEFF	TEXAS	M	W	

INMATE	STATE	SEX	RACE	JUVENILE

EMIL, RODNEY NEVADA M W

On June 17, 1984 Rodney Emil and several friends were riding in a pickup truck in Las Vegas, Nev., when they pulled up to a parked vehicle occupied by Emil's stepfather, Charles Emil. The younger Emil stood up in the truck and shot his stepfather four times with a pistol. Approximately one year later, Emil was linked to the shooting by statements his companions made to officials.

Responsible for previous murders, the slaying of Charles Emil, 46, is the crime that ultimately landed Rodney Emil on Nevada's Death Row. Emil, a 31-year-old Pueblo, Colo., native, is pursuing his appeal in federal court.

EMMONS, MARK NEVADA M W

On December 8, 1984, Mark Emmons, 23, and his co-defendant, Edward Hassett, were hitchhiking in Tuscon, Ariz., when 19-year-old Jack Perkins Jr. picked them up. When the driver asked the two to leave his vehicle, Emmons and Hassett tied Perkins' hands behind his back. Perkins wrestled with Emmons when he could not untie his hands but could not break free.

Emmons and Hassett threw the struggling, bound victim into a culvert in the Nevada desert. Emmons found a rifle in the victim's car and shot him because he said Perkins had been uncooperative. The victim was also robbed and stabbed.

Emmons, of Topeka, Kan., has filed a petition in the Eighth Judicial District Court. He awaits his execution by lethal injection on Nevada's Death Row.

INMATE	STATE	SEX	RACE
ENGLE, GREGORY	FLORIDA	M	W
ENIS, ANTHONY	ILLINOIS	M	B
ENOCH, WILLIE	ILLINOIS	M	B
EPHRAIM, SYLVESTER	ALABAMA	M	B
EPPERSON, ROGER D.	KENTUCKY	M	W
ERICKSON, PAUL	ILLINOIS	M	W
ERVIN, CURTIS	CALIFORNIA	M	B
ESCOBAR, DENNIS	FLORIDA	M	H
ESCOBAR, DOUGLAS	FLORIDA	M	H
ESPARZA, GREGORY	OHIO	M	H
ESPINOSA, HENRY	FLORIDA	M	H
ESPINOZA, ANTONIO	CALIFORNIA	M	H
ESTES, RICKEY	TENNESSEE	M	W
ETHERIDGE, GARY	TEXAS	M	W
EVANS, CHARLES	INDIANA	M	B

INMATE	STATE	SEX	RACE	JUVENILE
EVANS, DERRICK	OHIO	M	B	
EVANS, JOHNNIE LEE	ILLINOIS	M	B	
EVANS, JONATHAN	TENNESSEE	M	B	
EVANS, VERNON	MARYLAND	M	B	
EYLER, LARRY	ILLINOIS	M	W	
FAHY, HENRY	PENNSYLVANIA	M	W	

FAIN, CHARLES	**IDAHO**	**M**	**W**	

Charles Fain was convicted and sentenced to death February 1984 for the 1982 abduction, sexual assault and drowning of 9-year-old Daralyn Johnson. She was abducted while walking to school.

FAIR, ROBERT	ILLINOIS	M	B	
FAIRBANK, ROBERT	CALIFORNIA	M	W	

FAIRCHILD, BARRY	**ARKANSAS**	**M**	**B**	

Barry Fairchild was convicted and sentenced to death by lethal injection for the Feb. 26, 1983, abduction, beating, rape and murder of 2nd Lt. Marjorie "Greta" Mason, a nurse at Little Rock Air Force Base. Fairchild abducted Mason, 22, outside a Little Rock furniture store and took her to an abandoned farmhouse. Her body was later found inside. Fairchild is also serving a 25-year term for aggravated robbery. He pleaded guilty to those charges as part of a plea bargain that dismissed an attempted murder charge. Fairchild said he would rather be executed than spend his life in prison, and has told his attorney not to request his death sentence be commuted to life in prison during his appeals.

FARAGA, LAZARO	MISSISSIPPI	M	H	
FARLEY, RICHARD	CALIFORNIA	M	W	

FARMER, ROBERT	**NEVADA**	**M**	**W**	

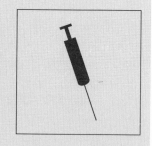

On Jan. 18, 1982, 36-year-old Farmer fatally stabbed a Las Vegas resident, Greg Gelunas, 35, in Gelunas' home. Farmer, born in Florida, had an appeal to the Nevada Supreme Court denied in February 1992. His sentence was upheld once by the U.S. Supreme Court in 1989.

INMATE	STATE	SEX	RACE	JUVENILE
FARNAM, JACK GUS	CALIFORNIA	M	W	
FARR, VICTOR	FLORIDA	M	W	
FARRIS, TROY D.	TEXAS	M	W	
FAUBER, CURTIS	CALIFORNIA	M	W	

FAULDER, JOSEPH S.   **TEXAS**   **M**   **W**

On July 8, 1975, 75-year-old Inez Phillips was beaten and stabbed with a butcher knife during a burglary of her home. Joseph Stanley Faulder and Lynda Ziegler "Stormie" McCann entered her home to break into a floor safe they had been told was in the house. McCann testified that Faulder beat and stabbed the victim. Faulder, now 53, is close to his first date with the executioner, though his lawyer is expecting the court of criminal appeals to grant a stay of execution.

FAULKNER, ARTHUR	PENNSYLVANIA	M	B	

FAUNTENBERRY, JOHN   **OHIO**   **M**   **W**

John Fautenberry was convicted of killing two people in two separate states during two separate trials. He is charged with killing three more people in two other states. Those trials are pending. Fautenberry was sentenced to 99 years in prison for the brutal stabbing murder of Jeffrey Diffee, an Alaskan silver miner who befriended Fauntenberry in March 1991. Fauntenberry, who was fleeing the police that he suspected was on his trail, wanted Diffee's truck and money so he could leave Juneau. After his Alaska conviction, Fauntenberry was extradited to Ohio to stand trial for killing Joseph Daron, an Ohio insurance executive and father of two. Fauntenberry hitched a ride with Daron, who was just returning from an ice-skating party with his two daughters. Fauntenberry said he decided to kill Daron because Daron was successfully employed and he was not. Fauntenberry unsuccessfully argued against Ohio's death penalty by saying he was a victim of child abuse. He was found guilty of murder and sentenced to death Sept. 17, 1992. Trials remaining include the murder of Gary M. Garmer, a Tennessee truck driver found shot in New Jersey; Christine Guthrie, an Oregon woman who was found shot in Oregon; and Don Ray Nutley, a Texas man also found shot in Oregon. Fauntenberry has admitted to all of the murders. Although Oregon, New Jersey and Ohio have active death penalty laws, Fauntenberry does not believe he will be executed. "The death penalty is just two words — death penalty. They don't execute people. I don't expect to die."

FEARANCE, JOHN	TEXAS	M	B	
FELDER, SAMMY	TEXAS	M	B	
FELKER, ELLIS	GEORGIA	M	W	
FELTROP, RALPH	MISSOURI	M	W	

FERGUSON, JOHN **FLORIDA** **M** **B**

John Ferguson received eight separate death sentences. In 1977, he and three accomplices killed six people in an execution-style shooting in a home where they thought drugs were hidden. Two of these accomplices, Marvin Francois and Beauford White, have been executed. Five months after these murders, Ferguson kidnapped and killed two teenagers.

FERRELL, DALLAS C.	SOUTH CAROLINA	M	W
FERRELL, ERIC	GEORGIA	M	B
FETTERLY, DONALD	IDAHO	M	W
FIELDS, NATHSON	ILLINOIS	M	B
FIELDS, STEVIE	CALIFORNIA	M	B
FIELDS, ZANE	IDAHO	M	W
FIERRO, CESAR R.	TEXAS	M	H
FIERRO, DAVID	CALIFORNIA	M	H
FINNEY, EDDIE	GEORGIA	M	B
FIRST, KENNETH W.	TEXAS	M	W
FISHER, DAVID LEE	VIRGINIA	M	W

FISHER, JAMES C. **ARIZONA** **M** **W**

James Fisher and his wife, Ann, managed an apartment complex in Phoenix for Marguerite Bailey, a 71-year-old woman. As part of their duties, the Fishers collected the rent from the other tenants and delivered the money to Bailey each Saturday. On September 12, 1981, Fisher and his wife decided to kill Bailey for the money she carried in addition to the rent money. When Bailey arrived shortly after noon to collect the rent, Fisher told his wife to go into the bathroom. Fisher then took a claw hammer and struck Bailey on the head three times, splintering the skull and driving the fragments into the cortex of the brain. Fisher wrapped the victim's bloody head in a plastic shower curtain. Fisher then bound Bailey's arms and legs, wrapped her in a blanket, and dumped her body in an alley some distance away. Fisher and his wife were arrested five days later in Iowa. Mrs. Fisher pled guilty to hindering prosecution. She received a $2^{1}/2$ - year sentence.

FISHER, ROBERT	PENNSYLVANIA	M	W
FITZGERALD, EDWARD	VIRGINIA	M	W
FLAMER, WILLIAM	DELAWARE	M	B

INMATE	STATE	SEX	RACE	JUVENILE

FLANAGAN, DALE **NEVADA** **M** **W**

In order to collect on an inheritance, 26-year-old Flanagan killed his grandparents, Carl and Colleen Gordon in Las Vegas. Also involved in the 1984 crime, was 27-year-old Randy Moore. Both men received the death penalty. Flanagan, of Santa Ana, Calif., and Moore, of Encino, Calif., had their cases reviewed by the U.S. Supreme Court to reconsider the sentences.

FLEENOR, D.H. INDIANA M W

FLEMING, SON **GEORGIA** **M** **B**

Son Fleming and two others were convicted on charges related to the Feb. 11, 1976, murder of Ray City (Ga.) Police Chief Ed Giddens. Giddens was abducted and shot to death after he stopped a car matching the description of one used in a robbery. Also convicted were Henry Willis III, who was executed May 18, 1989, and Larry Fleming , who was sentenced to life in prison. Son Fleming's appeals have been based in part upon claims that he is retarded.

INMATE	STATE	SEX	RACE
FLETCHER, MARCUS	ALABAMA	M	B
FLORES, MARIO	ILLINOIS	M	H
FLORES, MIGUEL	TEXAS	M	H
FLOYD, JAMES	FLORIDA	M	B
FONTENOT, KARL	OKLAHOMA	M	W
FORD, CLAY	ARKANSAS	M	B
FORD, GLENN	LOUISIANA	M	B
FORD, KENNETH	PENNSYLVANIA	M	B
FORD, MELBERT RAY	GEORGIA	M	W
FORD, PERNELL	ALABAMA	M	B

FORD, PRISCILLA **NEVADA** **F** **B**

Priscilla Ford was convicted and sentenced to death for the 1980 Thanksgiving Day massacre of six people in downtown Reno, Nevada. Ford drove her car down a crowded Reno sidewalk. In addition to killing six, she injured 21 other people.

INMATE	STATE	SEX	RACE	JUVENILE
FORTENBERRY, TOMMY	ALABAMA	M	W	

FOSTER, CHARLES **OKLAHOMA** **M** **B**

On April 1, 1983, Muskogee, Okla., grocer Claude Wiley failed to return home after delivering groceries to the home of Eula Mae and Charles Adrian Foster. His body was found in a wooded area 11 days later by a man searching for wild onions. Eula Mae testified that she saw her husband beat Wiley with a baseball bat more than seven times. After leaving the room in disgust, she could hear Foster continuing to hit the grocer. She testified Wiley was still breathing as Foster removed his body, wrapped in a blanket. The Fosters burglarized Wiley's house before leaving town.

Officer Tim Gibson testified that he decided to enter the Fosters' house after seeing blood on the porch and a tooth next to the door. When he entered the house, he found blood splattered on the ceiling, the walls, and the baby's crib. The Fosters were captured in Texas. Charles Foster was convicted of first-degree murder in the slaying.

FOSTER, CHARLES K.	FLORIDA	M	W	
FOSTER, EMMITT	MISSOURI	M	B	
FOSTER, JAMES	ILLINOIS	M	B	

FOSTER, LAFONDA FAY **KENTUCKY** **F** **W**

On the night of April 23, 1986, 23-year-old LaFonda Fay Foster stabbed and shot five people for no apparent reason. She then ran over them with a car and set fire to two of their bodies. At one point, Foster and an accomplice, Tina Hickey Powell, stopped to order chicken dinners in the midst of leaving corpses strewn in parts of southern Lexington, Ky. It ended when one of the bodies became lodged underneath the car.

Powell was given five life sentences after it was determined she was not the instigator.

Foster was given five death sentences and is the only woman in Kentucky facing the electric chair. While in prison, Foster was accused of throwing human waste on another inmate who testified against her. She is still under investigation for a security breach at the institution. Although officials decline to discuss the situation. She has suits pending against the Corrections Cabinet of Kentucky for failing to provide her the same facilities as the men on death row at the Kentucky State Penitentiary at Eddyville.

FOSTER, RICHARD DONALD	TEXAS	M	W	
FOSTER, RON	MISSISSIPPI	M	B	*
FOSTER, TIMOTHY	GEORGIA	M	B	
FOTOPOULOS, KOSTA	FLORIDA	M	W	
FOWLER, MARK	OKLAHOMA	M	W	
FOX, BILLY	OKLAHOMA	M	W	

INMATE	STATE	SEX	RACE	JUVENILE

FOX, RICHARD   OHIO   M   W

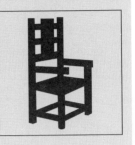

Richard Fox was convicted and sentenced to death in 1990 for the September 1989 murder of 18-year-old Leslie Keckler. Fox lured Keckeler into his car on the pretext of showing her a sales route for a fictitious job. He then made sexual advances, which Keckler rebuffed. Fox stabbed her as she she attempted to flee then strangled her "just to make sure she was dead."

FRANK, THEODORE   CALIFORNIA   M   W

In 1978, 2¹/2 -year-old Amy Sue Seitz was kidnapped from her aunt's back yard. The toddler was beaten, tortured with pliers, raped and strangled, and her body was dumped in a canyon. Theodore Frank was convicted in 1980 of murder, rape and other charges. Frank, now 56, is still in the appeals process.

FRANKLIN, WILLIAM	ILLINOIS	M	B	
FRANKLIN, GEORGE	OHIO	M	B	
FRAZIER, LEONARD	GEORGIA	M	W	

FRAZIER, RICHARD   ALABAMA   M   W

Richard Wayne Frazier was convicted in February 1986, of capital murder for the slaying of Jesse and Irene Doughty, a Mobile couple who were shot to death in their home January 22, 1977. Frazier was one of three hitmen hired by Doughty's business associate to kill Doughty for $5,000. Yet Frazier intended to leave no witnesses — Irene was killed because she happened to be home with her husband.

FRAZIER, RICHARD	OHIO	M	W	
FRAZIER, WAYNE	OHIO	M	B	
FREE, JAMES	ILLINOIS	M	W	
FREEMAN, DARRYL	ALABAMA	M	B	
FREEMAN, DAVID	ALABAMA	M	W	
FREEMAN, FRED	CALIFORNIA	M	W	
FREEMAN, JOHN	FLORIDA	M	W	
FRETWELL, BOBBY	ARKANSAS	M	W	
FREY, RODERICK	PENNSYLVANIA	M	W	
FRIERSON, LAVELL	CALIFORNIA	M	B	
FRONCKIEWICZ, MARK	TEXAS	M	W	

INMATE	STATE	SEX	RACE	JUVENILE
FRYE, JERRY G.	CALIFORNIA	M	W	
FUDGE, KEITH	CALIFORNIA	M	B	
FUENTES, JOSE	CALIFORNIA	M	H	
FUGATE, WALLACE	GEORGIA	M	W	

FULLER, AARON	**TEXAS**	**M**	**W**	

On March 18, 1989, 21-year-old Aaron Lee Fuller broke into 68-year-old Loretta Stephens' home. Her partially clad body was found four days later, in a patch of weeds less than 100 feet from U.S. 87. She had been beaten and suffocated.

Testimony during the trial indicated that Fuller robbed Stephens of more than $500 in cash. He stole her car and dumped her body. The abandoned vehicle was found near a bus station three days later. Fuller was arrested at his girlfriend's home after police received a tip. The defendant had been convicted on two separate burglary charges prior to this conviction. He was released from prison in September 1988 after serving about two years of a 15-year sentence.

FULLER, TYRONE	TEXAS	M	B	
FULLWOOD, MICHAEL LEE	NORTH CAROLINA	M	B	

FURMAN, MICHAEL	**WASHINGTON**	**M**	**W**	

Michael Furman was convicted and sentenced to death for the April 1989 murder of Anne Presler.

GACY, JOHN WAYNE	**ILLINOIS**	**M**	**W**	

John Gacy was convicted and sentenced to death for the murders of 33 people. Luring his victims into his home, Gacy often handcuffed and tortured them until they died. Twenty-seven bodies were found buried in a crawl space beneath his home. Gacy, who once volunteered as a clown at children's hospital, now clowns with the legal system. He has fired several appeals lawyers, causing a restart in the appeals process each time. Many of Gacy's fees have been paid for by federal and state programs for indigent defendants in capital cases. When asked if he thought he'd ever be executed, Gacy said he'd probably die of natural causes. His gruesome story has been retold in books and television movies.

GADDIS, BOBBY GENE	GEORGIA	M	W	

INMATE	STATE	SEX	RACE	JUVENILE
GADDY, RICHARD	ALABAMA	M	W	
GALL, EUGENE	KENTUCKY	M	W	

GALLEGO, GERALD CALIFORNIA M W

In April 1980, Karen Chipman-Twiggs and Stacey Redican, both 17, were lured into a van from a shopping mall in Sacramento, Calif. Charlene Gallego drove the van 200 miles to Nevada while her common-law husband sexually assaulted the girls in the back. In the remote hills outside of Lovelock, Nev., he beat the girls to death with a hammer.

In addition to the Nevada death sentence, Gallego also has been sentenced to die in California for the 1980 murders of Mary Beth Sowers and Craig Miller.

Shortly after the California decision, the Pershing County district attorney said he would try Gallego in Lovelock for the murders of Twiggs and Redican, because he had no faith in the California criminal justice system's ability to execute Gallego. When the comments were publicized, people from around the nation sent thousands of dollars to the Pershing County court clerk to defray the cost of the trial.

Gallego, 45, who sits on death row in Nevada, is the son of a man who was executed in Mississippi.

GALLEGOS, MICHAEL S.	ARIZONA	M	H	
GAMES, JAMES	INDIANA	M	W	
GANUS, VICTOR	ILLINOIS	M	W	
GARCEAU, ROBERT	CALIFORNIA	M	W	
GARCIA, ENRIQUE	FLORIDA	M	H	
GARCIA, FERNANDO	TEXAS	M	H	
GARCIA, GUSTAVO	TEXAS	M	H	
GARCIA, HECTOR L.	TEXAS	M	H	
GARCIA, HENRY	FLORIDA	M	H	
GARDNER, BILLY CONN	TEXAS	M	W	
GARDNER, DAVID A.	TEXAS	M	W	

GARDNER, JOHN NORTH CAROLINA M W

John Gardner was convicted and sentenced to death in 1983 for the first-degree murders of Kimberly Miller, 23, and Richard A. Adams Jr., 21. Gardner shot and killed Miller and Adams during a robbery in December 1982. "I had shot Richard Adams in his face. I remember Kim Miller begging me not to shoot her, but I wasn't myself for a few minutes. But when things came clear to me I was standing over the bodies of Kim Miller and Richard Adams," Gardner wrote in his confession.

GARDNER, MARK	ARKANSAS	M	W	
GARDNER, RONNIE.L.	UTAH	M	W	

GARRETT, DANIEL R.   **TEXAS**   **M**   **W**

Daniel Garrett was convicted, with Karla Faye Tucker, 29, of participating in the 1983 pickax killings of Jerry Lynn Dean, 26, and Deborah Ruth Thornton, 32. Tucker is also on death row.

| GARY, CARLTON | GEORGIA | M | B | |
| GASKIN, LOUIS | FLORIDA | M | W | |

GATES, JOHNNY LEE   **GEORGIA**   **M**   **B**

Johnny Gates was convicted and sentenced to death for the shooting of Katrina Wright. In a videotape at the crime scene, Gates admitted to the rape, robbery and murder of Wright. Gates posed as a gas company employee to enter Wright's apartment, then pulled out a gun and raped the woman. He then demanded money from Wright, who gave him $480. Gates blindfolded, gagged and bound Wright then shot her in the right temple with a .32-caliber pistol.

GATES, OSCAR	CALIFORNIA	M	B	
GAY, KENNETH	CALIFORNIA	M	B	
GAY, YVETTE	NORTH CAROLINA	F	B	

GENTRY, JONATHAN LEE   **WASHINGTON**   **M**   **B**

Jonathan Gentry was convicted and sentenced to death for the 1988 murder of Cassis Holden.

GENTRY, KENNETH E.	TEXAS	M	W	
GEORGE, MICHAEL C.	VIRGINIA	M	W	
GERALDS, MARK	FLORIDA	M	W	
GERISCH, JOHN	OHIO	M	U	

GERLAUGH, DARRICK LEONARD   ARIZONA   M   N

On January 24, 1980, Darrick Gerlaugh, Joseph Encinas and Matthew Leisure decided to hitchhike from Chandler, Ariz., to Phoenix and rob whoever offered them a ride. Their victim turned out to be Scott Schwartz. Schwartz had a leg injury, wore a leg brace, and used crutches. At a deserted location on the outskirts of Mesa, the group attacked Schwartz. Gerlaugh had Encinas and Leisure hold Schwartz on the road while he drove the car over him several times. Gerlaugh positioned the left rear tire on Schwartz' body and revved the engine so the spinning wheel would kill him. When the victim still seemed to be alive, Gerlaugh and Leisure stabbed him 30 to 40 times in the head, neck and shoulders with a screwdriver. The killers hid Schwartz' body in a nearby field, took $36 from him, and left in his car. Gerlaugh and Encinas were convicted of the murder following a joint trial. Encinas received a life sentence. Leisure pled guilty to first-degree murder and also received a life sentence.

GHENT, DAVID	CALIFORNIA	M	A
GIBBS, DAVID E.	TEXAS	M	W
GIBBS, RENWICK	NORTH CAROLINA	M	B

GIBSON, EXZAVIOUS   GEORGIA   M   B

Exzavious Gibson was convicted and sentenced to death for the February 1990 murder and armed robbery of grocer Douglas Coley. Gibson, who said he was high on cocaine, marijuana and beer when he went to Coley's Grocery to buy soft drinks and cookies, stabbed Coley 39 times during the mid-day robbery.

GIBSON, RONALD	PENNSYLVANIA	M	B
GIBSON, THOMAS	IDAHO	M	W
GILBERT, LARRY	SOUTH CAROLINA	M	B
GILES, ARTHUR	ALABAMA	M	B
GILES, WILLIAM	MISSISSIPPI	M	B
GILLARD, JOHN	OHIO	M	W
GILLIAM, BURLEY	FLORIDA	M	W
GILLIAM, TYRONE	MARYLAND	M	B
GILLIARD, ROBERT	MISSISSIPPI	M	B

INMATE	STATE	SEX	RACE	JUVENILE

GILLIES, JESSE   **ARIZONA**   **M**   **W**

On January 29, 1981, Suzanne Rossetti locked herself out of her car at a Phoenix convenience store. Jesse James Gillies and Mike Logan helped her get into her car. To show her gratitude, Rossetti bought the men a six-pack of beer and offered them a ride to a riding stable where Gillies worked. En route, one of the men grabbed Rossetti, stopped the car, and pulled her to the ground where they both raped her. Gillies and Logan drove Rossetti to Papago Park and then to her apartment, raping her at both locations. The men rifled her purse and scavenged her apartment for valuables. The attackers ultimately pushed Rossetti from a cliff.

Then, gillies and Logan pursued their victim and found her still alive. Rossetti begged for mercy, told the men she was going to die anyway, and asked them to let her die in peace. The victim was then bashed on the head with rocks until she lost consciousness. Gillies and Logan covered her with rocks and drove back to Phoenix in her car. Logan pled guilty to first-degree murder in exchange for a life sentence.

GILREATH, FRED   **GEORGIA**   **M**   **W**

On May 11, 1979, Fred Gilreath stabbed Linda Van Leeuwen Gilreath and Gerrit Van Leeuwen to death. On February 29, 1980, Gilreath was convicted in Dodge County, Ga., of two counts of murder. Gilreath, now 53, awaits execution by electric chair on Georgia's Death Row.

GLEATON, J.D.   SOUTH CAROLINA   M   B

GLENN, JOHN   **OHIO**   **M**   **B**

On October 22, 1981, Deputy John Litch Jr. was escorting a prisoner, Robert Glenn, to the local hospital for treatment of a leg wound. In an effort to free his older brother from custody, 19-year-old John Glenn bumped into the rear of the car. When the officer got out and began walking toward the other car, he was shot to death by John Glenn.

The U.S. Supreme Court refused to hear Glenn's appeal on October 7, 1991.

GLOCK, ROBERT D.	FLORIDA	M	W
GOAD, WILLIAM W. JR.	TENNESSEE	M	W
GOLDEN, ANDREW	FLORIDA	M	W
GOLLEHON, WILLIAM	MONTANA	M	W
GONZALES, ERNEST	ARIZONA	M	H

INMATE	STATE	SEX	RACE	JUVENILE

GONZALEZ, JESSE **CALIFORNIA** **M** **H**

On May 29, 1979, Jesse Gonzalez shot Deputy Sheriff Jack Williams to death at the home of Gonzalez's parents. Williams and about a dozen other officers had gone to search the home after an alleged drug sale had occurred there.

INMATE	STATE	SEX	RACE
GOODMAN, SPENCER	TEXAS	M	W
GOODWIN, ALVIN U.	TEXAS	M	W
GORBY, OLEN	FLORIDA	M	W
GORBY, THOMAS	PENNSYLVANIA	M	W
GORDON, PATRICK	CALIFORNIA	M	W
GORE, DAVID	FLORIDA	M	W
GORE, MARSHALL	FLORIDA	M	W
GOSCH, LESLEY LEE	TEXAS	M	W
GOSIER, HARRY	ILLINOIS	M	B
GOSS, CORNELIUS A.	TEXAS	M	B
GRAHAM, HARRISON	PENNSYLVANIA	M	B
GRAHAM, MICHAEL	LOUISIANA	M	W
GRANDISON, ANTHONY	MARYLAND	M	B
GRANNIS, DAVID	ARIZONA	M	W
GRANT, RICHARD	CALIFORNIA	M	W
GRANT, ROSALIE	OHIO	F	B
GRANVIEL, KENNETH	TEXAS	M	B
GRAY, COLEMAN WAYNE	VIRGINIA	M	B
GRAY, MARIO L.	CALIFORNIA	M	B
GRAY, RONALD	FEDERAL	M	B
GRAYSON, DARRELL	ALABAMA	M	B
GREEN, ALPHONSO	FLORIDA	M	B
GREEN, ALTON GARNER	NORTH CAROLINA	M	W

GREEN, ANTHONY **SOUTH CAROLINA** **M** **B**

On November 21, 1987, 20-year-old Anthony Green robbed and then fatally shot 36-year-old Susan Barbara Babich in the head. The slaying occurred moments after the woman parked her car in a Charleston, S.C., mall parking lot. Green was arrested a half-hour later with a rifle and Babich's checkbook in his vehicle. In March 1990, Green lost his first round of appeals. His defense claimed that jurors with reservations about the death penalty should have been allowed to serve and that one potential juror should have been disqualified because he admitted to racial bias (Green is black and his victim was white). The jury rejected those claims. Green remains in the appeals process on South Carolina's Death Row.

GREEN, CROSLEY	FLORIDA	M	B

INMATE	STATE	SEX	RACE	JUVENILE
GREEN, ELIZABETH	OHIO	F	B	
GREEN, GARY	NORTH CAROLINA	M	W	
GREEN, HARVEY LEE	NORTH CAROLINA	M	B	
GREEN, MICHAEL	OKLAHOMA	M	W	
GREEN, RICKY	TEXAS	M	W	
GREEN, SAMUEL	PENNSYLVANIA	M	B	
GREENWALT, RANDY	ARIZONA	M	W	
GREENWAY, RICHARD H.	ARIZONA	M	W	
GREER, PAUL	OHIO	M	B	

| GRETZLER, DOUGLAS | ARIZONA | M | W | |

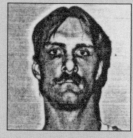

On November 3, 1973, Douglas Gretzler and Willie Luther Steelman escorted Michael Sandberg at gunpoint from the parking lot of his condominium complex into his home where his wife, Patricia, was studying. They bound and gagged the Sandbergs. When night fell, Gretzler shot Michael Sandberg, who was bound and lying on the bed. He then shot Patricia Sandberg in the head as she lay bound on the living room couch. Gretzler and Steelman then took the Sandbergs' credit cards, checks, a camera and their car, and left for California. Police apprehended Gretzler and Steelman there ending a crime spree that resulted in the deaths of at least nine people. Steelman was also convicted of first-degree murder and sentenced to death. He died in prison in 1987.

INMATE	STATE	SEX	RACE	JUVENILE
GRIBBLE, TIMOTHY L.	TEXAS	M	W	
GRIER, ERIC J.	PENNSYLVANIA	M	B	
GRIFFIN, DONALD	CALIFORNIA	M	W	
GRIFFIN, EVAN	ILLINOIS	M	B	
GRIFFIN, HENRY	ILLINOIS	M	B	
GRIFFIN, JEFFERY L.	TEXAS	M	B	
GRIFFIN, KENNETH	FLORIDA	M	B	
GRIFFIN, LARRY	MISSOURI	M	B	
GRIFFIN, MICHAEL	FLORIDA	M	W	
GRIFFIN, MILTON	MISSOURI	M	B	
GRIFFIN, REGINALD	MISSOURI	M	B	
GRIFFIN, RODNEY	PENNSYLVANIA	M	B	
GROOVER, TOMMY	FLORIDA	M	W	
GROSECLOSE, WILLIAM	TENNESSEE	M	W	
GROSSMAN, MARTIN EDWARD	FLORIDA	M	W	
GRUBBS, RICKY LEE	MISSOURI	M	W	
GUERRA, RICARDO A.	TEXAS	M	H	
GUEST, ANTHONY	ILLINOIS	M	B	
GUINAN, FRANK	MISSOURI	M	W	
GUNSBY, DONALD	FLORIDA	M	B	
GUNTER, JAMES LEE	TEXAS	M	W	
GURLEY, WILSON	ALABAMA	M	B	
GURULE, RAYMOND	CALIFORNIA	M	N	
GUTIEREZ, ISAAC	CALIFORNIA	M	H	
GUTIERREZ, JESSE	TEXAS	M	H	
GUTIERREZ, JOSE	TEXAS	M	H	

INMATE	STATE	SEX	RACE	JUVENILE

GUY, CURTIS　　　　　**NEVADA**　　　**M**　　**B**

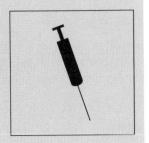

In 1990, Curtis Guy, 24, killed a Las Vegas transient who helped him buy drugs. Guy's partner, Larry Pendleton received life without parole for the shooting. Guy, a native of Kentucky, argued his case in January 1992 during an appeal to the Nevada Supreme Court.

HAAG, RANDY　　　　　PENNSYLVANIA　　M　　W

HABERSTROH, RICHARD　　**NEVADA**　　**M**　　**W**

In 1986, in the early morning hours, Donna Marie Kitowski was abducted from the parking lot of a supermarket in Las Vegas, Nev. Richard Haberstroh, a former Las Vegas mechanic, kidnapped, robbed and sexually assaulted Kitowski before killing her. Haberstroh was convicted October 13, 1987, of killing the 20-year-old mother and was given the death sentence. His case remains in the Nevada appeals process.

HACHETT, RICHARD　　　　PENNSYLVANIA　　M　　W

HAFDAHL, RANDAL WAYNE　　**TEXAS**　　**M**　　**W**

On November 11, 1985, Sgt. James Mitchell of the Amarillo (Texas) Police Department was on his way home from work, still dressed in uniform, when he was gunned down by Randall Wayne Hafdahl. The officer was approaching a car—that had left an expressway, jumped the access road and slammed through a fence before stopping in the back yard of a home—when the shooting occurred. Hafdahl was charged with capital murder because Mitchell was acting in the line of duty. Hafdahl remains in the appeals process awaiting his execution by lethal injection on Texas' Death Row.

HAIN, SCOTT	OKLAHOMA	M	W	*
HAKIM, YAQUB	FLORIDA	M	B	
HALE, ALVIE	OKLAHOMA	M	W	
HALE, THOMAS	TENNESSEE	M	B	
HALEY, KEVIN	CALIFORNIA	M	B	

INMATE	STATE	SEX	RACE	JUVENILE

HALIBURTON, JERRY FLORIDA **M** **B**

Jerry Haliburton was twice convicted and sentenced to death for the August 1981 burglary and murder of Donald Bohannon. Haliburton was first convicted in 1983, yet was granted a second trial because police officers refused to let Haliburton see his lawyer after his arrest. His second trial was held in January 1988 and again Haliburton was convicted and sentenced to death. Testimony from Haliburton's half-brother, Freddie, said Haliburton killed Bohannon "just to see if he had the nerve." Haliburton stabbed Bohannon 31 times while Bonhannon slept.

INMATE	STATE	SEX	RACE
HALL, ANTHONY	ILLINOIS	M	B
HALL, CARL	LOUISIANA	M	B
HALL, DENNIS	GEORGIA	M	B
HALL, DONALD	PENNSYLVANIA	M	B
HALL, FREDDIE	FLORIDA	M	B
HALL, LARRY	SOUTH CAROLINA	M	U
HALL, LEROY	TENNESSEE	M	W
HALL, WILLIAM	TENNESSEE	M	W
HALL, WILLIE JAMES	GEORGIA	M	B
HALLFORD, PHILLIP	ALABAMA	M	W
HALVORSEN, ARTHUR	CALIFORNIA	M	W
HALVORSEN, LEIF	KENTUCKY	M	W
HAMBLIN, DAVID	OHIO	M	W

HAMILTON, BERNARD CALIFORNIA **M** **B**

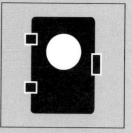

Bernard Hamilton was convicted of murdering Eleanore Buchanan in 1979. She was last seen alive walking toward her van in a parking lot after a college class. Her body was found, with its head and arms cut off, next to a road. Hamilton, then 28, was arrested eight days later in Oklahoma. Police tracked him down in Buchanan's van after he used Buchanan's credit cards. A jury found him guilty of first-degree murder, burglary, robbery and kidnapping and sentenced him to death.

INMATE	STATE	SEX	RACE
HAMILTON, BILLY RAY	CALIFORNIA	M	W
HAMILTON, MARCUS	LOUISIANA	M	B
HAMILTON, MICHAEL	CALIFORNIA	M	W
HAMILTON, THEWELL	FLORIDA	M	W
HAMILTON, TOMMY	ALABAMA	M	W
HAMILTON, WILLIAM	LOUISIANA	M	B
HAMM, DOYLE LEE	ALABAMA	M	W
HAMMON, RICHARD	OKLAHOMA	M	B
HAMMOND, EMMANUEL	GEORGIA	M	B
HAMMOND, JERRY	ALABAMA	M	B
HAMMOND, KARL	TEXAS	M	B

INMATE	STATE	SEX	RACE	JUVENILE

HAMPTON, LLOYD   ILLINOIS   M   W

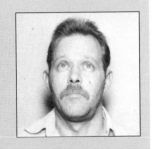

Lloyd Hampton was convicted and sentenced to death for the 1990 murder of 69-year-old Roy "Jasper" Pendleton. Hampton confessed to police that he killed Pendleton during a robbery because he did not want to risk capture by the police. Details of Pendleton's murder showed Hampton physically and psychologically tortured him: Hampton plunged a chef's knife repeatedly around the victim's head; he burned the victim's eyelid with a cigarette; he bound the victim's mouth, wrists and ankles with black tape, then "hogtied" Pendleton with a dog's leash before killing him with the knife. Hampton has prior convictions of robbery and assault with a deadly weapon. "My problem is, always has been, I don't give a damn," he said.

HANCE, WILLIAM HENRY   GEORGIA   M   B

HANEY, JUDY   ALABAMA   F   W

Judy Haney was sentenced to death November 18, 1988, for hiring a killer to murder her husband. She now spends much of her time on death row training a pet cockatiel.

HANNON, PATRICK	FLORIDA	M	W
HANSEN, TRACY	MISSISSIPPI	M	W
HAPP, WILLIAM	FLORIDA	M	W
HARBASON, EDWARD	TENNESSEE	M	B
HARDCASTLE, DONALD	PENNSYLVANIA	M	B

HARDING, DONALD   ARIZONA   M   W

Donald Harding, probably posing as a security guard, entered the Phoenix motel room of Allan Gage. Harding bound the victim's hands and feet with adhesive tape and stuffed a gag in his mouth. He then took Gage's wallet and identification, stole his car, and drove to Tucson. Gage was left lying face down on the floor of the motel room, where he died from asphyxiation. Harding used the same security guard ruse to kill and rob two men in a Tucson motel. Harding was arrested in Flagstaff two days later, and was in possession of Gage's wallet and identification.

INMATE	STATE	SEX	RACE	JUVENILE

HARDISON, RICHARD NEVADA **M** **B**

In 1986, 34-year-old Richard Hardison shot Pete Johnson, 42, to death. A motive was never established. The case of Hardison, who was born in Las Vegas, is under review in federal court.

INMATE	STATE	SEX	RACE	JUVENILE
HARDWICK, JOHN G.	FLORIDA	M	W	
HARDWICK, KENNETH	FLORIDA	M	W	
HARDY, JAMES	CALIFORNIA	M	W	
HARJO, GERALD	OKLAHOMA	M	N	
HARPER, EDDIE LEE	KENTUCKY	M	W	
HARRELL, ED	ALABAMA	M	B	
HARRIES, RONALD	TENNESSEE	M	W	

HARRIS, BENJAMIN WASHINGTON **M** **B**

Benjamin Harris was convicted and sentenced to death for the contract killing of Jimmy Turner June 14, 1984.

INMATE	STATE	SEX	RACE	JUVENILE
HARRIS, CURTIS PAUL	TEXAS	M	B	*
HARRIS, DANNY RAY	TEXAS	M	B	
HARRIS, DAVID R.	TEXAS	M	W	
HARRIS, EDWARD	TENNESSEE	M	W	
HARRIS, GEORGE	MISSOURI	M	B	
HARRIS, JAMES	ILLINOIS	M	B	
HARRIS, KENNETH B.	TEXAS	M	B	

HARRIS, LOUISE ALABAMA **F** **B**

Louise Harris hired three hitmen to kill her husband, Sgt. Isaiah Harris, a Montgomery County jailer. Sgt. Harris was shot to death with a 12-guage shotgun in March 1988. Mrs. Harris wanted her husband dead to collect money from a life insurance policy.

INMATE	STATE	SEX	RACE	JUVENILE
HARRIS, THEODORE	FLORIDA	M	B	
HARRIS, TIMOTHY	TENNESSEE	M	B	
HARRIS, VON M.	CALIFORNIA	M	B	
HARRISON, HENRY LEE	MISSISSIPPI	M	B	
HARRISON, JAMES	INDIANA	M	W	*
HART, GARY	ALABAMA	M	B	
HART, JOSEPH	CALIFORNIA	M	W	
HARTMAN, EDDIE	TENNESSEE	M	W	
HARVEY, HAROLD	FLORIDA	M	W	

HASKET, RANDY	CALIFORNIA	M	B

In 1978, Randy Haskett attacked his-half sister, Gwendolyn Rose, and murdered her two children, 11-year-old Keith, and his 4-year-old brother, Cameron. She survived to testify against Haskett. His original death sentence was overturned on appeal, but it has since been reinstated by another jury.

HATCH, STEVEN	OKLAHOMA	M	W
HATCHER, RICKY	GEORGIA	M	W
HATHORN, GENE WILFORD	TEXAS	M	W
HATTAWAY, MARK	LOUISIANA	M	W
HAWKINS, DON	OKLAHOMA	M	W
HAWKINS, EARL	ILLINOIS	M	B
HAWKINS, JEFFREY	CALIFORNIA	M	W

HAWKINS, SAMUEL	TEXAS	M	B

On Feb. 2, 1976, 12-year-old Rhonda DeAnn Keys was abducted, raped and murdered. Her body was found a week later lying in a concrete culvert with her hands tied behind her back and a pillowcase over her head. She died of head injuries.

On May 3, 1977, 19-year-old Abbe Rodgers Hamilton, a housewife who was six months pregnant with her first child, was stabbed as many as 20 times with a butcher knife. Samuel Christopher Hawkins was convicted of both murders and given two death sentences. He was given a life prison term for another 1976 rape. His case is currently in the appeals process.

HAWKINS, SHAWN L.	OHIO	M	B
HAWKINS, THOMAS	PENNSYLVANIA	M	B
HAWTHORNE, ANDERSON	CALIFORNIA	M	B
HAYES, BLUFFORD	CALIFORNIA	M	B
HAYES, CLARENCE	ILLINOIS	M	B

INMATE	STATE	SEX	RACE	JUVENILE
HAYES, ROBERT	FLORIDA	M	B	
HAYES, ROGER D.	OKLAHOMA	M	W	
HAYES, ROYAL	CALIFORNIA	M	W	
HAYES, TONY	FLORIDA	M	B	

HAYS, HENRY   **ALABAMA**   **M**   **W**

Henry Hays, a former Ku Klux Klansman, was sentenced to die in Alabama's electric chair for the 1981 kidnapping and murder of Michael Donald. Donald, a black, had been abducted from downtown Mobile, Ala., forced into a car at gunpoint, and taken to a wooded area where he was stabbed and beaten. After he was dead, Hays and an accomplice put Donald's body in the trunk of a car. Hays then cut Donald's throat, and the two tied a noose around his neck and brought him back to Mobile, where he was hanged from a tree.

HAYS, THOMAS	OKLAHOMA	M	W	
HEATH, RONALD	FLORIDA	M	W	
HEATWOLE, GEORGE	NORTH CAROLINA	M	W	
HEDGEPETH, ROLAND	NORTH CAROLINA	M	W	
HEIDNIK, GARY	PENNSYLVANIA	M	W	

HEINEY, ROBERT   **FLORIDA**   **M**   **W**

Robert Heiney was convicted and sentenced to die for the June 1978 slaying of Francis May Jr., who was beaten to death with a hammer. May's body was found near an interstate highway a day after witnesses saw Heiney and May together in Mississippi.

HEISHMAN, HARVEY	CALIFORNIA	M	W	
HENDERSON, CURTIS L.	ALABAMA	M	B	
HENDERSON, DEMETRIUS	ILLINOIS	M	B	
HENDERSON, JEROME	OHIO	M	B	
HENDERSON, JERRY	ALABAMA	M	W	
HENDERSON, ROBERT D.	FLORIDA	M	W	
HENDERSON, WILBUR	ARKANSAS	M	W	
HENDRICKS, EDGAR	CALIFORNIA	M	B	
HENDRICKS, ROBERT	FLORIDA	M	W	
HENLEY, STEVE	TENNESSEE	M	W	

HENRY, GRAHAM   ARIZONA   M   W

On June 6, 1986, at approximately 3 p.m., Graham Henry and Vernon Foote kidnapped Roy Estes from his Las Vegas apartment. The two men forced Estes into his truck and drove off with him. Estes, an elderly man, was partially paralyzed and used a walker. Henry and Foote took Estes to a desert area approximately 40 miles north of Kingman, Ariz., where they cut his throat and stabbed him in the heart. After hiding Estes' body behind a bush, Henry and Foote drove back to Highway 93. At approximately 5 p.m., police officers stopped Henry, who was driving the wrong way on the highway. Henry gave the police a false name and was arrested for drunk driving. On June 8, 1986, after learning Henry's true name and that Estes was missing, the police questioned Henry about Estes' whereabouts. Henry immediately blamed Foote for killing Estes and led police to the body. In a separate trial, Foote was convicted of robbery and theft, but the jury could not reach a verdict on the murder charge. Foote later pleaded guilty to attempted first-degree murder.

HENRY, IAN   MARYLAND   M   B

On Jan. 22, 1988, Ian George Henry and three other men went to an apartment with the intention of killing Leonard "Chief" Francis, the head of a drug gang. In an attempt to steal his money, Francis, three other men and one woman were shot to death. Another woman survived by pretending to be dead, after she was shot in the neck. Henry's death sentence was upheld Oct. 11, 1991.

INMATE	STATE	SEX	RACE
HENRY, JOSEPH	PENNSYLVANIA	M	B
HENRY, ROBERT	FLORIDA	M	B
HERMAN, DAVID	TEXAS	M	W
HERNANDEZ, ADOLPH	TEXAS	M	H
HERNANDEZ, FRANCIS	CALIFORNIA	M	H
HERNANDEZ, JESUS C.	CALIFORNIA	M	H
HERNANDEZ, JUAN	TEXAS	M	H
HERNANDEZ, MIGUEL	FLORIDA	M	H
HERNANDEZ, RODOLFO B.	TEXAS	M	H
HERNANDEZ, ROGELIO	TEXAS	M	H
HERRERA JR., WILLIAM	ARIZONA	M	H
HERRERA SR., WILLIAM	ARIZONA	M	H
HERRERA, LEONEL T.	TEXAS	M	H
HERRERA, MICHAEL	ARIZONA	M	H
HERRING, TED	FLORIDA	M	B
HICKS, DAVID	TEXAS	M	B
HICKS, JOHN	OHIO	M	B
HICKS, ROBERT KARL	GEORGIA	M	W

INMATE	STATE	SEX	RACE	JUVENILE

HIGH, JOSE GEORGIA M B

In 1978, Jose High was convicted of the murder of 11-year-old Bonnie Bulloch. High, the self-proclaimed mastermind of the crime family "Death Struck," had been previously charged with murdering Willina Hall and Leroy Linwood in August 1976, but was never prosecuted. High, now 32, is in the appeals process.

| HIGHTOWER, BOBBY RAY | NORTH CAROLINA | M | B |
| HIGHTOWER, JACINTO | NEW JERSEY | M | B |

HIGHTOWER, JOHN GEORGIA M B

John Hightower was convicted and sentenced to death for the 1987 slayings of his wife and her two daughters. Dorothy Hightower and her daughters Sandra and Evelyn Reaves were shot with a pistol that Hightower said he purchased because he and his wife were having marital problems.

HILDWIN, PAUL	FLORIDA	M	W
HILL, ALVIN	MISSISSIPPI	M	B
HILL, CLARENCE	ARIZONA	M	W

HILL, CLARENCE FLORIDA M B

Clarence Hill was convicted and sentenced to death for the October 1982 shooting death of Florida police officer Stephen Allen Taylor during a savings and loan robbery. Hill's accomplice in the robbery had been apprehended by Taylor and another officer, who were trying to handcuff him, when Hill approached them from behind and shot both officers. Hill killed Taylor, but the other officer, who was shot in the neck, managed to shoot Hill five times.

HILL, DANNY	OHIO	M	B
HILL, DARRELL	ARKANSAS	M	W
HILL, DONETTA	PENNSYLVANIA	F	B
HILL, GENESIS	OHIO	M	B

INMATE	STATE	SEX	RACE	JUVENILE

HILL, JAMES E.   **NEVADA**   **M**   **B**

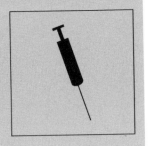

In 1983, Hill, 29, raped and killed wheelchair-bound Antonia Matthews, 56. The Mississippi native was sentenced to death for the crime. Hill is appealing to the Nevada Supreme Court for a second time.

HILL, MACK O.	TEXAS	M	W
HILL, MICHAEL	CALIFORNIA	M	B
HILL, SHAWN	CALIFORNIA	M	B

HILL, WALTER   **ALABAMA**   **M**   **B**

Walter Hill was 42 in 1977, but that did not keep him from wanting to marry the 13-year-old daughter of Mrs. Willie Mae Hammock, 60. Hammock refused her consent so Hill pulled out his .32-caliber pistol and shot Hammock in the back of the head while she was reaching into a closet. Hill then ran into the dining room and killed John Tatum, Hammock's 36-year-old son. When Lois Tatum, John's wife, returned from the bathroom, Hill chased her around the house and fatally shot her. Hill then abducted the 13-year-old, and was eventually captured by North Carolina police. Hill has resided on death row since convicted of the three killings in 1977.

| HILL, WARREN | GEORGIA | M | B |
| HILL, ZANE B. | NORTH CAROLINA | M | W |

HINCHEY, JOHN   **ARIZONA**   **M**   **W**

On October 29, 1985, John Hinchey and his common-law wife of 12 years, Marlyn Bechtel, got into an argument. After Marlyn had gone into the living room to sleep, Hinchey came in with a gun he had purchased that day, and shot Marlyn four times. He then ran to the bedroom where Marlyn's 17-year-old daughter, Tammy, was sleeping. Tammy's infant son, Nicholas, was sleeping beside her. Hinchey kicked in the door and shot Tammy in the face. Hinchey found out that Marlyn had run outside. He caught her and hit her over the head with the gun until he broke the gun. Then he picked up a rock and hit her. When he returned to the house, he heard Tammy moaning. He hit her in the face with a glass bottle until it shattered. He then grabbed a butcher knife from the kitchen and stabbed her several times, leaving the blade protruding from her stomach. Tammy died, Nicholas was unhurt, and Marlyn survived. Hinchey originally pled guilty to avoid the death penalty, but the trial court set aside his plea at his request.

| HINES, ANTHONY | TENNESSEE | M | W |

INMATE	STATE	SEX	RACE	JUVENILE
HINES, BOBBY	TEXAS	M	W	
HINES, GARY	CALIFORNIA	M	W	
HINTON, ANTHONY	ALABAMA	M	B	
HITCHCOCK, JAMES E.	FLORIDA	M	W	
HITCHINGS, KEITH	CALIFORNIA	M	W	
HITTLE, DANIEL	TEXAS	M	W	
HOBLEY, MADISON	ILLINOIS	M	B	
HOCHSTEIN, PETER	NEBRASKA	M	W	
HODGES, GEORGE M.	FLORIDA	M	W	
HODGES, HENRY	TENNESSEE	M	W	
HOEFERT, ROBERT	FLORIDA	M	W	
HOFFMAN, BARRY	FLORIDA	M	W	
HOFFMAN, MAXWELL	IDAHO	M	W	
HOGAN, KENNETH	OKLAHOMA	M	W	

HOGAN, MICHAEL	**NEVADA**	**M**	**W**	

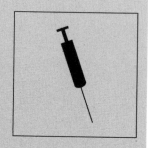

Hogan was sentenced to death for killing his live-in girlfriend, Heidi Hinckley, 39, and wounding her daughter, Shelly Brown, 16, after an argument in Las Vegas in 1984. Hogan, 43, an Iowa native, is arguing his case in district court.

HOGUE, JERRY L.	TEXAS	M	W	
HOKE, RONALD L.	VIRGINIA	M	W	
HOLDEN, RUSSELL	NORTH CAROLINA	M	B	
HOLIDAY, DALLAS	GEORGIA	M	B	

HOLLADAY, GLENN	**ALABAMA**	**M**	**W**	

Glenn Holladay was convicted on June 26, 1987, of the August 25, 1986, killings of his ex-wife, Rebecca Ledbetter Holladay, 31; her boyfriend, William David Robinson, 25; and a neighbor, Larry D. Thomas, Jr., 16. His death sentence was upheld in May 1989 by the Alabama Supreme Court.

HOLLAND, ALBERT	FLORIDA	M	B	
HOLLAND, DAVID L.	TEXAS	M	W	
HOLLAND, GERALD	MISSISSIPPI	M	W	
HOLLAND, JAMES	UTAH	M	W	
HOLLAND, WILLIAM	PENNSYLVANIA	M	W	
HOLLOWAY, ALLEN	OHIO	M	W	

INMATE	STATE	SEX	RACE	JUVENILE
HOLLOWAY, ARNOLD	PENNSYLVANIA	M	B	
HOLLOWAY, DUANE	CALIFORNIA	M	B	
HOLMAN, TAFFORD	ILLINOIS	M	B	
HOLMES, JAMES W.	ARKANSAS	M	W	
HOLT, JOHN LEE	CALIFORNIA	M	B	
HOLTON, RUDOLPH	FLORIDA	M	B	

HOMICK, STEVEN **NEVADA** **M** **W**

Steven Homick was convicted and sentenced to death for the 1985 murder of three people during a residential robbery. Homick forced the 50-year-old resident to provide the keys to a floor safe, then shot her and her maid, in the head. When the doorbell rang, Homick opened the front door, pulled a delivery man inside and shot him in the head twice.

HOOD, CHARLES	TEXAS	M	W	
HOOKER, JOHN	OKLAHOMA	M	B	
HOOKS, DANNY	OHIO	M	W	
HOOKS, JOSEPH	ALABAMA	M	W	
HOOKS, VICTOR	OKLAHOMA	M	B	
HOOPER, HAROLD	FLORIDA	M	W	

HOOPER, MURRAY **ARIZONA** **M** **B**

During the last months of 1980, Robert Cruz decided to have William Patrick Redmond murdered. To carry out the murder, Cruz hired William Bracy and Murray Hooper from Chicago and Edward Lonzo McCall, a former Phoenix police officer. On the evening of December 31, 1980, Bracy, Hooper, and McCall went to the Redmond home in Phoenix. Redmond, his wife Marilyn, and his mother-in-law Helen Phelps were at home preparing for a New Year's Eve party. The three men entered the house at gunpoint and forced the victims into the master bedroom. After taking jewelry and money, the killers bound and gagged the victims and made them lie face down on the bed. They then shot each victim in the head and also slashed Mr. Redmond's throat. Mr. Redmond and Mrs. Phelps died from their wounds, but Mrs. Redmond survived. Cruz and McCall were convicted of the murders following a joint trial. Cruz' conviction was reversed on appeal, but he was again convicted after two mistrials.

HOPE, EDGAR	ILLINOIS	M	B	

INMATE	STATE	SEX	RACE	JUVENILE
HORSLEY, EDWARD	ALABAMA	M	B	
HORTON, JAMES	CALIFORNIA	M	B	
HOUGH, KEVIN	INDIANA	M	W	
HOUSE, PAUL G.	TENNESSEE	M	W	
HOUSEL, TRACEY L.	GEORGIA	M	W	

HOUSEL, TRACEY L.	**GEORGIA**	**M**	**W**	

On April 7, 1985, Tracey Lee Housel murdered Jean Dellinger Drew. On February 7, 1986, Housel was convicted in Gwinnett County, Ga., of murder (strangulation and beating about head with a blunt instrument), rape and motor vehicle theft. Housel, now 33, awaits execution by electric chair on Georgia's Death Row.

HOUSTON, RICHARD	TENNESSEE	M	B	
HOVARTER, JACKIE R.	CALIFORNIA	M	W	
HOVEY, RICHARD	CALIFORNIA	M	W	
HOWARD, ALBERT	CALIFORNIA	M	B	
HOWARD, GARY	CALIFORNIA	M	W	
HOWARD, MELVIN K.	PENNSYLVANIA	M	B	

HOWARD, RONNIE	**SOUTH CAROLINA**	**M**	**B**	

Ronnie Howard and an accomplice were convicted in the August 1985 murder of Chinh Lee, a Vietnamese woman who authorities said had died of suffocation after a plastic bag had been tied around her head. Howard and another accomplice had been earlier convicted of the similar suffocation murder of another woman. In that case, Howard and his accomplice both received life sentences.

HOWARD, SAMUEL	**NEVADA**	**M**	**B**	

In 1980, Howard, 43, asked to test drive a van George Monahan, 39, was selling. During the encounter, Howard killed Monahan. Howard, a New York native, was sentenced to death. Howard is appealing his case in federal court.

HOWARD, STANLEY	ILLINOIS	M	B	

INMATE	STATE	SEX	RACE	JUVENILE
HOWELL, FRANKLIN	NORTH CAROLINA	M	W	
HOWELL, MICHAEL	OKLAHOMA	M	W	
HOWELL, MICHAEL W.	TENNESSEE	M	N	
HOWERY, BERNON	ILLINOIS	M	B	
HUBBARD, J.B.	ALABAMA	M	W	
HUDSON, DAVID	OHIO	M	W	
HUDSON, RENALDO	ILLINOIS	M	B	
HUDSON, TIMOTHY	FLORIDA	M	B	
HUFF, EVERETT R.	NORTH CAROLINA	M	W	
HUFF, JAMES	FLORIDA	M	W	
HUFFMAN, RICHARD	INDIANA	M	W	
HUFFSTETLER, DAVID	NORTH CAROLINA	M	W	
HUGHES, BILLY G.	TEXAS	M	W	
HUGHES, JAKE	ARIZONA	M	B	
HUGHES, KEVIN	PENNSYLVANIA	M	B	*

HUGHES, KRISTIN W.	**CALIFORNIA**	**M**	**W**	

On September 7, 1989, 31-year-old Kim Hickman was stabbed to death in her apartment. Kristin Hughes, on parole from a residential burglary conviction, entered a half-open door and attacked Hickman. She was stabbed 11 times, strangled and sexually assaulted.

HUGHES, PRESTON	TEXAS	M	B	
HUGHES, ROBERT	PENNSYLVANIA	M	W	

HULSEY, DEWAYNE	**ARKANSAS**	**M**	**W**	

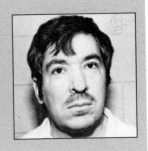

Dewayne Hulsey, now the senior inmate of Arkansas' death row, was convicted and sentenced to death for the 1975 killing of Johnny A. Easley Jr., a service station attendant. Hulsey shot Easley seven times during a robbery.

HUMPHREY, JACKIE	OKLAHOMA	M	W	
HUNT, DEIDRE	FLORIDA	F	W	
HUNT, FLINT	MARYLAND	M	B	
HUNT, HENRY LEE	NORTH CAROLINA	M	N	
HUNTER, BERT	MISSOURI	M	W	
HUNTER, JAMES	KENTUCKY	M	W	
HUNTER, MICHAEL	CALIFORNIA	M	W	
HUNTER, THOMAS	OKLAHOMA	M	W	

INMATE	STATE	SEX	RACE	JUVENILE
HURLEY, RANDY D.	TENNESSEE	M	W	
HUTCHINSON, EDWARD	TENNESSEE	M	W	
HUTTON, PERCY	OHIO	M	B	
INGRAM, NICHOLAS	GEORGIA	M	W	
IRICK, BILLY R.	TENNESSEE	M	W	
IRVIN, THOMAS	MISSOURI	M	W	
IRVING, JOHN BUFORD	MISSISSIPPI	M	B	
ISA, MARIA	MISSOURI	F	H	
ISA, VEIN	MISSOURI	M	A	

ISAACS, CARL	**GEORGIA**	**M**	**W**

In 1973, a bungled burglary at a mobile home resulted in the death of six family members. Gang members brutally killed Ned Alday; his brother Aubrey Alday; Ned's sons Jerry, Chester and Jimmy Alday; and Jerry's wife, Mary Alday, who was also raped in the attack. Carl Isaacs, convicted in 1973 and again in a 1988 retrial, was given six death sentences for the slayings. Isaacs' stepbrother, Wayne Coleman, and Coleman's prison buddy, George Dungee, were sentenced to six life terms. A fourth gang member, Isaacs' brother Billy, pleaded guilty to lesser charges and testified in both the 1973 and the 1988 trials. On November 30, 1989, the Georgia Supreme Court upheld Isaacs' six murder convictions and death sentences.

ISOM, JAMES M.	OREGON	M	W	
IVEY, BEN	IDAHO	M	W	
JACKSON, ANDRE	OHIO	M	B	
JACKSON, ANDREA H.	FLORIDA	F	B	
JACKSON, CARL	FLORIDA	M	B	
JACKSON, DONALD	INDIANA	M	W	

JACKSON, DOUGLAS	**FLORIDA**	**M**	**B**

Douglas Jackson was convicted and sentenced to death for murdering Walter Washington of Miami; his pregnant wife, Edna Manuel; their children, Terrence, 4, and Reggie, 14 months; and a friend, Larry Finney. The murders took place February 28, 1981, in a remote area of Florida. Jackson's ex-wife Karen testified Jackson forced the five into an abandoned car. He shot the adults then torched the car, leaving the children to be burned alive.

JACKSON, EARL	CALIFORNIA	M	B	
JACKSON, ETHERIA	FLORIDA	M	B	
JACKSON, HENRY C.	MISSISSIPPI	M	B	
JACKSON, KENNETH	ALABAMA	M	B	

JACKSON, LAWRENCE ILLINOIS M B

Described as "290 pounds of pure evil" by prosecutors during his trial, Lawrence Jackson was convicted of killing four people, including 4-year-old Dana Winder, during a home robbery in 1986. According to testimony, Jackson and an accomplice, Bobby Driskel, 29, were smoking cocaine the night of the slayings, but ran out of drugs and money. The two decided to kill 22-year-old Mark Brown, a cousin of Driskel. The other victims were Brown's fiancee, Vernita Winder, 22, and a friend of the couple, Shirley Martin, 23. A key witness against Jackson was Winder's 6-year-old daughter, Urica, who was stabbed 48 times, but survived by pretending to be dead. Jackson, now 28, received a death sentence and Driskel was sentenced to life in prison.

JACKSON, MICHAEL CALIFORNIA M B

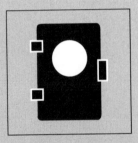

Michael Jackson was convicted and sentenced to death for shooting Kenneth Wrede, a California police officer, with the officer's shotgun on Aug. 31, 1983. Officer Wrede, on patrol by himself, had responded to a report of a man acting strangely. He found Jackson at an intersection. When Wrede tried to detain him, Jackson went berserk and the two struggled. The officer ran to his patrol car to call for assistance, but Jackson followed him, reached into the passenger side of the car and grabbed the 12-gauge shotgun. Wrede drew his revolver, and the two men aimed their weapons at each other across the roof of the patrol car. After a brief stand-off, Jackson fired the shotgun, striking Wrede in the head.

JACKSON, NOEL	CALIFORNIA	M	B
JACKSON, RONALD	FLORIDA	M	B
JACKSON, TOMMY RAY	TEXAS	M	B

JACKSON, WILLIE ALABAMA M B

Willie "Billy Boy" Jackson, confessed to killing Elmo Roberts, 87, in February 1989. Jackson said he was "broke, disgusted, and high as a kite" when he went to borrow money from Roberts, whom Jackson called "Pops." Jackson said Pops lent him money on prior occasions and also drove Jackson around town. On February 3, 1989, Jackson entered Pops' apartment, grabbed an iron used for a doorstop and struck Pops on the head. Pops remained alert and wrestled with Jackson, until Jackson grabbed a pair of scissors and slashed Pops' wrists and then his jugular vein. Jackson said he didn't want Pops to suffer, so he took a broom handle and slammed it across Pops' neck with enough force to break the handle. Although a jury recommended Jackson receive life in prison without parole, Circuit Judge Gary McAiley overruled their recommendation and sentenced Jackson to death. "The victim suffered substantial pain before he ultimately died," said McAiley, adding that the murder of Pops Roberts by Billy Boy Jackson was "the most heinous, atrocious, cruel" crime he has ever presided over.

INMATE	STATE	SEX	RACE	JUVENILE
JACOBS, BRUCE C.	TEXAS	M	W	
JACOBS, CLAWVERN	KENTUCKY	M	W	
JACOBS, JESSE D.	TEXAS	M	W	
JAMES, ANTONIO	LOUISIANA	M	B	
JAMES, DAVIDSON	FLORIDA	M	B	
JAMES, JOHNNY	TEXAS	M	W	

JAMES, STEVEN   **ARIZONA**   **M**   **W**

On November 16, 1981, Juan Maya picked up 14-year-old James Norton and made homosexual advances towards him. Norton rebuffed Maya, but suggested that he might find a more hospitable reception in a trailer belonging to Steven James. When Maya followed Norton into the trailer, James, Lawrence Libberton, and Norton took turns beating him. The three then forced Maya into the backseat of his own car and drove toward Salome, Ariz. where James' parents owned some property that included an abandoned mine shaft. En route, a police officer stopped them but Libberton threatened to kill Maya if he attempted to draw the officer's attention. After arriving at the Salome property around dawn, James ordered Maya to step up to the mine shaft. As Maya pleaded for his life, James shot at him from a distance of less than five feet. Maya charged James and tried to get the gun, so Libberton and Norton began striking Maya with large rocks and a board. They then dragged Maya to the mine shaft and threw him in, dropping rocks and railroad ties on top of him. Norton pled guilty to several charges and testified against Libberton and James.

INMATE	STATE	SEX	RACE	JUVENILE
JAMES, TERRENCE	OKLAHOMA	M	N	
JAMES, VINCENT	INDIANA	M	B	
JAMISON, DERRICK	OHIO	M	B	
JANECKA, ALLEN W.	TEXAS	M	W	
JANES, RON	ILLINOIS	M	W	
JARRELL, DAVID	GEORGIA	M	W	
JARRELLS, JONATHEN	GEORGIA	M	W	
JASPER, ALFRED	PENNSYLVANIA	M	B	
JAYNES, JAMES	NORTH CAROLINA	M	W	
JEFFERS, JIMMY	ARIZONA	M	W	
JEFFERSON, ALBERT	ALABAMA	M	B	
JEFFERSON, LAWRENCE	GEORGIA	M	B	

JEFFRIES, PATRICK   **WASHINGTON**   **M**   **W**

Patrick Jeffries was convicted and sentenced to death for the 1983 murders of Phil and Inez Skiff.

INMATE	STATE	SEX	RACE	JUVENILE
JELLS, REGINALD	OHIO	M	B	
JENKINS, ARTHUR	VIRGINIA	M	W	
JENKINS, DANIEL	CALIFORNIA	M	B	
JENKINS, LEO	TEXAS	M	W	
JENKINS, LEONARD	OHIO	M	B	
JENKINS, MARK	ALABAMA	M	H	
JENKINS, WILLIAM	MISSISSIPPI	M	W	
JENNINGS, BRYAN	FLORIDA	M	W	
JENNINGS, MICHAEL	CALIFORNIA	M	W	
JENNINGS, PATRICIA	NORTH CAROLINA	F	W	
JENNINGS, ROBERT M.	TEXAS	M	B	
JENNINGS, WILBUR	CALIFORNIA	M	B	
JERMYN, FREDERIC	PENNSYLVANIA	M	W	
JERNIGAN, JOSEPH P.	TEXAS	M	W	
JESTOR, WILLIE LEE	OHIO	M	B	

| JIMENEZ, VICTOR | NEVADA | M | H | |

In 1987, John Mynheir, 35, and Antonio Velasquez, 74, were attacked in a north Las Vegas bar during a robbery. Jimenez, 25, of Texas, was sentenced to die for attacking both men with knives and killing them. His appeals case is in federal court.

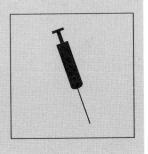

INMATE	STATE	SEX	RACE	JUVENILE
JIMERSON, VERNEAL	ILLINOIS	M	B	
JOHNS, STEPHEN	MISSOURI	M	W	
JOHNSON, ANDREW	ILLINOIS	M	B	
JOHNSON, ANTHONY K.	ALABAMA	M	W	
JOHNSON, CARL	TEXAS	M	B	
JOHNSON, CEASAR L.	NORTH CAROLINA	M	B	
JOHNSON, CECIL	TENNESSEE	M	B	
JOHNSON, CHARLIE	GEORGIA	M	W	
JOHNSON, CURTIS L.	TEXAS	M	B	
JOHNSON, DAVID	ARKANSAS	M	B	
JOHNSON, DEREK	TENNESSEE	M	U	
JOHNSON, DONNIE E.	TENNESSEE	M	W	
JOHNSON, DORSIE L.	TEXAS	M	B	
JOHNSON, EDDIE J.	TEXAS	M	B	
JOHNSON, EMANUEL	FLORIDA	M	B	
JOHNSON, ERSKINE L.	TENNESSEE	M	B	
JOHNSON, GARY	OHIO	M	B	
JOHNSON, GARY	TEXAS	M	W	
JOHNSON, GRAYLAND	ILLINOIS	M	B	
JOHNSON, GREGORY S.	INDIANA	M	W	
JOHNSON, JAMES	CALIFORNIA	M	B	
JOHNSON, JOE	CALIFORNIA	M	B	

INMATE	STATE	SEX	RACE	JUVENILE
JOHNSON, LARRY JOE	FLORIDA	M	W	
JOHNSON, LAVERNE	CALIFORNIA	M	B	
JOHNSON, LENARD	ILLINOIS	M	B	
JOHNSON, MALCOLM	OKLAHOMA	M	B	
JOHNSON, MARK	ILLINOIS	M	B	

JOHNSON, MARVIN	FLORIDA	M	W	

On June 7, 1978, 35-year-old Marvin Edwin Johnson escaped from a Tennessee prison. While robbing a pharmacy, Johnson confronted pharmacist Woodrow Moulton, 64, behind the prescription counter of the drugstore he had owned for more than 40 years. Johnson held a gun on him and demanded drugs and money. As Johnson started toward the front door, Moulton grabbed a revolver, fired and missed. Johnson then walked up to Moulton and said "You think you're a smart SOB" and fired a fatal bullet into his heart. Federal appeals courts have blocked Johnson's execution three times.

JOHNSON, MICHAEL	OHIO	M	W	

JOHNSON, MILTON	ILLINOIS	M	B	

Milton Johnson was twice convicted and sentenced to death for the 1983 killings of five people. His first conviction was for fatally shooting Anthony Hackett, 18, as Hackett and his fiancee slept in their car alongside an interstate highway. He raped the woman and left her for dead, but she lived to identify him to a jury. His second conviction was for the stabbing deaths for four women in a ceramics shop in August 1983. Johnson is suspected in more killings, yet Illinois prosecutors decided to stop taking the alleged murders to trail.

INMATE	STATE	SEX	RACE	JUVENILE
JOHNSON, PAUL BEASLEY	FLORIDA	M	W	
JOHNSON, RICHARD	SOUTH CAROLINA	M	W	
JOHNSON, RICKEY	ALABAMA	M	B	
JOHNSON, SAMUEL	MISSISSIPPI	M	B	
JOHNSON, TERRELL	FLORIDA	M	W	
JOHNSON, VINCENT	OKLAHOMA	M	B	
JOHNSON, WALTER	TENNESSEE	M	W	
JOHNSON, WILLIAM	PENNSYLVANIA	M	B	
JOHNSON, WILLIE D.	CALIFORNIA	M	B	
JOHNSTON, DAVID E.	FLORIDA	M	W	
JOHNSTON, JOE C.	NORTH CAROLINA	M	W	
JOHNSTON, TIMOTHY	MISSOURI	M	W	
JOINER, ORIEN C.	TEXAS	M	W	
JONES RONNIE LEE	FLORIDA	M	B	
JONES, AARON	ALABAMA	M	B	
JONES, ANDRE	ILLINOIS	M	B	
JONES, BENNY	OKLAHOMA	M	U	
JONES, BRANDON	GEORGIA	M	B	

INMATE	STATE	SEX	RACE	JUVENILE

JONES, CLARENCE   **FLORIDA**   **M**   **B**

Clarence Jones was convicted and sentenced to death for the July 1988 murder of Florida police officer Ernest Ponce De Leon. Jones, a one-time convicted felon serving a 25-year sentence for armed robbery with a deadly weapon, had escaped from the Maryland House of Corrections two weeks prior to Ponce De Leon's murder. He shot Ponce De Leon to avoid arrest and then robbed him. In addition to his death sentence, the judge also handed Jones three consecutive life sentences for attempted murder of another officer, robbery with a firearm, and burglary while armed. Five years were added for the aggravated assault with a firearm.

JONES, CLAUDE	TEXAS	M	W
JONES, D.L.	OKLAHOMA	M	W
JONES, DAMON	PENNSYLVANIA	M	B

JONES, DANIEL S.   **NEVADA**   **M**   **W**

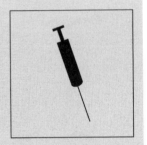

In July 1989, Don Woody was murdered in a casino parking lot. In an effort to steal his motorhome, Daniel Steven Jones shot Woody three times. Jones' previous convictions include an aggravated assault charge for beating his grandmother with a crowbar. His appeal to the Nevada Supreme Court was recently rejected.

JONES, DONALD ALLEN	SOUTH CAROLINA	M	B
JONES, EARL	CALIFORNIA	M	B

JONES, EDWARD   **NEVADA**   **M**   **W**

Pamela Williams, 22, was stabbed 37 times on August 22, 1991, following an argument with Jones. Jones, 29, was sentenced to die May 15, 1992, for killing Williams, his girlfriend. Jones' sentence will be automatically appealed to the Nevada Supreme Court.

JONES, GREGORY M.	MISSISSIPPI	M	B
JONES, JAMES	PENNSYLVANIA	M	B
JONES, JAMES	TENNESSEE	M	B
JONES, JEFFREY	CALIFORNIA	M	B
JONES, JOHN W.	NORTH CAROLINA	M	B
JONES, LEO	FLORIDA	M	B
JONES, MARVIN	MISSOURI	M	W

INMATE	STATE	SEX	RACE	JUVENILE
JONES, MICHAEL	CALIFORNIA	M	B	
JONES, MICHAEL STEVEN	TEXAS	M	B	
JONES, PATRICIA B.	OKLAHOMA	F	W	
JONES, RANDALL	FLORIDA	M	W	
JONES, RAYMOND	TEXAS	M	B	
JONES, RICHARD W.	TEXAS	M	W	
JONES, RONALD	CALIFORNIA	M	B	
JONES, RONALD	ILLINOIS	M	B	
JONES, SHELTON	TEXAS	M	B	
JONES, TROY	CALIFORNIA	M	B	
JONES, WILLIAM	ILLINOIS	M	B	
JONES, WILLIAM	MISSOURI	M	W	
JONES, WILLIAM Q.	NORTH CAROLINA	M	B	

JONES, WILLIE LEROY   **VIRGINIA**   **M**   **B**

In May 1983, Willie Leroy Jones robbed and murdered Graham and Myra Adkins. Graham Adkins, 77, was killed by a single shot in the face. Myra Adkins, 78, also was shot in the face, but she died of smoke inhalation while bound and gagged in a closet of their burning home.

Jones, now 33, was convicted in 1984, and is still in the appeals process.

JORDAN, CLARENCE	TEXAS	M	B	
JOSEPH, RICHARD	OHIO	M	W	

JOUBERT, JOHN   **NEBRASKA**   **M**   **W**

On August 22, 1982, a young boy, 11-year-old Richard Stetson, was abducted and murdered. His body was found near a bridge in Portland, Maine.

In the early morning hours of September 18, 1983, 13-year-old Danny Joe Eberle was delivering papers on his route in Omaha, Neb., when he was abducted. John J. Joubert, an airman at nearby Offutt Air Force Base, kidnapped, bound, stabbed and left the boy's body in a ditch.

On December 2, 1983, Joubert kidnapped another boy, 12-year-old Christopher Paul Walden, walking alone on his way to school in Faulkland Heights, Neb. Joubert strangled and stabbed Walden, after ordering him to strip down to his underwear.

Joubert, a former Boy Scouts troop leader, was convicted of killing the two Nebraska boys and he is accused of the Stetson killing. He now sits on Nebraska's Death Row.

KARIS, JAMES	CALIFORNIA	M	H	
KAURISH, JAY	CALIFORNIA	M	W	
KEARSE, BILLY	FLORIDA	M	B	
KEE, JOSEPH K.	NORTH CAROLINA	M	W	
KEEN, DAVID	TENNESSEE	M	W	

INMATE	STATE	SEX	RACE	JUVENILE
KEEN, MICHAEL SCOTT	FLORIDA	M	W	
KEENAN, MAURICE	CALIFORNIA	M	W	
KEENAN, THOMAS	OHIO	M	W	
KELLEY, WILLIAM	FLORIDA	M	W	
KELLY, ALVIN	TEXAS	M	W	

KELLY, CARL E.   TEXAS   M   B

On death row since July 1981, Carl Eugene Kelly was convicted of robbery and the slaying of 18-year-old Steven Pryor, a convenience store clerk. Pryor was abducted from the store and taken to a park and shot. Also killed in the incident was David Wade Reily, a transient who had been asleep in Pryor's car. After the two were shot, their bodies were thrown off Lover's Leap, a steep cliff in the park. Kelly, now 31, has escaped two execution dates.

KELLY, HORACE   CALIFORNIA   M   B

On Thanksgiving Day 1984, 11-year-old Daniel David Osentowski intervened when Horace Edwards Kelly tried to abduct his 13-year-old cousin. She was able to escape as a result, but Kelly shot the boy twice as he begged for his life. Previously, Kelly was convicted of two counts of first-degree murder when he shot two women to death after raping and robbing one of them and trying to rape the other.

KEMP, EMANUEL	TEXAS	M	B	
KENLEY, KENNETH	MISSOURI	M	W	
KENNEDY, STUART	INDIANA	M	W	
KENNEDY, VICTOR	ALABAMA	M	B	
KIGHT, CHARLES	FLORIDA	M	W	
KILES, ALVIE C.	ARIZONA	M	B	

KILGORE, BRUCE   MISSOURI   M   B

On October 23, 1987, Bruce W. Kilgore was sentenced to die for stabbing to death Marlyn Wilkins, 54. Wilkins had been abducted from the parking lot of a restaurant. Kilgore has been granted an indefinite stay of execution and sits on Missouri's Death Row.

KILGORE, DEAN	FLORIDA	M	B	

INMATE	STATE	SEX	RACE	JUVENILE

KILLSONTOP, VERN AND LESTER   MONTANA   M   N

At 2 a.m. on November 17, 1987, Marty Etchemendy, 23, left a Miles City, Mont., bar with Vern and Lester Killsontop. The two Cheyenne Indian brothers and their two female companions were going to give Etchemendy a ride to his home a mile away. Etchemendy was beaten to death during the course of a 13-hour drive, part of which he spent in the trunk of a black Dodge Duster, which carried him and his assailants from Miles City to an abandoned community hall 155 miles away in Gillette, Wyo. During frequent stops, Etchemendy had been dragged to the side of the road and beaten. After the first three assaults, the brothers ordered the blood-covered Etchemendy to strip and get in the car's trunk. The Killsontop brothers were both sentenced to death and sit in separate cells on Montana's Death Row.

INMATE	STATE	SEX	RACE
KIMBLE, ERIC	CALIFORNIA	M	B
KINDLER, JOSEPH	PENNSYLVANIA	M	W
KING, AMOS LEE	FLORIDA	M	B
KING, DANNY	VIRGINIA	M	W
KING, DERRICK	ILLINOIS	M	B
KING, ERIC	ARIZONA	M	B
KING, MACK ARTHUR	MISSISSIPPI	M	B
KING, TERRY	TENNESSEE	M	W
KING, THOMAS	TENNESSEE	M	B
KING, WILLIE	FLORIDA	M	B
KINLEY, JUAN	OHIO	M	B
KINNAMON, RAYMOND CARL	TEXAS	M	W
KINSMAN, RONALD	GEORGIA	M	W
KIPP, MARTIN	CALIFORNIA	M	N
KIRKPATRICK, FREDERICK	LOUISIANA	M	W
KIRKPATRICK, WILLIAM	CALIFORNIA	M	B
KIRKSEY, JIMMY	NEVADA	M	B
KITCHEN, RONALD	ILLINOIS	M	B
KITCHENS, WILLIAM J.	TEXAS	M	W
KNIGHTON, ROBERT	OKLAHOMA	M	W
KNOWLES, RANDALL	FLORIDA	M	W
KNOX, JAMES ROY	TEXAS	M	W
KOKAL, GREGORY	FLORIDA	M	W
KOKORALEIS, ANDREW	ILLINOIS	M	W
KOLBERG, BRYAN	MISSISSIPPI	M	W
KOLMETZ, JEFFREY	CALIFORNIA	M	W
KOON, RAYMOND	FLORIDA	M	W
KORNAHRENS, FRED	SOUTH CAROLINA	M	W
KRAFT, RANDY	CALIFORNIA	M	W
KRAMER, LARRY	FLORIDA	M	W
KRAWCZUK, ANTON	FLORIDA	M	W
KUENZEL, WILLIAM	ALABAMA	M	W

INMATE	STATE	SEX	RACE	JUVENILE
KUNKLE, TROY A.	TEXAS	M	W	
KYLES, CURTIS	LOUISIANA	M	B	
KYNARD, TERRY	ALABAMA	M	W	
LACAVA, MICHAEL	PENNSYLVANIA	M	W	
LACKEY, CLARENCE A.	TEXAS	M	W	
LADNER, JEFFREY	MISSISSIPPI	M	W	
LAFFERTY, RON	UTAH	M	W	
LAGRAND, KARL	ARIZONA	M	W	

LAGRAND, WALTER	ARIZONA	M	W	

Shortly after 8 a.m. on January 7, 1982, Walter LaGrand and his brother, Karl, entered the Valley National Bank in Marana, Ariz. Armed with a toy pistol, Karl tried to force Ken Hartsock, the 63-year-old branch manager, to open the vault. Hartsock couldn't open the vault because he only had half of the combination. The brothers then forced Hartsock and Dawn Lopez, a bank clerk, into Hartsock's office and bound them. After threatening Hartsock with a letter opener, the brothers began beating him. Hartsock died from 24 stab wounds. Karl and Walter tried to kill Lopez by stabbing her six times, then fled the bank.

LAIRD, RICHARD	PENNSYLVANIA	M	W	
LAMB, JOHN MICHAEL	TEXAS	M	W	
LAMBERT, JAMES	PENNSYLVANIA	M	B	
LAMBERT, MICHAEL	INDIANA	M	W	
LAMBERT, ROBERT	OKLAHOMA	M	W	
LAMBRIGHT, JOE	ARIZONA	M	W	
LAMBRIX, CARY	FLORIDA	M	W	
LANDRESS, CINDY	INDIANA	F	W	
LANDRIGAN, JEFFREY	ARIZONA	M	W	
LANDRUM, LAWRENCE	OHIO	M	W	
LANE, HAROLD	TEXAS	M	W	
LANEY, THOMAS G.	TENNESSEE	M	W	
LANG, KENNETH	CALIFORNIA	M	N	
LANGFORD, TERRY	MONTANA	M	W	
LANGLEY, ROBERT	OREGON	M	W	
LANIER, ARTHUR RAY	MISSISSIPPI	M	B	
LANKFORD, BRIAN	IDAHO	M	W	
LANKFORD, MARK	IDAHO	M	W	
LARA, MARIO	FLORIDA	M	H	
LARETTE, ANTHONY	MISSOURI	M	W	
LARK, ROBERT	PENNSYLVANIA	M	B	
LARKINS, ROBERT	FLORIDA	M	B	
LASHLEY, FREDERICK	MISSOURI	M	B	*
LAUTI, AUA	TEXAS	M	A	
LAVERS, ALFRED E.	ARIZONA	M	W	
LAWHORN, JAMES	ALABAMA	M	W	
LAWLEY, DENNIS H.	CALIFORNIA	M	W	

LAWRENCE, MICHAEL FLORIDA M W

On September 29, 1986, while on parole from a life sentence for killing his wife, 31-year-old Michael Alan Lawrence murdered Gail Tyree. The 37-year-old convenience store clerk's body was found in the storage room of the store with two bullet holes in the back of her head. The store was robbed of $58.

Lawrence was convicted in the strangulation murder of his wife in 1976. He was sentenced to life in prison, but paroled in 1985. His appeal has not yet been heard by the Florida Supreme Court.

LAWS, WAYNE ALAN NORTH CAROLINA M W

On August 21, 1985, Wayne Allen Laws was sentenced to die for the beating deaths of Ronnie Howard Waddell and James Lloyd Kepley on March 18, 1984.

LAWSON, CARL	ILLINOIS	M	B
LAWSON, DAVID	NORTH CAROLINA	M	W
LAWSON, JERRY	OHIO	M	W

LEAR, TUHRAN ILLINOIS M B

On Aug. 25, 1988, Terrence Doyle was finishing the final shift of his temporary job at a gas station. At about 5:45 a.m., 30-year-old Tuhran Lear robbed the station, murdering Doyle in the process. About a week later, Lear robbed another service station, murdered manager Greg McAnarney, and tried to kill station attendant Robert Bishop. Bishop feigned death after Lear shot him in the back of the neck, missing a major artery by one millimeter. Lear and his accomplice, 24-year-old Robert Thomas, were then interrupted by a couple who stopped to use the rest room. The couple called the police on their CB radio.

As a teen-ager in Chicago, Lear was convicted of killing another teen and served a juvenile prison sentence.

LEAVITT, RICHARD — IDAHO — M — W

Rick Leavitt held a steady job, was a husband, father, and son of law-abiding parents. In July 1984, he brutally stabbed Dannette Elg, an Idaho National Engineering Laboratory employee. Evidence showed Elg had numerous defense wounds on her body indicating she had struggled for her life. Her mutilated body was discovered in the bedroom of her parents' home by police after they received telephone tips from a man calling himself Mike Jensen. No one by that name was ever located, and police believe Leavitt was the one who actually made those calls. Leavitt received the death sentence December 19, 1985.

INMATE	STATE	SEX	RACE	JUVENILE
LECROY, CLEO	FLORIDA	M	W	*
LEDESMA, FERMIN	CALIFORNIA	M	H	
LEE, DANIEL BRIAN	NORTH CAROLINA	M	W	
LEE, JESSE	GEORGIA	M	B	
LEE, LARRY	GEORGIA	M	W	
LEE, PERCY	PENNSYLVANIA	M	B	*
LEE, TRACY	LOUISIANA	M	B	
LEGER, WILLIAM	ILLINOIS	M	W	
LEGO, DONALD	ILLINOIS	M	W	
LEISURE, DAVID R.	MISSOURI	M	W	

LEONARD, WILLIAM — NEVADA — M — W

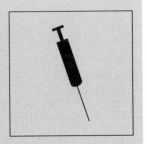

William Leonard stabbed to death Joseph Wright, an inmate at Nevada State Prison. Leonard was serving a life sentence for another murder when he killed Wright.

INMATE	STATE	SEX	RACE	JUVENILE
LESKO, JOHN	PENNSYLVANIA	M	W	
LESTER, EMANUAL	PENNSYLVANIA	M	B	
LETNER, RICHARD	CALIFORNIA	M	W	
LEWIS, ANDRE A.	TEXAS	M	B	
LEWIS, CINQUE	ILLINOIS	M	B	
LEWIS, DAVID LEE	TEXAS	M	W	
LEWIS, DONALD	OHIO	M	B	
LEWIS, LAWRENCE	FLORIDA	M	W	
LEWIS, MILTON	CALIFORNIA	M	B	
LEWIS, RAYMOND	CALIFORNIA	M	B	

INMATE	STATE	SEX	RACE	JUVENILE

LEWIS, ROBERT   **CALIFORNIA**   **M**   **B**

On October 27, 1983, Robert Lewis Jr. robbed and murdered Milton Estell. The victim was found in the bedroom of his home bound, gagged, stabbed and shot. Lewis was arrested driving Estell's Cadillac. Lewis, now 39, is in the appeals process.

LIBBERTON, LAWRENCE   ARIZONA   M   W

LIBBY, ROGER   **NEVADA**   **M**   **W**

In 1988, Libby shot and killed James Robertson, 24, and Charles Beatty, 28, both of Winnemucca, Nev. He then took a vehicle and an ATM card and drove to Missouri where he was arrested and extradited back to Winnemucca. Libby, a 26-year-old Montana native, has appealed his case to the Nevada Supreme Court.

INMATE	STATE	SEX	RACE
LIGHTBOURNE, IAN	FLORIDA	M	B
LILES, MARK	OKLAHOMA	M	W
LIM, KIM LY	TEXAS	M	A
LINCECUM, KAVIN W.	TEXAS	M	B
LINDSEY, TYRONNE	LOUISIANA	M	B
LINGAR, STANLEY	MISSOURI	M	W
LIPHAM, WILLIAM	GEORGIA	M	W
LITTLE, WILLIAM HAMILTON	TEXAS	M	W
LIVADITIS, STEVEN	CALIFORNIA	M	W
LIVELEY, JAMES	GEORGIA	M	W
LIVINGSTON, CHARLIE	TEXAS	M	B
LLOYD, OSCAR	NORTH CAROLINA	M	B
LOCKETT, CARL	MISSISSIPPI	M	B
LOCKHART, MICHAEL	FLA/IND/TX	M	W
LOGAN, RONALD	PENNSYLVANIA	M	B

INMATE	STATE	SEX	RACE	JUVENILE

LONCHAR, LARRY GRANT   GEORGIA   M   W

Larry Lonchar was convicted and sentenced to death for the 1986 triple murder of Charles Wayne Smith, 54, his son Steven Wayne Smith, 24, and the older man's girlfriend, Margaret Sweat, 45. Lonchar, a paroled armed robber with a lengthy criminal record dating back to his teens, owed the elder Smith $10,000 in gambling debts. He and an accomplice posed as law enforcement agents on a raid at Smith's condominium. Smith and his son were found handcuffed and shot to death. Sweat was also shot, but when she attempted to call 911, Lonchar slit her throat. An answering machine tape-recorded Sweat pleading for her life. Another son, Charles Richard Smith, saved his life by playing dead after being shot twice in the shoulder.

LONG, DAVID MARTIN	TEXAS	M	W	
LONG, MICHAEL E.	OKLAHOMA	M	W	

LONG, ROBERT   FLORIDA   M   W

Robert Joe Long, 35, a former X-ray technician, was arrested in November 1984 and confessed to the May 1984 murder of Michelle Denise Simms, 22, and nine other killings. Simms' body was found bound with rope and nearly decapitated from a throat slashing. In that case, Long pleaded guilty to first-degree murder, kidnapping and sexual battery. He was sentenced to be electrocuted.

LONGWORTH, RICHARD   SOUTH CAROLINA   M   W

Richard Longworth and David Rocheville were convicted in separate 1991 trials for the 1991 murders of theater workers Alex Hopps and Todd Green during a robbery. Both received the death sentence.

LOOKINGBILL, ROBERT	TEXAS	M	W	
LOPEZ, EDUARDO	FLORIDA	M	H	
LOPEZ, GEORGE	ARIZONA	M	H	

LOPEZ, MANUEL NEVADA M H

Manuel Lopez murdered his step-daughter in January 1985. The 4-year-old child died from prolonged torture as punishment for a bed wetting problem. Lopez was convicted and sentenced to death April 1985.

LOPEZ, SAMUEL ARIZONA M H

On October 29, 1986, Samuel Lopez broke into the home of 59-year-old Estafana Holmes. He raped her, beat her, and then murdered her. Her body was found nude from the waist down, with her pajama bottoms tied around her eyes. A lace scarf was crammed tightly into her mouth. She had been stabbed 23 times, and her throat was cut.

INMATE	STATE	SEX	RACE
LORD, BRIAN KEITH	WASHINGTON	M	W
LORRAINE, CHARLES	OHIO	M	W
LOTT, GREGORY	OHIO	M	B
LOVETTE, MICHAEL	FLORIDA	M	W
LOVING, DWIGHT J.	FEDERAL	M	B
LOWE, RODNEY	FLORIDA	M	B
LOWERY, JAMES	INDIANA	M	W
LOWERY, TERRY	INDIANA	M	W
LOYD, ALVIN	LOUISIANA	M	W
LOZA, JOSE T.	OHIO	M	H
LOZADA, DAVIS	TEXAS	M	H
LUCAS, CECIL D.	SOUTH CAROLINA	M	W
LUCAS, DAVID A.	CALIFORNIA	M	W
LUCAS, HENRY	FLA/TX	M	W
LUCAS, LARRY	CALIFORNIA	M	W
LUCAS, ROOSEVELT	ILLINOIS	M	B

LUCERO, PHILIP CALIFORNIA M H

On April 12, 1980, Phillip L. Lucero lured Christine "Chrissy" Hubbard, 7, and Teddy Elizabeth Engilman, 10, into his home in Yucaipa, Calif. Lucero, a Vietnam veteran, used a Pepsi bottle to crack the skull of Engilman. Hubbard was strangled with her necklace. Lucero then set fire to his own home, apparently to destroy evidence of the killings. He was sentenced in December 1981 to die in the California gas chamber. Lucero, now 42, remains in the California appeals process.

INMATE	STATE	SEX	RACE	JUVENILE
LUCKY, DARNELL	CALIFORNIA	M	B	
LUNDGREN, JEFFREY	OHIO	M	W	
LUSK, BOBBY	FLORIDA	M	W	
LY, CAM	PENNSYLVANIA	M	A	
LYNCH, FRANKLIN	CALIFORNIA	M	U	
LYNCH, GREGORY	NORTH CAROLINA	M	B	
LYND, WILLIAM	GEORGIA	M	W	
MACIAS, FEDERICO M.	TEXAS	M	H	
MACK, CLARENCE	OHIO	M	B	
MACK, JIMMY	MISSISSIPPI	M	B	
MACK, LARRY	ILLINOIS	M	B	
MACKALL, TONY	VIRGINIA	M	B	
MADDEN, ROBERT	TEXAS	M	W	
MADEJ, GREGORY	ILLINOIS	M	W	
MADISON, DERYL	TEXAS	M	B	
MADISON, VERNON	ALABAMA	M	B	
MAGWOOD, BILLY	ALABAMA	M	B	
MAGWOOD, KENNETH	ALABAMA	M	B	
MAHAFFEY, JERRY	ILLINOIS	M	B	
MAHAFFEY, REGINALD	ILLINOIS	M	B	
MAHALY, MARILYN	NORTH CAROLINA	F	W	
MAHARAJ, KRISHNA	FLORIDA	M	A	
MAHONE, STEVE	NORTH CAROLINA	M	W	
MAISONET, ORLANDO	PENNSYLVANIA	M	H	
MAJORS, JAMES	CALIFORNIA	M	W	

MAK, KWAN	**WASHINGTON**	**M**	**B**	

In 1983, Kwan Fai "Willie" Mak took part in a robbery at the Wah Mee gambling club in the International District of Seattle, Wash. Mak and his two friends left the club with $15,000, murdering 13 people in the process. Mak, a Hong Kong immigrant, was sentenced to death for his role in the murders. He sits on Washington's Death Row.

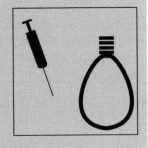

MALLETT, JEROME	MISSOURI	M	B	
MALONE, J.D.	OKLAHOMA	M	W	
MALONE, KELVIN	CA/MO	M	B	
MANN, ANTHONY	OKLAHOMA	M	W	
MANN, FLETCHER T.	TEXAS	M	W	
MANN, LARRY	FLORIDA	M	W	
MAPES, DAVID	OHIO	M	B	

MAQUEIRA, JOSE FLORIDA M H

Jose Maquiera was convicted and sentenced to death for the 1983 murder of Racquel Rodriguez during a home burglary. Miguel Rodriguez, Racquel's husband, was also killed when Maquiera and an unidentified accomplice burst into their home seeking $65,000 in cash. Maquiera was serving a 37-year term for attempted second-degree murder and attempted robbery when he confessed to the Rodriguez killings.

MAREK, JOHN R. FLORIDA M W

John Marek was convicted and sentenced to death for the 1983 murder of Adella Marie Simmons, a motorist stranded on a Florida turnpike. Marek and a friend, Raymond Wigley, offered to take Simmons to get help after her car broke down, but took her instead to a county beach. Marek and Wigley repeatedly raped Simmons, then strangled her.

INMATE	STATE	SEX	RACE
MARLOW, JAMES	CALIFORNIA	M	W
MARLOWE, HUGH	KENTUCKY	M	W
MARQUEZ, GONZALO	CALIFORNIA	M	H
MARQUEZ, HOWARD	OKLAHOMA	M	N
MARQUEZ, MARIO	TEXAS	M	H
MARSHALL, BARNEY	OKLAHOMA	M	N
MARSHALL, GEORGE	CALIFORNIA	M	B
MARSHALL, JEROME	PENNSYLVANIA	M	B
MARSHALL, JERRY J.	PENNSYLVANIA	M	B
MARSHALL, MATTHEW	FLORIDA	M	B

MARSHALL, ROBERT O. NEW JERSEY M W

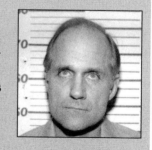

Robert Marshall was convicted of the 1986 murder of his wife, Maria. According to trial testimony, he killed her to collect on a sizeable insurance policy so he and his lover, Sarann Kraushaar, could live together. Kraushaar told the trial jury that Marshall had discussed with her his plans to kill his wife.

MARSHALL, RYAN	CALIFORNIA	M	W

INMATE	STATE	SEX	RACE	JUVENILE

MARSHALL, SAM CALIFORNIA M B

On April 13, 1986, Sam Marshall strangled Sharon Rawls. She was identified as a prostitute. Rawls was found tied and gagged in an abandoned building in Los Angeles. Marshall, now 45, has not yet filed his automatic appeal to the California Supreme Court.

MARTIN, ERNEST	OHIO	M	B	
MARTIN, JAMES	ALABAMA	M	W	
MARTINEZ, GILBERTO	OKLAHOMA	M	H	
MARTINEZ, MIGUEL	TEXAS	M	H	

MARTINEZ, RAMON ARIZONA M H

On an October weekend in 1982, Ramon Martinez-Villareal and an accomplice burglarized the Tumacacori, Ariz., home of Sarah Bailey, taking rifles and ammunition. On their way back to Mexico with the stolen goods, Martinez and his accomplice came upon James Thomas McGrew and Fernando Estrada-Babichi, who were grading a Salerno Ranch road. Martinez and his accomplice decided to rob the two men of their money and pickup truck, and waited overnight for them to return. When McGrew and Estrada returned on October 14, Martinez killed and robbed them with the rifles stolen from the Bailey residence.

MARTINI, JOHN	NEW JERSEY	M	W	

MASON, DAVID CALIFORNIA M W

In 1981, David Edwin Mason confessed to strangling four residents at their homes in 1980. In a tape recording titled "David E. Mason—Epitaph," he confessed to killing Joan Picard, 71, Arthur Jennings, 83, Antoinette Brown, 75, and Dorothy Lang, 72. The 1980 crimes were unsolved until Mason's confession. During a May 9, 1982, jail fight, he killed fellow inmate Boyd Johnson. Mason has been convicted of the five murders. His death sentence has been upheld by the California Supreme Court.

MASON, OSCAR	FLORIDA	M	B	
MASON, THOMAS	TEXAS	M	W	
MASSIE, ROBERT	CALIFORNIA	M	W	
MASTERS, JARVIS	CALIFORNIA	M	B	

INMATE	STATE	SEX	RACE	JUVENILE

MATA, LUIS   **ARIZONA**   **M**   **H**

On the evening of March 10, 1977, Luis Mata and his brother, Alonzo, were at their Phoenix, Ariz., apartment with Debra Lopez. When Lopez got up to leave, Luis stopped her and told her they were going to rape her. The brothers began beating her with a rifle and their fists, and each raped her. They drove the unconscious victim from the apartment and Luis killed her by cutting her throat with a knife, nearly decapitating her in the process. Alonzo Mata was also convicted for the murder of Lopez, but received a life sentence.

MATA, RAMON	TEXAS	M	H	
MATHENIA, CHARLES L.	MISSOURI	M	W	

MATHENY, ALLEN   **INDIANA**   **M**   **W**

In April 1990, Allen Matheney was convicted for killing his ex-wife, Lisa Marie Bianco. Matheney had been serving a seven-year sentence for assaulting Bianco, but during an eight-hour furlough from prison, he drove to Bianco's home and bludgeoned her to death with the butt of a shotgun.

MATHIS, JAMES	GEORGIA	M	B	
MATSON, JOHN, JR.	TEXAS	M	B	
MATSON, MICHAEL	TENNESSEE	M	W	
MATTHEWS, EARL	SOUTH CAROLINA	M	B	
MATTHEWS, KEVIN	PENNSYLVANIA	M	B	
MATTSON, MICHAEL	CALIFORNIA	M	W	
MATURNA, CLAUDE	ARIZONA	M	W	

MAULDEN, CHARLES   **FLORIDA**   **M**   **W**

Charles Maulden was convicted and sentenced to death for the murders of Tammy Maulden, his ex-wife, and her fiance Earl Duvall in June 1988. Maulden crawled through a bathroom window to gain admittance into Tammy's apartment, then crept upon and shot the sleeping couple to death. Maulden requested the death penalty instead of a life sentence. The judge granted him his wish.

MAURER, DONALD	OHIO	M	W	
MAURY, ROBERT	CALIFORNIA	M	W	
MAXWELL, ANDREW	ILLINOIS	M	B	
MAXWELL, CHESTER	FLORIDA	M	B	

INMATE	STATE	SEX	RACE	JUVENILE
MAXWELL, FREDERIC	PENNSYLVANIA	M	B	
MAY, FREEMAN	PENNSYLVANIA	M	W	
MAYES, WILLIAM	OKLAHOMA	M	W	
MAYFIELD, DEMETRIE	CALIFORNIA	M	B	
MAYFIELD, DENNIS	CALIFORNIA	M	B	
MAYHUE, FRED	PENNSYLVANIA	M	W	
MAYS, NOBLE D.	TEXAS	M	W	

MAZZAN, JOHN	**NEVADA**	**M**	**W**	

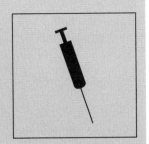

In 1978, Mazzan stayed the night at the house of his friend Richard Minor Jr. Mazzan, a 45-year-old a New York native, murdered the 26-year-old Minor and was convicted and sentenced to die. Mazzan was temporarily removed from Nevada's Death Row pending a new trial. He was convicted again and returned to Death Row. His case is being appealed in district court.

INMATE	STATE	SEX	RACE	JUVENILE
MC PHAIL, FREDERICK W.	NORTH CAROLINA	M	W	
MCBRIDE, MICHAEL L.	TEXAS	M	W	
MCCALL, EDWARD	ARIZONA	M	W	
MCCARTY, CURTIS E.	OKLAHOMA	M	W	
MCCOLLUM, HENRY	NORTH CAROLINA	M	B	
MCCORMICK, MICHAEL	TENNESSEE	M	W	
MCCRACKEN, JERRY	OKLAHOMA	M	W	
MCCULLOM, PHILLIP	INDIANA	M	B	
MCCULLUM, THOMAS	PENNSYLVANIA	M	B	

MCDERMOTT, MAUREEN	**CALIFORNIA**	**F**	**W**	

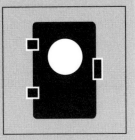

On April 28, 1985, Stephen Eldridge, 27, was stabbed more than 40 times in the home he co-owned with Maureen McDermott. His penis was cut off in attempt to disguise the slaying as a homosexual murder. McDermott, a 42-year-old registered nurse, was convicted of hiring James F. Luna, 36, to kill her roommate in exchange for a portion of a $100,000 mortgage insurance policy. McDermott and Eldridge had taken out the policy on the home they co-purchased. Following McDermott's orders, Luna made an attempt on Eldridge's life on March 21, 1985, but Eldridge escaped the first attack. Testimony indicated that Eldridge was not McDermott's first victim. Luna, who testified against McDermott, said McDermott also hired him to have a co-worker attacked so she could take the man's job.

INMATE	STATE	SEX	RACE	JUVENILE
MCDONALD, ROBERT	CALIFORNIA	M	W	
MCDONALD, SAM	MISSOURI	M	B	
MCDONNELL, MICHAEL	OREGON	M	W	

INMATE	STATE	SEX	RACE	JUVENILE
MCDOUGALD, ANTHONY	NEW JERSEY	M	B	
MCDOWELL, CHARLES	CALIFORNIA	M	W	
MCFADDEN, JERRY	TEXAS	M	W	
MCFARLAND, FRANK	TEXAS	M	W	

MCGAHEE, EARL	**ALABAMA**	**M**	**B**	

On Sept. 11, 1985, Earl Jerome McGahee entered a classroom and opened fired with a .357-Magnum handgun. Bullets hit his ex-wife, Connie McGahee, and a second student, Casandra Lee. McGahee savagely beat his ex-wife after ripping her clothes off and dragging her to the front of the classroom near the teacher's desk. Connie McGahee was pronounced dead at the scene, while Lee died 10 days later. McGahee was sentenced to die in 1986, but the ruling was set aside on a technicality and a new sentencing trial ordered.

MCGEE, JEWEL R.	TEXAS	M	B	
MCGOWEN, ROGER WAYNE	TEXAS	M	B	
MCGREGOR, BILLY K.	OKLAHOMA	M	W	

MCKAGUE, KENNETH	**NEVADA**	**M**	**W**	

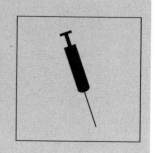

Kenneth McKague and his cousin, John McKague, murdered a husband and wife during a 1978 robbery. The victims, managers of a Reno motel, were shot in the back of their heads while on their knees and with their hands bound behind them.

MCKAY, DAVID WAYNE	TEXAS	M	W	
MCKAY, WILLIAM	TENNESSEE	M	B	

MCKENNA, PATRICK	**NEVADA**	**M**	**W**	

After an argument over a chess game in 1979, McKenna killed his cellmate, Jack Nobles, 20, in the Clark County (Nev.) Jail. McKenna, a 45-year-old Las Vegas native, had his death sentence overturned in 1992 in federal court. That ruling is on appeal by the state.

INMATE	STATE	SEX	RACE	JUVENILE
MCKENZIE, DUNCAN	MONTANA	M	W	
MCKINNEY, RANDY	IDAHO	M	W	
MCKOY, DOCK	NORTH CAROLINA	M	B	

MCLAIN, ROBERT	**CALIFORNIA**	**M**	**W**	

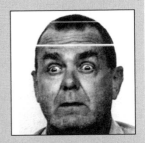

Robert McLain, his 17-year-old nephew, and a 16-year-old friend were on a crime spree in November 1979, when they abducted Diana Bazargani, 31, from a shopping mall where she worked. They drove her to a secluded area where they raped her, stabbed her in her heart and slashed her throat. At the time, McLain was on parole for raping two 11-year-old girls in 1971. McLain was also convicted of raping and murdering a young woman hitchhiker after killing Bazargani. He was sentenced to death in 1981.

INMATE	STATE	SEX	RACE	JUVENILE
MCLAUGHLIN, ELTON	NORTH CAROLINA	M	B	
MCMILLAN, RICHARD	MISSOURI	M	W	
MCMILLAN, WALTER	ALABAMA	M	B	

MCMURTREY, JASPER	**ARIZONA**	**M**	**W**	

On August 10, 1979, Jasper McMurtrey became involved in a fight at the Ranch House Bar in Tucson, Ariz. McMurtrey claimed he did not want any trouble so he armed himself for self-defense. He claimed that one of the victims pointed a gun at him so he opened fire killing Barry Collins and Albert Hughes, and wounding the third man.

INMATE	STATE	SEX	RACE	JUVENILE
MCNAIR, NATHANIEL	PENNSYLVANIA	M	B	
MCNAIR, WILLIE	ALABAMA	M	B	
MCNEIL, LEROY	NORTH CAROLINA	M	B	
MCNISH, DAVID	TENNESSEE	M	W	
MCPETERS, RONALD	CALIFORNIA	M	B	
MCPHERSON, LARRY	TEXAS	M	W	
MCQUEEN, HAROLD	KENTUCKY	M	W	
MCWILLIAMS, JAMES	ALABAMA	M	B	
MEADOWS, THOMAS	PENNSYLVANIA	M	B	
MEANES, JAMES R.	TEXAS	M	B	
MEASE, DARYL	MISSOURI	M	W	
MEDERS, JIMMY F.	GEORGIA	M	W	
MEDINA, JAVIER	TEXAS	M	H	
MEDINA, OSCAR G.	ARIZONA	M	H	
MEDINA, PEDRO	FLORIDA	M	H	

INMATE	STATE	SEX	RACE	JUVENILE

MEDINA, TEOFILO CALIFORNIA **M** **H**

Teofilo Medina was convicted for the 1984 murders of three young men. Two of the victims were employed at gas stations and a third was working at a drive-through dairy. Medina, having been paroled on a rape conviction from an Arizona prison, was on a three-week robbery spree. He was sentenced to death February 25, 1987.

INMATE	STATE	SEX	RACE
MEDLOCK, FLOYD	OKLAHOMA	M	W
MEDRANO, ANGEL	ARIZONA	M	H
MEEKS, DOUGLAS	FLORIDA	M	B
MELENDEZ, JUAN R.	FLORIDA	M	H
MELOCK, ROBERT	ILLINOIS	M	W
MELSON, HUGH	TENNESSEE	M	W
MELTON, ANTONIO	FLORIDA	M	B
MELTON, JAMES	CALIFORNIA	M	B
MEMRO, HAROLD	CALIFORNIA	M	W
MENDOZA, MANUEL	CALIFORNIA	M	H
MENDYK, TODD	FLORIDA	M	W
MENZIES, RALPH	UTAH	M	W
MESSIAH, KEITH	LOUISIANA	M	B
MEYER, JEFFREY	NORTH CAROLINA	M	W
MICHAELS, KURT	CALIFORNIA	M	W
MICKEY, DOUGLAS	CALIFORNIA	M	W
MICKLE, DENNY	CALIFORNIA	M	B
MIDDLEBROOKS, DONALD	TENNESSEE	M	W
MIDDLETON, FRANK	SOUTH CAROLINA	M	B
MIKELL, WILLIAM	PENNSYLVANIA	M	B
MILES, KENYATTA	PENNSYLVANIA	M	B
MILKE, DEBRA JEAN	ARIZONA	F	W
MILLER, DAVID	TENNESSEE	M	W
MILLER, DONALD A.	TEXAS	M	W
MILLER, DONALD	CALIFORNIA	M	B
MILLER, EDDIE LEE	ARKANSAS	M	B
MILLER, GARRY	TEXAS	M	W
MILLER, MICHAEL	GEORGIA	M	B
MILLER, PERRY	INDIANA	M	W
MILLER, ROBERT L.	OKLAHOMA	M	B
MILLER-EL, THOMAS JOE	TEXAS	M	B

MILLIGAN, RONNIE G. NEVADA **M** **W**

In 1980, Milligan killed a stranded motorist, Zolihan Voinski, 77, on Interstate 80 east of Reno, Nev. Then Milligan and his co-defendants returned to the victim's van, started it, and drove both vehicles to Golconda, Nev., where they were arrested. Milligan, a 42-year-old native of Tennessee, is appealing his death sentence in federal court.

INMATE	STATE	SEX	RACE	JUVENILE
MILLS, GREGORY	FLORIDA	M	B	
MILLS, JAMES E.	OHIO	M	B	
MILLS, JOHN	FLORIDA	M	B	
MILLWEE, DONALD	CALIFORNIA	M	W	
MINCEY, BRYAN	CALIFORNIA	M	W	
MINCEY, TERRY	GEORGIA	M	W	
MINES, CHARLES	TEXAS	M	B	
MINIEL, PETER	TEXAS	M	H	
MINNICK, WILLIAM	INDIANA	M	W	
MIRANDA, ADAM	CALIFORNIA	M	H	

MIRANDA, ROBERTO	NEVADA	M	H	

In 1981, Miranda stabbed to death Mexican national Manuel Torres during a burglary in Las Vegas. Miranda, a Cuban national, is appealing his case in federal court.

MITCHAM, STEPHAN	CALIFORNIA	M	B	
MITCHELL, ANDREW L	TEXAS	M	B	
MITCHELL, ANTHONY	ILLINOIS	M	B	
MITCHELL, GERALD LEE	TEXAS	M	B	
MITCHELL, NELSON E.	GEORGIA	M	B	
MITCHELL, WILLIE	FLORIDA	M	B	
MODDON, WILLIE MACK	TEXAS	M	B	
MONTEZ, MARCO	OREGON	M	H	
MONTGOMERY, RODNEY	NORTH CAROLINA	M	B	
MONTGOMERY, ULECE	ILLINOIS	M	B	
MONTGOMERY, WILLIAM	OHIO	M	B	
MONTIEL, RICHARD	CALIFORNIA	M	H	
MONTOYA, IRINEO	TEXAS	M	H	
MONTOYA, RAYMON	TEXAS	M	H	
MOODY, JOHN	TEXAS	M	W	
MOON, LARRY EUGENE	GEORGIA	M	W	

INMATE	STATE	SEX	RACE	JUVENILE
MOON, RICHARD	CALIFORNIA	M	W	
MOONEY, NELSON W.	TEXAS	M	W	
MOORE, BLANCHE T.	NORTH CAROLINA	F	W	
MOORE, BOBBY JAMES	TEXAS	M	B	
MOORE, BRIAN	KENTUCKY	M	W	
MOORE, BRUCE	GEORGIA	M	B	
MOORE, CAREY	NEBRASKA	M	W	
MOORE, CARZELL	GEORGIA	M	B	

MOORE, CHARLES   **CALIFORNIA**   **M**   **B**

In November 1977, Charles Edward Moore Jr. robbed and murdered Robert and Hettie Crumb. The Crumbs were managers of an apartment building where Moore, now 36, once lived. The case remains on appeal.

MOORE, DEWEY	OKLAHOMA	M	W	
MOORE, EDWARD	ILLINOIS	M	W	
MOORE, ERIC	TEXAS	M	B	
MOORE, GEORGE	NORTH CAROLINA	M	B	
MOORE, RANDOLPH	NEVADA	M	W	
MOORE, RICHARD	INDIANA	M	B	
MOORE, SCOTTY	OKLAHOMA	M	W	
MOORE, TYRONE	PENNSYLVANIA	M	B	
MOORMAN, ROBERT H.	ARIZONA	M	W	
MORALES, ALFRED	OHIO	M	N	
MORALES, MICHAEL	CALIFORNIA	M	H	

MORAN, RICHARD   **NEVADA**   **M**   **W**

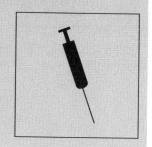

In 1984, Moran murdered part-time bartender Sandra Devere, 25, and off-duty cook Russell Rhodes, 27, at the Red Pearl bar in Las Vegas. Moran, 38, was sentenced to death for these murders and the subsequent killing of his former wife, 26-year-old Linda Vandervoort. Moran, a Texas native, is appealing his case in federal court.

MORAN, WILLARD	PENNSYLVANIA	M	W	
MORDENTI, MICHAEL	FLORIDA	M	W	
MORELAND, JAMES W.	TEXAS	M	W	
MORELAND, SAMUEL	OHIO	M	B	
MORENO, JOSE A.	TEXAS	M	H	
MORGAN, DERRICK	ILLINOIS	M	B	
MORGAN, JAMES	FLORIDA	M	W	*

INMATE	STATE	SEX	RACE	JUVENILE
MORGAN, SAMUEL	ILLINOIS	M	B	
MORRIS, BRUCE	CALIFORNIA	M	W	
MORRIS, KELVIN	PENNSYLVANIA	M	B	
MORRIS, TIMOTHY	TENNESSEE	M	W	

MORRISON, ERNEST	GEORGIA	M	W	

Ernest Morrison was convicted of the 1987 robbery, rape and strangulation of 54-year-old Mary Edna Griffin, who was related to Morrison by marriage. Morrison, who was staying with Griffin and her husband at the time of the killing, had escaped just four days earlier from a Georgia detention center where he was being held on charges involving the rape and robbery. At the time of the trial, Morrison asked the trial judge to impose the death sentence, calling it the right punishment.

INMATE	STATE	SEX	RACE	JUVENILE
MORRISON, JESSE	ALA/CA	M	B	
MORROW, RICKY E.	TEXAS	M	W	
MOSER, LEON	PENNSYLVANIA	M	W	
MOSS, BOBBY R.	NORTH CAROLINA	M	W	
MOTLEY, JEFFREY D.	TEXAS	M	W	
MU'MIN, DAWUD M.	VIRGINIA	M	B	
MUEHLEMAN, JEFFREY A.	FLORIDA	M	W	
MUELLER, EVERETT	VIRGINIA	M	W	
MUHAMMAD, ASKARI	FLORIDA	M	B	
MUNIZ, PEDRO CRUZ	TEXAS	M	H	
MUNOZ, JESUS	TEXAS	M	H	
MUNSON, ADOLPH	OKLAHOMA	M	B	
MURPHY, IRVIN	TEXAS	M	W	
MURPHY, JAMES	FEDERAL	M	B	

MURPHY, JOSEPH	OHIO	M	W	

On February 1, 1987, 73-year-old Ruth Predmore was stabbed to death in her home. She was found by a human services employee the next day. Joseph Dwayne Murphy was arrested by police days later and has been been convicted of the murder. Murphy, now 26, is in the appeals process.

INMATE	STATE	SEX	RACE	JUVENILE
MURRAY, ROBERT	MISSOURI	M	B	
MURTISHAW, DAVID	CALIFORNIA	M	W	
MUSGROVE, DONNIS	ALABAMA	M	W	
MUSSELWHITE, JOSEPH	CALIFORNIA	M	W	
NAKAHARA, EVAN TEEK	CALIFORNIA	M	A	
NAPIER, CARL E.	TEXAS	M	W	
NARVAIZ, LEOPOLDO	TEXAS	M	H	

INMATE	STATE	SEX	RACE	JUVENILE

NASH, VIVA LEROY **ARIZONA** **M** **W**

While serving two consecutive life sentences for murder and robbery in Utah, Viva Leroy Nash escaped. Three weeks later on November 3, 1982, he entered a coin shop in north Phoenix. He demanded money from an employee, Greggory West, and then shot West three times with a .357 handgun. As Nash fled, the proprietor of a nearby shop pointed a gun at him and told him to stop. Nash grabbed the weapon and the two men struggled over it. Police officers soon arrived and arrested Nash.

INMATE	STATE	SEX	RACE	JUVENILE
NAVARETTE, MARTIN	CALIFORNIA	M	H	
NAVE, EMMETT	MISSOURI	M	N	
NEAL, HOWARD	MISSISSIPPI	M	W	
NEAL, JOHN	ILLINOIS	M	W	
NEAL, JOHN L.	ALABAMA	M	B	*
NEELLEY, JUDITH	ALABAMA	F	W	
NEELY, CHARLES	CALIFORNIA	M	W	
NELSON, BILLIE	TEXAS	M	W	
NELSON, DAVID	ALABAMA	M	W	
NELSON, MARLIN E.	TEXAS	M	W	

NELSON, PETER D. **TEXAS** **M** **W**

After spending the night with him, Peter D. Nelson allegedly stabbed Lawrence Richardson 21 times, then fled with the dead man's car and wallet. Nelson, 36, an unemployed drifter, was arrested after using the dead man's credit cards. Police recovered the wallet and Richardson's driver's license with Nelson's photo laminated over it. The car was found along with a bag containing a bloodstained, 17-inch chef's knife and a lamination kit.

NETHERY, STEPHEN R. TEXAS M W

NEUSCHAFER, JIMMY **NEVADA** **M** **W**

Jimmy Neuschafer murdered inmate Willard Taylor while incarcerated at Nevada State Prison. Neuschafer strangled Taylor with a ligature fashioned from strands of bed sheets braided together. The victim died the next day at a hospital in Reno. At the time of this murder, Neuschafer was serving two consecutive life sentences for the rape and murder of two teenage girls in Carson City.

INMATE	STATE	SEX	RACE	JUVENILE

NEVIUS, THOMAS   **NEVADA**   **M**   **B**

During a 1980 burglary, Nevius shot 34-year-old David Lee Kinnamon, of Las Vegas. Nevius was arrested two years after the shooting. A New Jersy native, the 36-year-old Nevius is appealing his case in District Court.

| NEWLAND, ROBERT | GEORGIA | M | W | |
| NEWSTED, NORMAN L. | OKLAHOMA | M | W | |

NEWTON, FRANCES   **TEXAS**   **F**   **B**

Frances Newton, at 24 the youngest woman on Texas' Death Row, was convicted of murdering her 23-year-old husband, seven-year-old son, and 21-month-old daughter for insurance proceeds.

NGUYEN, TUAN A.	OKLAHOMA	M	A	
NICHOLS, HAROLD	TENNESSEE	M	W	
NICHOLS, JOSEPH B.	TEXAS	M	B	
NICKS, HARRY	ALABAMA	M	B	
NICOLAUS, ROBERT H.	CALIFORNIA	M	W	

NITZ, RICHARD   **ILLINOIS**   **M**   **W**

On April 6, 1988, Richard Nitz shot Michael David Miley, then decapitated him to potentially obscure the identification of the body. Miley's head has never been found. A prosecutor called Nitz "an obsessive homosexual hater." Miley was a homosexual. Nitz lost an October 21, 1991. Supreme Court appeal.

NIXON, JOE E.	FLORIDA	M	B	
NIXON, JOHN	MISSISSIPPI	M	W	
NOBLES, JONATHAN W.	TEXAS	M	W	
NOGUERA, WILLIAM	CALIFORNIA	M	H	
NOLAND, JOHN	NORTH CAROLINA	M	W	

INMATE	STATE	SEX	RACE	JUVENILE
NOLTE, MICHAEL	OKLAHOMA	M	W	
NORRIS, MICHAEL W.	TEXAS	M	B	
NUCKOLS, KENNETH	OKLAHOMA	M	W	
NUNLEY, RODERICK	MISSOURI	M	B	
O'DELL, JOSEPH	VIRGINIA	M	W	
O'GUINN, KENNETH W.	TENNESSEE	M	W	
O'MALLEY, JAMES	CALIFORNIA	M	W	

O'NEAL, ROBERT	**MISSOURI**	**M**	**W**	

On Feb. 3, 1984, 32-year-old Arthur Date was stabbed to death by fellow prison inmate, Robert E. O'Neal Jr. Authorities have said O'Neal is affiliated with the Aryan Nation, a white supremacist group. O'Neal is white; Dade was black. At the time of the fatal assault, O'Neal was serving a life sentence for killing an elderly man during a burglary. He has been granted an indefinite stay of execution.

O'ROURKE, MICHAEL	**ARKANSAS**	**M**	**W**	

Michael O'Rourke murdered his 61-year-old parents in 1983. His trial was delayed three years while he was in a state hospital. He had been judged incompetent to stand trial. O'Rourke was convicted of capital murder in 1986 and sentenced to death. In 1990, he said he didn't want to delay his execution any longer and requested that his attorney drop any appeals. His court-appointed attorney answered his requests by saying, "I don't know why he's doing this. It would be faster to just go through the appeals. By the time we get this [request for execution] heard he could have been through his appeal and been executed already."

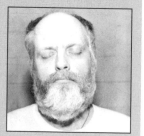

INMATE	STATE	SEX	RACE	JUVENILE
O'SHEA RONALD	PENNSYLVANIA	M	W	
OATS, SONNY BOY	FLORIDA	M	B	
OCCHICONE, DOMINICK	FLORIDA	M	W	
OCHOA, LESTER	CALIFORNIA	M	H	
ODLE, JAMES	CALIFORNIA	M	W	
ODLE, THOMAS	ILLINOIS	M	W	
OGAN, CRAIG	TEXAS	M	W	
OKEN, STEVE	MARYLAND	M	W	
OLINGER, PERRY	ILLINOIS	M	W	
OLIVER, JOHN WESLEY	NORTH CAROLINA	M	B	
OMELUS, ULRICK	FLORIDA	M	B	
ORANGE, LEROY	ILLINOIS	M	B	
ORNDORFF, MICHAEL	ARKANSAS	M	W	
ORTIZ, IGNACIO	ARIZONA	M	H	
OSBAND, LANCE	CALIFORNIA	M	B	
OTEY, HAROLD	NEBRASKA	M	B	
OWENS, GAILE	TENNESSEE	F	W	

INMATE	STATE	SEX	RACE	JUVENILE
OWENS, ROBIN	ILLINOIS	M	B	
OXFORD, RICHARD	MISSOURI	M	W	

PACE, BRUCE   FLORIDA   M   B

On November 4, 1988, 28-year-old Bruce Douglas Pace murdered an elderly taxi cab driver while on parole from an armed robbery conviction. Floyd Covington, 70, owner of Floyd's Taxi Service, was killed in his cab. Pace shot him once in the chest with a shotgun, then robbed him. Pace dumped the victim's body in a wooded area on the Eglin Air Force Base Reservation and ditched the blood-stained cab. Pace's appeal is pending before the Florida Supreme Court.

PADGETT, LARRY	ALABAMA	M	W	
PADILLA, ALFREDO A.	CALIFORNIA	M	H	

PADILLA, DANIEL   NEVADA   M   W

In 1986, Daniel Padilla, 31, and his half-brother, 27-year-old Dwayne Steven stabbed and shot to death Las Vegan Richard Holscher. Padilla and Stevens, both Los Angeles natives, are appealing their convictions in Nevada Supreme Court.

PADILLA, RAYMOND	FLORIDA	M	H	
PAGE, PATRICK	ILLINOIS	M	W	
PALMER, CHARLES	NEBRASKA	M	W	
PALMER, DONALD L.	OHIO	M	W	
PARADIS, DONALD	IDAHO	M	W	
PARDO, MANUEL	FLORIDA	M	H	
PARKER, BYRON	GEORGIA	M	W	
PARKER, HENRY	OKLAHOMA	M	W	

PARKER, J.B.   FLORIDA   M   B

J.B. "Pig" Parker was convicted and sentenced to death for the 1982 kidnapping and slaying of Frances Julia Slater, a teenaged convenience store clerk. Parker and three other men abducted Slater from the convenience store, then stabbed and shot her. She was left to die along an isolated road.

INMATE	STATE	SEX	RACE	JUVENILE
PARKER, JOHN	ALABAMA	M	W	
PARKER, JOHN	MISSOURI	M	B	
PARKER, NORMAN	FLORIDA	M	B	
PARKER, ROBERT L.	FLORIDA	M	W	

PARKER, STEVEN   **NEVADA**   **M**   **B**

In 1989, 24-year-old Parker killed Las Vegan Deborah Lynn Oscars, 23, in her home. A Henderson, Nev., native, Parker is appealing his sentence to the Nevada Supreme Court.

PARKER, WILLIAM   **ARKANSAS**   **M**   **W**

On November 3, 1984, in Rogers, Ark., Frankie Parker decided to get even with his wife Pam for leaving him. First, Parker tried to frame his wife's sister, Cindy Warren. He claimed that Warren shot him, but FBI detectives proved that Parker had hired someone else to do the shooting. Angered, Parker stalked Cindy and followed her to her parents house. He tried unsuccessfully to shoot Cindy, but managed to fatally shoot the girls' parents, James and Sandra Warren. Parker fled to his estranged wife's house where he picked up Pam at gunpoint. He drove to the local police station, shot and injured a police officer, and barricaded himself and Pam in the department. During the nearly three hours that followed, he shot Pam, and was wounded by police snipers. After treatment for the gunshot wounds, Parker was charged with two counts of felony murder (James and Sandra Warren), one count of attempted capital felony murder (Ofc. Ray Fejen), two counts of attempted first degree murder (Pam and Cindy), and one count of kidnapping. He was convicted on all charges and was sentenced to death by lethal injection on the capital murder charges. He remains on Arkansas' Death Row in the appeals process.

PARKUS, STEVEN J.	MISSOURI	M	W	
PARSONS, JOSPEH M.	UTAH	M	W	
PASCH, JOHN	ILLINOIS	M	W	
PATRICK, JESSIE	TEXAS	M	W	
PATTEN, ROBERT	FLORIDA	M	W	
PATTERSON, AARON	ILLINOIS	M	B	
PATTERSON, RAYMOND	SOUTH CAROLINA	M	B	
PATTILLO, KEITH	GEORGIA	M	W	
PAXTON, KENNETH W.	OKLAHOMA	M	B	
PAYNE, EDWARD	TEXAS	M	B	
PAYNE, JOSEPH	VIRGINIA	M	W	
PAYNE, PERVIS	TENNESSEE	M	B	

PAYNE, RANDY JOE   NORTH CAROLINA   **M**   **W**

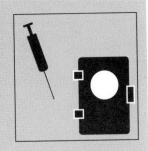

On November 9, 1983, Randy Joe Payne raped 69-year-old Kathleen Leonard Weaver and murdered her with a hatchet. He was given a death sentence January 26, 1985, in Davidson County, N.C. Payne, now 35, is waiting resentencing hearings. The previous conviction and death sentence was overturned by the North Carolina Supreme Court in July 1987 because Judge John Lewis talked to jurors without Payne being present. Payne's appeal concerns whether he was properly found guilty and whether he was properly sentenced.

PAYTON, WILLIAM	CALIFORNIA	M	W	

PAZ, FEDERICO   **IDAHO**   **M**   **H**

Federico Paz was convicted and sentenced to death for the 1987 murder of Gary Bright, 39. Paz was previously convicted for stabbing an Oregon man to death.

PECORARO, JOHN	ILLINOIS	M	W	
PEEDE, ROBERT	FLORIDA	M	W	
PEEPLES, WILLIAM	ILLINOIS	M	B	

PELLEGRINI, DAVID   **NEVADA**   **M**   **W**

In 1986, 25-year-old David Pellegrini killed a Las Vegas 7-Eleven clerk, Barry Hancock, 27. Pellegrini, a Missouri native, was sentenced to death. He is appealing his sentence to the Nevada Supreme Court.

PELZER, KEVIN	PENNSYLVANIA	M	B	
PENRY, JOHNNY PAUL	TEXAS	M	N	
PENSINGER, BRETT	CALIFORNIA	M	W	
PEOPLES, JOHN	ALABAMA	M	W	
PEREZ, AUGUSTINE	FLORIDA	M	H	
PEREZ, DOMINGO	ILLINOIS	M	H	
PEREZ, MANUEL J.	TEXAS	M	H	

INMATE	STATE	SEX	RACE	JUVENILE

PERILLO, PAMELA L.   TEXAS   F   W

Pamela L. Perillo, a former Houston, Texas, barmaid, was convicted of participating in the robbery-killing of 26-year-old Bob Skeens of Houma, La. In June 1989, the U.S. Supreme Court refused to hear her appeal. Perillo, now 32, sits on Death Row in Texas. Perillo is one of the four female inmates on Death Row in Texas.

PERRY, EUGENE   ARKANSAS   M   W

Eugene Perry was convicted and sentenced to death in July 1981 for the September 1980 shooting deaths of Kenneth Staton, 50, and his daughter Suzanne Staton Ware, 24, during the robbery of Staton's jewelry store.

| PERRY, MICHAEL OWEN | LOUISIANA | M | W | |
| PERRY, RANDY | OKLAHOMA | M | W | |

PERTGEN, WES   NEVADA   M   W

In 1986, 34-year-old Wes Pertgen killed his 44-year-old roommate, Eugene Kortkamp, in Las Vegas. Pertgen is appealing his sentence to the Nevada Supreme Court.

PETARY, DONALD	MISSOURI	M	W	
PETERKA, DANIEL	FLORIDA	M	W	
PETERKIN, OTIS	PENNSYLVANIA	M	B	
PETERSON, CHRISOPHER	INDIANA	M	B	

PETROCELLI, TRACY   NEVADA   M   W

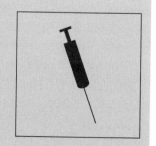

In 1982, Tracy Petrocelli killed James Wilson Sr., a 63-year-old Reno, Nev., man, during a robbery. Petrocelli, a 40-year-old native of Chicago, is appealing his case to the Nevada Supreme Court.

PETTIT, SAMUEL — FLORIDA — M — W

Samuel Pettit was convicted and sentenced to die for the August 1988 abduction and murder of assistant state attorney Norman Langston. Pettit approached Langston and Kathleen Finnegan, then also an assistant state attorney, at gunpoint as they were leaving a Howard Johnson's lounge. He forced them to drive to a remote area, where he shot each of the attorneys twice after robbing them. Langston, 27, died from head wounds two days later; Finnegan made a general recovery. Pettit has not appealed his case, but the Florida Supreme Court has filed his appeals for him anyway. Pettit has Huntington's disease — a degenerative brain disorder that eventually leads to death — and has said he would rather die than spend life in prison.

PHANOS, JOHN	MARYLAND	M	W
PHILLIPS, CLIFFORD X.	TEXAS	M	B
PHILLIPS, HARRY	FLORIDA	M	B
PHILLIPS, JOHN PAUL	ILLINOIS	M	W
PHILLIPS, RICHARD	CALIFORNIA	M	W
PHILLIPS, SHIRLEY	MISSOURI	F	W

PICKENS, CHARLES — ARKANSAS — M — B

Charles Pickens was sentenced to die in February 1976 for the 1975 slaying of Wesley Noble, 76, during a grocery store robbery. Witnesses said Pickens, one of three men who robbed the store and several customers, had fired the shots that killed Noble. During the robbery, another man was killed, five others were shot and one woman was raped.

PICKENS, DARRIN	OKLAHOMA	M	B

PIERCE, ANDY D. — ALABAMA — M — W

In 1988, Annie Ruth Brooks was bludgeoned to death by Andy Dwight Pierce. Pierce was hired by the 68-year-old Brooks, a prominent Geneva, Ala., widow, to do yard work at her home the day she was murdered. Brooks was found slain on her bed, bound and gagged with her bed linens. Brooks' body was found by a woman who called herself Pierce's commonlaw wife. Pierce was convicted in January 1989 and sentenced to die in Alabama's electric chair. Pierce, a white man, stated in court that he deserves a new trial because three blacks were not selected as jurors in his case. Pierce, now 32, is trying to arrange a new trial on the grounds of improper jury selection.

PIERCE, ANTHONY L.	TEXAS	M	B
PIERCE, MICHAEL	PENNSYLVANIA	M	W
PIETRI, NOBERTO	FLORIDA	M	H

PINCH, MICHAEL — NORTH CAROLINA — M — W

On October 18, 1979, Michael Pinch murdered two Greensboro, N.C., teenagers: Freddie Pacheco and Tommy Ausley. He was sentenced to death September 11, 1980. After spending 11 years on death row, Pinch is still among the 101 inmates in North Carolina currently awaiting their execution by lethal injection or the gas chamber.

INMATE	STATE	SEX	RACE
PINHOLSTER, SCOTT	CALIFORNIA	M	W
PINKNEY, BOBBY	MISSISSIPPI	M	B
PINNEL, MARK	OREGON	M	W
PIRELA, SIMON	PENNSYLVANIA	M	H
PITSONBARGER, JIMMY	ILLINOIS	M	W
PITTMAN, DAVID	FLORIDA	M	W
PITTS, JAMES L.	GEORGIA	M	B

PIZZUTO, GERALD — IDAHO — M — W

Gerald Pizzuto was convicted and sentenced to die for the bludgeoning deaths of Berta Herndon, 58, and her nephew Del Dean Herndon, 37. Pizzuto's 1990 appeal said his 1986 death sentence was flawed because it did not take into sufficient consideration that Pizzuto was continuously beaten as a child, may have suffered from epilepsy and could have sustained an injury to his brain that affected his thinking.

INMATE	STATE	SEX	RACE
PLANTZ, MARILYN K.	OKLAHOMA	F	W
PLATH, JOHN	SOUTH CAROLINA	M	W
PLESS, CARROLL	OHIO	M	W
POE, DAVID	TENNESSEE	M	W
POINDEXTER, DEWAINE	OHIO	M	B

POLAND, MICHAEL — ARIZONA — M — W

On the morning of May 24, 1977, two Purolator guards, Russell Dempsey and Cecil Newkirk, left Phoenix, Ariz., in an armored van on their scheduled run to banks in Prescott, Sedona and Flagstaff. At the Bumblebee Road exit on Interstate 17, the van was stopped by Michael and Patrick Poland, who were disguised as highway patrolmen and were driving a car with an emergency light bar on the top. The Polands took the guards captive, removed close to $300,000 in cash from the van, and left the scene. Around 6 a.m. on May 25, authorities found the abandoned Purolator van. That same morning, Michael Poland rented a boat at a Lake Mead marina. He then piloted the boat to a little-used landing where he met his brother. The Polands put the guards into canvas bags, took them across the lake and dumped them into the water. Three weeks later, the bodies surfaced in a cove on the Nevada side of the lake.

The Polands were convicted in federal court on robbery and kidnapping charges arising from these events. Their trial in state court on the murder charges followed.

INMATE	STATE	SEX	RACE	JUVENILE
POLAND, PATRICK	ARIZONA	M	W	
POLLARD, ROOSEVELT	MISSOURI	M	B	
PONTICELLI, ANTHONY	FLORIDA	M	W	
POPE, CARLTON	VIRGINIA	M	B	
POPE, JIMMIE	NORTH CAROLINA	M	W	
POPE, THOMAS DEWEY	FLORIDA	M	W	
PORTER, ANTHONY	ILLINOIS	M	B	
PORTER, ERNEST	PENNSYLVANIA	M	B	
PORTER, GEORGE J.	IDAHO	M	W	
PORTER, RALEIGH	FLORIDA	M	W	
PORTER, WILLIAM HOWARD	NORTH CAROLINA	M	N	
PORTER,GEORGE	FLORIDA	M	W	
PORTERFIELD, SIDNEY	TENNESSEE	M	B	
POST, RONALD	OHIO	M	W	
POTTS, JACK	GEORGIA	M	W	
POTTS, JACK HOWARD	GEORGIA	M	W	
POTTS, LARRY	INDIANA	M	B	
POWELL, DAVID	TEXAS	M	W	
POWELL, DUDLEY	OKLAHOMA	M	W	
POWELL, JAMES	TEXAS	M	N	

POWELL, KITRICH NEVADA M W

Kitrich Powell was convicted and sentenced to death for the November 1989 beating death of a 4-year-old child. The child was admitted to a Las Vegas hospital by Powell and the child's mother. An examination of the child revealed bruises and contusions about the forehead and left side of the throat. She also appeared to have been sexually abused. Powell, who was taking care of the child, stated she had fallen onto her neck and arms while he was playing with her. The victim died five days later. An autopsy revealed the child died from blunt trauma to the head, possibly on a recurring basis. Powell received the death sentence in May 1991.

POWELL, TIMOTHY	ALABAMA	M	B	
POWELL, TONY	OHIO	M	B	

POWELL, TRACY NEVADA M W

In 1989, Powell beat his girlfriend's 4-year-old daughter, Melie Allen, to death in Las Vegas. Powell is appealing his case to the Nevada Supreme Court.

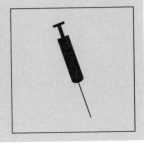

POWER, ROBERT	FLORIDA	M	W	
POYNER, SYVASKY	VIRGINIA	M	B	
PRATT, JAMES	IDAHO	M	W	

INMATE	STATE	SEX	RACE	JUVENILE
PRATT, JESSE	OREGON	M	W	
PRESNELL, VIRGIL	GEORGIA	M	W	
PRESTON, ELROY	MISSOURI	M	B	

PRESTON, ROBERT   FLORIDA   M   W

Robert Preston was convicted and sentenced to death for the 1978 robbery, kidnapping and murder of convience store clerk Earline Walker, 46. Walker's mutilated body was discovered about a mile away from the store in a field. Approximately $600 in cash and food was stolen from the store.

PRICE, CURTIS	CALIFORNIA	M	W	

PRICE, RICKY LEE   NORTH CAROLINA   M   W

Ricky Price was convicted and sentenced to death for the 1987 strangulation murder of Brenda Leigh Smith, 27. When sentenced to death, Price had already been convicted in the murder of Joan Brady in Virginia. He was sentenced to life in prison for her murder.

PRIDE, TIMOTHY	CALIFORNIA	M	B	
PROCTOR, ROGER	PENNSYLVANIA	M	B	
PROCTOR, WILLIAM	CALIFORNIA	M	W	
PROVENZANO, THOMAS	FLORIDA	M	W	
PRUETT, DAVID MARK	VIRGINIA	M	W	

PRUETT, MARION   ARKANSAS   M   W

Marion Pruett, the self proclaimed "mad dog killer," was sentenced to death September 1982 for the 1981 killing of Peggy Lowe, a Mississippi loan officer; the October 1981 abduction-slaying of Bobbie Jean Robertson, an Arkansas convenience store clerk; and three other murders in Colorado and New Mexico. In 1989 Pruett asked a Mississippi newspaper to pay him $20,000 in exchange for information on an engagement ring belonging to Lowe. The newspaper refused. In 1990, Pruett offered to reveal the whereabouts of a Florida victim's body for a paid appearance on the Geraldo Rivera show.

PRUITT, MARK ANTHONY	GEORGIA	M	W	
PUGH, WILLIE	ILLINOIS	M	B	
PUIATTI, CARL	FLORIDA	M	W	
PURSELL, ALAN	PENNSYLVANIA	M	W	

INMATE	STATE	SEX	RACE	JUVENILE
PURTELL, ROBERT MICHAEL	TEXAS	M	W	

PUTMAN, WILLIAM GEORGIA M W

William Putman was convicted of the shooting deaths of William G. Hodges, David N. Hardin and Katie C. Black. For the first murder he was given one life sentence (1981) and for the second two murders he received two death sentences (1982).

INMATE	STATE	SEX	RACE	JUVENILE
PYLES, JOHNNY D.	TEXAS	M	W	
QUARTERMAIN, DRAX	CALIFORNIA	M	W	
QUESINBERRY, GEORGE	VIRGINIA	M	W	
QUESINBERRY, MICHAEL	NORTH CAROLINA	M	W	
QUICK, HAROLD	NORTH CAROLINA	M	B	
QUINCE, KENNETH	FLORIDA	M	B	
QUINTERO, DERRICK	TENNESSEE	M	H	
RABBANI, SYED M.	TEXAS	M	A	
RADFORD, RONALD	GEORGIA	M	W	
RAGSDALE, EDWARD	FLORIDA	M	W	
RAINEY, MICHAEL	PENNSYLVANIA	M	B	
RALEY, DAVID	CALIFORNIA	M	W	
RAMEY, IRVING	ILLINOIS	M	B	
RAMIREZ, CARLOS	TEXAS	M	H	
RAMIREZ, DAVID M.	ARIZONA	M	H	
RAMIREZ, JOSEPH	FLORIDA	M	H	

RAMIREZ, RICHARD CALIFORNIA M H

In the summer of 1985, Richard "The Night Stalker" Ramirez terrorized residents of Southern California during a string of bizarre murders, sexual attacks and burglaries. Characteristics of Ramirez's murders included: scrawling pentangles, the sign of the devil, in a victim's blood across a wall; inscribing a pentagram in lipstick on another murder victim's thigh; gouging the eyes out of a murder victim (a form of mutilation sometimes practiced by devil worshipers); and shooting a victim's husband before raping her twice, and then sodomizing her eight-year-old son. On September 20, 1989, Ramirez was found guilty on 43 counts, including 13 murders counts and various other charges of burglary, sodomy and rape. He remains on California's Death Row and is in the appeals process.

INMATE	STATE	SEX	RACE	JUVENILE
RAMIREZ, RICHARD RAYMOND	CALIFORNIA	M	H	
RAMOS, MARCELINO	CALIFORNIA	M	H	
RAMSEY, ROY	MISSOURI	M	B	

INMATE	STATE	SEX	RACE	JUVENILE
RANDOLPH, RICHARD	FLORIDA	M	B	
RANSOM, KENNETH RAY	TEXAS	M	B	
RAY, CLARENCE	CALIFORNIA	M	W	

RAY, JOHN — SOUTH CAROLINA — M — W

John Ray was convicted and sentenced to death for the 1990 murder and kidnapping of Josylin Ballenger, 20. Ray and three other men were charged with killing Ballenger and dumping her body in an abandoned well.

REAVES, WILLIAM	FLORIDA	M	B	
RECTOR, CHARLES	TEXAS	M	B	

RED DOG, JAMES — DELAWARE — M — N

On February 14, 1992, James Red Dog was convicted of murder. He was sentenced to be executed on July 12, 1992. Red Dog is one of seven men on death row in Delaware. Delawares' Death Row inmates are not housed together like most other states. Each of the inmates cases are under appeal.

They are housed in two different prison facilities and at different security levels. In 1986 legislation was enacted to make lethal injection the mode of execution. The last time an attempt was made to abolish the death penalty in Delaware was 1955, however, the bill was voted on three times and defeated.

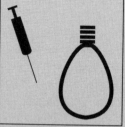

REDMEN, TIMOTHY — NEVADA — M — W

In 1990, Redmen killed and mutilated a 57-year-old Las Vegas tourist Max Biederman. Redmen, a native of West Virginia, had his appeal to the Nevada Supreme Court denied in March of 1992.

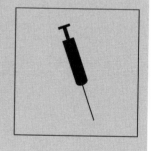

REED, GROVER	FLORIDA	M	W	
REED, JONATHAN B.	TEXAS	M	W	
REESE, DONALD	MISSOURI	M	W	
REEVES, MICHAEL	NORTH CAROLINA	M	W	
REEVES, RANDOLPH	NEBRASKA	M	N	
REGAN, DERRICK	PENNSYLVANIA	M	B	
REID, ANTHONY	PENNSYLVANIA	M	B	

INMATE	STATE	SEX	RACE	JUVENILE
REID, LLOYD	PENNSYLVANIA	M	B	
REILLY, MARK	CALIFORNIA	M	W	
REMETA, DANIEL	ARK/FLA	M	N	
RESNOVER, GREGORY	INDIANA	M	B	
REVILLA, DANIEL	OKLAHOMA	M	W	
REY, JOHNNY	TEXAS	M	H	
RHOADES, PAUL	IDAHO	M	W	
RHODES, RICHARD	FLORIDA	M	W	

RICE, DAVID LEWIS	WASHINGTON	M	W

David Rice was convicted and sentenced to death for the 1985 murders of Charles and Annie Goldmark and their two children, 10-year-old Colin and 12-year-old Derek. Rice killed the family December 24, 1985.

RICE, TONY	TEXAS	M	W
RICH, DARRELL	CALIFORNIA	M	N
RICHARDS, MICHAEL W.	TEXAS	M	B
RICHARDSON, DAMON	TEXAS	M	B
RICHARDSON, FLOYD	ILLINOIS	M	B
RICHARDSON, JAMES D.	TEXAS	M	B
RICHARDSON, MIGUEL A.	TEXAS	M	B
RICHARDSON, TOMMY	FLORIDA	M	B
RICHEY, KENNETH	OHIO	M	W
RICHLEY, DARYL	ARKANSAS	M	W

RICHMOND, WILLIE LEE	ARIZONA	M	B

On August 25, 1973, Willie Richmond and two female accomplices took Bernard Crummett to the outskirts of Tucson. Crummett believed one of the women was going to commit an act of prostitution with him. At the scene, Richmond knocked Crummett to the ground, then hit him over the head with some rocks. One of the women took Crummett's wallet. Then either Richmond or one of the girls killed him by running over him with the car.

RICKMAN, RONALD	TENNESSEE	M	W
RIDDLE, ERNEST	SOUTH CAROLINA	M	W
RIDDLE, GRANVILLE	TEXAS	M	W
RIECHMANN, DIETER	FLORIDA	M	W
RIEL, CHARLES D.	CALIFORNIA	M	W
RIGGINS, DAVID	NEVADA	M	W

INMATE	STATE	SEX	RACE	JUVENILE
RILES, RAYMOND	TEXAS	M	B	

RILEY, BILLY R.   **NEVADA**   **M**   **B**

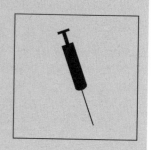

In 1989, during a drug-related argument, Riley shot to death 26-year-old Albert Bolin of Las Vegas. Riley, a native of Louisiana, is appealing his case in district court.

INMATE	STATE	SEX	RACE	JUVENILE
RILEY, JAMES	DELAWARE	M	B	
RILEY, MICHAEL LYNN	TEXAS	M	B	
RIOS, JOE	TEXAS	M	H	
RIVERA, ANGEL	TEXAS	M	H	
RIVERA, MICHAEL	FLORIDA	M	H	
RIVERA, SAMUEL	FLORIDA	M	H	
RIVERS, DELORES	PENNSYLVANIA	F	B	
RIVERS, WARREN	TEXAS	M	B	
ROBBINS, MALCOLM	CALIFORNIA	M	W	
ROBBINS, PHILLIP	NORTH CAROLINA	M	B	
ROBEDEAUX, JAMES	OKLAHOMA	M	N	
ROBERSON, BRIAN A.	TEXAS	M	B	
ROBERTS, LARRY	CALIFORNIA	M	B	
ROBERTS, MICHAEL	OKLAHOMA	M	B	
ROBERTS, RICKEY	FLORIDA	M	B	
ROBERTS, ROY	MISSOURI	M	W	
ROBERTS, SAMMY	SOUTH CAROLINA	M	W	
ROBERTS, VICTOR	GEORGIA	M	B	
ROBERTSON, ALLEN	LOUISIANA	M	B	

ROBERTSON, ANDREW   **CALIFORNIA**   **M**   **W**

Andrew Robertson was convicted of killing two women, Karen Ann Litzau, 20, and Kimberly Gloe, 19, in October 1977. Their nude bodies, found dumped along a freeway, had been stabbed and slashed more than 100 times. Both women were prostitutes Robertson picked up at a San Bernardino truck stop. Robertson claimed that delayed stress from his U.S. Army experience in Vietnam led him to rape and kill the two women. He was sentenced to die in 1978.

INMATE	STATE	SEX	RACE	JUVENILE

ROBERTSON, LAVARITY   FLORIDA   M   B

Lavarity Robertson was convicted and sentenced to death for the double murders of two young lovers. Frank Najarro, 19, and Isilia Paguada, 18, were parked in a lovers' lane in November, 1988. Robertson, armed with a shotgun, approached their car and demanded money. He shot Najarro, who died in the lap of his beloved, then repeatedly shot Paguada. Robertson was 20 when he committed the killings.

ROBERTSON, MARK	TEXAS	M	W	

ROBINS, CHARLES   NEVADA   M   B

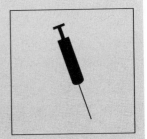

Charles Robins caused the 1988 death of his girl friend's 11-month-old baby daughter when he repeatedly hit and shook the baby. Robins caused a broken back, subdural hematoma and multiple hemorrhages to the head, abdomen, back and legs of the baby. Robins had physically abused the baby on several prior occasions. He was convicted and sentenced to death December 1988.

ROBINSON, DWIGHT	NORTH CAROLINA	M	B	
ROBINSON, EDDIE	NORTH CAROLINA	M	B	
ROBINSON, FRED	ARIZONA	M	B	
ROBINSON, JOHNNY	FLORIDA	M	B	
ROBINSON, TIMOTHY	FLORIDA	M	B	
ROBINSON, WALANZO	OKLAHOMA	M	B	
ROBINSON, WILLIAM	TEXAS	M	B	

ROBISON, LARRY K.   TEXAS   M   W

On August 10, 1982, Larry Robison began avenging a homosexual affair that turned sour. Six hours later, five people—including an 11-year-old boy—lay dead in the outskirts of Fort Worth, Texas. All of the victims had their throats slashed, were shot in the head and were stabbed repeatedly. His former lover, Bruce Gardner, was decapitated, sexually mutilated and cannibalized. His other victims were the next-door neighbors whom Robison killed and robbed, in order to obtain a getaway car. Eleven months later, Robison was tried for capital murder in Gardner's death: he had been charged on all five deaths, and details of the savage murders came out in his trial. After jurors rejected the defense's argument of guilty by reason of insanity, they sentenced him to death by lethal injection. He remains on Texas' Death Row in the appeals process.

ROCHE, CHARLES	INDIANA	M	W	

ROCHEVILLE, DAVID SOUTH CAROLINA M W

On January 7, 1991, David Rocheville and Richard Longworth, both 23, stole $3,000 from a theater safe in Spartanburg, S.C. In the process, two theater workers, Alex Hopps, 19, and Todd Green, 24, were murdered. After his arrest, Longworth told police that he first struggled with Hopps in an effort to knock him out. Later, Longworth admitted holding Hopps over a bar behind the theater as Hopps was shot in the head with Longworth's .44-caliber pistol. Todd Green was driven away from the theater, then ordered to get out of the van, walk five paces and kneel down. According to Longworth, Rocheville shot Green. Both men later split the money from the burglary. Arrests were made after the Westgate theater manager's son remembered seeing Rocheville in Green's car in the parking lot on the night of the shootings. Convicted of capital murder, both men are currently on South Carolina's Death Row in the appeals process.

INMATE	STATE	SEX	RACE	JUVENILE
RODDEN, JAMES	MISSOURI	M	W	
RODRIGUES, JOSE	CALIFORNIA	M	H	

RODRIGUEZ, FRANK COLORADO M H

Frank Rodriguez and his brother, Chris, were convicted in the 1984 abduction, rape, robbery and murder of Denver bookkeeper Lorraine Martelli, 54. Rodriguez, a parolee with three felony convictions at the time of the murder, abducted Martelli 10 blocks away from the courthouse where he was tried. He then beat, raped, gagged and tortured Martelli, stabbing her 28 times. Both Rodriguez brothers were found guilty of Martelli's murder. Frank, however, was sentenced to death by a jury who found he committed the brutal stabbings. Another jury spared his brother's life and sentenced him to life in prison.

INMATE	STATE	SEX	RACE	JUVENILE
RODRIGUEZ, LIONEL	TEXAS	M	H	
RODRIGUEZ, LUIS	CALIFORNIA	M	H	
RODRIGUEZ, STEVE	TEXAS	M	H	
RODRIQUEZ, JUAN	FLORIDA	M	H	
ROE, JOHN GLENN	OHIO	M	W	
ROGERS, DAVID	ALA/CA	M	W	
ROGERS, DAYTON	OREGON	M	W	
ROGERS, JAMES	GEORGIA	M	W	

ROGERS, JERRY L. FLORIDA M W

Jerry Rogers was convicted and sentenced to death for the murder of David Eugene Smith, an assistant manager of a grocery store. Rogers and his cohort, Thomas McDermid, shot Smith in the aftermath of an aborted armed robbery. Rogers and McDermid escaped and returned to their homes in Orlando. They were charged with the murders later, with McDermid given immunity from prosecution by acting as state's witness against Rogers.

INMATE	STATE	SEX	RACE	JUVENILE
ROGERS, KELLY	OKLAHOMA	M	B	

ROGERS, MARK NEVADA M W

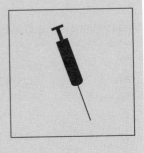

Mark Rogers, 32, was sentenced to death in 1981 for the December 1980 murders of an elderly couple and their adult daughter in a mining camp outside Lovelock, Nev. Rogers, an aspiring actor known also as "Teepee Fox," was convicted of repeatedly stabbing and shooting Emery and Mary Strode, a couple in their 70s, and their 41-year-old daughter, Meriam Strode Treadwell.

ROGERS, PATRICK	TEXAS	M	B	
ROGERS, ROCKY D.	VIRGINIA	M	W	
ROGERS, STANLEY	FLORIDA	M	W	

ROJAS, MARTIN OHIO M H

Jesse Rojas was convicted and sentenced to death for the May 1987 murder of Rebecca Scott, 28, who befriended Rojas at a Christian center. When Scott rebuffed Rojas' sexual advances, he went to her apartment and stabbed her repeatedly. He also raped her while she was dying.

ROJEM, RICHARD	OKLAHOMA	M	W	
ROLAN, FLORENCIO	PENNSYLVANIA	M	H	
ROLLINS, SAHARRIS	PENNSYLVANIA	M	B	

ROMANOSKY, JOHN ARIZONA M W

On the night of May 17, 1986, John and Sara Smith were staying at a Travel Lodge motel in Phoenix. That same night John Romanosky, Debra Summerville, and Charles Shepherd came to the motel looking for money. Romanosky told Summerville to begin knocking on doors. When she knocked on the Smiths' door, John Smith answered and Summerville told him that she had the wrong room. A few minutes later, Summerville knocked again, and this time Sara Smith answered. When she opened the door, Romanosky pushed into the room and pointed a gun at Mr. Smith. Romanosky demanded money. As Mr. Smith reached for his wallet, Romanosky shot him in the chest. Romanosky ordered Mrs. Smith to get her dead husband's wallet, but she was unable to do so. Summerville then took the wallet and left with Romanosky. Summerville pleaded guilty to second-degree murder and testified against Romanosky. Shepherd was convicted of first-degree murder and received a life sentence.

INMATE	STATE	SEX	RACE	JUVENILE
ROMINE, LARRY	GEORGIA	M	W	
ROMPILLA, RONALD	PENNSYLVANIA	M	W	
RONDON, REYNALDO	INDIANA	M	H	
ROPER, JAMES E.	NORTH CAROLINA	M	W	
ROSALES, MARIANO JUAREZ	TEXAS	M	H	
ROSE, CLINTON	NORTH CAROLINA	M	W	
ROSE, JAMES	FLORIDA	M	W	
ROSE, JASON	OREGON	M	W	
ROSE, JOHN	NORTH CAROLINA	M	M	
ROSE, MILO A.	FLORIDA	M	W	
ROSS, ARTHUR	ARIZONA	M	W	
ROSS, BOBBY LYNN	OKLAHOMA	M	B	
ROSS, CRAIG	CALIFORNIA	M	B	
ROSS, JAMES C.	TEXAS	M	B	

ROSS, MICHAEL   CONNECTICUT   M   W

On May 12, 1981, Michael Bruce Ross, a student at Cornell University, assaulted and raped 25-year-old Dzung Ngoc Tu. On June 13, 1984, Ross was driving when he spotted 17-year-old Wendy Baribeault walking along the rode. After unsuccessfully trying to offer her a ride, he jumped out of his car, dragged her 200 yards into the woods, raped and strangled the girl. When Ross was finally picked up by police in June 1984, he provided the keys to 11 unsolved assaults and murders in Connecticut, New York and North Carolina. On December 13, 1985, he was sentenced in Windham County, Conn., to 120 years in prison—two consecutive life terms—for the 1982 murders of Tammy Williams and Debra Taylor. And on July 6, 1987, in Bridgeport, Conn., Ross became the first man sentenced to die in the state's electric chair since Connecticut's last execution in 1960. He was charged with the murders of Wendy Baribeault, Robin Stavinsky, April Brunais and Leslie Shelley. He has petitioned, unsuccessfully, for a change in the law requiring mandatory review of death sentences and his public defenders continue to prepare his appeal to the Connecticut Supreme Court.

ROSSI, RICHARD   ARIZONA   M   W

Around 12:30 p.m. on August 29, 1983, Richard Rossi went to the Scottsdale, Ariz., home of Harold August, supposedly to sell a typewriter. Instead, he shot August three times. After the first two shots, August said, "You've got my money and you've shot me, what more do you want?" Rossi then shot August in the mouth, killing him. A neighbor, Sherrill Nutter, heard the shots and walked into the August home. Rossi hit her over the head with a blackjack and shot her twice in the chest. Nutter survived.

INMATE	STATE	SEX	RACE	JUVENILE
ROUGEAU, PAUL	TEXAS	M	B	
ROUSE, KENNETH	NORTH CAROLINA	M	B	
ROUSSEAU, ANIBAL	TEXAS	M	H	

INMATE	STATE	SEX	RACE	JUVENILE
ROUSTER, GREGORY	INDIANA	M	B	
ROUTLY, DANIEL	FLORIDA	M	W	
ROWLAND, GUY	CALIFORNIA	M	W	
ROY, LARRY	ALABAMA	M	W	
RUDD, EMERSON	TEXAS	M	B	
RUESCHER, ED	MISSOURI	M	W	
RUIZ, ALEJANDRO	CALIFORNIA	M	N	
RUIZ, LUIS	ILLINOIS	M	H	
RUIZ, PAUL	ARKANSAS	M	H	
RUNDLE, DAVID	CALIFORNIA	M	W	
RUNNING EAGLE, SEAN	ARIZONA	M	N	

RUPE, MITCHELL	**WASHINGTON**	**M**	**W**	

Mitchell Rupe was convicted and sentenced to death for the 1981 shooting deaths of bank tellers Twila Capron and Candace Hemmig.

INMATE	STATE	SEX	RACE	JUVENILE
RUSSELL, CLIFTON CHARLES	TEXAS	M	W	
RUSSLE, WILLIE	MISSISSIPPI	M	B	
RUST, JOHN	NEBRASKA	M	W	

RUTHERFORD, ARTHUR	**FLORIDA**	**M**	**W**	

On Aug. 22, 1985, 26-year-old Arthur D. Rutherford killed 63-year-old Stella Salamon. Salamon had employed Rutherford to do odd jobs around her house for about 10 years. A doctor testified Salamon died by asphyxiation, either by drowning or having a hand put over her mouth. She also suffered three blows to the head that the doctor said could have rendered her unconscious. A witness testified that Rutherford said he hit the victim in the head with a hammer. Her beaten body was found in a bloody bathtub at her home.

INMATE	STATE	SEX	RACE	JUVENILE
RYAN, MICHAEL	NEBRASKA	M	W	
SAKARIAS, PETER	CALIFORNIA	M	W	
SALAZAR, ALPHONSO	ARIZONA	M	H	
SALAZAR, MANUEL	ILLINOIS	M	H	
SALAZAR, MAXIMO	OKLAHOMA	M	N	
SALCIDO, RAMON	CALIFORNIA	M	H	
SALLIE, WILLIAM	GEORGIA	M	W	
SAMAYOA, RICHARD	CALIFORNIA	M	H	
SAMPLE, MICHAEL	TENNESSEE	M	B	
SAN MIGUEL, JESSE	TEXAS	M	H	
SANBORN, PARRAMORE	KENTUCKY	M	W	

INMATE	STATE	SEX	RACE	JUVENILE
SANCHEZ, HECTOR	ILLINOIS	M	H	
SANCHEZ, TEDDY	CALIFORNIA	M	H	
SANCHEZ-VELASCO, R.	FLORIDA	M	H	
SANDERS, DAVID L.	KENTUCKY	M	W	
SANDERS, NORMAN	LOUISIANA	M	H	
SANDERS, RAYMOND	ARKANSAS	M	B	
SANDERS, RICARDO	CALIFORNIA	M	B	
SANDERS, RONALD	CALIFORNIA	M	W	
SANDERS, STANLEY	NORTH CAROLINA	M	B	
SANDERSON, RICKY LEE	NORTH CAROLINA	M	W	
SANDOVAL, ALFRED	CALIFORNIA	M	H	
SANTANA, CARLOS	TEXAS	M	H	
SANTOS, CARLOS	FLORIDA	M	H	
SAPP, JOHN	CALIFORNIA	M	W	
SATCHER, CHARLES M.	VIRGINIA	M	B	
SATTERWHITE, JOHN T.	TEXAS	M	B	
SATTIEWHITE, VERNON	TEXAS	M	B	
SAUNDERS, WILLIAM	VIRGINIA	M	B	
SAVINO, JOSEPH J.	VIRGINIA	M	W	

SAWYER, ROBERT **LOUISIANA** **M** **W**

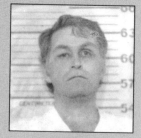

In 1978, 23-year-old Frances Arwood was attacked while babysitting the children of Robert Wayne Sawyer's girlfriend. Testimony showed that Sawyer and Charles Lane beat her, poured hot coffee on her, scalded her with boiling water, and then doused her with lighter fluid and set her on fire. She later died of severe burns and brain damage.

Lane was convicted of first-degree murder in Arwood's death and given life in prison. Sawyer was sentenced to die in the electric chair. Since Louisiana changed its method of execution to lethal injection, a new execution date has not been set for Sawyer as of Oct. 12, 1991.

SAWYERS, JOHN C.	TEXAS	M	W	
SCHAAF, STEVEN R.	ARIZONA	M	W	

SCHACKART, RONALD **ARIZONA** **M** **W**

Ronald Schackart and Charla Regan had known each other since high school and they continued to be friends at the University of Arizona. On March 8, 1984, Schackart told Regan he needed a place to stay since his parents had kicked him out of their house. He also told her he needed to talk to her about his wife's filing rape charges against him. They went to a Tucson Holiday Inn where Schackart raped Regan at gunpoint, hit her in the face with the gun, strangled her, and stuffed a sock into her mouth. He reported the killing to the police and claimed he had not intended to kill Regan.

INMATE	STATE	SEX	RACE	JUVENILE

SCHAD, EDWARD   ARIZONA   **M**   **W**

On August 1, 1978, Lorimer "Leroy" Graves, a 74-year-old Bisbee resident, left home in a new Cadillac. He was on a trip to Everett, Wash., to visit his sister. Eight days later, Graves' badly decomposed body was discovered hidden in the brush just off U.S. Highway 89 south of Prescott. Graves had been strangled with a rope that was still knotted around his neck. A month later, Edward Schad was stopped for speeding in New York. Schad was driving Graves' Cadillac, and many of Graves' personal belongings were in the car.

SCHIRO, THOMAS   INDIANA   **M**   **W**

In February 1981, Thomas Schiro pretended to have car trouble, knocked on Laura Jane Luebbehusen's door, and asked to use a telephone. During the next several hours, Schiro, 20, raped, mutilated and strangled Luebbehusen, 28, and then continued to beat, chew and have sexual relations with her body. Convicted in 1981, Schiro, now 30, is still in the appeals process.

SCHLUP, LLOYD	MISSOURI	M	W
SCHMECK, MARK L.	CALIFORNIA	M	W
SCHNEIDER, ERIC	MISSOURI	M	W
SCHURZ, ELDON M.	ARIZONA	M	N
SCHWAB, MARK	FLORIDA	M	W
SCOTT, ABRON	FLORIDA	M	B
SCOTT, JAMES	CALIFORNIA	M	B
SCOTT, JAY D.	OHIO	M	B
SCOTT, JEREMY L.	FLORIDA	M	W
SCOTT, LARRY	ILLINOIS	M	B
SCOTT, PAUL	FLORIDA	M	W
SCOTT, ROGER	ARIZONA	M	W
SCOTT, SIDNEY	OKLAHOMA	M	W
SCUDDER, KEVIN	OHIO	M	W
SCULL, JESUS	FLORIDA	M	H
SEATON, RONALD H.	CALIFORNIA	M	B
SECHREST, RICKY	NEVADA	M	W
SEIBER, LEE	OHIO	M	W

INMATE	STATE	SEX	RACE	JUVENILE

SELLERS, SEAN — OKLAHOMA — M — W

On September 8, 1985, Robert Paul Bower, a 36-year-old convenience store clerk, was shot to death in the middle of the night with a .357-caliber pistol by Sean Richard Sellers. Sellers later confessed that the motive was to see how it felt to kill someone.

On March 6, 1986, 16-year-old Sellers, clad only in his underwear and armed with a .44-caliber pistol, crept into his parents bedroom and shot them to death. He tried to disguise the murder as a homicidal burglary. His defense at trial was that he was under the influence of Satan.

He was convicted of three counts of first-degree murder and sentenced to death. He has since claimed that he has found Jesus and has appeared with Geraldo, Oprah and on the CBS news show "48 Hours." He remains on Oklahoma's Death Row.

SELVAGE, JOHN HENRY	TEXAS	M	B	

SERNA, JOHN — ARIZONA — M — H

John Serna was an inmate at the Perryville, Ariz., prison. On June 21, 1985, Patrick Chavarria was transferred from the Florence, Ariz., prison to Perryville. When Serna learned Chavarria was at Perryville, he decided to kill him. Serna was able to find a length of steel pipe and corner Chavarria in the laundry room. He broke Chavarria's kneecap with the pipe, and then beat him over the head, killing him.

SESSION, JAMES	TEXAS	M	B	
SEUFFER, JAMES	ILLINOIS	M	W	
SEXTON, MICHAEL	NORTH CAROLINA	M	B	
SHARP, MICHAEL E.	TEXAS	M	W	
SHARPING, MICHAEL	SOUTH CAROLINA	M	W	

SHAW, ROBERT — MISSOURI — M — B

On July 16, 1979, 61-year-old correctional officer Walter Farrow was stabbed by inmate Bobby Lewis Shaw. Authorities said Shaw grabbed two butcher knives in a kitchen area of the state penitentiary and stabbed Farrow. Farrow bled to death. Another prison employee was injured. According to reports, Shaw had been offered a diamond ring to carry out the murder. Shaw was serving a life sentence for killing his sister's boyfriend, Calvin Morris, in 1975.

SHELDON, JEFFREY	CALIFORNIA	M	W	
SHELL, ROBERT LEE	MISSISSIPPI	M	B	
SHEPHERD, JOE	TENNESSEE	M	W	

INMATE	STATE	SEX	RACE	JUVENILE
SHERE, RICHARD E.	FLORIDA	M	W	
SHERRIDAN, DARYL	ARKANSAS	M	W	
SHURN, DARYL	MISSOURI	M	B	
SHURN, KEITH	ILLINOIS	M	B	
SIDEBOTTOM, ROBERT T.	MISSOURI	M	W	
SIEBERT, DANIEL	ALABAMA	M	W	
SIGLER, DALE	TEXAS	M	W	
SILAGY, CHARLES	ILLINOIS	M	W	
SILVA, BENJAMIN	CALIFORNIA	M	A	
SILVA, MAURICIO	CALIFORNIA	M	H	

SIMKO, JOHN JR.   **OHIO**   **M**   **W**

John Simko Jr. was convicted in June 1991 of kidnapping and aggravated murder in the death of Mary Jane Johnson. The 58-year-old janitor purchased a .357-caliber handgun less than a week before the slaying, telling his cousin he needed it because he thought a prowler was coming around his home. Johnson, Simko's former girlfriend, was held at gunpoint and then shot as she fled from the elementary school where they were both employed as janitors. He was also convicted of kidnapping another janitor, Howard "Bud" Baker, who tried to intervene when he found Simko holding Johnson at gunpoint in the teachers' lounge.

Witnesses testified that Simko spent the evening before the slaying drinking and executing his will, and wrote a check to his son, Jim, for the remaining balance in his checking account. He also made arrangements with a cousin, Larry Simko, to take his boat. He told his cousin he planned to kill two people that evening.

SIMMONS, BEORIA	KENTUCKY	M	B	
SIMMONS, JONATHAN	SOUTH CAROLINA	M	B	
SIMMS, DARRYL	ILLINOIS	M	B	
SIMON, RICHARD	TENNESSEE	M	B	
SIMON, ROBERT	MISSISSIPPI	M	B	
SIMONSEN, DAVID	OREGON	M	W	
SIMPSON, PERRIE	NORTH CAROLINA	M	B	

SIMS, MITCHELL   **CALIF./S.C.**   **M**   **W**

On December 2, 1985, former Domino's pizza restaurant manager Mitchell Sims entered a Hanahan, S. C., Domino's, tied up the two employees, took money out of a safe, and fatally shot Chris Zerr and Gary Melke. Sims and his girlfriend, Ruby Padgett, fled to California. The pair, later called "The Killing Team" by prosecutors, devised another plan of attack against Domino's to occur a week later. After purchasing ammunition for the gun, rope for tying people up, socks to use as gags, a knife for "general purposes" and Vodka for courage, the two checked into a motel just a few minutes from a Glendale, Calif., Domino's. They called for a pizza to be delivered, and waited for their next victim to show up. After he arrived with the pizza, he was held at gunpoint, bound and gagged, then drowned in a bathtub with a pillowcase over his head. The two returned to the Domino's, wearing the boy's uniform shirt and name tag underneath his jacket. After

INMATE	STATE	SEX	RACE	JUVENILE

robbing the store, Sims left the two remaining employees bound and suspended by their necks in the walk-in cooler. A chance arrival of another employee saved them. Sims was sentenced to death in California and then tried, convicted and sentenced to death in South Carolina. It took less time for the complete trial in South Carolina than it had taken California to pick a single juror. He is in the appeals process in both states, but is likely to remain in South Carolina.

SIMS, TERRY	FLORIDA	M	W	

SINGLETON, CHARLES   **ARKANSAS**   **M**   **B**

Charles Singleton fatally stabbed Mary Lou York, 62, during the robbery of her grocery store June 1, 1979. He twice stabbed her in the neck as she yelled to her niece, "Go get help. Charles Singleton is killing me." A police officer later testified in court that York also identified Singleton when the officer found York bleeding on the floor of her store. York died en route to the hospital.

SINGLETON, CORNELIUS   **ALABAMA**   **M**   **B**

Cornelius Singleton was sentenced to die in 1981 for the 1977 robbery and murder of Sister Ann Hogan, a Roman Catholic nun. Her body was found bound and gagged under a pile of debris in a Catholic cemetery. Singleton confessed the murder to Mobile police officers.

SINGLETON, FRED	SOUTH CAROLINA	M	B	
SIRECI, HENRY	FLORIDA	M	W	
SIRIPONGS, JATURUN	CALIFORNIA	M	A	
SIVAK, LACEY	IDAHO	M	W	
SIX, ANDREW	MISSOURI	M	W	

SKAGGS, DAVID   **KENTUCKY**   **M**   **W**

During a May 6, 1981, robbery, Herman and Mae Matthews were shot to death. David Leroy Skaggs was convicted of killing the elderly couple. On October 7, 1991, the Supreme Court upheld his conviction and death sentence.

INMATE	STATE	SEX	RACE	JUVENILE
SKIPPE, SHERMAN	NORTH CAROLINA	M	W	
SLAGEL, BILLY	OHIO	M	N	
SLATON, NATHAN	ALABAMA	M	W	*
SLAUGHTER, MICHAEL	CALIFORNIA	M	B	
SLAWSON, NEWTON	FLORIDA	M	W	
SLAWTER, JAMES	KENTUCKY	M	B	
SLOAN, JEFFREY	MISSOURI	M	W	
SMITH, ANDY	SOUTH CAROLINA	M	B	

SMITH, BERNARD   **ARIZONA**   **M**   **B**

Shortly after midnight on August 22, 1983, Bernard Smith entered the Low Cost Market in Yuma, Ariz. He purchased cigarettes, and paid with a $5 bill. When the transaction was rung up and the cash drawer opened, Smith pointed a pistol at Charles Pray, the 57-year-old cashier, and demanded the money. When Pray turned and called out the name of a fellow employee, Smith raised the pistol and fired one .22-caliber bullet through the base of Pray's head, severing the spinal cord. Smith walked around the counter and removed the paper money from the cash register and left. Two women outside the store watched Smith walk to his car, and called the police with his license number. Smith was arrested within minutes of the shooting.

SMITH, BOBBY D.	OKLAHOMA	M	W	
SMITH, BRIAN	PENNSYLVANIA	M	W	
SMITH, CHARLES	TEXAS	M	W	
SMITH, CLIFFORD	PENNSYLVANIA	M	B	
SMITH, DAVID	ILLINOIS	M	W	
SMITH, DAVID	KENTUCKY	M	W	
SMITH, DERRICK	FLORIDA	M	B	

SMITH, FRANK E.   **FLORIDA**   **M**   **B**

Frank Smith Jr. was convicted and sentenced to death for the December 1978 robbery, abduction and murder of Sheila Porter, 19. Smith and two other men robbed Porter then drove her to a motel where she was raped. Her body was found three days later with three bullets in the back of her head.

SMITH, FRANK L.	FLORIDA	M	B	
SMITH, GERALDINE	ILLINOIS	F	B	
SMITH, GREGORY	CALIFORNIA	M	U	
SMITH, JACK HARRY	TEXAS	M	W	
SMITH, JAMES	PENNSYLVANIA	M	B	

SMITH, JOE ARIZONA M W

Shortly before midnight on December 30, 1975, 18-year-old Sandy Spencer finished work at a fast food restaurant and began hitchhiking home. Joe Smith picked her up and drove her to a desert location north and west of Phoenix. There he bound her, forced dirt into her mouth and nostrils, and taped her mouth closed. Spencer died of asphyxiation. To satisfy himself that she was actually dead, Smith stabbed her numerous times and embedded a 2-inch sewing needle in her breast. Spencer's nude body was found January 1, 1976.

In late January of 1976, Smith picked up another hitchhiker, 14-year-old Neva Lee. Smith took the girl to another desert location and killed her in similar fashion. Her nude body was discovered on February 2, 1976. Smith was tried and convicted of both murders.

INMATE	STATE	SEX	RACE
SMITH, KENNETH E.	ALABAMA	M	W
SMITH, KERMIT	NORTH CAROLINA	M	W
SMITH, LAROYCE	TEXAS	M	B
SMITH, LEONARD	TENNESSEE	M	W
SMITH, LOIS	OKLAHOMA	F	W
SMITH, MIKELL P.	OKLAHOMA	M	W
SMITH, OSCAR F.	TENNESSEE	M	W
SMITH, PHILLIP	OKLAHOMA	M	B
SMITH, RANDALL	OREGON	M	W
SMITH, REBECCA	SOUTH CAROLINA	F	W
SMITH, RICHARD	OKLAHOMA	M	W
SMITH, RICKY G.	TENNESSEE	M	B

SMITH, ROBERT ARIZONA M W

Sometime between March 11 and March 14, 1980, Robert Smith, Joe Leonard Lambright and Kathy Foreman picked up Sandra Owen, who was hitchhiking near Tucson, Ariza. They subsequently kidnapped Owen and Smith raped her twice. They took the victim to a remote area in the mountains outside Tucson. Lambright and Smith then killed Owen by choking her, stabbing her, and hitting her in the head with a large rock. They concealed her body by covering it with rocks, and the body was not discovered until one year later.

Lambright and Smith were tried in a joint trial before two separate juries. Foreman testified against them in exchange for a grant of immunity.

INMATE	STATE	SEX	RACE
SMITH, ROBERT	KENTUCKY	M	W
SMITH, ROBERT	TEXAS	M	B

SMITH, ROGER LYNN — ARIZONA — M W

On June 6, 1981, Roger Smith, along with Alfredo and Antonio Abila, decided to rob Farmer's Liquor Store in Phoenix. While the Abila brothers waited outside in the car, Smith entered the store carrying a sawed-off shotgun. Smith pointed the weapon at the clerk, Herman Helfand, and demanded money. Helfand opened the cash register and stepped back. Smith took approximately $150 from the register and then shot Helfand once in the head. The Abila brothers pleaded guilty to armed robbery and were sentenced to prison.

INMATE	STATE	SEX	RACE
SMITH, ROGER	NORTH CAROLINA	M	B
SMITH, RONALD	MONTANA	M	W

SMITH, ROY B. — VIRGINIA — M W

On July 24, 1988, Manassas (Va.) Police Sgt. John Conner left his mother's house to check on a call that a man was firing shots in front of his home. Conner, 37, was shot to death by Roy Bruce Smith. Smith, 42, had several previous run-ins with the law, mostly alcohol related. He was known to loathe authority figures, especially police and had a record of being a violent drunk. Smith was suicidal and intoxicated at the time of the murder. Smith was convicted of capital murder and now sits on Virginia's Death Row.

INMATE	STATE	SEX	RACE
SMITH, ROY G.	TEXAS	M	B
SMITH, SAMUEL D.	MISSOURI	M	B
SMITH, SYLVESTER	TENNESSEE	M	B
SMITH, TERRY WILLIAM	NORTH CAROLINA	M	W
SMITH, TOMMIE	INDIANA	M	B
SMITH, WILLIAM H.	OHIO	M	B
SMITH, WILLIE ALBERT	MISSISSIPPI	M	B
SMITHEY, GEORGE H.	CALIFORNIA	M	W
SNEED, DAVID	OHIO	M	B
SNELL, RICHARD	ARKANSAS	M	W
SNELSON, RICKY	MISSISSIPPI	M	W

SNOW, JOHN — NEVADA — M B

In 1983, Snow was hired to kill a Las Vegas lounge owner, Harry Wham, 63. Snow, 49, was convicted of the contract killing and sentenced to death. The Ohio native is appealing his sentence in district court.

INMATE	STATE	SEX	RACE	JUVENILE
SNOW, PRENTIS	CALIFORNIA	M	B	
SNOW, ROCKY D.	OKLAHOMA	M	W	
SOCHOR, DENNIS	FLORIDA	M	W	
SOCKWELL, MICHAEL	ALABAMA	M	B	
SOFFAR, MAX A.	TEXAS	M	W	
SOKE, THEODORE	OHIO	M	U	
SONION, CHARLES	TEXAS	M	W	
SORIA, JUAN SALVEZ	TEXAS	M	H	
SOSA, PEDRO S.	TEXAS	M	H	
SOUTH, ROBERT W.	SOUTH CAROLINA	M	W	
SOUTHERLAND, ROBERT	SOUTH CAROLINA	M	W	
SOWELL, BILLIE	OHIO	M	B	
SPANN, STERLING B.	SOUTH CAROLINA	M	B	
SPARKS, WILLY	TENNESSEE	M	B	

INMATE	STATE	SEX	RACE	JUVENILE
SPAZIANO, JOSEPH	**FLORIDA**	**M**	**W**	

Crazy Joe Spaziano was convicted and sentenced to death in July 1976 for the 1973 murder of Laura Lynn Harberts, 18, a hospital clerk. She disappeared after going out with a man named Joe, and her mutilated body was found two weeks later in a trash dump. The body of a second woman was also found in the trash, but no charges were filed in that killing because the body was never identified. Spaziano had a prior rape conviction, where he cut the eyes of his 16-year-old victim in an attempt to keep her from identifying him. He was sentenced to life plus five years for that attack.

INMATE	STATE	SEX	RACE	JUVENILE
SPEARS, BRIAN	OKLAHOMA	M	W	
SPENCE, DAVID WAYNE	TEXAS	M	W	
SPENCE, MORRIS	PENNSYLVANIA	M	B	
SPENCER, CLINTON	ARIZONA	M	W	
SPENCER, JAMES	GEORGIA	M	B	
SPENCER, LEONARD	FLORIDA	M	B	
SPENCER, TIMOTHY	VIRGINIA	M	B	
SPIRKO, JOHN G.	OHIO	M	W	
SPISAK, FRANK	OHIO	M	W	
SPIVEY, RONALD	GEORGIA	M	W	
SPIVEY, WARREN	OHIO	M	B	
SPRANGER, WILLIAM	INDIANA	M	W	
SPREITZER, EDWARD	ILLINOIS	M	W	
SPRUILL, JONNIE LEE	NORTH CAROLINA	M	B	
SQUIRES, WILLIAM	FLORIDA	M	W	
ST. PIERRE, ROBERT	ILLINOIS	M	W	
STAFFORD, ROGER	OKLAHOMA	M	W	
STAGER, BARBARA	NORTH CAROLINA	F	W	
STALEY, STEVEN	TEXAS	M	W	
STAMPER, CHARLES	VIRGINIA	M	B	

INMATE	STATE	SEX	RACE	JUVENILE

STANFORD, KEVIN — KENTUCKY — M — B

Kevin Stanford was sentenced to die in Kentucky's electric chair for the 1981 abduction and murder of Baerbel Poore, a 20-year-old gas station attendant. Stanford was 17 at the time of the crime. His case was a key element in the U.S. Supreme Court ruling permitting the execution of killers as young as 16. Stanford and two others robbed the gas station of $143.07 in cash, 300 cartons of cigarettes, and two gallons of gasoline, Then, according to police reports, Stanford and another teen-ager sexually abused and terrorized Poore before Stanford gave her a last cigarette, then shot her twice in the head.

STANKEWITZ, DOUGLAS	CALIFORNIA	M	N	
STANLEY, DARREN	CALIFORNIA	M	B	
STANLEY, GERALD	CALIFORNIA	M	W	

STANLEY, MILO — ARIZONA — M — W

On the evening of June 19, 1986, Milo Stanley and his wife, Susan, were arguing about his drinking problem. He drove Susan; his five-year-old daughter, Seleste; and his one-year-old son, Chad, to a remote area outside Cottonwood, Ariz. Stanley and Susan continued to argue as they sat in the car. Stanley ended the argument by shooting Susan three times in the head. He then shot Seleste once in the top of the head. He did not shoot Chad because the boy was too young to tell what he had seen. After dumping the bodies of Susan and Seleste off the side of the road, Stanley went home and put Chad to bed. Several hours later, he called the police and told them that Susan and Seleste were missing. The police began a search that ended late the following day when Stanley confessed. Stanley received the death penalty for the murder of Seleste, and a life sentence for the murder of Susan.

STANO, GERALD	FLORIDA	M	W	
STANSBURY, ROBERT	CALIFORNIA	M	W	

STARR, DAVID LEE — ARKANSAS — M — B

David Starr was sentenced to die for the June 1985 beating, rape and murder of Gladys Ford, 76, during a robbery at her home.

STARR, GARY	PENNSYLVANIA	M	W	
STATEN, DEONDRE	CALIFORNIA	M	B	

INMATE	STATE	SEX	RACE	JUVENILE
STEELE, RAYMOND	CALIFORNIA	M	W	
STEELE, ROLAND	PENNSYLVANIA	M	B	

STEFFEN, DAVID **OHIO** **M** **W**

On August 19, 1982, David Joseph Steffen, a door-to-door salesman with a troubled past, killed Karen Range. She was found lying on a bathroom floor in a pool of blood.

STEIDL, GORDON	ILLINOIS	M	W	
STEIN, STEVEN	FLORIDA	M	W	
STEINHORST, WALTER	FLORIDA	M	W	
STEPHENS, VICTOR	ALABAMA	M	B	

STEPHENS, W. KENNY **GEORGIA** **M** **B**

William Stephens was convicted and sentenced to death for the 1979 murder of Sheriff's Investigator Larry Douglas Stevens. The investigator stopped Stephens' car, and was shot by Stephens in the right elbow with a high-powered rifle. Letter carrier William Cleek, an eyewitness to the murder, said the investigator tried to hide in his car after he was shot. "I saw a man standing there, pointing a rifle or shotgun. He walked around the back of the car and raised the gun up and he shot. He was just standing there, cool, calm and collected. It didn't seem like he had a care in the world."

STERLING, GARY	TEXAS	M	B	
STERLING, TERRY NASH	TEXAS	M	B	
STEVENS, DALLAS	OREGON	M	W	
STEVENS, DWAYNE	NEVADA	M	W	
STEVENS, RUFUS	FLORIDA	M	W	
STEVENS, THOMAS	GEORGIA	M	W	
STEVENSON, JOHN	TENNESSEE	M	W	
STEWARD, JAMES W.	ARIZONA	M	B	
STEWART, CHARLES	ALABAMA	M	W	
STEWART, DARRYL E.	TEXAS	M	B	
STEWART, KENNETH	FLA/VA	M	W	
STEWART, RAYMOND	ILLINOIS	M	B	
STEWART, ROY	FLORIDA	M	W	
STEWART, WALTER	ILLINOIS	M	B	
STEWART, RICHARD	CALIFORNIA	M	W	
STILES, RUSSELL	OKLAHOMA	M	W	
STOCKTON, DENNIS	VIRGINIA	M	W	
STOKER, DAVID W.	TEXAS	M	W	

STOKES, RALPH PENNSYLVANIA M B

Ralph Stokes was sentenced to death for killing three people on March 11, 1982, when he held up a city restaurant. Stokes shot and killed two employees and a letter carrier.

INMATE	STATE	SEX	RACE	JUVENILE
STONE, RAYMOND	FLORIDA	M	W	
STOREY, JOSEPH	MISSOURI	M	W	
STOUFFER, BIGLER	OKLAHOMA	M	W	
STOUT, BILLY	OKLAHOMA	M	W	
STOUT, LARRY A.	VIRGINIA	M	B	
STREET, CHARLES	FLORIDA	M	B	
STRICKLAND, TYRONE	ILLINOIS	M	B	
STRICKLER, TOMMY D.	VIRGINIA	M	W	
STRINGER, JAMES R.	MISSISSIPPI	M	W	

STRIPLING, ALFONSO GEORGIA M B

On October 16, 1988, Alfonso Stripling shot Gregory Bass and Anthony Evans to death during a robbery. On July 7, 1989, Stripling was convicted in Douglas County, Ga., of two shooting counts, armed robbery and aggravated assault. Stripling, now 36, awaits execution by electric chair on Georgia's Death Row.

INMATE	STATE	SEX	RACE	JUVENILE
STROUTH, DONALD	TENNESSEE	M	N	
STUART, EUGENE	IDAHO	M	W	
STUMPF, JOHN	OHIO	M	W	
STYERS, JAMES L.	ARIZONA	M	W	
SUGGS, ERNEST	FLORIDA	M	U	
SULLY, ANTHONY J.	CALIFORNIA	M	W	
SUMMERLIN, WARREN	ARIZONA	M	W	
SUMMERS, GREGORY	TEXAS	M	W	
SUTHERLAND, CECIL	ILLINOIS	M	W	
SUTTON, NICHOLAS	TENNESSEE	M	W	
SWAFFORD, ROY	FLORIDA	M	W	
SWEET, GLENNON	MISSOURI	M	W	
SWEET, WILLIAM	FLORIDA	M	B	
SYRIANI, ELIAS H.	NORTH CAROLINA	M	A	
SZABO, JOHN	ILLINOIS	M	W	
SZUCHON, JOSEPH	PENNSYLVANIA	M	W	
TART, WILLIAM	LOUISIANA	M	B	

INMATE	STATE	SEX	RACE	JUVENILE
TARVER, BOBBY	ALABAMA	M	B	
TARVER, ROBERT	ALABAMA	M	B	
TASSIN, ROBERT	LOUISIANA	M	W	
TATE, KENNETH	OKLAHOMA	M	W	
TAYLOR, BRIAN K.	GEORGIA	M	B	
TAYLOR, C.W.	MISSISSIPPI	M	B	
TAYLOR, DARRYL	TENNESSEE	M	W	
TAYLOR, FELTUS	LOUISIANA	M	B	

TAYLOR, FREDDIE LEE　　CALIFORNIA　　M　　B

On January 22, 1985, Carmen Vasquez was beaten to death in her Richmond, Calif., home. Freddie Lee Taylor was convicted of the slaying. On October 7, 1991, the U.S. Supreme Court rejected his appeal and let stand the murder conviction and death sentence.

Taylor remains on Death Row in California, along with 305 other Death Row inmates currently awaiting execution in the gas chamber.

TAYLOR, JOHN A.	UTAH	M	W	
TAYLOR, MICHAEL	MISSOURI	M	B	
TAYLOR, NORRIS	NORTH CAROLINA	M	B	
TAYLOR, PAUL	PENNSYLVANIA	M	B	
TAYLOR, PERRY A.	FLORIDA	M	B	
TAYLOR, RAYVON	OHIO	M	B	
TAYLOR, RICHARD C.	TENNESSEE	M	W	

TAYLOR, ROBERT　　CALIFORNIA　　M　　B

Robert "T-Bone" Taylor and friend Norman DeWitt were convicted of the January 1991 murder, assault, burglary and robbery of Kazumi, 65, and Ryoko Hanano, 60. Taylor shot Ryoko, then shot Kazumi twice in the head. Kazumi survived, but is now paralyzed from the waist down. DeWitt, who testified against Taylor, received life sentence without possibility of parole. Taylor was sentenced to death January 31, 1992.

TAYLOR, STEVEN	FLORIDA	M	W	
TAYLOR, VICTOR	KENTUCKY	M	B	
TAYLOR, VON	UTAH	M	W	
TEAGUE, DELBERT BOYD	TEXAS	M	W	
TEAGUE, RAYMOND	TENNESSEE	M	W	
TEDFORD, DONALD	PENNSYLVANIA	M	W	
TEEL, BOULDIN	TENNESSEE	M	W	
TEFFETELLER, ROBERT	FLORIDA	M	W	
TENNARD, ROBERT J.	TEXAS	M	B	
TENNER, JAMES	ILLINOIS	M	B	
TERRELL, DREW	ILLINOIS	M	B	
TERRY, BENJAMIN	PENNSYLVANIA	M	B	

INMATE	STATE	SEX	RACE	JUVENILE
TERRY, JOHN D.	TENNESSEE	M	W	
THANOS, JOHN	MARYLAND	M	W	
THARPE, KEITH	GEORGIA	M	B	
THAVIRAK, SAM	PENNSYLVANIA	M	A	
THOMAS, ALFRED	KENTUCKY	M	W	
THOMAS, BRIAN	PENNSYLVANIA	M	B	
THOMAS, CHRIS	VIRGINIA	M	W	*
THOMAS, DANNY DEAN	TEXAS	M	N	
THOMAS, DARRELL	OKLAHOMA	M	W	
THOMAS, DAVID	FLORIDA	M	B	

THOMAS, DONRELL	**CALIFORNIA**	**M**	**B**	

On March 31, 1986, Donrell Thomas murdered Avery Lawson after robbing Lawson outside the victim's apartment. Thomas, now 29, is waiting for the Supreme Court to hear his appeal.

INMATE	STATE	SEX	RACE
THOMAS, JAMES EDWARD	NORTH CAROLINA	M	B
THOMAS, JESSE LEE	NORTH CAROLINA	M	B
THOMAS, JOSEPH L.	FEDERAL	M	W
THOMAS, KENNETH G.	ALABAMA	M	W
THOMAS, KENNETH W.	TEXAS	M	B
THOMAS, LEROY	PENNSYLVANIA	M	B
THOMAS, PATRICIA	ALABAMA	F	B
THOMAS, RALPH	CALIFORNIA	M	B
THOMAS, WALTER	ILLINOIS	M	B
THOMAS, WILLIE	ILLINOIS	M	B
THOMPKINS, WILLIE	ILLINOIS	M	B
THOMPSON, CHARLIE	FLORIDA	M	B
THOMPSON, CRAIG	TENNESSEE	M	B
THOMPSON, EUGENE W.	KENTUCKY	M	W
THOMPSON, GREGORY	TENNESSEE	M	B
THOMPSON, JOHN	LOUISIANA	M	B
THOMPSON, LOUIS	PENNSYLVANIA	M	B

THOMPSON, MICHAEL	**ALABAMA**	**M**	**W**	

Michael Thompson was convicted for the December 10, 1984, robbing, kidnapping, and murder of Maisie Gray, a 57-year old store clerk. Gray's body was found in a well three weeks after the crime. Court evidence proved that Thompson forced Gray into the well then shot her.

INMATE	STATE	SEX	RACE	JUVENILE
THOMPSON, RAYMOND	FLORIDA	M	W	
THOMPSON, RICKY	TENNESSEE	M	W	

THOMPSON, ROBERT CALIFORNIA M W

Robert Thompson was convicted in the 1981 murder of 12-year-old newspaper boy Benjamin Brenneman. Thompson, who has a lifelong history of molestations, was in the fourth month of his parole from another molestation conviction when he abducted the boy, sexually assaulted him, then killed him. Brennman's sandals were later found in Thompson's apartment and helped lead to his arrest. In 1983, a jury recommended Thompson receive the death penalty. When Superior Court Judge Francisco Briseno followed the jury's recommendations and sentenced Thompson to die in California's gas chamber, he commented, "Mr. Thompson was picked up long ago as being a danger to our children, and we let him out. We knew when we let him out that he had not been rehabilitated. And why did we let him out? Budgetary reasons. One of the richest states in the country cannot keep a person this dangerous away from others."

THOMPSON, STEVEN	ALABAMA	M	W	
THOMPSON, THOMAS	CALIFORNIA	M	W	

THOMPSON, WILLIAM NEVADA M W

William Thompson, 46, was convicted in 1984 of killing a 28-year-old transient. He has insisted that he will forego appeals, and wishes to be executed for the killing of Randy Waldron at Waldron's campsite on the banks of the Truckee River in Reno, Nev. At the time of that killing, Thompson was wanted for the murder of two California brothers. Thompson had spent 23 years in reform schools or prisons in Texas, New York and Florida.

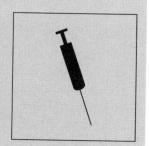

THORSON, ROGER	MISSISSIPPI	M	W	
TIGER, THOMAS	OKLAHOMA	M	N	
TILLEY, WILLIAM	PENNSYLVANIA	M	W	
TILLMAN, ELROY	UTAH	M	B	
TITONE, DINO	ILLINOIS	M	W	
TOBIN, CHRISTOPHER	CALIFORNIA	M	W	

TODD, ROBERT ILLINOIS M W

Robert Todd was convicted and sentenced to death for the 1989 murder of Sandra Shelton. Todd strangled and stabbed Shelton to death in her home. Her nude body, found by Shelton's 15-year-old daughter, was covered with vegetable oil, candlewax droplets and feces. This was Todd's first conviction. Although the death sentence is usually administered to repeat offenders, authorities believe it applies to this case because of the brutality of Todd's crimes.

TODD, WILLIAM L. GEORGIA M W

William Todd was convicted and sentenced to die for robbing and hammering Randy Allen Churchill to death. Todd testified at his trial that Churchill had befriended him and allowed Todd to live in his home.

TOMPKINS, WAYNE FLORIDA M W

Wayne Tompkins was convicted and sentenced to death for the March 1983 strangulation murder of Lisa DeCarr. Tompkins lived with the victim, her mother and children for two years. He admitted killing DeCarr and burying her body under their house because she refused to have sex with him.

TORRES-ARBOLEDO, OSCAR	FLORIDA	M	H
TOWNES, RICHARD	VIRGINIA	M	B
TOWNS, TERRENCE	ILLINOIS	M	B
TOWNSEL, ANTHONY	CALIFORNIA	M	B
TOWNSEND, JOHNNY	INDIANA	M	B
TRAN, HECK VAN	TENNESSEE	M	A
TRAVAGLIA, MICHAEL	PENNSYLVANIA	M	W
TRAWICK, GARY	FLORIDA	M	B
TREPAL, GEORGE	FLORIDA	M	W
TREVINO, JOSE MARIO	TEXAS	M	H
TRICE, EDDIE	OKLAHOMA	M	B
TROTTER, MELVIN	FLORIDA	M	B

TRUEBLOOD, MICHAEL INDIANA M W

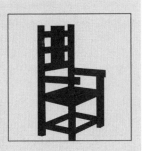

In August 1988, Michael Trueblood shot his girlfriend, 22-year-old Susan Bowsher of Lafayette, Ind., and her two children, Ashelyn Hughes, 2, and William Bowsher, 1. The victims' bodies were found in a shallow grave in rural Fountain County, Ind. In 1990, Trueblood admitted to the killings.

TRUESDALE, LOUIS	SOUTH CAROLINA	M	B
TUCKER, JEFFERY	TEXAS	M	W

INMATE	STATE	SEX	RACE	JUVENILE

TUCKER, KARLA FAY **TEXAS** **F** **W**

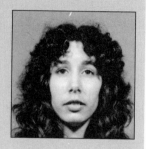

Karla Fay Tucker, 29, was convicted in 1983 of participating in the pickax killings of Jerry Lynn Dean, 26, and Deborah Ruth Thornton, 32. A co-defendant in the trial, Daniel Garrett, is also incarcerated on the Texas Death Row.

TUCKER, MICHAEL	OREGON	M	W
TUGGLE, LEM	VIRGINIA	M	W

TUILAEPA, PAUL **CALIFORNIA** **M** **A**

On October 6, 1986, Paul Tuilaepa murdered Melvin Whiddon during the robbery of a bar in Long Beach, Calif. Tuilaepa, now 26, is waiting for the Supreme Court to hear his appeal.

TURNER, CLAUDE	NORTH CAROLINA	M	W
TURNER, DOUGLAS	MONTANA	M	W
TURNER, ERIC	FLORIDA	M	B
TURNER, JESSEL	TEXAS	M	B
TURNER, MELVIN	CALIFORNIA	M	B
TURNER, RICHARD	CALIFORNIA	M	W
TURNER, ROBERT	ILLINOIS	M	W
TURNER, THADDEUS	CALIFORNIA	M	B
TURNER, WILLIAM	FLORIDA	M	B
TURNER, WILLIE LLOYD	VIRGINIA	M	B
TWENTER, VIRGINIA	MISSOURI	F	W
TYE, JIMMIE	ILLINOIS	M	B
TYLER, ARTHUR	OHIO	M	B
TYREE, TROY	GEORGIA	M	W
UNDERWOOD, HERBERT	INDIANA	M	W
UPCHURCH, JAMES	NORTH CAROLINA	M	W
UPTON, JACKIE WAYNE	TEXAS	M	W
URBANO, GILBERT	TEXAS	M	H
VALDES, FRANK	FLORIDA	M	H
VALDEZ, ALBERTO	TEXAS	M	H
VALDEZ, ALFREDO	CALIFORNIA	M	H
VALDEZ, GERALDO	OKLAHOMA	M	H
VALENTINE, TERANCE	FLORIDA	M	B

INMATE	STATE	SEX	RACE	JUVENILE

VALERIO, JOHN — NEVADA — M — H

In 1986, Valerio stabbed Las Vegas prostitute, 26-year-old Sue Blackwell, to death. Valerio, 27, of Utah, has appealed his sentence to the Nevada Supreme Court.

INMATE	STATE	SEX	RACE
VALLE, MANUEL	FLORIDA	M	H
VAN CLEAVE, GREG	INDIANA	M	B
VAN DENTON, EARL	ARKANSAS	M	W
VAN HOOK, ROBERT	OHIO	M	W

VAN POYCK, WILLIAM — FLORIDA — M — W

During a 1987 botched escape attempt, William Van Poyck shot to death Fred Griffis, a Glades Correctional Institution officer. According to testimony, Van Poyck shot him in an attempt to free an old prison friend, James O'Brien. Griffis was transporting O'Brien in a prison van, because O'Brien needed to see a doctor. Griffis, a highly decorated U.S. Army Ranger, was shot three times in the chest and head when he refused to cooperate. Van Poyck also shot at West Palm Beach, Fla., police cars while fleeing in a stolen Cadillac.

VAN WOUDENBERG, SAMMY — OKLAHOMA — M — N

VANDERBILT, JIM — TEXAS — M — W

Jimmy Vanderbilt, a former Amarillo, Texas, police officer is a long-time resident of the Texas Death Row. Vanderbilt was convicted of the April 1975 killing of 16-year-old Katina Moyer whose body was found on a rural road with a single gunshot wound to the head.

INMATE	STATE	SEX	RACE
VAUGHN, ROGER	TEXAS	M	W
VEASLEY, CHAUNCEY	CALIFORNIA	M	B
VEGA, MARTIN	TEXAS	M	H
VENTURA, PETER	FLORIDA	M	W

VICKERS, ROBERT ARIZONA M W

In 1977, Vickers was just a small time thief when he was sent to prison in Arizona. There, he adopted the nickname, "Bonzai Bob," and committed the acts that would land him on death row. In October 1978, Vickers strangled his cell mate, Frank Ponciano, 21, with a knotted bed sheet. Ponciano apparently had failed to awaken Vickers for lunch and drank his Kool-Aid. Vickers then used a sharpened toothbrush to stab Ponciano six times and carve his nickname in the man's back. Prior to this, Vickers had stabbed another inmate and subsequently received another 10 to 15 years on his original sentence. Vickers was sentenced to death in August 1979. While on death row in March 1982, Vickers threw a firebomb into fellow death row inmate Buster Holsinger's cell, killing him. When guards asked Vickers what happened, he said "I burned Buster." Among his many colorful letters, he sent a message to the medical examiner relishing the crime and inquiring whether Holsinger looked and smelled like a burnt piece of toast. Vickers remains in the appeals process on Arizona's Death Row.

VICTOR, CLARENCE	NEBRASKA	M	B
VIEIRA, RICHARD	CALIFORNIA	M	H
VIGNEAULT, DONALD LEE	TEXAS	M	W

VILLAFUERTE, JOSE ARIZONA M H

On February 22, 1983, Jose Villafuerte was arrested near Ash Fork, Ariz. He was in possession of a car belonging to Amelia Scoville. When Phoenix police officers went to Villafuerte's home, they found her body, clad only in a blouse, bra, and panties. Her hands were tied behind her back and a strip of bedding bound one of her ankles to her hands. Scoville's head was wrapped in a sheet, a bedspread, and long thermal underwear, all of which were bloodstained. A ball made of a tightly wrapped strip of bedsheet was found in her throat. Scoville had died as a result of gagging. Lab tests showed the presence of seminal fluid in her vagina.

VILLAREAL, R. MARTINEZ	ARIZONA	M	H

VINING, JOHN FLORIDA M W

On November 18, 1987, 39-year-old Georgia Caruso, a manicure shop owner and part-time gems dealer, disappeared after meeting George Williams. According to testimony, Caruso had expected to sell Williams $60,000 worth of diamonds. Her remains were found in a field a month later. John Vining, 59, was convicted of posing as George Williams and shooting Caruso in the head. The crime occurred while he was on parole for land fraud and forgery.

INMATE	STATE	SEX	RACE	JUVENILE
VISCOTTI, JOHN	CALIFORNIA	M	W	
VON DOHLAN, HERMAN	SOUTH CAROLINA	M	W	
VUONG, HAI KIEN	TEXAS	M	A	
WADDY, WARREN	OHIO	M	B	
WADE, FORREST K.	OKLAHOMA	M	N	
WADE, JOHNNY	GEORGIA	M	W	

WADE, MELVIN   **CALIFORNIA**   **M**   **B**

Melvin Wade, 33, was sentenced to die for the 1981 torture-murder of his 10-year-old stepdaughter. Evidence indicated that during a 20-hour period, he beat the child with his fists and a board, put her in a duffle bag, choked her with a dog leash, and punched and stomped on her stomach. Wade carried out the deed while drinking a bottle of wine. He shouted that he was an archangel and would kill the child because she was a devil.

INMATE	STATE	SEX	RACE	JUVENILE
WADER, MICHAEL	CALIFORNIA	M	W	
WAIDLA, TAYNO	CALIFORNIA	M	W	
WAINRIGHT, KIRT	ARKANSAS	M	B	
WALDON, BILLY	CALIFORNIA	M	N	
WALDROP, BILLY	ALABAMA	M	W	
WALKER, ALLEN	MISSISSIPPI	M	W	
WALKER, ANTHONY	OHIO	M	U	
WALKER, GARY	OKLAHOMA	M	W	
WALKER, JACK D.	OKLAHOMA	M	W	
WALKER, JERRY	GEORGIA	M	B	
WALKER, MARVIN	CALIFORNIA	M	B	
WALKER, MAXINE	ALABAMA	F	W	
WALKER, RICHARD	GEORGIA	M	B	
WALKER, SHAWN	PENNSYLVANIA	M	B	
WALKER, THOMAS	CALIFORNIA	M	U	
WALKER, TOMMY JOE	TENNESSEE	M	W	

WALLACE, DONALD   **INDIANA**   **M**   **W**

On January 14, 1980, Donald Ray Wallace Jr. murdered Patrick and Theresa Gilligan, both 30, and their two children, Lisa, 5, and Gregory, 4. The adult family members were killed after they returned home unexpectedly and discovered a burglary in progress. According to trial testimony, the children were killed so they wouldn't have to grow up as orphans. Wallace, now 42, has been ordered to die in Indiana's electric chair January 17, 1992.

INMATE	STATE	SEX	RACE	JUVENILE
WALLACE, GEORGE	OKLAHOMA	M	W	

WALLACE, JAMES ARIZONA M W

James Wallace lived with Susan Insalaco and her two children, 16-year-old Anna and 12-year-old Gabe. On the night of January 31, 1984, Insalaco and Wallace had an argument and Wallace planned to leave the next day. However, when Anna returned from school that day, Wallace killed her by striking her repeatedly with a baseball bat until it broke and then pushing the broken end of the bat through her throat. He then placed her in the bathroom and cleaned up. Wallace decided he needed a better killing instrument, so he went to a shed where he obtained a steel pipe wrench. When Gabe arrived home, Wallace killed him by striking him with the pipe wrench. When Susan arrived home a few hours later he killed her with the same wrench. The next day Wallace called the police and confessed. He refused a trial and pleaded guilty to first-degree murder.

WALLACE, WILLIAM	PENNSYLVANIA	M	B	
WALLS, ROBERT	MISSOURI	M	W	
WALTON, JASON DIRK	FLORIDA	M	W	

WALTON, JEFFREY ARIZONA M W

On March 2, 1986, Jeffrey Walton, Sharold Ramsey, and Robert Hoover, were waiting for the opportunity to rob someone. When Thomas Dale Powell became their prey, Walton pointed a pistol at Powell and ordered him to lie down and empty his pockets. The trio then forced Powell into his car and drove to a remote area west of Tucson. Powell was tied up, taken away, and shot in the head by Walton. The shot blinded Powell but did not kill him. When Powell regained consciousness, he floundered in the desert for approximately one week before he died from exposure and pneumonia. Ramsey pled guilty to a lesser offense and testified for the state. Hoover was convicted and received a life sentence.

WALTON, TYRONE	OREGON	M	B	
WARD, CARMEN	CALIFORNIA	M	B	
WARD, DAVID	NORTH CAROLINA	M	B	
WARD, JAMIE	GEORGIA	M	W	
WARD, JERRY	ILLINOIS	M	B	
WARD, THOMAS	LOUISIANA	M	B	
WASH, JEFFERY DAVID	CALIFORNIA	M	W	
WASHINGTON, EARL JR.	VIRGINIA	M	B	
WASHINGTON, JOHN P.	OKLAHOMA	M	B	
WASHINGTON, TERRY	TEXAS	M	B	
WASHINGTON, THEODORE	ARIZONA	M	B	

INMATE	STATE	SEX	RACE	JUVENILE

WASHINGTON, WILLIE   TEXAS   **M**   **B**

Willie Washington was sentenced to death in 1986 for killing Kiflemariam Tareh, 27, an Ethiopian political refugee. Tareh was working at a grocery store in 1985 when Washington robbed about $100. Another employee was shot in the face, but lived to testify at the trial. Previous crimes by Washington, included burglary and rape.

INMATE	STATE	SEX	RACE
WATERHOUSE, ROBERT	FLORIDA	M	W
WATERS, EURUS	GEORGIA	M	W
WATKINS, DARRYL	ALABAMA	M	B
WATKINS, JOHINNY	VIRGINIA	M	B
WATKINS, PAUL	CALIFORNIA	M	U
WATKINS, RONALD	VIRGINIA	M	B
WATSON, HERBERT	PENNSYLVANIA	M	B
WATSON, KEN	FLORIDA	M	B
WATSON, PAUL	CALIFORNIA	M	B
WATTS, TONY R.	FLORIDA	M	B
WAY, FRED	FLORIDA	M	W
WEAVER, WARD FRANCIS	CALIFORNIA	M	W
WEAVER, WILLIAM	MISSOURI	M	B

WEBB, DANIEL   CONNECTICUT   **M**   **B**

Daniel Webb was sentenced to death for the August 1989 kidnap and murder of bank executive Diane Gellenbeck. Webb abducted Gellenbeck from a parking garage during her lunch hour, drove her to a golf course where he attempted to rape her, then repeatedly shot her as she fled barefoot across a city park, screaming for help.

INMATE	STATE	SEX	RACE
WEBB, DENNIS	CALIFORNIA	M	W
WEBB, FREDDIE	TEXAS	M	B
WEBB, MICHAEL	OHIO	M	W
WEBSTER, DANIEL	ARIZONA	M	W
WEBSTER, LARRY	CALIFORNIA	M	N
WEEKS, VARNELL	ALABAMA	M	B
WEISS JESSE	MISSOURI	M	B
WELCH, DAVID E.	CALIFORNIA	M	B
WELCOME, HERBERT	LOUISIANA	M	B
WELDON, DANA	SOUTH CAROLINA	M	B
WELLS, MICHAEL	IDAHO	M	U
WEST, PAUL	ILLINOIS	M	B
WEST, ROBERT W.	TEXAS	M	N

INMATE	STATE	SEX	RACE	JUVENILE
WEST, STEVEN	TENNESSEE	M	W	
WEST, THOMAS	ARIZONA	M	W	
WESTLEY, ANTHONY RAY	TEXAS	M	B	
WHARTON, GEORGE	CALIFORNIA	M	B	
WHARTON, ROBERT	PENNSYLVANIA	M	B	
WHEAT, KENNETH	MISSISSIPPI	M	B	
WHEATFALL, DARYL	TEXAS	M	B	

WHISENHANT, THOMAS   **ALABAMA**   **M**   **W**

In 1963, Thomas Whistenhant was 16 when he robbed and murdered a 72-year-old widow. While in the U.S. Air Force in 1965, he was sentenced to 20 years for assault with intent to kill. After serving eight years, he was paroled. In November 1975, he killed Mobile convenience store clerk Patricia Hitt with a gunshot to her head. Whistenhant then disfigured her body. In April 1976, he abducted and shot Venora Hyatt, 44, another Mobile store clerk. Whistenhant returned to her body several times to mutilate it. In October 1976, he abducted Cheryl Lynn Payton, 24, from yet another Mobile convenience store. He raped her, then ordered her into a cornfield, where he shot her in the head. He again returned several times to mutilate her corpse. Whistenhant was caught by Alabama authorities when a deputy spotted him leaving the scene of Payton's mutilated body. Whistenhant later admitted kidnapping, assaulting and killing the three Mobile women. He received life in prison sentences for the Hitt and Hyatt murders, and was convicted and sent to death row in 1977 for the Payton murder. That conviction was thrown out on appeal. Whisenhant was convicted and sentenced to death a second time in 1981. However, a 1984 Alabama Supreme Court decision ordered Whisenhant to be resentenced. He was sentenced to death a third time in 1984.

INMATE	STATE	SEX	RACE	JUVENILE
WHITE, CLIFTON A.	NORTH CAROLINA	M	W	
WHITE, EXCELL	TEXAS	M	W	
WHITE, JERRY	FLORIDA	M	B	
WHITE, KARU	KENTUCKY	M	W	
WHITE, LARRY WAYNE	TEXAS	M	W	
WHITE, LEAMON	MISSOURI	M	B	

WHITE, LEROY   **ALABAMA**   **M**   **B**

Leroy White was sentenced to death for the 1988 shotgun slaying of his estranged wife, Ruby, a schoolteacher. During sentencing, the judge said White's acts were "especially heinous and atrocious compared to other capital offenses." White approached his wife's home with shotgun in hand, then blasted through her front door. He shot his wife's sister, Stella, four times as she fled out the door and fell into the yard. White then told Ruby, "You made me kill your sister. Now I have to kill you." As Ruby pleaded for her life, White threatened to blow her legs off unless she stopped crying. He shot her, walked into the house, and returned to fatally shoot her in the neck.

INMATE	STATE	SEX	RACE	JUVENILE

WHITE, MICHAEL — ARIZONA — M — W

Michael White, Susan Minter and David Johnson were involved in a love triangle. Although Minter married Johnson, she and White plotted to kill Johnson and collect his life insurance money.

On Dec. 12, 1987 White shot Johnson as he returned home from work. Minter, who was inside the home at the time of the shooting, refused to allow Johnson in despite his cries for help. Johnson died as a result of his injuries. White received the death penalty and Minter was sentenced to life in prison.

WHITE, REGINALD	FLORIDA	M	B	

WHITE, RONALD — COLORADO — M — W

In September 1987, Ronald Lee White was in the midst of a cocaine psychosis, according to a psychiatrist's testimony. Within five months, after moving to Pueblo, Colo., White killed three men. He has said he could testify to perhaps a dozen more, although White has been convicted of just the three murders. White now spends his time drawing pictures and reading religious tracts. Currently, White remains in the appeals process on Colorado's Death Row.

WHITE, STEPHEN	OKLAHOMA	M	N	
WHITE, WILLIAM	FLORIDA	M	W	
WHITEHEAD, JOHN	ILLINOIS	M	W	
WHITFIELD, JOSEPH	MISSOURI	M	B	

WHITMORE, JONAS — ARKANSAS — M — W

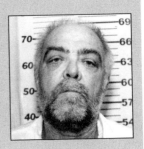

Jonas Whitmore was sentenced to death for the August 1986 stabbing murder of Essie Mae Black. Approximately $250 was taken from her home, where Whitmore killed her.

WHITNEY, RAY	PENNSYLVANIA	M	B	
WHITT, CHARLES	CALIFORNIA	M	W	
WICKHAM, JERRY	FLORIDA	M	W	
WICKLINE, WILLIAM	OHIO	M	W	
WIGGINS, KEVIN	MARYLAND	M	B	

INMATE	STATE	SEX	RACE	JUVENILE

WIKE, WARFIELD FLORIDA M W

On July 14, 1989, Raymond Warfield Wike abducted two girls from their apartment. The two sisters and their mother were asleep when Wike forced his way into their home. Wike took the sisters, one six and the other eight, to a pine thicket, where he sexually assaulted the older girl and cut both girls' throats. The older girl survived. Wike's appeal is pending before the Florida Supreme Court.

WILCHER, BOBBY MISSISSIPPI M W

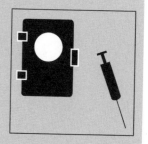

Bobby Wilcher was twice convicted and sentenced to death for the 1982 murders of Katie Bell Moore and Odell Noblin. Wilcher asked the two women for a ride home from a local nightspot. He gave the women false directions to lure them to a secluded spot. Both women begged, then fought for their lives. Wilcher later confessed to stabbing the women multiple times. A cup containing their jewelry was found in Wilcher's room by his father.

INMATE	STATE	SEX	RACE
WILCOXSON, BOBBY	TENNESSEE	M	W
WILES, MARK WAYNE	OHIO	M	W
WILEY, HOWARD	ILLINOIS	M	B
WILEY, WILLIAM	MISSISSIPPI	M	B
WILKENS, JAMES JAY	TEXAS	M	W
WILKERSON, PONCHAI	TEXAS	M	B
WILKERSON, RICHARD J.	TEXAS	M	B

WILKINS, HEATH MISSOURI M W

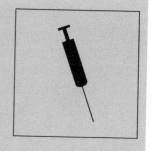

Heath Wilkins was sentenced to die for murdering Nancy Allen, a liquor store clerk, during a 1985 robbery. Allen, a 26-year-old mother of two, was stabbed in the chest and back, then, as she pleaded for mercy, was stabbed four times in the throat. Wilkins, who was 16 years old when he killed Allen, was instrumental in the U.S. Supreme Court ruling permitting execution of killers as young as 16.

INMATE	STATE	SEX	RACE
WILLACY, CHADWICK	FLORIDA	M	B
WILLE, JOHN FRANCIS	LOUISIANA	M	W

WILLIAMS, ALEXANDER — GEORGIA — M — B

In March 1986, 17-year-old Alexander Williams kidnapped Aleta Carol Bunch. Bunch, a 16-year-old high school junior and part-time model, had gone shopping for a birthday present for her mother on the day she disappeared. She was driving a 1984 metallic blue mustang she recently received for her 16th birthday. Investigators never found the car.

Bunch was raped, shot four times in the head and was shot once in the chest. Eleven days after her disappearance, Police found her by following a trail of purchases made with her credit cards. The people who had the cards said they got them from Williams.

In July 1989, the U.S. Supreme Court decided 16- and 17-year-olds may be sentenced to death. This ruling permitted Georgia to sentence Willams to die in the state's electric chair.

Williams now sits on Georgia's Death Row.

INMATE	STATE	SEX	RACE
WILLIAMS, ANDRE	OHIO	M	B
WILLIAMS, ANTOINE	PENNSYLVANIA	M	B
WILLIAMS, ARTHUR LEE	TEXAS	M	B
WILLIAMS, BARRY	CALIFORNIA	M	B

WILLIAMS, CARY — NEVADA — M — B

In 1982, Williams killed Katherine Carlson, 27, in her home during a burglary. Carlson, a nurse in Reno, Nev., was pregnant at the time of her murder. Williams, born in Los Angeles, is appealing his case in federal court.

INMATE	STATE	SEX	RACE
WILLIAMS, CLIFFORD	OHIO	M	B
WILLIAMS, CRAIG	PENNSYLVANIA	M	B
WILLIAMS, DARNELL	INDIANA	M	B
WILLIAMS, DARREN C.	CALIFORNIA	M	B
WILLIAMS, DENNIS	ILLINOIS	M	B
WILLIAMS, DOBIE	LOUISIANA	M	B
WILLIAMS, DONALD	OHIO	M	B
WILLIAMS, DOROTHY	ILLINOIS	F	B
WILLIAMS, DOUGLAS	NORTH CAROLINA	M	B
WILLIAMS, DOYLE	MISSOURI	M	W
WILLIAMS, EDDIE	ILLINOIS	M	B
WILLIAMS, FREDDIE LEE	FLORIDA	M	B

WILLIAMS, HERBERT ALABAMA M B

In November 1988, Herbert Williams Jr. broke into Timothy Copley Hasser's residence and hid in the attic until Hasser came home. Williams, 22, was "obsessed" with owning Hasser's Porsche 928 and had made entries in his personal diary that he was going to take the car. After Hasser came home, Williams forced him to drive to Creola, Ala., where he was shot to death. Williams was arrested after he was stopped by a Jackson, Ala., police officer for driving suspiciously slow on a bridge. Williams was driving Hasser's car and had Hasser's body with him. The victim had been shot three times in the head and had weights attached to his legs. Williams was found guilty of robbing and murdering Hasser.

INMATE	STATE	SEX	RACE
WILLIAMS, HERNANDO	ILLINOIS	M	H
WILLIAMS, JEFFREY	OREGON	M	W
WILLIAMS, JESSE	MISSISSIPPI	M	W
WILLIAMS, KEITH	CALIFORNIA	M	W
WILLIAMS, KENNETH	PENNSYLVANIA	M	W
WILLIAMS, LARRY D.	NORTH CAROLINA	M	B
WILLIAMS, LEWIS	OHIO	M	B
WILLIAMS, LUTHER	ALABAMA	M	B
WILLIAMS, MARVIN	NORTH CAROLINA	M	B
WILLIAMS, MICHAEL	CALIFORNIA	M	W
WILLIAMS, RICKY	TENNESSEE	M	B
WILLIAMS, ROBERT	NEBRASKA	M	B

WILLIAMS, RONALD L. FLORIDA M B

On Sept. 20, 1988, the leader of the Miami Boys cocaine ring, 25-year-old Ronald Williams, ordered the murders of two drug dealers who had stolen a safe containing cocaine and cash. His underlings, Michael Coleman, 27, and Timothy Robinson, 22, plus brothers Darrell Frazier, 25, and Bruce Frazier, 19, burst into a Gulf Beach Highway apartment where the two thieves lived. The intruders forced the six people who were there to strip, bound them with electric cords and sheets, and gagged them. The Frazier brothers freed one woman after she led them to the stolen cash. Robinson and Coleman slashed the five others with knives and shot them in the head. One woman who survived testified. Williams was not present at the murder scene, but he paid the killers plus the two others who were with them after the murders.

Bruce Frazier was sentenced to 50 years in prison and Darrell Frazier to life in prison after testifying against Williams. Williams, Coleman and Robinson were sentenced to death. Supreme Court appeals have not yet been heard.

INMATE	STATE	SEX	RACE	JUVENILE

WILLIAMS, RONALD T. ARIZONA M W

On the morning of March 12, 1981, Ronald Williams kicked in the front door of a home in Scottsdale, Ariz., and began to burglarize it. A short time later, a neighbor John V. Bunchek, went to the home to investigate. He confronted Williams and Williams killed Bunchek by shooting him in the chest. Williams fled and was apprehended three months later in New York City.

WILLIAMS, ROY ALABAMA M W

Roy Williams was convicted and sentenced to death in 1983 for the brutal murder of William Claude Parker on June 22, 1982. Parker's body was discovered in the Alabama woods two days after his murder. He had been beaten about the head 15 times with a 2-by-4, stabbed in the chest six times, and his throat was slit from ear to ear. Williams had met Parker earlier at a local lounge.

WILLIAMS, STANLEY	CALIFORNIA	M	B
WILLIAMS, TERRANCE	PENNSYLVANIA	M	B
WILLIAMS, TERRY	VIRGINIA	M	B
WILLIAMS, TOBY LYNN	TEXAS	M	B
WILLIAMS, WALTER KEY	TEXAS	M	B
WILLIAMS, WILLIE	ALABAMA	M	B
WILLIAMS, WILLIE RAY	TEXAS	M	B

WILLIAMSON, JOHNNY FLORIDA M W

Johnny Williamson was convicted and sentenced to death May 1986 for the 1985 murder of Daniel Inman Drew. Williamson was serving nine years for armed robbery when he was found guilty of the stabbing death of Inman. Williamson claimed Drew owed him money.

WILLIAMSON, RONALD	OKLAHOMA	M	W
WILLIE, MICHAEL	MISSISSIPPI	M	B

WILLIS, ERNEST RAY TEXAS M W

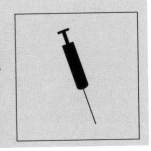

In June 1986, Elizabeth Grace Belue, 25, and Gail Allison, 24, were killed in a fire. The two women were visiting in the Iran, Texas, home where the fire took place. Ernest Ray Wilson was convicted in 1987 of arson and murder in connection with the fire. Willis' conviction and death sentence were both affirmed by the Court of Appeals in Austin in 1989. A motion was filed Oct. 1, 1991, for a stay of execution.

INMATE	STATE	SEX	RACE	JUVENILE
WILLIS, JAMES EARL	NORTH CAROLINA	M	W	
WILLIS, ROBERT	TEXAS	M	B	*
WILLOUGHBY, MITCHELL	KENTUCKY	M	W	
WILSON, DANIEL	OHIO	M	U	

WILSON, EDWARD NEVADA M W

In June 1979 Edward Wilson led a plot to rob Reno Police Department Narcotics Officer James Dean Hoff during a narcotics transaction in Reno, Nevada. Wilson and accomplices David Lani, Fred Stites and John Olausen murdered officer Hoff by stabbing him nine times. They then drove to an isolated area and buried the victim's body. Wilson received the death sentence in December 14, 1979.

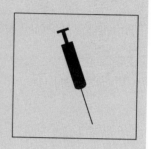

WILSON, GLEN ILLINOIS M B

Glenn Wilson was convicted and sentenced to die for the 1988 murders of Robert Webb, 31; Scott Burton, 30; and Whitney Cole, 24, during an armed robbery. His half brother, Alvin Alexander, was convicted and sentenced to life in prison.

WILSON, GREGORY	KENTUCKY	M	B	
WILSON, HAROLD C.	PENNSYLVANIA	M	B	
WILSON, JACKIE B.	TEXAS	M	H	
WILSON, JAMES	SOUTH CAROLINA	M	W	
WILSON, MICHAEL R.	NORTH CAROLINA	M	W	

WILSON, ROBERT CALIFORNIA M W

On Sept. 6, 1984, Robert Paul Wilson murdered Roy M. Swader. After robbing the Tucson tool vendor, Wilson shot him to death in his van. Wilson, now 40, is waiting for the Supreme Court to hear his appeal.

WILSON, WILLIE	GEORGIA	M	B	
WILSON, ZACHARY	PENNSYLVANIA	M	B	
WISE, JOE	VIRGINIA	M	B	
WISEHART, MARK	INDIANA	M	W	
WOOD, JOSEPH	ARIZONA	M	W	
WOODARD, EUGENE	OHIO	M	B	
WOODRUFF, DAVID	OKLAHOMA	M	W	
WOODS, BILLY JOE	TEXAS	M	W	
WOODS, DAVID	INDIANA	M	W	
WOODSON, SHAWN	MARYLAND	M	B	
WOODWARD, PAUL	MISSISSIPPI	M	W	

WORATZECK, WILLIAM   ARIZONA   M   W

Linda Louise Leslie was a 36-year-old woman with the mental capacity of a 15-year-old. She lived in a small room she rented from William Woratzeck in Pinal County, Ariz. On March 6, 1980, at approximately 2:30 a.m., Woratzeck broke into this room, strangled, stabbed and beat the victim to death, and robbed her of approximately $107. He then set the room on fire.

INMATE	STATE	SEX	RACE	JUVENILE
WORKMAN, PHILLIP	TENNESSEE	M	W	
WORKMAN, WINDEL	OKLAHOMA	M	W	
WREST, THEODORE	CALIFORNIA	M	W	
WRIGHT, BRONTE	CALIFORNIA	M	B	
WRIGHT, CHARLES	TENNESSEE	M	B	
WRIGHT, DWAYNE	VIRGINIA	M	U	*
WRIGHT, FREDDIE	ALABAMA	M	B	
WRIGHT, JOEL	FLORIDA	M	W	
WRIGHT, PATRICK	ILLINOIS	M	W	
WUORNOS, AILEEN	FLORIDA	F	W	
WYATT, THOMAS	FLORIDA	M	W	
WYNNE, CARL	NORTH CAROLINA	M	W	
YARBOROUGH, JOHN	TEXAS	M	W	
YARRIS, NICHOLAS	PENNSYLVANIA	M	W	

YBARRA, ROBERT   NEVADA   M   H

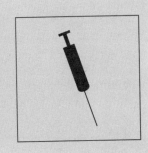

Robert Ybarra was convicted and sentenced to death for the 1979 murder of a young girl. Ybarra had sexually assaulted, severely beaten and burned her entire body. Yet the young girl was found alive sitting in the brush and waving her arms. She later died as a result of her injuries. Ybarra received his death sentence July 23, 1981.

INMATE	STATE	SEX	RACE	JUVENILE
YEATTS, RONALD	VIRGINIA	M	W	
YEOMAN, RALPH	CALIFORNIA	M	W	
YOUNG, DAVID	FLORIDA	M	B	

YOUNG, DAVID   UTAH   M   W

On July 27, 1989, Teresa Ann Young left her mother's home in Loogootee, Ind., and agreed to go for a walk with her husband, David Franklin Young. She had left him after he had beaten her and stabbed her in the throat. A few minutes later, Young returned alone, got into his truck and sped off. His estranged wife was beaten to death with a bicycle fork. At the time of his wife's murder, Young was on parole. He had served 37 months for voluntary manslaughter in the 1982 murder of his fiancee, Teresa Schmittler.

About three weeks after his wife's slaying, on Aug. 19, 1987, Young raped and murdered 27-year-old Ember Kimberly Mars of Kearns, Utah. Young planned to rob her and steal her

INMATE	STATE	SEX	RACE	JUVENILE

truck so he could return to his wife's home and murder her parents. Eight days later, Young was picked up by authorities in Indiana.

Young was sentenced to 35 years for the murder of his wife. He was sentenced to death for the murder of Mars. Currently, he is serving the 35-year sentence in Indiana. When that sentenced is completed, he will most likely be sent back Utah for execution.

YOUNG, JOSEPH   **PENNSYLVANIA**   **M**   **B**

In the early morning hours of May 27, 1986, Joseph L. Young, also known as Yusuf Ali, entered the Wyncote, Pa., home of a world-renowned Islamic scholar and his wife. Young fatally stabbed Dr. Ismail al Faruqi and Dr. Louis al Faruqi.

Young was sentenced to death for the murders of the two Temple University professors. Still in the appeals process, Young is scheduled for re-sentencing in Montgomery County Court.

YOUNG, MOSES	MISSOURI	M	B	
YOUNG, ROBERT	CALIFORNIA	M	B	
YOUNG, WILLIAM	ILLINOIS	M	B	
ZAGORSKI, EDMUND	TENNESSEE	M	W	
ZAPIEN, CONRAD J.	CALIFORNIA	M	H	

ZARAGOSA, RUBEN   **ARIZONA**   **M**   **H**

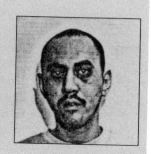

On May 26, 1981, Ruben Zaragoza encountered Winifred Duggan in downtown Phoenix. Duggan was an elderly woman with limited mental capabilities due to a lobotomy she had undergone years before. Zaragoza sexually assaulted her before bludgeoning her with a wine bottle. He then left her in an alley to bleed to death.

ZEIGLER, WILLIAM	FLORIDA	M	W	
ZEITVOGEL, RICHARD	MISSOURI	M	W	
ZETTLEMOYER, KEITH	PENNSYLVANIA	M	W	
ZIMMERMAN, KEVIN	TEXAS	M	W	
ZOOK, ROBERT	PENNSYLVANIA	M	W	

ZUERN, WILLIAM   **OHIO**   **M**   **W**

William Zuern was convicted and sentenced to death for the murder of a sheriff's jail officer. Zuern stabbed Officer Phillip Pence with what was believed to be a sharpened piece of a bucket handle during a weapons check at a Cincinnati jail.

| ZUNIGA, BERNARDINO | NORTH CAROLINA | M | H | |

252

INMATE	STATE	DATE OF EXECUTION	INMATE	STATE	DATE OF EXECUTION
GARY GILMORE	UTAH	1-17-77	CHARLES MILTON	TEXAS	6-25-85
JOHN SPINKELLINK	FLORIDA	5-25-79	MORRIS MASON	VIRGINIA	6-25-85
JESSE BISHOP	NEVADA	10-22-79	HENRY M. PORTER	TEXAS	7-9-85
STEVEN JUDY	INDIANA	3-9-81	CHARLES RUMBAUGH	TEXAS	9-11-85
FRANK COPPOLA	VIRGINIA	8-10-82	WILLIAM VANDIVER	INDIANA	10-16-85
CHARLIE BROOKS	TEXAS	12-7-82	CARROLL COLE	NEVADA	12-6-85
JOHN EVANS	ALABAMA	4-22-83	JAMES T. ROACH	S. CAROLINA	1-10-86
JIMMY LEE GRAY	MISSISSIPPI	9-2-83	CHARLES WILLIAM BASS	TEXAS	3-12-86
ROBERT SULLIVAN	FLORIDA	11-3-83	ARTHUR LEE JONES	ALABAMA	3-21-86
ROBERT W. WILLIAMS	LOUISIANA	12-14-83	DANIEL THOMAS	FLORIDA	4-15-86
JOHN ELDON SMITH	GEORGIA	12-15-83	JEFFREY A. BARNEY	TEXAS	4-16-86
ANTHONY ANTONE	FLORIDA	1-26-84	DAVID FUNCHESS	FLORIDA	4-22-86
JOHN TAYLOR	LOUISIANA	2-29-84	JAY PINKERTON	TEXAS	5-15-86
JAMES AUTRY	TEXAS	3-14-84	RONALD STRAIGHT	FLORIDA	5-20-86
JAMES HUTCHINS	N. CAROLINA	3-16-84	RUDY ESQUIVEL	TEXAS	6-9-86
RONALD O'BRYAN	TEXAS	3-31-84	KENNETH BROCK	TEXAS	6-18-86
ARTHUR GOODE	FLORIDA	4-5-84	JEROME BOWDEN	GEORGIA	6-24-86
ELMO SONNIER	LOUISIANA	4-5-84	MICHAEL SMITH	VIRGINIA	7-31-86
JAMES ADAMS	FLORIDA	5-10-84	RANDY WOOLLS	TEXAS	8-20-86
CARL SHRINER	FLORIDA	6-20-84	LARRY SMITH	TEXAS	8-22-86
IVON STANLEY	GEORGIA	7-12-84	CHESTER WICKER	TEXAS	8-26-86
DAVID WASHINGTON	FLORIDA	7-13-84	JOHN ROOK	N. CAROLINA	9-19-86
ERNEST DOBBERT	FLORIDA	9-7-84	MICHAEL WAYNE EVANS	TEXAS	12-4-86
TIMOTHY BALDWIN	LOUISIANA	9-10-84	RICHARD ANDRADE	TEXAS	12-18-86
JAMES DUPREE HENRY	FLORIDA	9-20-84	RAMON HERNANDEZ	TEXAS	1-30-87
LINWOOD BRILEY	VIRGINIA	10-12-84	ELISIO MORENO	TEXAS	3-4-87
THOMAS BAREFOOT	TEXAS	10-30-84	JOSEPH MULLIGAN	GEORGIA	5-15-87
ERNEST KNIGHTON	LOUISIANA	10-30-84	EDWARD EARL JOHNSON	MISSISSIPPI	5-20-87
VELMA BARFIELD	N. CAROLINA	11-2-84	RICHARD TUCKER	GEORGIA	5-22-87
TIMOTHY PALMES	FLORIDA	11-8-84	ANTHONY WILLIAMS	TEXAS	5-28-87
ALPHA OTIS STEPHENS	GEORGIA	12-12-84	WILLIAM BOYD TUCKER	GEORGIA	5-29-87
ROBERT LEE WILLIE	LOUISIANA	12-28-84	BENJAMIN BERRY	LOUISIANA	6-7-87
DAVID MARTIN	LOUISIANA	1-4-85	ALVIN MOORE	LOUISIANA	6-9-87
ROOSEVELT GREEN	GEORGIA	1-9-85	JIMMY GLASS	LOUISIANA	6-12-87
JOSEPH CARL SHAW	S. CAROLINA	1-11-85	JIMMY WINGO	LOUISIANA	6-16-87
DOYLE SKILLERN	TEXAS	1-16-85	ELLIOTT JOHNSON	TEXAS	6-24-87
JAMES RAULERSON	FLORIDA	1-30-85	RICHARD WHITLEY	VIRGINIA	7-6-87
VAN R. SOLOMON	GEORGIA	2-20-85	JOHN R. THOMPSON	TEXAS	7-8-87
JOHNNY PAUL WITT	FLORIDA	3-6-85	CONNIE RAY EVANS	MISSISSIPPI	7-8-87
STEPHEN P. MORIN	TEXAS	3-13-85	WILLIE CELESTINE	LOUISIANA	7-20-87
JOHN YOUNG	GEORGIA	3-20-85	WILLIE WATSON	LOUISIANA	7-24-87
JAMES BRILEY	VIRGINIA	4-18-85	JOHN BROGDON	LOUISIANA	7-30-87
JESSE DE LA ROSA	TEXAS	5-15-85	STERLING RAULT	LOUISIANA	8-24-87
MARVIN FRANCOIS	FLORIDA	5-29-85	BEAUFORD WHITE	FLORIDA	8-28-87

INMATE	STATE	DATE OF EXECUTION	INMATE	STATE	DATE OF EXECUTION
WAYNE RITTER	ALABAMA	8-28-87	RICKY BOGGS	VIRGINIA	7-19-90
DALE PIERRE SELBY	UTAH	8-28-87	ANTHONY BERTOLOTTI	FLORIDA	7-27-90
BILLY MITCHELL	GEORGIA	9-1-87	GEORGE C. GILMORE	MISSOURI	8-31-90
JOSEPH STARVAGGI	TEXAS	9-10-87	CHARLES T. COLEMAN	OKLAHOMA	9-10-90
TIMOTHY MCCORQUODALE	GEORGIA	9-21-87	CHARLES WALKER	ILLINOIS	9-12-90
ROBERT STREETMAN	TEXAS	1-7-88	JAMES W. HAMBLEN	FLORIDA	9-21-90
WAYNE FELDE	FLORIDA	3-15-88	WILBERT L. EVANS	VIRGINIA	10-17-90
WILLIE DARDEN	LOUISIANA	3-15-88	RAYMOND R. CLARK	FLORIDA	11-19-90
LESLIE LOWENFIELD	LOUISIANA	4-13-88	BUDDY EARL JUSTUS	VIRGINIA	12-13-90
EARL CLANTON	VIRGINIA	4-14-88	LAWRENCE L. BUXTON	TEXAS	2-26-91
ARTHUR BISHOP	UTAH	6-10-88	ROY A. HARICH	FLORIDA	4-24-91
EDWARD BYRNE	LOUISIANA	6-14-88	IGNACIO CUEVAS	TEXAS	5-23-91
JAMES MESSER	GEORGIA	7-28-88	JERRY JOE BIRD	TEXAS	6-18-91
DONALD GENE FRANKLIN	TEXAS	11-3-88	BOBBY M. FRANCIS	FLORIDA	6-25-91
JEFFREY DAUGHERTY	FLORIDA	11-7-88	ANDREW LEE JONES	LOUISIANA	7-22-91
RAYMOND LANDRY	TEXAS	12-13-88	ALBERT CLOZZA	VIRGINIA	7-24-91
GEORGE "TINY" MERCER	MISSOURI	1-6-89	DERICK PETERSON	VIRGINIA	8-22-91
THEODORE BUNDY	FLORIDA	1-24-89	MAURICE BYRD	MISSOURI	8-23-91
LEON RUTHERFORD KING	TEXAS	3-22-89	DONALD GASKINS	S. CAROLINA	9-6-91
AUBREY ADAMS	FLORIDA	5-4-89	JAMES RUSSELL	TEXAS	9-19-91
HENRY WILLIS	GEORGIA	5-18-89	WARREN MCCLESKEY	GEORGIA	9-25-91
STEPHEN MCCOY	TEXAS	5-24-89	MICHAEL MCDOUGALL	N. CAROLINA	1-18-91
MICHAEL LINDSEY	ALABAMA	5-26-89	G.W. GREEN	TEXAS	11-12-91
WILLIAM THOMPSON	NEVADA	6-19-89	JOE ANGEL CORDOVA	TEXAS	1-22-92
LEO EDWARDS	MISSISSIPPI	6-21-89	MARK HOPKINSON	WYOMING	1-22-92
SEAN P. FLANNAGAN	NEVADA	6-23-89	RICKY RAY RECTOR	ARKANSAS	1-24-92
HORACE F. DUNKINS	ALABAMA	7-14-89	JOHNNY GARRETT	TEXAS	2-11-92
HERBERT RICHARDSON	ALABAMA	8-18-89	DAVID CLARK	TEXAS	2-28-92
ALTON WAYE	VIRGINIA	8-30-89	EDWARD ELLIS	TEXAS	3-3-92
JAMES "SKIP" PASTER	TEXAS	9-20-89	ROBYN PARKS	OKLAHOMA	3-10-92
ARTHUR JULIUS	ALABAMA	11-17-89	OLAN ROBISON	OKLAHOMA	3-13-92
CARLOS DELUNA	TEXAS	12-7-89	STEVEN PENNELL	DELAWARE	3-14-92
GERALD SMITH	MISSOURI	1-18-90	LARRY HEATH	ALABAMA	3-20-92
M. JEROME BUTLER	TEXAS	4-21-90	DONALD E. HARDING	ARIZONA	4-6-92
RONALD R. WOOMER	S. CAROLINA	4-27-90	ROBERT A. HARRIS	CALIFORNIA	4-21-92
JESSIE TAFERO	FLORIDA	5-4-90	WILLIAM W. WHITE	TEXAS	4-23-92
WINFORD STOKES	MISSOURI	5-11-90	JUSTIN LEE MAY	TEXAS	5-7-92
LEONARD LAWS	MISSOURI	5-17-90	STEVEN D. HILL	ARKANSAS	5-7-92
JOHNNY RAY ANDERSON	TEXAS	5-17-90	NOLLIE L. MARTIN	FLORIDA	5-12-92
DALTON PREJEAN	LOUISIANA	5-18-90	JESUS ROMERO	TEXAS	5-20-92
THOMAS BAAL	NEVADA	6-3-90	ROGER K. COLEMAN	VIRGINIA	5-20-92
JOHN E. SWINDLER	ARKANSAS	6-18-90	ROBERT BLACK	TEXAS	5-22-92
RONALD SIMMONS	ARKANSAS	6-25-90	EDWARD D. KENNEDY	FLORIDA	7-21-92
JAMES SMITH	TEXAS	6-26-90	EDWARD FITZGERALD	VIRGINIA	7-23-92
WALLACE N. THOMAS	ALABAMA	7-13-90	WILLIAM ANDREWS	UTAH	7-30-92
MIKEL DERRICK	TEXAS	7-18-90			